THE SWISS AND THE NAZIS

THE
SWISS
AND THE
NAZIS

*How the Alpine Republic Survived in
the Shadow of the Third Reich*

By
STEPHEN P. HALBROOK

CASEMATE
Philadelphia & Newbury

Published in 2010 by
CASEMATE
908 Darby Road, Havertown, PA 19083
and
17 Cheap Street, Newbury, Berkshire, RG14 5DD

Copyright 2006 © Stephen P. Halbrook

ISBN 978-1-935149-34-7

Cataloging-in-publication data is available from the Library of Congress
and the British Library.

10 9 8 7 6 5 4 3 2 1

Printed and bound in the United States of America.

For a complete list of Casemate titles please contact:

CASEMATE PUBLISHERS (US)
Telephone (610) 853-9131, Fax (610) 853-9146
E-mail: casemate@casematepublishing.com

CASEMATE PUBLISHERS (UK)
Telephone (01635) 231091, Fax (01635) 41619
E-mail: casemate-uk@casematepublishing.co.uk

Mixed Sources
Product group from well-managed
forests and other controlled sources
www.fsc.org Cert no. SW-COC-002283
© 1996 Forest Stewardship Council

CONTENTS

INTRODUCTION

By every strategic rationale, Switzerland should have fallen to the Nazis in World War II. She lies directly exposed on the German border, and during the course of the war became completely surrounded by the Axis powers. The majority of her people are ethnically German, and her population was outnumbered by the Axis at least thirty to one. While the Swiss Alps were eminently defensible, the north of the country, containing most of its population and industry, was relatively flat and easily accessible to mechanized forces. As a landlocked nation in the heart of Europe, Switzerland was beyond the reach of potential allies.

Further, to Adolf Hitler, political neutrality meant nothing, and national borders were no obstacle to his Wehrmacht. Pre-war Nazi theorists drew up maps that depicted Switzerland's obliteration, most of it incorporated into Germany with smaller parts designated for client states along ethnic lines. By 1940, every country surrounding Switzerland was either a member of the Axis or under Nazi rule. The Wehrmacht finalized plans for blitzkrieg attacks against Switzerland.

But Switzerland was not overrun. Its army hunkered down at the border and in its Alpine fortresses, swearing to exact a high price in blood from any invader. The Nazis constantly sought opportunities to subvert and to strike, but dissuaded by Swiss resistance and skillful Swiss diplomacy, and with overwhelming distractions elsewhere, the opportune time to wreak destruction never came.

The reasons for Switzerland's survival in World War II are several, and in the final analysis the gigantic scale of the Nazi war in Russia, which began in June 1941, holds first place. If Hitler had achieved the quick victory over the Soviet Union that he expected, traditional Swiss courage, along with the country's elaborate defensive preparations, would have been overwhelmed by brute force. Instead, as the war seesawed back and forth in the East, and later in the West, the Swiss were left with a waiting game, their mobilizations timed against each rise of Axis fortunes, the Swiss themselves never knowing when a Wehrmacht onslaught would finally be launched.

Switzerland's policy of deterrence took three major forms. The first consisted of its unique military system, in which every able-bodied man served in the army and was well trained in firearms. This allowed Switzerland to field a greater percentage of its population than other countries, and far more than the other small states that had fallen to Hitler. Second, and less well known, is the fact that the Swiss wired their infrastructure, particularly their transportation system—bridges, rails, and their strategically vital Alpine tunnels—informing the Germans that it would be destroyed the minute an invasion began. Though the cost of such destruction would have been incalculable to the country itself, the Germans were left with no doubt that the Swiss would go to any lengths to defy an invader, even to the point of devastating their own country.

The third primary form of deterrence was improvised during the war by Commander-in-Chief of the Swiss Army Henri Guisan, after the fall of France resulted in German panzers arrayed along the country's exposed western border. In 1940 Guisan decided to negate the tactics and machinery of Nazi blitzkrieg by moving the bulk of Swiss forces to a fortified zone in the Alps called the *Réduit National* (National Redoubt). Involving a massive movement of troops as well as a colossal construction enterprise, this strategy meant that, henceforth, German armor and airpower would be useless against Switzerland's main forces. Instead of a quick war using mobile tactics, the Wehrmacht would be faced with a protracted struggle amid the Alps, with Swiss marksmen and hidden artillery emplacements pre-targeting every narrow approach.

These measures, along with others taken by the Swiss, both spiritual and material, succeeded in deterring Hitler in his desire to absorb the Alpine Republic, until in the end the Nazis themselves were destroyed by more powerful outside forces.

The result was that there was no Holocaust in Switzerland, no slave labor, and no seizure of Swiss machinery or transit systems for unrestrained Nazi use. The thousands of refugees who found shelter in Switzerland were never stigmatized, much less deported to the death camps of the Reich. Switzerland was and is a multicultural, multiethnic, multireligious democracy with a tradition of tolerance. Nazi Germany, with its institutional racism and leadership cult, represented everything the Swiss abhorred.

Given her geographical location at the heart of central Europe, as well as her multilinguistic composition, Switzerland's neutrality had been codified in European councils as early as 1515. Once considered the foremost warriors of Europe (and drawn upon for centuries afterward as mercenaries) the Swiss received ratification by the international Treaty of Vienna after the Napoleonic Wars as comprising an independent confederation that should take no part in future European wars. Thus, Switzerland adopted political neutrality as the primary principle of her foreign policy, through the Franco-Prussian War and World War I, until her concept of armed neutrality was put to the ultimate test in the 1940s, when she found herself surrounded by Axis forces. During this period the Swiss, standing fast to their independence, were called upon to duplicate the courage of their forebears.

In a December 1944 memo to Anthony Eden, a supremely circumspect Winston Churchill wrote: "Of all the neutrals Switzerland has the greatest right to distinction. . . . She has been a democratic State, standing for freedom in self-defense among her mountains, and in thought, in spite of race, largely on our side."[1]

Led by General Henri Guisan, the Swiss armed forces spent the war prepared to resist invasion at any cost. When General Guisan died in 1960, the largest and most magnificent wreath was sent by General Dwight D. Eisenhower, who was then President of the United States. Five years earlier, Eisenhower had occasion to review a company of Swiss troops and wrote: "Rarely in my military experience have I had the opportunity to see a more perfectly trained unit."[2] Switzerland was the centuries-old "Sister Republic" of the United States, and her ubiquitous military force—in which every male was armed and trained as a marksman—enjoyed a unique reputation.

Allen Dulles, head of America's spy network operating against Germany from his base in Switzerland during World War II, wrote: "At the peak of its mobilization Switzerland had 850,000 men under arms or standing in reserve, a fifth of the total population. . . . That Switzerland did not have to fight was thanks to its will to resist and its large investment of men and equipment in its own defense. The cost to Germany of an invasion of Switzerland would certainly have been very high."[3] German intelligence reports indicate with grim clarity that Switzerland would not roll over and capitulate like other neutrals, and even some of the Allies. The Swiss, as in the tradition of their famed mercenary regiments, would fight to the death.

Today, it is easy to criticize Switzerland for remaining neutral throughout the war. Why did the Swiss not join the Allied military campaigns against Germany? What about Swiss commerce, including manufactured exports and coal and food imports from Germany? Why were not all refugees at the Swiss border admitted? By holding fast to its independence, did the Swiss Confederation somehow prolong the war?

These were the charges that suddenly emerged some fifty years after World War II had ended and which quickly gained public currency, even though they were based on carefully chosen anecdotes or highly selective interpretations of the record. The charges reflected very little in-depth knowledge of the realities of the war, the positions taken by the Allies, or the options available to Switzerland. Most importantly, the accusations failed to take into consideration the patriotic nature of the wartime Swiss, whose army was determined to resist aggression.

Sparking the charges were lawsuits filed in New York in the mid-1990s claiming that, after the war ended, Swiss banks refused to pay the dormant accounts of Holocaust victims to survivors. The banks responded that the deposits were paid to all persons who provided evidence of legal entitlement. (Switzerland has never had escheat laws, which allow the government to confiscate money in dormant accounts after a specified number of years.) After a negative politico-media campaign and the threat of a financial boycott, but no judicial trial of any of the claims, two large commercial Swiss banks agreed to pay $1.25 billion.[4] The Swiss National Bank, supported by an overwhelming majority of the Swiss public, refused to take part.

The merits of these charges against banks and financiers will not be reviewed here, but rather, the history of the Swiss people's clear determination during World War II to remain independent and preserve their democratic institutions.

At this writing, the wartime generation is passing, but their living memories and their firsthand knowledge of real-life conditions in Switzerland during the war remain invaluable. Life then was not easy and neither were the choices. The Federal government in Bern had the difficult task of restraining the Swiss press—in fact, the defiant nature of the entire country—so as not to provoke a Nazi onslaught. Many civilians feared an invasion, but there were also thousands of young men trained in marksmanship, stationed in carefully prepared positions, who thought to themselves, "Let them come." It is difficult to relate the complete story of Switzerland in World War II, but reviewing the firsthand experiences of the country's own wartime generation, as well as German archives that contain the Nazis' attack plans, is essential.

This author sought to bring some balance to the historical record in English with the publication of *Target Switzerland: Swiss Armed Neutrality in World War II* (1998),[5] which recounted the Nazi threat and Switzerland's military and political response, together with the plight and the will to resist of the Swiss people at large. That book took a chronological approach, interweaving Swiss ideological defiance and military preparations in reaction to the Nazi menace for the entire life of the Third Reich.

Target Switzerland filled a void in World War II history and generated considerable interest in the United States as well as abroad, where it has appeared in German, French, Italian and Polish language editions.[6] The book won the 2000 Max Geilinger Foundation award for works contributing to Swiss and Anglo-American culture and the 2002 Foundation for Western Thought (*Stiftung für Abendländische Besinnung*) award.[7]

The following pages can be viewed as a sequel, although perusal of *Target Switzerland* is definitely not a prerequisite. This new work presents an additional, more intimate picture of significant attitudes, plans and events which could only be treated briefly in the previous work but which are critical to understanding how the Swiss dissuaded a Nazi invasion and occupation. It presents the recollections of scores of survivors of that epoch, and its oral history contains perspectives and experiences not found in official documents or historical overviews. It also reveals Nazi plans for subversion and conquest based on comprehensive research in the German military archives.

This book is organized into four units. The first, *A War of Words and Nerves*, depicts how the Swiss mobilized an active "spiritual defense" of their country as war clouds gathered and broke. Chapters describe the use of the press and cabaret as satirical weapons against totalitarianism, and the role of Swiss newsreels in building the spirit of resistance. German prewar subversion plans and reports on the negative mood of the Swiss people toward the Third Reich are also analyzed.

The book's second unit, *Preparing for Invasion*, concerns military preparations by both the Swiss and the Germans against each other. In a series of interviews, Swiss soldiers and officers recall their experiences about an epoch when every day could have been "the day" when all hell would break loose and they would meet the enemy. Blitzkrieg plans against Switzerland devised by the German Wehrmacht in 1940, including German assessments of Swiss resistance, are described in detail. Switzerland was an armed camp, with countless fortifications along rivers and in the highly defensive Alpine terrain, against which the Axis could have attempted access only with extreme costs in blood.

Struggle for Survival: Food, Fuel, and Fear, the third unit, presents oral histories of daily life during the war with its shortages and alarms, rumors and tedium. Jokes and slurs the Swiss devised to characterize Hitler's "Swabians" across the Rhine are retold. The role of women in the military and the economy are probed. A chapter on the refugee crisis investigates what role Swiss officials played in Germany's prewar adoption of the "J" stamp on Jewish passports, how Switzerland became a lifeboat for thousands of refugees, and how asylum policies were liberalized as the persecution of Jews escalated and was publicized.

Espionage and Subversion, the fourth and final unit, covers larger strategic issues as well as fascinating intelligence activities in Switzerland during the war. Aggressive intentions against Switzerland—from attack plans to bickering within the Gestapo about who would rule the conquered Swiss territory—persisted throughout the war. One chapter focuses on Davos, today's international meeting site, where the Swiss struggled against an active fifth column and which became an internment site for American airmen who managed to bring down their crippled bombers in the safety of Swiss territory. The final chapter profiles Switzerland as America's window on the Reich—how from Bern, Allen Dulles operated the OSS (the U.S. spy agency), helped at crucial junctures by clandestine information from Switzerland's own intelligence services.

None of these critical topics was addressed in the 25 volumes issued by the Bergier Commission. The Bergier reports, mistakenly perceived as exhaustive, actually addressed only certain issues, such as Switzerland's economic relations with Germany, and did not utilize firsthand accounts by ordinary Swiss citizens still living or give a systematic analysis of Swiss experience during the war.[8] Without trade, Switzerland could not manufacture arms to defend itself against the Axis, feed its population, prevent collapse, or host refugees. While most European countries were conquered by the Nazis, provided slave labor to them, and failed to prevent the deportation of their Jews to death camps, Switzerland successfully avoided all of these horrors.

The Bergier reports include no volumes on some fundamental aspects of Swiss life during the war, including Nazi blitzkrieg plans, Swiss military defenses, Swiss ideological resistance against Nazism, and the patriotic willpower of an Alpine democracy that survived intact when every surrounding nation had fallen to Nazi arms or intimidation. These topics are covered in this book, and bring to the attention of scholars and the public alike aspects about the role of Switzerland during World War II that are little known in the U.S.

It is pleasing to note that in recent years interest in the actual record of Switzerland in World War II has increased. A growing body of impeccable scholarship on Switzerland during the Second World War is emerging, including both original works and others translated from German or French.[9]

Americans in particular should realize that while their own homeland was not threatened by invasion during the war, Switzerland was under constant threat. If Hitler had found the opportunity to concentrate his main forces against the Alpine republic, it surely would have been conquered, albeit at the cost of a gigantic number of casualties. The fact that the war flowed around Switzerland, rather than through it, is tribute enough to Europe's oldest democracy, and America's "Sister Republic."

* * *

This book could not have been written without the help and cooperation of scores of people, particularly members of Switzerland's "active service" generation who gave interviews to the author. Other individuals provided tours of military fortifications, arranged conferences with historians and military officials, and furnished a steady stream of out-of-print books and documents. Many such persons are identified in the text or endnotes. The author is grateful for the assistance of all such persons, regardless of whether their names are mentioned.

The author is especially grateful to Jürg Stüssi-Lauterburg and the staff at the Swiss Military Library in Bern for helping to locate documents. George Gyssler, Paul Rothenhäusler, and Peter Baumgartner-Jost assisted in arranging interviews for the oral history portions of the book. Similarly helpful was Hans Wächter, who was an artillery officer in the war and now is President of *Aktion Aktivdienst 1939–1945*, which promotes awareness of the Swiss army during the war. Sebastian Remus, a professional German archive researcher, shifted through thousands of documents pertaining to planned hostilities against Switzerland in the German Military Archives. Therese Klee-Hathaway assisted with translations from German, including Swiss German dialect. Lisa Halbrook indefatigably scoured through reams of archival documents. Tom Ryan and Steve Smith provided invaluable and diligent editorial assistance. Needless to say, the author is solely responsible for the interpretations and any inaccuracies in the work.

PART I
A WAR OF WORDS AND NERVES

CHAPTER 1

THE EYES OF GERMAN INTELLIGENCE

An essential starting point for understanding Switzerland's politico-military stance during World War II is to see how it was analyzed by contemporary agents of the Third Reich. For this study, exhaustive searches were made in the German military archives for documents pertaining to Switzerland during the time of the Hitler regime.[1] The military, diplomatic, and intelligence documents found reveal the intentions and attitudes of both the Germans and the Swiss during these years.

German intelligence kept a close eye on Switzerland during the entire period of the Third Reich. The Nazi hierarchy saw Switzerland as a land in which the ideals of freedom and federalism posed a threat to their New Order. At various times, operations specialists from the German armed forces made detailed plans for blitzkrieg attacks against Switzerland. Administrators were likewise put to work preparing a new civil organization for the country once it had been overrun.

Having seized power in early 1933, Hitler's first task was to consolidate his regime within Germany itself. A year later, he increasingly turned his attention to other parts of Europe. German diplomatic and military reports coming back to the planning centers began to reflect his priorities and concerns. Germany's neighbors were all potential enemies. Hitler himself knew that sooner or later there would be war.

France would be a major target. Switzerland was neutral, but the country offered a relatively direct southern route into France. How the country would respond to German—or French—initiatives was recognized as critical. If the French sensed that a German offensive was imminent, they might move into Switzerland to block it or to counterattack. For their part, the Germans had to know whether the neutral Swiss would allow or support a French attack against Germany's southern flank, and whether they would oppose German troops moving against France. The French, who in 1923 had occupied the Ruhr over Germany's non-payment of war debts, had begun to pour the bulk of their defense resources into constructing the Maginot Line, a massive network of fortifications along the French-German border. Successful as a deterrent against head-on attack, the existence of this line placed new importance on the smaller countries to both the north and south, on whose territory the only mobile operations could take place.

On April 14, 1934, the German envoy to Bern, Ernst von Weizsäcker, wrote to the Ministry of Foreign Affairs in Berlin that Switzerland saw the peace of Versailles as unfair or unwise but preferred it to a new war. "National Socialism was regarded as warlike." The Swiss feared that a revived Germany might attack France through Switzerland, moving through Geneva to fall upon the French from behind their Maginot Line. They would likely annex German-speaking Switzerland in the process. Swiss Foreign Minister Motta told Weizsäcker: "In 1934 there will be no war in Europe. But later?" He wanted to add that France would not wage a preventative war but that, if Germany rearmed, the danger would return.[2]

Under the Treaty of Versailles, Germany had to pay enormous reparations to France and England. But the chaotic aftermath of the Great War, the runaway inflation of 1923, and the Great Depression left the German economy in ruins. Indeed, the Depression left the entire world's economy in shambles. Disaffected, unemployed workers threatened stability in every country. Hitler sought to repudiate both the reparations imposed by the disgrace of Versailles and commercial debts. As for the latter, Weizsäcker wrote that Germany owed the "bourgeois" Swiss some 21 billion marks.

Switzerland had to realize that the Nazi regime was securely in place and therefore must accommodate it. As Weizsäcker put it, "Switzerland needed many years in order to get used to Fascism in the south. Likewise she must get used to National Socialism in the north. The Swiss still see as criminal the conversion of their small, democratic Austrian neighbor into a dictatorship, and then how trouble looms westward into France." (Austria had just become a dictatorship under the rule of Engelbert Dollfuss.)

Germany's envoy stressed that two elements of National Socialism were wholly unacceptable to the Swiss: "The Führer principle, for

Switzerland is still today built on federalism; and the race principle, because neither race nor *Volkstum* [folk power] as we think of them holds Switzerland together." He sought to find common ground between Swiss values and National Socialism based on their mutual opposition to Marxism. However, the Swiss, with their centuries-old resistance to emperors, instinctively opposed the centralized statist regimes they saw in both Germany and the Soviet Union.

Weizsäcker cautioned that "the total balance admittedly remains negative for the time being," and that, in a European conflict, Switzerland would lean toward France and against Germany. "Our left flank would be pressed up against a country with 300,000 rifles, which would be ready to be used sooner against us than against France."

The Swiss had ample reason to fear German aggression. Their German-speaking region was appearing in Nazi maps of a "Greater Germany," and an alleged German plan to attack France through Switzerland had been published in Swiss French-language newspapers.[3] German Envoy Weizsäcker addressed this propaganda in a note to the Ministry of Foreign Affairs in Berlin on June 20, 1934, entitled "Annexation of German-speaking Switzerland: French propaganda, German carelessness."[4] The trouble began as follows:

> After German statements had spread fear last fall that the new Germany was aiming at splitting the Confederation and annexing the German-speaking part of Switzerland, we were able to clear up these fantasies in discussions between the Foreign Minister of the Reich and the head of Swiss foreign policy, Mr. Motta, as well as with the publication of the content of these discussions. . . . For a while, Swiss circles remained nervous because ill-meaning elements had spread rumors about an alleged new plan of Germany to march through Switzerland. After a statement by the War Minister of the Reich put out that fire, things calmed down a bit.

However, "new concerns about German annexation desires" were being stirred up by "a certain French source that is in close contact with the French Embassy here," and "careless statements by certain German personalities who visited Switzerland about a month ago revived the fear of annexation." A previously friendly high-ranking Swiss military officer had become an enemy of the new Germany.

Weizsäcker continued: "While those cases could be explained as being

intentionally malicious or just stupid, there can be no excuse for a publication like the one I am sending in the attachment." He enclosed a map
that was included in the June issue of *Der Auslanddeutsche* (*The German
Abroad*) published by the German Foreign Institute in Stuttgart and the
German People's Association for Germandom Abroad. The map, he
exclaimed, "designates German-speaking Switzerland and even areas
beyond that as 'German land withheld or taken away from Germany.'"
What was worse, the map was marked as having been reprinted from yet
another publication of the new Germany. Similar instances had been
noted in a Swiss newspaper. Weizsäcker concluded: "If we keep assisting
French propaganda in this manner, we should not be surprised that neither public nor private opinion in Switzerland, even those that are based
on good will, show any trust in the new Germany."

Weizsäcker appears here less the ideological Nazi than professional
diplomat. As events would show, he would waiver between the two roles.
In fact, it became ever more clear that the Nazis intended to subvert and
annex Switzerland.

The alleged influence of the French in Switzerland was an important
intelligence topic from this period all the way through the war years. The
military attaché of the German envoy in Vienna, Austria, reported on July
16, 1934, that he had attended a tournament in Thun, Switzerland, and
then stayed in Bern. He claimed to have talked to high-ranking Swiss officers, but his report is based primarily on discussions with the Italian military attaché, who was the source for the following:

> The latter thinks that French influence on the Swiss army is
> increasing constantly, also within the corps of German-speaking
> Swiss officers. Apparently, this influence is promoted with a very
> skillful anti-German propaganda and in particular because very
> many Swiss officers are dispatched to French military schools.
> That has become a permanent institution and has created a cer-
> tain connection between the two armies. Swiss officers start think-
> ing along French political lines without even noticing it. The fear
> of National Socialist ideas taking over in Switzerland and threat-
> ening the basis of Swiss statehood also fosters anti-German senti-
> ments.[5]

To the extent possible, this might be counterbalanced, noted the
attaché, by giving Swiss officers more opportunities to learn about

Germany and its military. However, "the Italian military attaché was very concerned that the Swiss government would not be truly willing to maintain neutrality in case of war." The leading officers in the Swiss General Staff, Colonel Combé and Lieutenant Colonel Dubois, were extremely friendly toward the French. The French influence was exemplified by a recent decree of the Swiss Federal Council on military training periods, which was based on a decree by French General Clément-Grandcour, director of the war college, *Ecole Supérieure de Guerre*. The general owned an estate in Switzerland on Lake Murten and had observed Swiss military maneuvers.

Swiss Lieutenant General Wille, who was considered pro-German (but not pro-Nazi), reportedly had lost influence, while the influence of his successor as chief of arms of the infantry, the pro-French Major General Borel, had increased. The Italian attaché quoted Federal President Pilet-Golaz as saying: "Wille is a danger to our neutrality." However, the German attaché warned against the security danger of forging too close relations with the Swiss. "I have been told confidentially that officers dispatched to Switzerland are speaking too openly to Swiss officers about our armament plans. Apparently they tend to forget that just because Swiss officers speak German they are not necessarily pro-German and that there are numerous connections to the French army."

The same German military attaché filed a further report with the *Oberkommando der Wehrmacht* (Armed Forces High Command, or OKW) on September 27, 1934, concerning talks he heard at Swiss military maneuvers. In his welcoming remarks, Federal President Pilet-Golaz stated that the Swiss had the will to defend their country against any attack. Federal Councilor Rudolf Minger, head of the Swiss Military Department, and Corps Commander Roost indicated that the situation in Europe was prompting improvements in Swiss national defense.

Apprehension was expressed that any Italian foothold in Austria would be a threat to Switzerland's southern front. Fortifications needed to be constructed, he said, on all fronts. A one-sided fortification against Germany ignored the danger that a socialist government at the rudder in France could march against anti-democratic neighbors. "Switzerland must form a hedgehog against all sides," offering each of her neighbors the assurance of a certain flank in event of an armed conflict, without compromising Swiss neutrality.[6] Indeed, there was only a theoretical threat from France. The Swiss spokesmen well knew that the only real threat was from Germany.

In the mid-1930s, Germany escalated its rearmament program. Well aware of the danger across the border, Switzerland's militia army was reorganized, modernized, and enlarged. The Swiss public willingly bought defense bonds to support these efforts. German military intelligence carefully watched these developments.[7]

A Wehrmacht intelligence report of March 11, 1937, stated that the Führer had publicly "guaranteed unconditional independence and neutrality to Switzerland. The explanation has appeared exceptionally calming in Switzerland. Federal President Motta explained that neutrality is also guaranteed by the League of Nations."[8] Hitler would later make similar assurances to other neutral European states, only to launch unprovoked attacks against them.

Rabble-rousing Swiss propaganda against Germany was the subject of a report from the German Legation in Bern on April 13, 1937, concerning allegations in the Geneva socialist paper *Le Travail* that Hitler was preparing a war to be unleashed soon at the Czechoslovak border. The German Legation protested to the Political Department of the Swiss Confederation against the Swiss press influencing public opinion against Germany.[9]

This particular prediction came true the following year. The *Anschluss* of Austria in March 1938 was achieved through intimidation and did not require a war. But the following September Hitler massed forces on the border of Czechoslovakia, and war was avoided only when England and France gave Hitler what he wanted at the Munich conference, causing the dissolution and German occupation of that country. It appeared that small countries could expect no help from the major powers. Switzerland redoubled its military and ideological preparations to avoid a similar fate.[10]

Lieutenant Colonel Iwan von Ilsemann was the German military attaché assigned to Bern. He reported regularly to his commanding general in the *Oberkommando des Heeres* (Army High Command, or OKH). His report of October 24, 1938, reiterated previous concerns about a Swiss military alliance with France:

> Attached please find a copy of the Envoy's report concerning "Swiss Neutrality in Times of Tension," which among other things deals with military issues that I discussed in detail earlier. At the time, my news about certain French advances to clarify Switzerland's position with regard to a potential march of French

troops through that country was not considered appropriate here. The discussion of the Envoy with Lieutenant General Wille confirmed, however, that France has in fact taken some steps in that direction. I doubt that they were merely intended as bluff because if they served only bluffing purposes, they would not have been kept secret as anxiously as they were and would have been brought to our attention in one form or another. In addition, [German consul] Mr. von Bibra by chance a few days ago learned from a Scandinavian diplomat accredited in Belgium that France had taken similar steps in Belgium.[11]

Leaks and alleged misrepresentations in the Swiss press continued to infuriate Hitler. The Nazi press waged a relentless campaign against Swiss newspapers. Indeed, members of the Swiss press were openly threatened with death by the German media, and were undoubtedly on blacklists compiled for the time of invasion. Matters that first appeared in intelligence reports spilled over into attacks in German newspapers. The article "Agitation of the Swiss Confederation Against Germany" graced the pages of the *Völkische Beobachter (People's Observer)*, Hitler's newspaper, in December 1938.[12] It began by noting that Swiss Federal Councilors Baumann and Motta had only pretended to respond to the agitation against Germany:

So far there have been only words, no actions. The federal government has taken actions, energetic actions, only against pro-German efforts. A wave of persecution of anything suspected of being pro-Third Reich has been tolerated and assisted by the Federal Council in the past months. House searches, confiscations, arrests and prohibitions have been common. Swiss were even considered traitors if they were friendly to a Reich party member.

On the other hand, neither the Federal Council nor the Cantons have done anything to counter the unbridled agitation and the psychosis of hatred which have seized the Confederation. The Swiss press, such as the *Neue Zürcher Zeitung*, the *Basler Nachrichten*, the *Nationalzeitung* in Basle or the *Bund* in Berne writes negatively about the Reich without any inhibition and has not been warned or reprimanded. The publishers *Europa, Oprecht* and *Reso* [?] are able to print emigrants' outbursts against the Reich without any problems. A prohibition was issued against the pro-

German *Internationale Presse-Agentur* of Franz Burri from Lucerne, but in the same place a Jew named Waldemar Curian who converted to Catholicism was allowed to publish his *German Letters* without encountering any difficulties from the authorities. Nobody has thought of making life hard for the *Katholische Internationale Presseagentur* in Freiburg either. A group called *Youth Action Community* has begun to get rid of the "German poison" in books and newspapers flowing into Switzerland. A film association has set up with the same goal. In addition, a volunteer news service directed exclusively against the Reich was set up. This service has a connection to Swiss living abroad, is subject to a certain foreign influence and has personal ties to the *Bund* in Bern, which is part Jewish.

The *Neue Basler Zeitung*, which is not particularly pro-German and cannot be suspected of bringing National Socialist thoughts to Switzerland, but is solely trying to be objective toward Germany, has great difficulties. It has been investigated and persecuted, while the Communist paper *Freiheit*, whose agitation in Germany could not be any greater, has been tolerated. We have even reached the point where a paper that contains nothing but agitation against the Reich, namely the [illegible] *am Sonntag*, was allowed to start publishing again without the federal government intervening. We could fill many columns talking about the Swiss activities against Germany if we wanted to show how fertile the Confederation is for enemies of Germany and how shamelessly the Swiss neglect their simplest neighborly duties.

The fact is that Switzerland is more and more becoming a ground for hatred and agitation against the Reich. . . .

But what the Reich may demand with determination from a small neutral state is that it have an objective and just attitude towards all things German. . . . [T]he Reich has to demand from Switzerland to stop the shameless agitation that Switzerland has been conducting over the years concerning domestic matters of the Reich. Since the *Anschluss* of Austria and the Sudetenland have taken place, there have been strange contacts between the [deposed Austrian] Schuschnigg government and Switzerland, and the agitation has become unbearable. We may tell the Swiss with determination that they are no longer neutral if they persecute and condemn everything pro-German, but allow the worst agitators to conduct their activity against the Reich; that there is no neutrality when the *Nationalzeitung* in Basle openly welcomes the French influence in Switzerland, and the federal government does not even take note of it.

As war approached in 1939, German military intelligence was busy not only gathering information on obvious enemies such as Poland and France, but also obtaining the most detailed knowledge of Swiss defenses. Today, at the German military archives in Freiburg am Breisgau, one may examine a large box filled with numerous local maps showing fortifications and troop dispositions compiled by *"Nachrichtendienst Ic: Schweiz"* (Intelligence Service Ic [Army Group C]: Switzerland), dated August 18 through December 28, 1939.[13]

Included are tourist maps, official maps, topographical maps and military maps of all kinds. Intelligence agents drew in pen the positions of machine-gun nests, bunkers, munitions storage points and every other known defensive shelter. To gather this intelligence, German spies and informants were obviously present in every village, town and city. The only reason to gather detailed intelligence of this kind was to prepare for an attack. Swiss authorities, aware of this activity, forbade the sale of maps.

Just a week before Hitler launched World War II by attacking Poland on September 1, 1939, the German legation in Bern reported: "Federal Councilor Motta expressed his joy and gratitude over the categorical explanation of the Führer and Chancellor [Hitler] today to [Swiss] Professor Burckhard, that Germany will maintain Swiss neutrality under all circumstances."[14] However, the Swiss were privately not so naïve as to take chances, and continued to prepare for a Nazi invasion.

Once the war started, diplomatic channels were filled with pledges to respect neutrality. The day after Hitler attacked Poland, the German legation in Bern reported that the Italian emissary assured Swiss Federal Councilor Motta that Italy would respect Swiss neutrality. The Germans knew that French General Maurice Gamelin had confirmed respect for Swiss neutrality to the Swiss embassy in Paris.[15] French Foreign Minister Bonnet told the Swiss envoy who handed over the Swiss declaration of neutrality in Paris that the French government would respect the neutrality of the Swiss Confederation and the intactness of its territory pursuant to the treaties of 1815 and supplemental agreements.[16] The French statement was particularly appropriate since France had been the last country to invade Switzerland, occupying much of the country from 1798 until

Napoleon's final defeat at Waterloo. However, diplomatic assurances notwithstanding, it was clear that Switzerland was threatened only by Germany. Germany had not invaded Switzerland since the Swabian War of 1499, but the disregard of the Nazis for what they saw as merely administrative divisions of territory prompted Switzerland to negotiate a secret alliance with France concerning French support in the event of a German invasion.

The German legation reported from Bern on September 6 that "in the Swiss population and also in officer circles, the apprehension is still very great that they will be pulled into the war through France."[17] However, France was not prepared to attack Germany through Switzerland or anywhere else, despite her mutual defense treaty with Poland. Hitler kept his options open in the war of nerves that lasted until the following year.

German intelligence reported on September 18 that the Federal Council had reproached the army's leadership for not sufficiently fortifying Switzerland's western border. Thus, the Swiss were now erecting additional fortifications in the Jura mountains so the Federal Council and the military could legitimately maintain that they were prepared to resist an attempted incursion by the French.[18] It was only a show, however, to impress the Germans that their southern flank was secure and thus to remove any motivation to pull Switzerland into German war plans. The Swiss stressed their neutrality, but they were in fact seriously preparing for invasion from the only possible enemy: the Germans to their north.

As the mismatched conflict ended in Poland, the German military kept a close eye on and constantly updated maps detailing Swiss defenses. A map first prepared on October 12, 1939, showed nine Swiss divisions, nine border brigades, and three mountain brigades.[19] Updates through mid-November, each inscribed with a different colored pencil, indicated changing positions and the demobilization of two border brigades in the south. Question marks at some Swiss troop positions on the map indicate that Wehrmacht intelligence was not perfect. Moreover, German intelligence knew that "the deliveries of armament matériel of different types promised for a long time from France have not arrived."[20]

On October 30, the first of a regular series of intelligence reports written by or submitted to the OKW, the Wehrmacht high command, reported the following:

In case of a German attack Switzerland will apply total chemical warfare and use mustard gas. The Swiss troops therefore conduct daily marching exercises and practice attacks with gas masks so that they will be able to keep the gas masks on all day.

All along the border several thousand mines have been put into the grassy soil. They will explode at the slightest touch. In addition, trip wires have been set everywhere.

Should vital locations (train stations, gas utilities, ammunition factories, etc.) be bombarded, all Germans will be immediately interned.[21]

While it is unclear whether the Swiss actually planned to use chemical munitions, the remainder of the report was accurate. Meanwhile, the Germans were bristling from anti-German attacks in the Swiss press. Iwan von Ilsemann, the German military attaché in Bern, reported on November 3, 1939, that he complained to Lieutenant Colonel Roger Masson of the "Information Section" (actually, espionage section) of the Swiss General Staff Division that military reporters were deviating from "a press attitude worthy of Swiss neutrality."[22] Meanwhile, the Wehrmacht itself was hardly staying neutral. It continued to keep close watch on deployment of Swiss forces, preparing detailed maps.[23]

Swiss arms exports were also closely watched. In its regular intelligence report of November 11, the OKW had this to say about one of Switzerland's leading arms manufacturers:

a) The *Machine Tool Manufacturer Orlikon* made deliveries mostly to neutral countries, namely Turkey, Yugoslavia, Denmark, and Holland.

b) Delivery contracts have been executed with England with a value of CHF [Swiss francs] 100,000,000 for 20mm anti-aircraft guns and ammunition, mostly for the navy. These deliveries are scheduled to begin in March 1940. Trade negotiations are ongoing between England and Switzerland. England is exerting strong pressure on Switzerland regarding these deliveries and both sides have emphasized that the deliveries will take place no matter what. . . .

c) It is interesting to note that the admiralty is attaching extremely great importance to obtaining 20mm anti-aircraft guns for the navy. We know from discussions with British officers that their current anti-aircraft guns are unable to cope with dive bombers. . . .

The British hope to fill that gap with the automatic rapid-fire
20mm guns.

d) France has received seven [?] Orlikon deliveries since the beginning of the war. There is an order pending worth CHF
80,000,000. It is scheduled to be executed in the spring of 1940
(20mm anti-aircraft guns, airplane cannon, and ammunition).[24]

German intelligence reports also provide a comprehensive picture of
what the Swiss thought of the Third Reich. A remarkably candid assessment was distributed by the OKW with the date of November 17, 1939.
It began:[25]

a) Reliable sources tell us that the *Swiss Government is without any
doubt neutral* and strives to implement the country's neutrality and
the resulting obligations in public life.

b) *Reportedly, however, the Swiss population is very hostile toward Germany.*
People are of the opinion that Germany caused this war with its
ruthlessness. After all, the demands for Danzig and the corridor
could have been met by way of negotiations. It was not necessary
to pull the entire world into disaster.

It was, of course, fully consistent with international law that the government be "formally" neutral while individual citizens favor one or the
other side. Official political neutrality was necessary for Switzerland's survival, but the Swiss people were anything but neutral, as the OKW recognized. The report continued:

The Swiss population believes that Germany is alone responsible
for the inconveniences and the financial damages caused by its
mobilization. For these reasons, 90% of the population has a negative attitude toward Germany, 5% are indifferent, and at best 5%
have a positive attitude.

The prevalence of negative attitudes toward Germany would only
increase in 1940, when France collapsed and Switzerland became surrounded by the Axis. Similar statistics would be suggested by correspon-
dents from the Allied countries. The intelligence report continued:

Reports show that the 5% with a positive attitude toward

Germany would have to fear for their jobs should they in fact dare to support Germany. Reich citizens are reportedly called bad names such as "*Sauschwob*" [Swabian pig] and "*Nazihund*" [Nazi dog], and German business people are threatened with boycotts. In the recent past, a number of such upright Germans have been expelled from the country. The 140,000 Reich Germans current- ly living in Switzerland are considered dangerous because under pressure from the Reich they identify with Hitlerism. Neither French nor British citizens have this problem because their home countries do not exert any similar influence.

Again, this intelligence report prepared by Germans for Germans frankly acknowledges Swiss rejection of Nazism. (For their part, the Swiss were alert to the threat of a fifth column posed by citizens or foreign resi- dents with Nazi sympathies.) Reflecting the attitude of their regime, the German intelligence report would naturally be incomplete without an anti-Semitic attack: "Jewish emigrants in their blind hatred are inciting people against anything German and, of course, they are not open to objective arguments." This charge would escalate throughout the war. Goebbels' propaganda machine regularly attacked Switzerland as a land of "mountain Jews" and under Jewish influence.[26] The report continued: "Sources tell us that the hatred against Germans is so great that Swiss driving German cars are exposed to insults."

Press censorship was adopted by Swiss authorities both to decrease the chances of provoking a Nazi attack and to prevent disclosure of infor- mation useful to the Germans. At the same time, the military was making all efforts in preparation to resist an attack. The intelligence report stated:

> c) We have learned that *the Federal Council is striving to impose neutral- ity on the press.* General Guisan recently warned the press in this regard and threatened censure should the press fail to comply.
>
> Reportedly, the press showed a certain reluctant restraint after that, but the tone toward Germany was still spiteful and nasty. Reuter and Havas are dominating the newspapers. The German Press Bureau is represented almost exclusively with army reports. As for the rest, news favorable to Germany is weakened or not reported at all.
>
> Reportedly, *Paris Soir* appears daily with an edition of more than 100,000, while the German press is allegedly able to sell only

300 papers a day. The only paper sympathizing with Germany, the *Neue Basler Zeitung*, reportedly has few readers in Switzerland. Swiss papers carrying German pictures are in danger of being canceled.

d) Given the population's attitude, German propaganda is showing little effect. According to the reports, the Swiss simply do not believe the Germans anymore and even think that the German radio is lying.

Through their choice of newspapers, Swiss citizens were expressing their sympathy toward the Allies and antipathy toward the Nazis, whose propaganda was failing. The OKW report continued with the following concerning the military:

e) *The attitude of the Swiss general staff toward Germany reportedly is not unfriendly.* The officers were very impressed with [Germany's] successes in Poland. We have, however, learned that the Swiss military routinely refers to the Führer using the most obscene terms. A recently issued army decree threatens persons who insult foreign heads of state with draconian punishment so that the public grumbling should stop.

Some members of the Swiss general staff were admittedly oriented toward Germany and proven German military theories, albeit not toward Nazism itself. However, the Swiss army command saw the danger and sought to weed out or transfer such officers to positions where they would not pose a risk to Swiss resistance or to sensitive information. The German report does not mention a Swiss-French alliance, which the Germans strongly suspected. Most telling is the comment that, despite official orders, military personnel continued to insult Hitler. In any case, while formal press censorship was a filter for negatives, it could not force the Swiss to print pro-German stories. Moreover, it would not and could not curtail negative comments about Hitler by individual soldiers and citizens. The report continued:

f) Reports show that Poland enjoys great sympathy all over Switzerland. In order to help, some Swiss have set up a charitable organization called "Pro Polonia." According to information received, the press keeps describing the destruction of Warsaw caused by

the German bombardment and the suffering of the Polish population. This, too, shows the attitude set against Germany.

g) France and England are said to be appreciated because the
Swiss reportedly assume that Switzerland will retain its current
size if the Western forces win, while they fear that the German-
speaking part of Switzerland will be annexed by Germany if
Germany wins.

As noted, since Hitler came to power, the more rabid Nazis had been
printing maps showing Switzerland as part of *"Grossdeutschland"* (Greater
Germany). German intelligence thought such carelessness was needlessly
provoking to the Swiss. In fact, a 1939 Swiss publication entitled *"Gau
Schweiz"* (a *Gau* meaning a Nazi administrative district) compiled several
such maps and Nazi threats of annexation to show where Nazi plans were
heading.[27] Concerning the Hitler-Stalin agreement, the OKW report
noted: "The Russian-German friendship pact had a similarly unfavorable
effect, particularly in church circles. Those circles are speaking of a pact
with the devil."

This November 17, 1939, intelligence report ends with a pithy sum-
mation of the prevailing mood in Switzerland after the fall of Poland:

Frankreich Wird geliebt,	France is loved,
England bewundert,	England is admired,
Deutschland gehasst.	Germany is hated.

No doubt Hitler himself read some of these reports, reinforcing his
animosity toward Switzerland. The continuing resistance of a German-
speaking population that should have had a natural affinity to the Reich,
the absence of any significant pro-Nazi political elements within
Switzerland, and what he regarded as Swiss duplicity frustrated and
angered him. As the year 1940 approached, however, he had bigger fish to
fry. His underlings in OKW intelligence were given responsibility for dealing with Switzerland, and intelligence reports continued to pour in. This
one is from November 29:

Based on our extensive experience, the current Swiss neutrality is
a neutrality of the state, not of the people. Even if the Federal
Council tries to convince the Swiss press to adopt the official policy of neutrality, the press nevertheless goes its own way.

According to the reports, the English-Jewish influence on the newspapers is very strong because the large Swiss papers are paid by the British and also because Freemasonry plays a large role. We should not overlook that the Freemasons are a branch of the English Freemasons. It is well known that the latter are working closely with the English "Intelligence Service," the far-reaching espionage organization.[28]

The report complained that English influence affected the Swiss justice system and the police, and that the policies of the Office of the Attorney General of Switzerland "have nothing to do with neutrality." No specifics are stated, but this could refer to actions against Nazi organizations. Further, the report alleged, regulations provided that all incoming newspapers were supposed to be inspected when they cross the border. However, "German newspapers are held back and sometimes forwarded to their destination after a wait of ten days, while French newspapers are hardly even checked and are sent through in their entirety." Further, "British newspapers are confiscated only in exceptional cases."

An OKW report by Lieutenant Colonel Jacobsen dated January 10, 1940, stated that the mood seen in Swiss mail (obviously some snooping was taking place) could be expressed: "One waits." The general attitude against Germany was accompanied by the hope for an English victory. A Swiss border soldier wrote that he was concerned about unemployment in Switzerland and added, "When I think of the future, it does not seem good to live in Switzerland, one does not know what will come, Germany and Italy have us fully in hand." The greater part of the populations in the neutral countries were favorable to England because she remained defiant and to France out of old sympathies.[29]

As to the Hitler-Stalin pact, the German Army High Command, OKH, wrote to German military attaché Iwan von Ilsemann in Bern on January 13, 1940, about rumors in Switzerland that Germany was sending large numbers of officers to Russia. The attaché was told to deny the charge but not to "create the impression that we are bluntly distancing ourselves from the Russians. The leitmotif remains that with our new relationship to Russia we have crushed the planned encirclement. Russia is a welcome economic partner, and we have a non-aggression treaty, but no military treaty."[30] That last comment would be proven false after the war, when it was discovered that Hitler and Stalin had agreed to dismember Poland.

In January 1940 the Army Printing Office in Berlin published the pocket book *Schweizerisches Heer* (The Swiss Army). In mid-month, the OKH General Staff, Division of Foreign Armies West, wrote to Army Group C (Ic) that it would shortly receive a quantity of the book. It was to be distributed as follows:

Army Group C	10 copies
Army Headquarters 7 (and army troops)	50 ``
Corps Command XXV (and corps troops)	40 ``
96 Infantry Division (up to and incl. battalions)	30 ``
50 Infantry Division (up to and incl. battalions)	30 ``
205 Infantry Division (up to and incl. companies)	150 ``
260 Infantry Division (up to and incl. companies)	150 ``
	460 copies[31]

The books were promptly sent.[32] The need to prepare the troops for an invasion of Switzerland was the only reason to distribute such a book in such a quantity. Army Group C was positioned at the Swiss border and, as will be seen, would be assigned the task of preparing for an attack on Switzerland later in the year.

Much of the planning turned on the disposition and intent of what was thought to be the much more powerful French army. The Germans were highly suspicious of cooperation between the French and Swiss. An officer in the 260th Division—one of those listed above—reported on January 31 about French-Swiss contacts. A Frau Brugger returned from Rheinfelden, Switzerland, and revealed having seen a black car with French tags in an area not accessible to the public near the Rhine bridge. Inside were two French officers wearing tall, dark-blue caps and four Swiss officers with steel helmets.[33] The report was repeated up the chain of command by Army Group C.[34]

A top-secret "Case Switzerland" was submitted by the Operations Division Ia, Army Headquarters, on February 9, 1940. It was entitled "Overview of probable measures to be taken by Army High Command 7 in the case of a French invasion of Switzerland."[35] Under Case A, "Switzerland resists the French." "In Case A we would not have to expect the French forces to rush to the Reich border. German troops would probably invade Switzerland. It is impossible to set a time frame for possible necessary measures." Switzerland would become a battleground.

Under Case B, "Switzerland does not resist the French or joins them."

This could happen "after a short or longer period of tensions" or "as a surprise with no preceding period of tensions." Case B "is the most likely scenario. Accordingly, preparatory measures that could be executed partially or entirely during the period of tension must be shortened as much as possible. Operational measures, which must be taken at the latest at the beginning of the French invasion of Swiss territory, should be ordered as soon as possible." The Operations Division was directed: "Order to fight if enemy attacks Reich territory from Switzerland."

As a result, the Wehrmacht monitored Swiss troop positions ever more carefully so as to be able to attack on short notice. Among the surviving German invasion plans is a map dated February 5, 1940, drawn on tracing paper, showing the Swiss forces in red and black pencil, including any that were demobilized.[36] Accompanying it is a large map of southwestern Europe on which the tracing paper map was placed. Such small maps could be changed regularly to provide the latest updates on targets and objectives for actual battle plans.

Giuseppe Motta, a member of the Federal Council who sought to maintain an even-handed neutrality in foreign affairs, died on January 23, 1940. Despite the fact that Motta supported the suppression of Nazi groups within Switzerland, the German Foreign Office in Bern sent Berlin a pessimistic report saying that the country would become even more anti-Reich now that the moderate Motta was gone: "That the Swiss public sides with the Western forces and the authorities allow this to happen can be explained primarily by the fact that the authorities themselves are convinced that Germany will ultimately lose."

The military attaché noted that since 1933 Switzerland had been fearful of the German Reich. The Reich's increasing display of power and the influence of the National Socialist philosophy on the German population led to an intentional Swiss policy to isolate itself from the Reich. Fueled by the left, the Swiss movement against National Socialism, and by implication against the German people, was taken up by the entire Swiss population.

German political leaders tried to stop this development. "The Führer had repeatedly made representations about the inviolability of Switzerland. However, to allow a basic discussion of the relationship between the two countries, the Germans insisted that the Swiss government control the Swiss press."

The report alleged that before he died Federal Councilor Motta understood that it was necessary to make public opinion less poisonous against the Germans. When one issue or another became hot in the press, he repeatedly intervened with official declarations that sought to cool things down. However, Motta was not, by and large, successful.

Beginning in 1939, due to his illness, Motta was forced to become less active politically. According to the German envoy, in the winter of 1938–39, Motta also began to change his mind and to disapprove of German policies. As a firm enemy of Communism, he could not understand why the Germans entered into a treaty of non-aggression with the Soviet Union. The envoy noted that, for years, Switzerland's "good neighbor" policy toward Germany had its best and perhaps its only supporter in Motta. His death could only mean the end of an already weak hope that a single strong personality with political vision could maintain a good German-Swiss relationship, even during war.[37]

In both intelligence and agitation, the Soviets were useful to the Germans. Particularly in socialist-oriented France, Soviet-backed organizers and agents were to prove very effective in undermining the morale of French troops. As revealed in an OKW intelligence report dated February 16, 1940, "The Communist propaganda is said to be extremely skillful and to have reached the most advanced [French] lines. Soldiers apparently find leaflets in all kinds of locations. Officers look for the distributors, but are unable to find them. Most likely they are soldiers themselves."[38]

The same OKW report noted that the Swiss federal government decreed that the export of any kind of war matériel to foreign countries now required a special permit. The Swiss were moving increasingly toward wartime control measures. It also stated that the Federal Council determined that a German edition of the banned book *Guillemots' Conversations with Hitler (Gespräche mit Hitler)* by Hermann Rauschnigg had been published in Switzerland, contrary to a statement made in the book. Apparently, the Federal Council decided to confiscate that edition.[39]

Meanwhile, German intelligence was making every effort to extract information on French forces from Swiss officers. Iwan von Ilsemann, German military attaché in Bern, discussed the problem in a letter to his commanding general dated February 17, 1940. Even assuming that the Swiss general staff was informed about the French forces on all fronts and about operational reserves, only a very small circle would have this knowledge. "These officers will, however, be particularly unwilling to inform German representatives. In addition, officers who used to belong to the army staff and were especially interested in good relations with the Germans were recently transferred elsewhere."[40]

To the chagrin of von Ilsemann, Swiss officers who previously had been friendly "deflected all attempts at steering the discussion to military details in France. . . . Further, we cannot help but notice that since the beginning of the war Swiss officers have avoided being alone with Germans." Indeed, they would not meet with representatives of the envoy. The attaché observed that the Swiss saw Germany as the enemy: "Without any doubt, the main reason is that even officers who so far had not participated in the campaign against Germany and whose hearts may be on the German side even today cannot avoid their country's mood. Germany, after all, is its only conceivable enemy."

The attaché noted that Admiral Canaris, the chief of Germany's military intelligence agency, the *Abwehr,* discussed the issue with Herr von Bibra, counselor to the envoy, and von Chamier, the press counselor. Bibra thought he might obtain information from certain Czechs and Poles, who would be bribed with guarantees that their former possessions in Bohemia or Poland would be preserved. "Chamier has close relationships with the so-called Swiss Frontists who have, however, lost their importance and do not include any high-ranking officers anymore." The Frontists, supporters of National Socialism, had been weeded out. In short, the Swiss would not be sources of intelligence on the French forces.

A February 22 memorandum from Army High Command 7 to the Command of Army Group C concerned "T" measures—the abbreviation for *Täuschung,* meaning "deception." It covered Wehrmacht troop movements in southern Germany:

> The execution of the T [deceptive] measures last week has proven that [news] about large military movements or even just rumors about planned military measures from the area south of the line between Freiburg and Donauechingen reach the French intelligence service within 2 to 3 days by way of Switzerland. There is no doubt that this happens because of the more than 2,000 commuters crossing the border daily in the sector between Basle and Constance.[41]

In a follow-up to the above, Army High Command 7 reported the interception of a French message sent over a transmitter identified as "Rennes." The intercepted message said that German agents in Zurich had spread the rumor of a German offensive to be initiated soon, along the Rhine, but that deployments of German troops had not changed. The same German report also stated that the Swiss General Staff did not anticipate a German attack against France through Switzerland. That was factually incorrect and could well have been a rumor circulated by the Swiss. In any event, the intelligence report concluded that "T" measures worked only when corroborated by observations in the field.[42]

On March 8, 1940, as invasion plans against France were moving into high gear, the German Frontier Protective Force Sector Command reported that 70,000 Swiss troops had been called to arms. Officers with pro-German sympathies had been removed, and preparations had been made at the German-Swiss frontier to facilitate the march of French troops through Switzerland. "Not only the press but also the Swiss government are inciting the Swiss population against Germany. The Swiss think that the field of operations between the warring forces will be between Lake Constance and Basle."[43] That is, of course, along the Swiss border with Germany.

A few days later, the same headquarters reported that an informant returning from Switzerland had stated: "From the Finnish defeat, the Swiss population has concluded that in case of war England and France will abandon Switzerland."[44] Even so, the Swiss were greatly inspired by the manner in which tiny Finland had held out against vastly superior numbers of Russian troops for so long. They knew that the hope of receiving help from the West was illusory. Poland had gotten no support, despite the fact that she had a mutual defense agreement with both England and France.

On March 26, the German commander at Lake Constance reported that the troops of Swiss border brigades 6 and 7 stationed opposite his position had been replaced. The towns behind the border were more densely occupied than before. He sensed an entirely anti-German sentiment among the population:

> The mood in Switzerland is everywhere strongly against us. The press is in large part responsible. Parts of the population are suffering from a delusion of persecution! Basically Germany is made responsible for everything. Sometimes the Germans are said to be coming from the north across the Rhine, sometimes through Vorarlberg (see article in the newspaper *La Suisse*). People do not expect any danger from the West![45]

Concern about Swiss-French cooperation was again the topic of a report by German military attaché von Ilsemann on April 8. While General Guisan and other officials apparently denied any connection, the report noted:

> Nevertheless, rumors persist about unilateral agreements of the Swiss military with the French. Recently, someone even alleged that General Guisan had met with General Gamelin the month before. Neither the Envoy nor I believe this to be true. [Air Attaché Friedrich] Hanesse, however, who does not think too highly of the Swiss anyway, is convinced that the allegations are true.
>
> From all I have heard I think it plausible that there have been certain discussions between the Swiss and French military. But those discussions probably covered only any assistance the French might provide in case the Germans attempt to march through Switzerland, something that is still believed possible here.[46]

Von Ilsemann expressed gratitude that his requests to send "a competent intelligence officer to G."—apparently Geneva—had been followed. "F. will be very useful in that location. . . . It is very important to obtain more detailed records on the French and English reserves."

What von Ilsemann knew of the coming offensive is not known. But as the uncertainties of winter gave way to spring 1940 in this war of nerves, Hitler was putting all his military assets at risk with a sudden, massive attack to flank the northern—not southern—end of the Maginot Line. All hell was about to break loose.

CHAPTER 2

HANGING HITLER IN SATIRE

From Charlie Chaplin's *The Great Dictator* and the Three Stooges' *You Nazty Spy* to the underground Russian *Samizdat* satires, humor has been a powerful weapon against the bombast of totalitarian rulers. After the rise of Adolf Hitler, the ability of the Swiss population to ridicule the pretensions of the Nazis—combined with defensive preparations and the ability of Swiss soldiers to shoot straight—was an important part of resistance to the Axis. It also infuriated Hitler and his circle, who never quite managed to silence this Swiss laughter once and for all.

Hitler did make many attempts to "shut up" the Swiss. German diplomats and agents in Switzerland before and during the war made constant complaints—often brazen threats—against what they considered Swiss violations of neutrality. From newspaper articles and speeches to plays and satires, the Germans monitored expressions of Swiss independence and put pressure on Bern to suppress them. The Swiss government had to walk a narrow line between offending its own high-spirited patriots or the ranting Nazis to the north.

This chapter examines the two leading sources of satire in Switzerland which—in the face of shrill German protests—lampooned and infuriated the Nazis. One was the *Nebelspalter*, Switzerland's leading magazine of humor and political cartoons since 1875. It took no prisoners, publishing hugely popular caricatures of the totalitarian systems of both Germany and Russia. *Cabaret Cornichon* was the other. Its writers and actors kept audiences in stitches with rollicking live performances that openly mocked the pretensions of the Third Reich, even in the darkest days.

Nebelspalter was published weekly. It roared at both the Brown (Nazi) and Red (Communist) totalitarians. *Nebelspalter*'s political cartoons were so insulting to Hitler and Stalin that it is difficult to understand why the magazine was not censored, or even banned as overly provocative. Following are descriptions of a few examples, identified by date.[1]

August 1932: Months before the Nazis even came to power, a cartoon depicts a ghastly spider with a swastika spinning a web around a cadaverous human. The caption: "Biology. Among all spiders it is the swastika spider which weaves the most beautiful webs." In Germany itself, such a barb would have been sufficient to get the creator beaten up—or killed—and his offices firebombed.

June 1933: Hitler is now in power. Storm Troopers hurl rocks labeled "Nazi propaganda," "anti-Semitism," and "Fascism" at a woman protecting children under an overcoat with a Swiss cross. The caption reads: "Helvetia has to assume new duties as a mother!" This was an early warning that Switzerland must resist the dangerous ideology to the north.

October 1933: "Germany's Rise" portrays brownshirts marching, concentration camps, hypnotized masses, and rotting corpses. "By way of *Gleichschaltung* [a Nazi term meaning 'forcing into line'] of shirts, countryside and brains," the caption says, "the path leads to the next real and final *Gleichschaltung*." This foresaw the grisly events that would take place in the future.

November 1934: A marching black swastika in step beside a marching red hammer-and-sickle, both with boots, are accompanied by a poem:

> Though the black child feels unease
> Beside her big red bravo,
> Her flirting manner tells her heart,
> We're sure it is not sorrow.
> This pair is clearly heaven-starred,
> The wedding comes tomorrow!

Once again, Nazis and Communists are shown marching toward common totalitarian goals. Amazingly, *Nebelspalter* seems to have anticipated the Hitler-Stalin Pact a half decade later which formed the basis for the attack on Poland and the beginning of World War II.

July 1935: A threatening fist with swastika shakes at a small man wearing a milking hat with Swiss cross. The caption: "Since you clench your fist against me all the time, I think I'd better roll up my sleeves." And a sub-caption: "All Swiss newspapers are prohibited [in Germany]! Consequently Switzerland banned the German newspapers—the *Reichsdeutsche*, the *Alemanne,* and the *Stürmer.*" Nazi Germany's banning of Switzerland's newspapers provided a convenient opportunity for Switzerland to protect herself by keeping out the most strident organs of Nazi propaganda.

November 1937: Hitler and Mussolini with knives and forks have the globe on their dinner table. "Intimate issues being considered. '. . . do you think we can manage this steak?'" *Nebelspalter* again saw the handwriting on the wall, in this case the Pact of Steel of May 1939, in which the Führer and the Duce joined in a military alliance.

July 1938: The flags of Germany and Italy as well as the other major powers seem to overwhelm a boy waving a small Swiss cross. "Don't be shy, little Hans. It's not the size of your flag that matters!" The *Anschluss* of Austria had recently taken place, and Switzerland was in her traditional David against Goliath role.

November 1938: A jester redraws a picture of a frowning Hitler into a demonically smiling Hitler at the prodding of a sinister advisor. The caption: "Drawing lessons. 'More charm, please.'" The impetus for this cartoon was the Munich agreement, in which British Prime Minister Neville Chamberlain agreed to Germany's annexation of the western part of Czechoslovakia.

December 1938: In the aftermath of the anti-Jewish *Kristallnacht* (Night of the Broken Glass), Nazi Propaganda Minister Josef Goebbels sits in an easy chair pushing buttons on automatic devices for "concentration camps, inquisition chambers, expropriation, deprivation, outrage, pogroms, and asset confiscation" as well as "*Gleichschaltung*" and "elimination." The seeds of war and genocide had been planted.

February 1939: A powerful Swiss kicks out a weakling bearing the sign, "*Gau Schweiz NSDAP*" (Switzerland as a future Nazi administrative unit). The caption: "'Prepare to dismiss' as opposed to 'Ready for action.'" In the days before this cartoon, German propaganda organs had launched a series of anti-Swiss attacks. The cartoon's message was that the Swiss must expel Nazi subversives before they could act.

September 1939: A smiling British Prime Minister Neville Chamberlain shows Hitler to a door marked "Stalin." Chamberlain says, "After you, Sir." Little did the world know that Hitler and Stalin had already made an alliance which included the carving up of Poland.

September 1939: Nazi Germany and Communist Russia had just attacked and partitioned Poland. The picture shows a gruesome Nazi hugging an equally gruesome Communist. Both are laughing and dripping with blood. The caption reads: "The New Friends. 'We now have to wipe off the dirt we threw at each other for so long!'"

October 1939: "Polka." Stalin merrily dances over Poland's corpse with a woman wearing a swastika ribbon. While the Allies would not discover the military agreements set forth in the Hitler-Stalin pact until after the war, just weeks after it was signed a Swiss satirist depicted in this cartoon a pact without limits.

August 1940: Western Europe has fallen to the German blitzkrieg. Switzerland is surrounded but armed and determined. In this cartoon, a short, fat Swiss man, his dog at his feet, folds his hands before a sharp Nazi face. The main caption: "If need be, pretend to be deaf!" The subcaption is a little lesson on "playing dumb" and thwarting the Nazis:

"Isn't it true that every man possesses his own rifle?" "No no, my dog is called Mopsli not Trifle." "Don't you keep your rifle ready all the time?" "Unfortunately, Mopsli eats more than he can handle at one time." "Will you please listen: a heavy rifle and rounds of ammunition?" "Well, this is true, for Mopsli food is always a temptation." "As far as I know, you also maintain an *Ortswehr* (local guard)?" "I agree, Mopsli is too fat by far."

Such obfuscation is exactly what the Swiss did in countless confrontations with the Nazis that followed. They played dumb, answered and didn't answer, delayed and evaded, and proved in the end to be skilled and tenacious negotiators. Against the military strength of the Nazis, it was often better to pretend to be the bumbling idiot who only wants to talk about his dog, but who has a pistol in his pocket.

Once Switzerland was surrounded and locked in, however, Nazi threats had to be taken seriously. Not only did German leaders openly make death threats against Swiss writers, but attacks in the Swiss press provoked the Nazi leadership to threaten trade sanctions on essential goods such as food and coal, and to consider military action to wipe out the republic once and for all. While formal neutrality did not require moral neutrality on the part of the country's people and media, as a measure of self-defense the Swiss government established an official—if mild—form of censorship to make it appear that it was cracking down. It applied to published writings depicting either of the combatants. The censorship did not involve any prior restraint, but was applied after publication took place; items which were overly "biased" would result in a warning, and might even be seized. However, no censorship existed of oral or private communications, which became the primary methods in which political sentiments were expressed.

The censorship explains why, in the last year of peace, *Nebelspalter* published 54 caricatures of Hitler, but in the next five years featured only eight. Attacking Hitler personally in print became "illegal," and he vanished from political cartoons in the public media.[2] Indicative of the emotional tilt of the Swiss people toward the Allies, unfavorable caricatures of Churchill and Roosevelt were virtually non-existent from the start.

Within Switzerland, censorship itself became a subject of satire. Yet, apparently only a single issue of *Nebelspalter* was officially censored during the war. Heidi Moore, a childhood friend of the daughter of the publisher Ernst Löpfe-Benz, recounted the incident as she heard it from her friend. "We both remember the consternation in the country when this happened. Her father was at a loss why [the censorship] happened. The only objectionable cartoon and text was actually taken from a German (underground) publication and was identified as such. Apparently that was the reason why the German ambassador lodged a threatening protest with the Foreign Affairs Department in Bern."[3]

Toward the war's end, however, open vehemence returned. *Nebelspalter* published a whole series of cartoons like the following:

January 1945: "The Shoes of the Dead in Maidanek." Nazi Propaganda Minister Goebbels gestures to a sea of dead victims' shoes. The further caption: "Dr. Goebbels writes in *Das Reich*: 'Among the peoples the Germans of today are the pioneers of new convictions and hence of a better and nobler human race.'"

February 1945: Ridiculous looking musketeers with swastikas and bent swords are surrounded by gigantic shadows of American, British, and Russian soldiers with bayonets. The only caption, "Redoubt," mocked the hope of a Nazi "Fortress Europe" strategy.

April 1945: Hitler, Himmler, Göring, and Goebbels smiling around a table while being served cake, champagne, and fruit. "Why capitulate?" To the end, the Nazi leadership denied that the war was lost.

May 1945: With the Axis finally defeated, *Nebelspalter* could lambaste with no holds barred. One cartoon is captioned, "The very last reunion." The deceased Hitler and Mussolini, with black wings, ascend over ruins of cities and piles of corpses. In another cartoon, a train falls over a cliff, Hitler as driver and skulls as passengers. The caption reads: "We are grateful to our Führer."

With the liberation of concentration camps by the Allies, a cartoon appeared of the ghosts of Goethe, Bach, Schiller and Beethoven looking down on the devil portrayed by Himmler. "Viewing the concentration camps in Germany. 'And this is what is left of Germany.'" On the same theme is another cartoon with the caption, "Buchenwald. Himmler being awarded the highest German order of the '*Rote Buche*' [Red Beech]." This is a word play on "Buche" and "Buchenwald." Happy devils kiss and surround Himmler.

Marking the guilty verdicts in the war crimes trials, a cartoon in the October 1946 edition bears the caption: "The end of dastardliness." A hydra with all its Swastika-marked snakeheads hangs from the gallows. The war is over and Nazi war criminals condemned at Nürnberg have been executed.

Nebelspalter is still published today, but its greatest achievements were its caricatures during the period of the Third Reich. It took on all forms of totalitarianism, lambasting Soviet Russia as roughly as it did Nazi Germany. A book of leading *Nebelspalter* cartoons entitled *Gegen Rote und Braune Fäuste (Against Red and Brown Fists)* was published just after the war and was recently reprinted.

Despite the censorship of public newspapers and radio during the worst years of Axis encirclement, in private one could insult the Führer freely or otherwise say one's piece. In those years, there was a lively cultural life reflecting both directly and indirectly on Switzerland's predicament and the nature of her enemies. It ran from the constant lectures given both for and by members of the military to a wide range of entertainments for civilians. Of the latter, the most intriguing was cabaret.

Although it may seem to reach a smaller audience, cabaret, or stage-produced satire, can be far more revealing of the mindset of the times than official proclamations or political speeches. In cabaret, performers use dialogue, poetry, songs, dance, music, and props to express parody, mockery, farce, melodrama, and tragedy.

In the world of cabaret, it would be difficult to surpass the anti-Nazi spirit of Zurich's *Cabaret Cornichon* (The Pickle Cabaret), the stage of Elsie Attenhofer (1909–99), the grande dame of all Swiss cabaret.[4] Attenhofer's book on the Cornichon—symbolized by a smiling pickle with chicken legs and an umbrella walking a high wire—presents a side of Swiss defiance that complemented the country's military preparations.

On December 9, 1938, the Federal Council declared: "Although the preparation and organization of the military and economic defense of the country is a matter for the state, we would like to leave the *geistige Verteidigung* [mental or spiritual defense] to the initiative of our citizens." Through its satirical attacks, the Cornichon played that role to the maximum. Indeed, when German diplomats protested against its anti-Axis invective and the Swiss censors would come to inquire, the Cornichon pointed to the declaration by the Federal Council.[5]

In 1933, Hitler's seizure of power drove many of Germany's prominent intellectuals and artists from the country. Poet Thomas Mann moved to Zurich with his family, including his daughter Erika, a blossoming cabaret star.[6] Erika Mann established herself in the Cabaret *Pfeffermühle* (Pepper Mill), which was constantly satirizing the pretensions of the Germans. Seeing the success of the *Pfeffermühle*, Walter Lesch and his colleagues Emil Hegetschweiler, Alois Carigiet, and musician Billy Weilenmann decided to found the Cornichon. Two very talented beginners applied to play leading roles, and Lesch chose both: Elsie Attenhofer and Mathilde Daneggers.[7] From its first performances in September 1934, the Cornichon became a thorn in the side of the Nazis.

Its attacks were both ingenious and hilarious. Already some Swiss publications, including the *Nebelspalter*, had been prohibited in Germany. The cabaret's first program featured children singing what was ostensibly a folk song but which asked the question, "How many Swiss newspapers are prohibited in the Reich? Only [Nazi Propaganda Minister] Goebbels can count them." The smallest newspaper "from the smallest Swiss village gnaws like a worm at the Third Reich."[8]

The 1935 program "These Are the Days of Roses" contained a special presentation "for which we will charge a bit more," said the Master of Ceremonies in Basel when the Cornichon started its first tour of several Swiss cities. "The Cornichon unfortunately failed to contribute anything to the wedding of Reich Marshal Göring and Emmy Sonnemann. We want to correct that now. Maybe you have heard that the noble bride and groom received a wild boar as a gift. We are now collecting money for a collar and a leash so that Mrs. Göring can walk the wild boar every evening."[9] Calling one of the highest officials of Nazi Germany a pig brought howls of laughter from the Swiss and howls of protest from Germany.

In a 1937 newspaper interview, Cornichon founder Walter Lesch said that he wrote the skits with Max Werner Lenz, who was then living in St. Gall but had been a long-time actor and producer in Germany. It was a perfect match—an exile from the Third Reich and a Swiss from the

German-speaking part of Switzerland, where antipathy toward the Hitler regime was most pronounced. Yet, it still took courage to denounce Nazism, for, as Lenz well knew, the path to the concentration camp could be short.[10]

But ridicule and taunt the Third Reich they did. The 1937 production *"Landesausstellung"* (Foreign Exhibition) featured a Nazi bookseller hawking *Mein Zwist* (My Strife, a parody on Hitler's *Mein Kampf*) and other books with twisted titles. A skeptical Swiss, speaking dialect filled with double meanings, is not buying. The NSDAP (Nazi party), the Gestapo, and the SA (Storm Troopers) are jeered by name.[11]

Nazi agents and stenographers sat at the back of the theater recording the dialogue and listing performers and even enthusiastic members of the audience who booed Nazi symbols. The information was passed on to Berlin.[12] The Nazis fully expected to take revenge when the Führer got around to dealing with Switzerland.

A 1938 production depicted "a duel between fascism and democracy." A Swiss with only an umbrella fights a huge armored figure. The Swiss falls back, but when he utters the word "freedom," the fascist figure collapses. The victor examines the fallen giant and finds that there is nothing at all inside the armor.[13] The same program featured a song, sung to a street organ, entitled "It's All His Fault." It made fun of the Nazis blaming the Jews for all social ills while imposing totalitarianism upon everyone else. The lyrics run as follows:[14]

> In Nazidonia, Nazidonia,
> where the ancient Aryans live,
> there in the Reich of a thousand years
> and of the people of pure race,
> a great and strong leader is standing guard,
> over butter, blood and cottage cheese. . . .
> And the Führer is doggedly searching
> for the evil assassin,
> because there is no question
> that this whole mess is someone's fault.
> And of course,
> that's it:
> Isidor, who has always been degenerate,
> has committed this crime too.
> And to punish him for his hatred,

the Führer seizes his money and his passport.
And the people, even though exploited,
at least feel they have been saved.
And the moral of this story
is very short and simple:
were it not for the hated Jew,
who would we have to blame?
German and Italian and Japanese,
pure and pious and Franco-Spanish,
the people will only degenerate,
unless we give them someone to execute.
Jew or Communist,
Gypsy or Christ —
nothing but enemies all around,
take them away, kill them!
And so we gain some time,
until it is our turn.
And the people, even though they have been betrayed,
still do not smell the bacon.
And the moral for all times
until eternity:
were it not for the hated Jew,
who would we have to blame?

Why is the Führer guarding "butter, blood and cottage cheese"? Butter (as in "guns and butter") probably referred to a prosperous economy, in other words, "the goodies." Blood meant the supposed purity of the Aryan race. Cottage cheese was thrown in to make the lines rhyme while at the same time making fun of Hitler.

The Cabaret Cornichon became so popular that the Zurich police feared that its shows might provoke the Germans to take measures to punish all of Switzerland. A police report dated May 1, 1939, described a performance as follows:

The entire piece is directed solely against the Axis powers and their heads of state. Individual acts ridicule Hitler, Mussolini and their policies, especially Act 4, "Little Aspirations," and Act 5, "The Rat Catcher." In Act 4, actors do grotesque impersonations of Hitler and Mussolini. It concludes when a nurse and a physician from a mental hospital enter and declare both of them incurable. In Act 5, the Rat Catcher of Hammeln appears as the "Idea of National Socialism," hypnotizes several persons and makes them dance to his tune.[15]

On May 25, the police reported that the German Consul General in Zurich had complained about the performance, which by that time had rocked the city with its defamatory satire. Anti-German sentiment ran high, and the Swiss play was filled with dangerous wordplay. The report explained:

> In "The Rat Catcher," an announcer opens by telling Swiss children that Switzerland has become a part of the Third Reich. The Rat Catcher then enters and uses his flute to hypnotize the children to determine how they react to the Anschluss. Then actress Voli Geiler comes on the stage. She declares that her mother, a very fashionable French-speaking Swiss, had strongly favored the Anschluss. But now, she laments, all her jewelry has been stolen. Her *broches* [brooches] and all her money went to the "*boches*" [slang for Germans]. This entire sketch is directly anti-German . . . and the applause of the audience shows that it has had its intended effect.[16]

The very same day, Zurich police sought the advice of Confederation legal counsel in Bern on whether they should intervene. The German Consul General was outraged that "The Rat Catcher" could be performed on stage in a supposedly neutral country: "The expression '*Boches*' is the worst insult that there is for a German."[17]

Confederation counsel responded the next day, admitting the Consul General's protest was justifiable. The expression "*Boches*" insulted a foreign people and should not be allowed.[18] Notably, he did not go on to suggest that speaking ill of Nazism was forbidden.

The portion of the "Rat Catcher" that caused the most commotion follows a Nazi plot to overcome Swiss resistance and establish a police state. Voli Geiler, referring to her mother, delivered the following lines in a typically topsy-turvy mixture of Swiss-German and French:

Wer hät ere de Bolle gstucht	Who took all her money
et toutes les broches?	and all her brooches?

Wer hät namal Devise brucht?	Who needed currency?
C'étaient les boches!	The Germans [*les boches*]!
Jetzt äntli merkts mis Mami gwüss	Now my mother finally understands:
Les Nazi sont	The Nazis
encore plus rouge que les Russes!	Are even more red than the Russians!
Elle a raison . . .	She is right . . .
O lala![19]	O lala!

The Zurich police duly admonished the Cornichon, and author Walter Lesch, that it was "not nice" to disparage foreign peoples. Lesch didn't give an inch. He held his ground and refused to strike anything from the scene. He did issue a written explanation in response to the charge that the cabaret had insulted the German people.[20] Pointing out that the performance portrays a Swiss woman who uses some French words, Lesch (who himself was an exile from Germany) brazenly declared that he had never written a direct insult in his five years with the Cornichon. Artistic freedom cannot be suppressed: "If you take away our artistic freedom, you take away any effectiveness we have as an instrument of *geistige Verteidigung* [spiritual defense]. That freedom is protected by the authorities and sanctioned by the public." Therefore, Lesch concluded, "we refuse to alter a single word of the text in question."

The Cornichon actors also stood their ground and continued performances, although they had good reason to fear the Germans.[21] Like many other Swiss citizens, their names were on Nazi blacklists. Actress Trudi Schoop's entire life history, including her family tree and the details of her acting career, was written up in Berlin. Lenz, who had worked at the Dessau Theater in Germany, was told by a man returning from Dessau that the new theater director was a Nazi who had been promoted to Gauleiter. When talk turned to Switzerland he had said: "So, you are from Zurich? Isn't that where Lenz is! The pig! Tell him, when we get there, we will hang him!" But Lenz was waiting for them, not only with his satire but with his rifle: as a member of the military's Local Defense.

The Cornichon also showed no mercy to Swiss politicians who were perceived as weak toward the Axis. In 1940, Swiss Federal President Pilet-Golaz acceded to a demand for a meeting with a small group of Swiss who supported collaboration with Germany. Although the meeting might have well been a Machiavellian ploy to "play dumb" and allow dangerous elements to let off steam, Pilet-Golaz was roundly attacked. In one Cornichon skit, "*Frischi Weggli*" (Fresh Buns), an actor steps in front of the curtain and exclaims, *"Me sött de Pilet goh-lah!"* This wordplay used "goh-lah" (Swiss dialect for "to get rid of") which sounded like "Golaz" to cry "Pilet-Golaz must go!" [22]

A performance in May 1942 drove the Nazis to distraction. Two actors are standing in front of the curtain. One of them is selling the Nazi newspaper, *Signal*. The other, a passerby, notices that a picture is printed on the paper. He shouts "Is that *him*?" meaning Adolf Hitler. "Yes, that is him"—"I want to cut out this picture and frame it!"—"What, do you want to hang it on the wall at home?"—"I do not know yet—either I will hang it or put it on the wall [for execution]."[23] The audience roared, but in most of Europe at that time jokes about killing Hitler would have gotten the humorist hung or put up against the wall to be shot.

German Ambassador Freiherr von Bibra discussed the slanders with the German Consul General Voigt, and a memorandum of their conversation was sent to Swiss authorities. The German officials stated:

> *von Bibra:* I have heard that there is an unbelievably filthy hole in Zurich at the Cornichon. People there are insulting the Führer in the most impudent and impertinent manner. . . .
> *Voigt:* Yes, I have heard about that too.
> *von Bibra:* Couldn't you send someone to listen to this? Our agent from the Reich Ministry who has seen it thought that this was entirely undignified and shameless!
> *Voigt:* At any rate, these people are Jews.
> *von Bibra:* That is what I thought! The agent compared this to the measures of censorship that the Swiss allow. They say verbatim: "to the gallows with the man, he should hang or be put against a wall and executed." It is clear that this kind of speech is directed against Adolf Hitler. That is what they allow themselves in a so-called neutral country!

The Swiss Federal Attorney, playing the usual game, sent a note to the Zurich police with the remark: "Please monitor one performance and send detailed report. *Urgent!*"

German Consul General Voigt reported to German Ambassador von Bibra on May 16, 1942, that their concerns had been raised with the head of the Zurich Cantonal Police, named Briner.[24] But Briner took no action, saying the cabaret program would last only a week. Voigt found the Swiss explanation unacceptable, pointing out that the same program was running in Basel and Bern, where the cabaret had been recently expanded. He added:

> We have complained repeatedly that Cabaret Cornichon continues to present inflammatory material. The Italians have also protested. But our complaints have had no effect, as the current program shows. Half the program is filled with disparaging remarks about Germany, while Germany's enemies are barely mentioned and, if they are, are seldom criticized. Compared to the treatment of the Allies, the remarks targeted at Germany are outrageous outbursts of hatred and hostility. They are never softened by humor or even a trace of good will. The Führer is not expressly mentioned, but the references to him are perfectly clear.

Walter Lesch explained the Cornichon's position in a letter dated July 21, 1942, to the Federal Political Police.[25] He denied knowledge of the joke about "hanging" Hitler, saying it was a spontaneous improvisation made by an actor on a day he was not present. Lesch asserted that another scene featuring Swiss dialect had been misunderstood to mock nasal-sounding German officers. "To the sentence 'certainly not him' in response to the question who will be the winner of this war, we would like to point out that the text shows clearly that the sentence can mean either Churchill or Hitler." And, he added, not every short man who wears a mustache is the Führer. Such twinkling denials by Lesch were as much game-playing as were the original performances.

In this period the Cabaret Cornichon in Zurich began a series of "Fireside Chats" inspired by Roosevelt's radio broadcasts. Stricter censorship took its toll, shifting performances toward domestic topics like rationing and air raid blackouts, but the Germans still objected.[26] Invariably, the spirit of resistance crept into these programs, too. "Cheap Jacob" featured suspenders and the crossbow, "the symbol for our ability to put up a fight, the symbol for our freedom, the symbol for our country."[27] The Cornichon evoked William Tell with a contemporary twist, amidst the ever acid, outrageous humor of the cabaret.

Despite censorship and reminders from the Swiss authorities, the Cornichon would not stop targeting current political events, although hot topics were given a slight cover. In November 1942, "Green is the Color of Hope" implied that Hitler would lose the war in Russia.[28] It was indirect, but the more subtle the innuendos, the more the audience laughed.

And truth followed humor: in December an entire German army was encircled at Stalingrad.

In September 1943, the German envoy shot off a new series of complaints against the performance of "Salem Aleikum," which was characterized by "mockery of the Third Reich."[29] In one segment, as he described:

A fakir entered the stage, his arm frantically raised in the German greeting. He said that he had sworn to keep his arm stretched out for one thousand years so that, if he could keep his pledge, he would become the most famous fakir. When someone told him that he was not the only fakir of this kind, he became discouraged and dropped his arm. He complained bitterly that he had given 10 years of his life for nothing.

The Swiss ridiculed both the Hitler salute and the fantasy of the "thousand year Reich." Ironically but typically, the German envoy ended the above letter with the obligatory "Heil!" In any event, the envoy also included the following further grievance:

This act was followed by a factious diatribe against Swiss censors. The act featured a Swiss as a target dummy in a shooting gallery. The dummy was blindfolded and gagged, and his ears were covered. After sharp verbal attacks against Swiss censors by the actress playing a shooting gallery attendant, the attendant fired at the dummy several times, shooting off his blindfold, the gag on his mouth, and the covers over his ears.

Thus, while the Germans were annoyed at the ineffectual nature of censorship in Switzerland, they considered it outrageous to suggest that the Swiss people would liberate themselves from any censorship at all. Such a policy would have meant no bounds on open Swiss attacks on the Nazis and their Axis partners.

These antics continued through the end of the war and beyond. The Cabaret Cornichon helped to buoy morale within Switzerland and thereby may have contributed indirectly to dissuading an attack. Humor and the ability to wage ideological war against one of the most aggressive and powerful states in history were the characteristics of the Cornichon. Men and women armed with satire may well have been as effective as military preparedness in the grand strategy of resistance. The caricatures of *Nebelspalter* and the antics of the Cabaret Cornichon were unique in Switzerland, and in fact not replicated elsewhere in central Europe. Everywhere else one would face execution for expressing disrespect for the Nazis.

CHAPTER 3

COUNTERATTACK OF THE NEWSREELS[1]

"National Defense and the *Ortswehren* [Local Forces]" is the title that flashes across the screen in movie theaters in Switzerland in August 1943. A dramatic voiceover intones: "May 1940: Attack on Belgium and Holland; breakthrough of Panzer forces far into the hinterland. Paratroopers, saboteurs, evacuation of the civil population . . . . call of the General for the formation of the *Ortswehren*."[2] Three long years have passed since Western Europe collapsed and the Swiss republic has been surrounded by German Nazi and Italian Fascist forces. Under General Henri Guisan's leadership, all of Switzerland—down to each local village—is armed and ready to resist invasion.

The film begins with an urgent phone call to a Swiss military officer; he sends three youngsters in Boy Scout uniforms rushing off on their bicycles with old Model 1889 rifles on their backs. One bursts into an office where an older man is dictating to a secretary; he grabs his tattered military coat and a holstered pistol from the hat rack; the alarm spreads like wildfire.

One young boy alerts a man at home; instantly the man and his wife run out, both in uniform; men sprint with rifles in hand; one positions himself at a window above some railroad tracks; two others take sniper positions at a bridge; still others await on high ground behind obstructions. Barricades of heavy logs are thrown up on roads; a crane-like device sets up concrete tank obstructions; women and children are warned away; a tent hospital is readied.

An alarm signal sounds and a ready unit of *Ortswehr* men grab their rifles and run out, secreting themselves along a barricaded road with Molotov cocktails or other explosive devices at the ready. An enemy vehicle appears; the devices are lit and several are hurled at the vehicle; the vehicle explodes. Nightfall comes with the sound of heavy weapons fire; camouflaged *Ortswehr* members hide in the deepening shadows; finally larger units of the Swiss army are shown moving into position.

The accompanying voiceover intones that total war requires total defense, commitment, and engagement. The lessons are: Don't evacuate! Remember what happened in France and Belgium. Immediate first-line defense by every *Ortswehr* unit is essential for Switzerland's survival.

The above is a typical example of the hundreds of Swiss newsreels made during World War II.[3] The message of this Army Film Service (AFD) film could not have been lost on anyone: the entire Swiss population would rise up against a Nazi invasion. Films like these were crafted to give the Swiss confidence that total resistance was the only possible response to invasion. That resistance would be uncompromising and relentless, in contrast to the demoralization and collapse of the rest of Western Europe in the face of blitzkrieg attacks. This particular film was aimed at the teenage boys and older men who made up the *Ortswehr*, highlighting their role of harassing and delaying advancing enemy forces until the regular army could launch counterblows.

Participation in the official and arm-banded *Ortswehr* served another purpose. As Federal Councilor Karl Kobelt, head of the Swiss military department, noted in a recruiting call, soldiers in uniform—though that uniform be no more than an armband—were entitled to protection under international law should they become prisoners of war.[4] They could not legally be shot as guerillas or unlawful combatants if captured by an invader.

It goes without saying that the only invader would have been the German Wehrmacht, which could not be explicitly named because of official Swiss neutrality. Based on a leak from Hitler's own headquarters, Swiss intelligence had believed that an attack would take place in March 1943. An assault did not materialize then. However, in early July the Anglo-American invasion of Sicily began. Mussolini was soon deposed and Hitler began rushing additional troops into northern Italy.[5] He didn't want an exposed rear in Switzerland. Thus, when this newsreel was shown in August, the Swiss had every reason to anticipate a Nazi invasion. The Swiss did not want to provoke Germany, but they intended to send a clear message that any incursion would be fiercely opposed. It was common knowledge that German intelligence viewed Swiss newsreels.

THE GERMAN WEEKLY NEWSREELS

The Swiss newsreels were designed in part to counter those produced by the Nazis. A weapon of Josef Goebbels' propaganda ministry, the German *Wochenschau* (Weekly Film) was filled with glowing accounts of the successes of the Reich.[6] Produced by the Reich's film producer Fritz Hippler, each edition of the newsreel was carefully reviewed by Goebbels and then personally approved by Hitler.[7]

A typical edition, shown in May 1940, entertained viewers with Wehrmacht attacks on Holland, Belgium and France. Enemy soldiers are always shown dead or in the process of surrendering, while Wehrmacht soldiers rarely seem to get a scratch. Civilians happily greet German tanks, except that posters are put up demanding that they surrender all firearms within 24 hours or face the death penalty. Hitler promises that this great war will be the harbinger of a thousand-year Reich. A patriotic song— against a background of artillery barrages, Luftwaffe bombings, and panzer assaults—builds to a grand finale.[8]

After the attack on the Soviet Union in June 1941, the German *Wochenschau* shows many dead Soviets and not one dead German. Rarely, there is seen a German casualty walking with the help of a comrade, and an occasional elaborate state funeral of a high leader. No dead German bodies or caskets were ever shown, even after Stalingrad.

The German regime made special *Auslandwochenschauen* (Foreign Weekly News) which included local topics for each country it sought to influence. In the post-war report of *Heer und Haus* (Army and Home), the Swiss agency whose mission was to promote military morale, Swiss Major Roland Ziegler noted about the German newsreels: "The purpose was to prove to the Swiss that the German Wehrmacht could not be stopped from crushing every enemy and that the Swiss were still under a kind of idyllic Seldwyla illusion regarding their defense readiness." (Seldwyla is an imaginary Swiss town in a novel by 19th-century Swiss author Gottfried Keller.) The German films denigrated everything about Switzerland. Ziegler explained:

> For example, the infantry. While the newsreels intended for Germany showed infantry battles at length, they were almost completely missing on the newsreels destined for Switzerland. On the other hand, the Swiss were shown in detail what they did not

have. For example, the newsreels would show the following potpourri: (i) huge bombers bombarding cities and train stations followed by the "*Zibelemärit*" [November onion festival] in Bern, followed by attacks by large tanks; (ii) submarines in attack mode followed by the *Knabenschiessen* [annual boys' shooting match] in Zurich, followed by dive-bombers; (iii) large tanks followed by a miniature train installation built by a man in Aarau followed by pictures from the air war with numerous airplanes and paratroops. The purpose was clear: Swiss moviegoers should leave the theater with the impression that nothing could be done against the German army and all the Swiss were doing was play.[9]

The dive-bombers in the German films were invariably accompanied by the shrill, piercing sound of their steep attack runs followed by devastating explosions. An intelligence report by the Wehrmacht High Command (OKW) of October 29, 1940, complained that the Swiss were doctoring the German films: "The sound made by dive bombers is eliminated from Universum Film AG's (Ufa) weekly broadcasts to tone down the action so as to avoid undermining the population's will of resistance."[10]

The Swiss developed their own newsreels to counter these German messages. Newsreels from Britain and other Allies were also regularly shown in Switzerland. Radio broadcasts from both sides brought both the encouraging words of Winston Churchill and the constant threats of Adolf Hitler. Swiss anti-Nazi sentiment was evident in the movie theaters. In 1941, when the United States was still neutral, reporters for *Fortune* magazine returning from Germany via Switzerland humorously recounted why the Hitler salute was removed from the German newsreels shown in the Swiss republic:

There are 360 movie houses in Switzerland . . . . The movie houses show both American and German newsreels. The Nazi reels move with a peculiar jerkiness, a result of the removal of all "*Heil*ing" for the Swiss market. The Germans are still puzzled, but found that Swiss audiences laughed uproariously at every sight of a grim-faced German shooting up his hand like a railroad signal and grunting "*Heil, Hitler!*" One theatre had to stop the film to restore calm after a scene in which Hitler himself had said "*Heil, Hitler!*"[11]

In a recent interview, Paul Ladame, the first director of the Swiss *Wochenschau*, confirmed the accuracy of the above account. He added that, at the time, the American newsreels were not well liked because they were not clearly against Hitler. The United States was neutral. The American position changed abruptly after Pearl Harbor. Both American and British films were smuggled into Switzerland and shown during the war.[12] While the pre-war American newsreels may have been superficially neutral, a German military intelligence report in November 1940 nonetheless complained of American bias:

> The Swiss weekly newsreels of October 7 to 12 did not show any war pictures, but an American weekly newsreel, which ran at the same time, did. The pictures had all been taken by the British side and showed destroyers sold by the United States putting to sea, visits by the English King and the shelling of a convoy under attack in the vicinity of Dover.[13]

THE SWISS WEEKLY NEWSREELS

An assessment of the Swiss newsreels over a half-century after the fact is not easy. No analysis or even summary of the films has ever been published. Only portions of the original films exist on videotape, and these are accessible only to the determined researcher. This analysis of selected films seeks to contribute to this uncharted history by describing their contents and evaluating their role in the struggle to survive and the will to resist. The opportunity to communicate with the two successive heads of the Swiss weekly film service during the war, while they were still alive, adds an important dimension.

Two official Swiss entities produced films: the civilian *Schweizer Filmwochenschau* or *Ciné Journal Suisse* (Swiss Weekly News) and the military *Armeefilmdienst* (Army Film Service). The films of both entities were shown to the populace throughout the entire country. Both sought to present facts, to give hope, and to engender a spirit of resistance. They would engage in a lively David and Goliath battle with the mighty German propaganda ministry.

Paul Ladame, the first Swiss *Wochenschau* director, recorded his experiences in *A Camera Against Hitler* (*Une caméra contre Hitler*).[14] When talkies began in Europe in 1929, Ladame acted in several movies and learned screenwriting, casting and directing. He earned a diploma in Berlin at the famed Reimannschule. When he returned in 1936 to cover the Olympic Games, his school had been closed and its Jewish professors expelled. He even found he was being watched by the SS.

Mobilized into the Swiss Army when World War II erupted, Ladame's prewar experience would lead to his appointment as *Wochenschau* director. "I was in my gray army uniform at 3,000 meters guarding a pass when I was called and offered the task of being director of the newsreel. I signed the contract the day the Germans captured Paris," he explained.[15] "My civilian job was to counteract, and if possible to neutralize, the shrewd German propaganda. In theory my job was simple: the Nazis fomented fear and hopelessness with their films. Their army appeared so strong, young, well armed and well trained that any resistance seemed doomed. My job was to instill hope, courage and confidence."[16]

With only Ladame, two cameramen and a secretary, they began by producing short documentary films. The budget was low and the equipment minimal. Only three meters of raw film could be used for each meter projected in the cinemas. There were national security restrictions as well. Films could not be made abroad, in military areas, or in refugee camps. The first edition of the Swiss *Wochenschau* was shown in Bern on August 1, 1940, Swiss National Day, to members of Parliament, the press, and dignitaries. A great success, it included five subjects: passage over the border into Switzerland by units of the defeated French army, including Polish and African soldiers; daily life of these internees in a camp in central Switzerland; 1,600 volunteers sorting out thousands of letters at the prisoner-of-war agency run by the International Committee of the Red Cross (ICRC) in Geneva; a speech by ICRC President Max Huber; and a spectacular explosion of landmines in Valais in the south of Switzerland.[17]

The *Wochenschau* was shown in all cinemas of the country in German, French and Italian languages. The typical episode had three to five subjects including, besides news, sporting events and various types of documentaries. At the beginning, the newsreel had a duration of three minutes, but was later extended to six minutes. All cinemas in Switzerland were obliged to show the films.

The numbers varied, but about 40 copies of each edition were produced, 30 in German, eight in French, and two in Italian. With a few exceptions, the film negative was the same for all three versions. The number of copies for each version would vary depending on the number of movie theaters that played the films in the first week. It was up to the cinema associations and the film distribution association to come up with the distribution scheme. The *Wochenschau* organization had no part in those decisions. There were never enough copies for all Swiss movie theaters to show the most recent film upon its release. Each number went through a chain of cinemas, with the rental fee declining from the first to the tenth week of presentation.[18]

As the Swiss newsreels effectively countered the German ones, viewers cheered the former and booed the latter. While it was not required by law to show the German films, viewers were used to German movies and were naturally curious about what the Germans were saying about the war. Still, there was concern that Nazi propaganda not overwhelm the Swiss newsreels. Funding shortages led in March 1941 to a meeting of concerned citizens with the theme *"Wir kämpfen gegen die deutsche Propaganda wie mit einer Korkpistole gegen Panzerwagen"* (We're fighting with a cork pistol against the tanks of German propaganda).[19] The assembly passed a resolution to the Federal Council requesting more funding, which was soon supplied. Ladame served as head of the newsreel, making 200 films until 1944, when he was replaced by Hans Laemmel (who remained head until 1961).[20] While it is unclear why the change took place, it was not unusual in Switzerland for a French-speaking Swiss to serve in an office and then be replaced by a German-speaking Swiss, or vice versa.

Laemmel wrote the following account in response to this author's request for information.[21] His reflections illustrate Switzerland's respect for its multilingual tradition even under the most threatening of wartime circumstances:

> As a soldier, I was dispatched to the division "Army and Home" (the military's morale-boosting agency) for a while and wrote articles about the work of the Army Film Service. I did not become editor-in-chief of the newsreel until 1944. I considered our *Wochenschau* a means to just *show* Switzerland in its diversity on the screens of our domestic movie theaters. I always preferred to emphasize that the *Wochenschau* supplemented the Swiss part of the movie programs at the time, not that it fought against the German and Italian weekly reviews. It was sufficient to show the living presence of our country. As editor I always tried to avoid making the *Wochenschau* sound like the "voice of Bern" or a weapon. That was important because many movie theater owners and a large part of the Swiss-French population believed that

Bern had created the Swiss *Wochenschau* as a means for official indoctrination, a tool for the centralistic shaping of public opinion.

The distrust of French Switzerland for any kind of overbearing centralism came from the long-standing concern of western Switzerland about its French language and culture. The French-speaking cantons traditionally felt threatened by the more numerous German-speaking cantons. Many felt that a weekly show set up and funded by Bern could be an attempt to force centralization on movie theater owners and their customers. Paul Ladame, whose native language was French, was well aware of this distrust. However, he knew German-speaking Switzerland well and did not share the concerns of his compatriots in the west. As a Swiss patriot, he realized the danger emanating from Hitler's Germany more clearly and earlier than many of his compatriots in western Switzerland, where the threat was less direct and tangible. As a result, he emphasized the importance of the Swiss *Wochenschau* as a means for all of Switzerland to fight the Nazi influence.

In the German-speaking and Italian-speaking parts of Switzerland, most of the owners of movie theaters welcomed the Swiss newsreels, and their associations made subscriptions to it mandatory. For German-speaking Switzerland, the Nazi danger was right across the border, while for many Swiss in the western part it was at first still far away. Then, even when the Germans were standing at the western border of Switzerland too, many French-speaking Swiss thought that the pact between [Vichy] French Marshall Pétain and Hitler reduced the danger.

Italian-speaking Switzerland experienced the threats and *irredenta* [Fascist claims to territory] coming from Mussolini's Italy. From the beginning, the Ticinesi and the Italian-speaking people in Graubünden were determined to resist Italy. [22]

THE ARMY FILM SERVICE

Beginning in the late summer of 1940, the *Armeefilmdienst* (AFD, or Army Film Service), a component of *Heer und Haus* (Army and Home), decided to go beyond the army and take its message directly to the people. They started preparing materials for civilian moviegoers and also for pupils of elementary and secondary schools.[23] The carefully produced AFD documentaries, like domestic and foreign weekly reviews, were shown as previews at some but not all movie theaters. They were not part of the *Wochenschau*.[24] Rather, they contained military themes, complementing the predominantly civilian themes of the *Wochenschau*.

The acting head of the *Abteilung Presse und Funkspruch* (Department of Press and Radio), Herr Fueter, had pointed out to the Chief of the General Staff as early as April 1940 that German newsreels sought to create the impression that resistance to superior German power was senseless. Since Switzerland was neutral, it could not prohibit German films, but something had to be done to counter the German propaganda, especially in the military area.

Colonel Oscar Frey wrote to the Adjutant General in May 1941 that Swiss films must confront the German film initiatives directly and as quickly as possible. "Example: The German newsreel shows a tank attack. Answer: Swiss Ik. [*Infanteriekanone*—infantry antitank cannon] exercises, going into position, shooting. Final picture: a shot-through tank armor." When viewers left movie theaters, they would be making comments such as "Did you know that we also have flamethrowers? The medical service and avalanche-dog service take care of our soldiers."[25]

Such short films of no more than five minutes—"answers" to the German newsreels—began to appear, sometimes at two-week intervals, and were shown in all cinemas in Switzerland. Longer films were also made, such as the 40-minute *"Schulung zum Nahkampf"* (Training in Close Combat).[26] Swiss military attachés in foreign countries, particularly in the Axis, made the Swiss films available as part of the strategy emphasizing the high potential casualties of a German invasion.

The relationship between the Army Film Service and civilian film organizations was set out in a September 1941 directive. The primary focus of the Army Film Service was to make films for actual military instruction, both to strengthen trust in the army and educate the civilian population. This entailed cooperation with *Wochenschau* production and distribution units in order to widen exposure to the civilian population.[27] The *Wochenschau* could also make films with military themes that would be shown in the framework of its normal program. The *Wochenschau* indeed treated military subjects, and its first 30 editions all included segments on some aspect of national defense.

The *Armeefilmdienst* was operated by Army and Home. It always remained separate from the civilian *Wochenschau*. However, a movie theater could show the films of both. Sometimes a projectionist would glue the two together for convenience, and that could have left the impression that one was part of the other. At any rate, the army films were, first and fore-most, meant to be viewed by the troops for training in tactics and specific weapons.[28]

A number of the editions of the *Wochenschau* and *Armeefilmdienst* pro-ductions have been reproduced in whole or part on videotape. The video-tapes do not always identify and distinguish the source of specific footage, but it can be assumed generally that the *Wochenschau* produced the civilian themes and the *Armeefilmdienst* produced the military themes (particularly those of longer length).

According to one source, most of the *Wochenschau* films were sold after the war to a comb factory. The celluloid was considered more valuable than the historic content. Hans Laemmel, the *Wochenschau* editor-in-chief, maintains that the Swiss film archives in Lausanne kept a copy of each edition in German, French, and Italian. However, because those reels con-tained acetate and nitrate, there was a danger they would deteriorate and pose a risk of spontaneous combustion. As a result, they were copied over onto videotape and deposited with the Swiss Federal Archives in Bern.[29]

Following are descriptions of some of the newsreels, once so avidly viewed by the wartime generation of Swiss, but unseen in public since the fall of the Third Reich.

Mobilization

The Swiss military was formally mobilized on September 1, 1939, the day of Hitler's attack on Poland. The *Wochenschau* edition flashes to the mobi-lization poster seen on walls throughout the country and then to a church bell ringing in a village. With the beautiful Alps as background, a farmer and his wife or daughter in traditional attire rush down the hillside. Grabbing one of four rifles on a rack, his helmet, and a bayonet, the man hurries in uniform from his house to the village.[30] This scene, which with individual variations was part of the memory of every Swiss family, exudes hope, duty, love of family and homeland.

Then the film is all business. Soldiers rush to a road; weapons covers are pulled off; anti-tank obstacles are positioned; mines are laid and care-fully covered with sod; cannon are moved into prepared emplacements; barbed wire is spread. There is a cut to the supreme commander, General Henri Guisan, being sworn in before Parliament. A further mobilization is announced; with intensive, backbreaking labor, soldiers move logs and stones to build additional fortifications.

There is footage of the period of the so-called Phony War, the winter of 1939–40 between Germany's conquest of Poland and her spring offensives against the West. England and France had declared war on Germany over Poland, but aside from naval actions there were only feints and gestures on both sides. It was, however, a time of preparation for war. In the films of this period, Swiss winter soldiers trot on horseback through the snow. When spring comes, they practice gymnastics, jump over barbed wire and obstacles, do bayonet drills and work through mock assaults on tanks and trenches.[31]

With the massive blitzkrieg against Western Europe in May 1940, the newsreel has to compress many events into just a few minutes of film. The *Wochenschau* depicts German fighter planes, General Guisan speaking, Swiss maneuvers with live ammunition, soldiers racing up steep hills, pistol competitions, swimming races, horse obstacle courses and practice with heavy artillery. Then come scenes of demoralized French soldiers entering Switzerland, laying down their arms and being interned. A map shows Switzerland in white surrounded by Axis black—as if in a contrast between good and evil.[32] Music and other sound effects enhance the visual message and voiceovers are used at dramatic points.

The September 1940 episode *"Krieg"* (War) said it all: France has fallen, and everywhere people wonder what the next target of German aggression will be. The Swiss response is to flash back to May 10, the day Germany attacked Belgium, Holland, and France, and the Federal Council had ordered Switzerland's second great mobilization. A farmer hangs up a large scythe, grasps his rifle, and quickly bids farewell to his family; shops close; soldiers take oaths; more building of fortifications and defenses. On mountain roads, near rivers, and in city streets, barbed wire, tank obstacles and all manner of impediments go up; air raid alarms go off as women pull down shutters; anti-aircraft guns limber up. The scene shifts to war games—explosions, blazing machine guns, firing tanks. A soldier running through a trench is suddenly knifed from behind; next General Guisan is giving a speech on national defense; the film then flashes to some children, and the announcer admonishes viewers to protect freedom and the Fatherland; patriotic music ends the episode.[33] Once again the message is clear: the Swiss can and will resist attack, and the costs to Nazi Germany—which need not and cannot be mentioned—will be heavy.

Industry, Agriculture, and Shortages
Throughout the war, the *Wochenschau* reiterated two basic messages. First, the Swiss situation was dangerous: cut off from her normal trading part-

ners, Switzerland lacked fuel and natural resources, and did not produce sufficient food. Shortages were inevitable. Second, the core Swiss values of persistence, hard work, and the application of technology to solve problems would make survival possible. These episodes, compared with the shrill bombast of the German *Wochenschau*, may appear dry today, but they were exactly what the Swiss needed to endure.

Many segments focused on specific tasks. For instance: the recycling of old tires and parts from junk cars (classic old cars by today's standards);[34] wedding guests use the electric tramway to save fuel;[35] old tubes collected by school children are melted and used for soldering wire;[36] brown coal is mined with chisels and picks (no machine tools are shown);[37] gas is made from wood;[38] zinc coins replace copper coins (pouring out of a stamping machine like water);[39] reeds are harvested for the building industry;[40] and fence scrapings and household scrap are collected for the metal industry.[41]

One rather amusing episode covers the children's harvest of cockchafer (a large scarab beetle) for processing as pig feed. Children violently shake the branches of a tree, causing cockchafer to rain down onto a tarpaulin on the ground. They are poured into huge burlap sacks—care must be taken because they eat their way out!—and then transported to a machine, which processes huge quantities into feed. In the final scene, pigs eagerly devour the delicious delicacy.[42] The implied lesson: even children must work in the struggle for food.

One newsreel segment entitled "Cultivation War" featured the national food plan devised by Dr. F. T. Wahlen. Every man, woman, and child participated in this plan, which entailed growing potatoes and other crops on every available bit of land, no matter how small. Charts in the film show that, in 1938, 83% of agricultural land was used for livestock and only 17% for crops, but by 1942 the numbers changed to 54% and 46% respectively. In 1934, 183,000 hectares of land were under cultivation, but that number later more than doubled to 500,000. The film shows scientists in laboratories conducting futuristic-looking experiments in agriculture.[43] Besides reporting news, this episode was intended to reassure the population that everything possible was being done to produce an adequate, if Spartan, food supply.

Several episodes were devoted to this unending agricultural "war," emphasizing that Switzerland would never experience famine because of the hard work of all citizens, young and old.[44] Many years later, Paul Ladame reminisced that the best of the *Wochenschau* were the homey films on Dr. Wahlen's campaigns to increase production of the lowly potato.[45]

Sometimes relief was needed from news about the war, hardship, and shortages. One episode featured a ladies fashion show, depicting innovations of the textile industry. Beautiful models display the latest styles to a crowd of admiring women. The models then retire to lounge chairs, smoke cigarettes, laugh and chat. This must have been a kind of therapeutic window-shopping—a chance to forget the war and hope for a better future.[46]

Humor also played a part. The theme of another episode was the preparation of tasty meals in the midst of shortages. The episode purported to show housewives that help was on the way in the form of a sci-fi-looking tape recording device filled with food ideas and recipes. It was, of course, a joke to relieve the tension.[47]

One of the staples of the Swiss wartime diet was the ubiquitous two-day-old potato bread. A 1944 episode was devoted to its production and rationing. A Swiss-flagged ship on the high seas—a little known supplier of products from abroad—is shown, but as a reason for shortages. (A handful of Swiss-flagged ships did in fact transport goods from countries outside the Axis, with the cargos arriving in Switzerland via overland routes through Italy.) Land is cleared by animals or tractors pulling up roots and by rows of men with picks. Women then do the final hoeing. The rationing plan for the month is explained, and the edition ends with the exhortation "*Zusammenhalten und Disziplin wahren!*" (Hold together and keep discipline!).[48]

The *Wochenschau* dealt with the poor as well. One episode contrasts the relative well-being of the average Swiss with the plight of the poor. There are flashes of a wheat harvest, people employed, a soccer game and healthy children; shop windows full of food and watches are contrasted with six somber people living in a single room. A woman washes clothes on a scrub board; children have holes in their shoes and torn clothes; newspapers are used in a wood stove; the family is down to its last potato; there is not enough bread; the ration cards are running out; the bills cannot be paid. Help arrives—suddenly there are plenty of potatoes, the children get new clothes, there is wood for the stove. The edition ends: "*Wenn Du zögerst frage Dein Herz*" (When you hesitate, ask your heart).[49] Such appeals to charity and goodwill helped the Swiss support one another, aid the thousands of refugees in Switzerland, and fund the work of the International Committee of the Red Cross in many other countries during the war.

Episodes about shortages and hardship often featured women and children. They, after all, were the ones who had to make it on their own while husbands and fathers were away on military service. "The Woman in Our Time" flashes *"Das Swing-Girl"*—caricatures of stylish women— but quickly shifts to Swiss women in military service and in ordinary walks of life. The housewife sees the basket of eggs shrink; she bundles hay; she runs low on ration coupons; and just when she is feeling low, the air raid alarm sounds; she checks on her precious sleeping child; the alarm awakens her at 6:00 a.m. and she is at once on the run; she dons her apron; throws wood in the stove; feeds the children; her daughter's shoe has a huge hole; she sends the children off to school and goes to the pharmacy, where a crowd competes to redeem ration coupons—then back home for housework and more ration coupon clipping. This depiction of the obviously exhausting routine was clearly designed to be a tribute to the hard work of women in Swiss wartime society.[50]

Women in Service
Several episodes are devoted to women in hospitals, factories, the military, farms and the home. Women from all walks of life joined the *Frauenhilfsdienst* (FHD), the Women's Auxiliary Service. FHD women awake in hotels or apartments turned into barracks; they don their military uniforms; practice marching; they work as aides for the General Staff, scan the skies for enemy aircraft and serve all along the communications line for air defense.[51] The FHD films were intended to celebrate and affirm their work as well as to recruit.

The FHD included contingents of dispatch carriers on skis. In one episode, a group of women are sleeping in a barn; an alarm awakens them and they rush outside and strap on their skis; while delivering an important message from a soldier, a woman falls and is injured; six women come to her rescue; the snow is deep, the scenery beautiful.[52] The adventure depicted here, while simplistic, was intended to attract young women to join the FHD and perform tasks which could release men for actual combat.

Another military assignment for FHD women was with the carrier pigeon units which were still a part of the Swiss army.[53] They also ran kitchens and canteens for soldiers who were mobilized.[54] These films were little different in their themes from, for example, American advertisements for the Women's Army Corps (WACS) later made and distributed to the U.S. population.

The 650th Anniversary of the Confederation

In 1941, the *Wochenschau* seized upon the opportunity of celebrating the 650th anniversary of the founding of the Swiss Confederation in 1291 by creating productions depicting Switzerland's medieval victories against the great European powers of the day.[55] Praising the production *"Notre pain quotidien"* (Our Daily Bread), Federal Councilor Philippe Etter wrote Ladame requesting an all-out effort for the anniversary:

> Switzerland must survive, as our ancestors wished. We will fight until the end so that the red flag with white cross flies over the Gotthard. You made excellent movies so that our people do not die of hunger. You helped Dr. Wahlen to fill stomachs. For myself, I ask you to help save the spirit, the courage, and the will to resist. Little Switzerland, curled up like a hedgehog, must draw strength through courage and confidence from her over six-hundred-year history, in order to support the soldiers who are feverishly working to fortify the Réduit, our ultimate defense.[56]

The result was the production of the film *La Suisse héroique* (Heroic Switzerland), the script of which was personally reviewed by Councilor Etter. The "Pact of the Rütli" concerned the founding events occurring around the lakes of the first Alpine Cantons—Uri, Schwyz and Unterwald. The film depicted the medieval battles of Morgarten, Sempach, and Morat, where small numbers of Swiss peasants defeated large armies of knights. The film featured the breast-plated cavaliers of the *Remonte fédérale* (Federal Troop), the best horsemen of Switzerland, with standards and pennants flowing, attacking Habsburg cavalry. Ladame remembered the production:

> Everywhere we went, people received us with joy and cooperated with zeal. I will always remember the mountaineers of the Muotathal interpreting, truer than nature, the pact of the three Cantons Uri, Schwyz and Unterwald. They believed in it. They relived it. 1291, for them, was like yesterday. The Duke of Habsburg who wanted to invade their country was Hitler today.[57]

By the end of the year, the film would be shown to over 100,000 Swiss children. The film was generally met with spontaneous applause. While some critics questioned whether its depiction of events was historically accurate,[58] the film successfully contributed to the program of *geistige Landesverteidigung* (spiritual national defense).

Sports Films

A soccer match between Switzerland and Germany in Zurich depicted in film in April 1941 had obvious symbolic value. Crowds swamp the stadium and citizens anxiously listen on the radio; the German players line up and give the Heil Hitler salute as a band plays; the members of the Swiss team coolly keep both arms down at their sides; the game is filled with exciting plays; the crowd is ecstatic as Switzerland wins 2 to 1.[59] Once again little Switzerland has defeated the giant to the north. The fans were thinking of more than a soccer match.

Another episode encouraged every Swiss, man or woman, to participate in sports and to earn the Swiss sport medal for general fitness. It contrasted group calisthenics on an athletic field with factory work. The choices: gymnastics, 100-meter sprinting, swimming, biking, fencing, pistol shooting, wrestling, rowing, skiing, horseback riding, long-distance racing with rifle on back, track and field.[60] The message was that active participatory sports contributed strong defenders and encouraged a spirit of resistance.

The collapse of the tourism industry, which thrived before the war, resulted in massive unemployment in hotels throughout the country. One film encourages Swiss to take advantage of various outdoor recreational activities available at or near these hotels.[61]

Refugees and Humanitarian Aid

Helping refugees and humanitarian priorities were distinguishing characteristics of Switzerland for the entire war, and the *Wochenschau* created several episodes highlighting these themes. One featured Switzerland's program to bring children from occupied countries into Switzerland for three months of rest and recuperation. Trains arrive with the children, who are taken by nuns to a mess hall to eat what must have been their best meal since the war began; they are then taken by individual families, who depart by horse-drawn wagons or taxis; each child receives medical attention; attends educational classes; helps out with household chores; gains about five kilograms in weight; and there are tearful scenes when they depart for home.[62] This film does not identify the country of origin of the children, but in fact most came from France.

Tragedy struck at home in 1944 when the American Eighth Air Force accidentally bombed the Swiss city of Schaffhausen, which lies on the northern side of the Rhine. As shown in the newsreel, parts of the city are in flames and 37 are dead; firemen, soldiers, Scouts, and citizens of all kinds are putting out fires and looking for loved ones; buildings are shown completely bombed out and gutted. The film barely mentions that it was American bombers and expresses no animosity. Three days later, a funeral service is held at a church; a column of mourners marches to a mass grave, a circular trench with coffins facing the center; a child's coffin is seen beside an adult one; people crowd around expressing their sorrow.[63]

As the war ebbed and flowed, refugees by the thousands continued to flow into Switzerland. Basel appears first in these films as a city enjoying peace and security, without hunger. Then, images from December 1944 depict deafening artillery and machine gun fire from across the border. Elderly people, children, women, and the wounded—some 5,000 of them—are fleeing across from Germany. Swiss soldiers help them enter; nurses examine the babies.[64]

Switzerland was a neutral zone where severely wounded soldiers of both sides could be exchanged. Sponsored by the International Committee of the Red Cross, trains transported wounded Americans, English, Middle Easterners, Indians, and Africans as well as Germans into Switzerland, where they were exchanged and put on other trains to be returned to areas under the control of the Allies and Axis respectively. Doctors and nurses treated those in immediate need.[65] The facial expressions of the wounded in these films show the reality of war close up.

Just after the war in Europe ended, the *Wochenschau* featured Russian soldiers who were still interned in Switzerland. They had apparently escaped to Switzerland from German POW or work camps. Perhaps some were deserters seeking to escape from Communism. Located in Wallis Canton, the internees are shown picking potatoes, singing, hearing a harangue by a Bolshevik political commissar under a picture of Stalin, and then doing the Russian step dance. After meeting with Swiss authorities, the Russian military delegate informs the assembled internees that they will be returning to Russia, which leads to wild applause; they leave in trains, still singing.[66]

The events which transpired after their departure, however, were not so happy. Although the Soviet Union had never joined the Geneva Convention Covering Treatment of Prisoners of War, the Swiss protected the Russian internees as if they had. Russian internees were given very limited leave and their Slavic language did not facilitate their getting acquainted with the Swiss people. However, the freedom these internees witnessed in Switzerland was believed to be too subversive. In blatant violation of the assurances given to the Swiss who negotiated with the Soviets about the treatment of the Russian internees, the vast majority were sent to Gulags—labor camps—instead of being returned home to their families.[67] It is believed that some may have simply been shot for surrendering rather than dying for the Motherland in combat. In fact, most of them were never heard from again once they reentered the Soviet Union.

Military Exercises

Military activities were the common theme of Army Film Service productions and were also featured in the *Wochenschau*. This was calculated to give the Swiss people confidence and to encourage participation while at the same time sending the message to Germany that the Swiss military was prepared and would resist fiercely.

Alpine snow scenes were highlighted in various military episodes. The message was that Switzerland was a rugged land where certain death awaited invaders. In one edition, soldiers in white camouflage sweep the terrain with binoculars; they spot something and take off on their skis, executing high jumps; the scene flashes to hard farm work with hand tools and plows pulled by animals.[68] In another, soldiers ascend snow-capped mountains, using picks and climbing gear.[69]

One episode showing snow maneuvers features live firing of rifles, machine guns, and mortars. Soldiers sprint out of small holes in the snow-covered mountainside and move to the attack; ski troops swoop down from steep inclines in full battle gear; a mortar is loaded and fired into a mountainside, causing an avalanche.[70]

An edition on units of Swiss cavalry appears strangely anachronistic in the age of the tank and the fighter plane, although horse troops would have been useful in certain terrain. However, the film shows classic horse training in various gaits, as well as movements through uneven ground. The grand finale is a troop of mounted soldiers with helmets, carbines on their backs, and swords hanging from their sides![71]

Even a militia army needs a band. One newsreel featured a performance in a large hall. However, it is a strange concert indeed, because the band members are all wearing helmets, totally ready for action of another kind. The music they play, moreover, sounds every bit as martial and bombastic as anything on the German *Wochenschau*.[72]

Some training exercises were created as public demonstrations for both military and civilian visitors—including, no doubt, spies who carried their observations back to Germany. One such exercise, in which the audience of men, women, and children included General Guisan himself, was a "mini D-Day" conducted by pontoon troops. It begins with shock troops swimming across a river; then three-man paddleboats are launched from concealed locations along the wooded shore; once a bridgehead is secure, larger boats with more soldiers cross to assault fortified positions on the other side. Gunfire and artillery fire punctuate the attack.[73]

"Shhhhh!" Spies . . .

Wochenschau episodes did not tend to be overly dramatic. They were matter-of-fact. One film from 1941 began innocuously enough. From rugged Alps with glaciers the camera moves to hard farm work with hand tools and plows pulled by animals. This is the usual fare. However, the tone suddenly changes to the dramatic and surreal. A phantom human skull, growing ever larger, is superimposed over a Swiss city.[74] The message is the danger of espionage in Switzerland.

"*Wer nicht schweigen kann, schadet du Heimat!*" (Whoever cannot be silent, you harm the Homeland!), an oft-repeated slogan, was the basis for the title of a film shown in May 1943,[75] just after the "March Alarm" in which a Wehrmacht invasion was expected. It was No. 145 of the *Wochenschau*, and the topic was ordered by General Guisan.[76] This film is a masterpiece of drama, visualization, and contrast. Its story: day and night, our army guards our borders and country for "*Verteidigung, Freiheit und Arbeit, Heim und Familie*" (defense, freedom and work, country and family). Soldiers march and sing patriotic songs; a mother tucks in a girl, who says a prayer; the father is standing guard on a dark, rainy night.

The father's guard unit is relieved, a train rushes through a tunnel, and the guards slosh to a dry building filled with other soldiers. The guards unchamber the rounds in their rifles and take off their soaked raincoats; a foxtrot plays; the camera sweeps across the room; soldiers are sleeping or reading on their blankets in the straw, with pinups to keep them company. An American might title this film "Swiss GIs." These scenes set a mixed tone of deadly earnest and carefree relaxation, the two sides of army life.

The film then moves to the easy dangers of talking too much about military matters. Soldiers at a train station mix with the general public; soldiers at a table in a restaurant are laughing and talking; a man sits listening at the next table—is he suspicious? A soldier is getting a shave—

what is he saying to the barber? Another soldier walks out of a store talking to a female clerk; another walks by three pretty women. Anyone can
be a spy! Men are playing cards; the music becomes ominous. Men and
women are talking on the telephone laughing; talking at a bowling alley;
what are they saying? A messenger reports to an officer, who checks a map
and then tells the messenger too much; in the next scene, that messenger
repeats every word to another soldier during a card game.

The camera returns to the scene where the mother was tucking in her
daughter . . . to soldiers deep in thought . . . to a grandmother and grandfather . . . to the soldiers' quarters, where they are all asleep on the hay . . .
and each one is dreaming now . . . one dreams of his loved ones; then the
sergeant wakes him up; once more it is time to relieve the other guards. A
rendition of the Swiss patriotic song "My Fatherland" concludes this dramatic and stimulating film.

The War for Europe
With the Normandy invasion of June 1944, newsreel episodes begin to
reflect the dramatically changed security risks for Switzerland. There is
again war on the very borders. A Swiss officer lectures his men about the
new perils now that the Allies are battling the Axis in France. Mountain
troops with ropes and picks climb up massive vertical cliffs; Swiss Me-109
fighters fly over rugged mountains with machine guns blazing; assault
troops fire and move forward as flamethrowers blaze away; an explosion
causes huge logs to roll down a steep slope and block a tank speeding along
a mountain road. The war is not over but it is entering a new phase.[77] This
film is designed to depict the Swiss as ready to repulse an attack by "any
invader."

The army needs wireless operators, announced the newsreel, which
proceeded to show potential recruits the adventures to be expected.
Airmen sprint to their Me-109s and, once airborne, communicate observations to ground personnel via telegraphic Morse code (the Swiss had
no voice radio communication with their aircraft); the ground operators
pass the message to a courier, who sprints away to another radio station,
where the message is retransmitted to troops in the field; soldiers rush
to their preassigned positions and prepare for an attack; a mock battle
commences; assault troops cross a shallow river; messages about enemy
positions are passed from one unit to another in the field; maps are
surveyed, calculations are rapidly made and heavy camouflaged guns
begin firing; riflemen with fixed bayonets advance under the cover of

machine guns through smoke, flames and barbed wire.[78]

After all the excitement, in town a man hangs a poster notifying young men about recruit school. Then a class in Morse code is shown. "We need wireless transmitters; learn the Morse signals; they are essential." This film has plenty of action, but the theme throughout is the importance of wireless telegraph to communicate threats and to prepare counterattacks. While the German newsreels were filled with the intimidating power of barrages, Swiss films emphasized good communications, precision firing and coordinated tactics.

Another episode featured Swiss grenadiers—light infantry units like American Rangers. The Swiss Army had made great strides in weapons and training since 1940. A map portrays a steep mountain valley where enemy forces must advance through the narrow fire zones; they are subjected to attacks from above; soldiers attempt to use ropes to climb down and cross the river as bullets crackle in the water around them; snipers hidden behind rocks on the mountainside take well-aimed shots; grenades are thrown from above; rubber floats are used to carry men and weapons downstream. These mock battles—with explosions, automatic weapon fire and flamethrowers—have the feel of real battle.[79]

The newsreels produced intriguing episodes on Swiss antiaircraft defenses and the Swiss Air Force. It is night, and soldiers on duty hear aircraft, plot their course, and telephone the data to the antiaircraft center, where it is received by one of perhaps twenty uniformed women auxiliaries; the speed and direction of attacking aircraft are plotted on maps, and an air raid alarm sounds in the city; a soldier on watch cries "Alarm! Alarm!" to rows of soldiers sleeping in haylofts; they swarm to antiaircraft guns; gigantic spotlights search the skies; an aircraft is spotted! The observation and aiming instruments appear highly sophisticated. Fire! Shot after shot explodes around the attacking aircraft.[80]

Another segment deals with Swiss defenses in the air. Pilots rev their motors while the control tower personnel look on; on the ground, they communicate by voice radio—which was unavailable in the air; the scene shifts to pilot school, where students learn air acrobatics in biplanes; then come Me-109s and a Swiss-made and -designed C-36, distinguished by its two vertical stabilizers with rudders; the fighters practice machine-gun fire at targets in a lake; an alarm sounds; pilots race to their planes while ground personnel plot coordinates; the Swiss fighters pursue and close in on a damaged American bomber, signaling it to land by dipping their wings. After an exchange of signals, the fighters guide the bomber to a safe landing at the military airfield at Dübendorf, where ground crews rush out to assist the damaged aircraft.[81]

Features on the Swiss military also depicted the human side. In one, under torchlight, General Guisan addresses assembled troops on the fifth Christmas of the war; a band plays "Silent Night"; the mood is somber; the soldiers are not with their families, yet appear confident. In one scene, soldiers exchange gifts with their helmets on! Viewers would know that the militia army was ready for combat even during a Christmas ceremony.[82]

"Open your doors for soldiers when off-duty" is a plea for solidarity with the army at the local level. In a small town in the Jura, where Swiss troops are concentrated in early 1945 across from the battle zone, soldiers throw snowballs and flirt with women. Morale is boosted when they are taken into homes, served bread and wine, and invited to play board games with the children. The snow begins to fall, and the soldiers again stand guard.[83]

The War Ends

The *Wochenschau* celebrated the end of the war along with the entire population. The capitulation of the Wehrmacht meant the end of a long nightmare. Thousands of Swiss, American, British, and French flags are waved by masses of rejoicing people in the streets. They sing "Heil Dir Helvetia," which has the same melody as "My Country 'Tis of Thee" and "God Save the Queen." A bell rings, celebrating the peace. There is a parade before the Parliament with General Guisan and the members of the Federal Council. The grand finale is a beautiful mountain scene with patriotic commentary: the Alpine democracy has survived.[84]

Europe remained a chaotic and potentially dangerous place, and active duty had not yet ended. A mid-summer 1945 episode featured a day with General Guisan at Schloss Jegensdorf. After a friendly "bonjour" to the guards, the General must decide the punishment for cases of misconduct. He grants amnesty in a minor case and refuses it for a traitor. After a horse ride through farm and forest, the General hears reports of a crisis at the Italian border and meets with Chief of the General Staff Jakob Huber. After a flashback to the Rütli meeting of 1940 in which the General admonished all of the high officers to resist to the end, the episode shows Guisan observing war maneuvers, with explosions, machine-gun fire, and assaulting troops. When night falls, the General plays cards with officers of the General Staff and then is alone reviewing reports.[85]

In August, Japan surrendered, and at last *"Der Krieg ist Vorüber"*—the war is over. The period of active service officially ended. The *Wochenschau* covered the jubilant celebration and parade in Bern. It was enormous.[86] This was the end of an era—the newsreels thereafter addressed the post-war epoch, and with it the reconstruction of Europe and a return to normalcy.

The newsreels of the *Wochenschau* and the *Armeefilmdienst* were significant ideological weapons that kept hope alive. The ability of the Swiss people to maintain their freedom and independence during World War II may be attributed in no small part to a fierce attitude of defiance against the New Order and confidence in their capacity to survive. It seems incredible that these newsreels of the tough-minded Swiss could be shown for the entire war right in the center of a Europe otherwise occupied by the Axis.

The newsreels were limited to domestic affairs, particularly economic matters and military demonstrations. Neither political news nor "late-breaking" news items typical of television newscasts of today were included. War news was widely published in newspapers, leading to constant Axis protests of bias because the papers allegedly played up Allied victories and Axis defeats. However, the *Wochenschau* was funded by the government—which was officially neutral—and did not cover foreign affairs or the results of battles. The populace could keep informed of the progress of the war by watching the films made by both Allies and Axis at the cinemas and, on a daily basis, by tuning in to the BBC and to German radio. Further, names could be named and anything could be said against the Nazis in both written and oral communications within the military and among private civilian groups.

The Swiss films instilled confidence that the people could and would survive economically and promoted the imperative that the armed Swiss populace would wage total war against any invader. The films were not "neutral" in that they embodied unquestioned normative premises. If Swiss political neutrality and encirclement by the Axis prohibited the naming of names of the only likely aggressor, film viewers hardly needed to ask "guess who."

Were the Swiss newsreels truly informative, as suggested by the authorities at the time, or were they mere propaganda? The Nazi version of "propaganda" contained little truthful information and many big lies. The Swiss newsreels contained no falsehoods, but did always encourage resistance.

PART II

PREPARING FOR INVASION

CHAPTER 4

I WAS A MILITIA
SOLDIER THEN

The reminiscences of Swiss who actually lived through the period of the Third Reich provide a rich source of information on life in those dark days, particularly concerning resistance to the fifth column within Switzerland and the ever-present threat of a German invasion.

Listening to persons who actually experienced and survived an historical epoch presents a unique opportunity to understand how ordinary people reacted to larger events. Unfortunately, the Independent Commission of Experts, in preparing its recently published 25-volume report, decided not to interview World War II era Swiss citizens about their personal experiences and recollections. Chaired by Professor Jean-François Bergier, the Commission's final report has been published in English as *Switzerland, National Socialism and the Second World War* (2002). Many Swiss of the wartime generation regard the negative picture painted therein as incomplete.

This chapter is a small effort to allow survivors of that epoch to relate some of their experiences in their own words. While hardly comprehensive, such personal accounts often tell more than sterile documents. Rather than attempting to slice up the topics discussed under formal categories, the following permits the speakers to present the array of attitudes and experiences they found most important to relate.

Hans Köfer-Richner, a Swiss who was born in 1927 and who went on to author two books on the depression and war years,[1] shared his experiences in a 1999 interview. "We lived in the village of Mellingen, not far from the German border. We were a poor family with seven to nine mouths to feed at the table every day. Father was a mechanic and often unemployed. He was too proud to get welfare. Until 1942, I slept on straw in the cellar or the schoolroom, and never in a bed. I served at mass every morning at 6 or 7, and then went to school."[2]

Food was a constant concern for most Swiss families as cross-border trade diminished and strict rationing was imposed. Everyone tried to find ways to supplement rations. Hans was one. "I owned 220 rabbits. Rabbit meat was not rationed, and I supplied it to stores. One store was owned by an Italian named Moneta. At first I didn't know that Moneta was a fascist. When I told my father I got the contract, he was furious, saying, 'You're not going to sell rabbits to a fascist!' My father stormed off to see him and I was afraid there was going to be a terrible row. But Moneta announced: 'I stopped being a fascist when Mussolini went with Hitler!'"

Grown men were pulled away from farm work and factory lines for active duty, and boys were recruited to construct fortifications. "I was in the *Ortswehr* (Local Defense). We built bunkers in 1939—even in rain and mud. We were always exhausted. I helped cook for my brother's military unit and got leftovers to take home for Mother. General Guisan was like a god. I saw him three times at the Limmat Line when he came through to inspect bunkers."

Germans who resided in Switzerland were frequently shunned. "I knew two pro-Nazi Germans about my age. Both left Switzerland—one to fight in the East—and were never heard of again. My friends and I took it for granted that we would be killed, but we always said: 'At least one German goes first!'"

This was no idle boast. They trained to do just that. "In 1944, we were at the Limmat Line. This was a major defensive position south of the Rhine, the north side of which was occupied by Germany. *Ortswehr* members who knew the Limmat River planned to swim across and plant charges to blow up bunkers. I was a good athlete. In one practice run six of us attempted the swim. We all made it and planted dynamite. The regular Swiss soldiers positioned there moved back and we blew up all the practice targets."

Hans Köfer grimaced as he turned the subject to the enemies at home. "There were a dozen fifth columnists in town. They planned to set up a prison camp in Tigerfelden [for Swiss]. Their Gauleiter (head of a Nazi administrative unit) was named. In 1944, the *Ortswehr* commander gave me, a boy of 15, a list of five names, including a German named Disch. The commander ordered: 'Take two names of the five. If I or my troops give the order, arrest your two and bring them to the commander of the *Ortswehr* or the battalion.' I asked, 'What if they start shooting?' He replied, 'You shoot first!'"

Over a half-century later, Hans Köfer still seemed to relish the idea of a shootout with Nazis. He continued: "There were Nazis in Baden, Aarau, and Ortmarsingen. My father worked in the Luftschutz (Auxiliary Air Defense) in Mellingen and was a member of Swiss intelligence. He kept close tabs on them and sent the information on to Bern.

"When we heard about German V-1 and V-2 rockets reaching London, we were afraid Zurich and Bern could be the next targets, especially if the Germans started to invade." The fear of some kind of terrible German super weapon did not abate until the war ended.

Much Swiss wartime material remained secret until long after the end of the war. "In 1966, just after my father had a heart attack, he told me to go into the attic and find a box of his papers from the war years. The box was one foot high and two feet wide. He told me to read everything in the box and then burn the documents. One document, apparently written by someone in the fifth column, said that, if the Germans came, 'Joseph Köfer and his son Hans should be killed immediately.' There was also a list with 12 names. It said, 'If the Germans come, as many as possible of them [these traitors] must be killed.'" Hans burned the contents of the box, but his education on the war years was not over. He described how, years later, he traveled to Germany and had a conversation with one of the highest-ranking officers of Hitler's Wehrmacht: "I had moved up in the retail business, and in 1951 I got a letter from a Stuttgart department store offering me a job as department head. I went for an interview. That night I was at a bar, and none other than former Generalfeldmarschall von Rundstedt was there. We happened to strike up a conversation, which I later recorded in my diary."

Gerd von Rundstedt had been the leader of the blitzkrieg against France in 1940. He commanded the forces that made the unexpected attack through the supposedly impenetrable Ardennes, while Guderian crossed the Meuse and Rommel drove through France. He then commanded Army Group South in Russia. After a brief period falling out of Hitler's favor, he took command of German armies in the West, presiding over Germany's last great offensive in the Battle of the Bulge. All together, Rundstedt was quite a person for the young Swiss to run into.

"That night he told me: 'I always respected Switzerland. In the spring of 1943, we received an order to prepare for an invasion. We needed three weeks to work up a plan for Hitler. I and my staff recommended against it. We would have lost three to five hundred thousand men in such an attack. We knew that all bridges were mined and that everything would be blown up. It wasn't worth the price we'd have to pay, and we needed every resource we could spare for Russia. We Germans knew every Swiss has a gun. How old were you when you got your first gun?'

"I replied: 'At age 12, when I became a Kadet.' I had poor eyesight, so my father got me an air rifle, and I practiced every day. Finally I did become a good shot with the military rifle. I could shoot scores of 80 in competitions held by the Swiss Shooting Federation.

"Von Rundstedt asked: 'If you were 12 in 1939, would you have fired had we come?'

"I replied: 'As clear as water! Our slogan was, for every Swiss, two Germans!'

"The General laughed and said: 'We were strong. But maybe we would have lost.'"

This noteworthy encounter is also related in Hans Köfer's book, where he wrote: "Von Rundstedt emphasized that he and a few of his generals had a very hard time convincing Hitler to abandon his military preparations for an attack on Switzerland. He said that he was convinced of the Swiss army's willingness to defend its country and added: 'By the spring of 1943 we were under tremendous pressure on all fronts and could not afford Hitler's craziness.'"[3]

Indeed, from the very beginning of the war the Swiss militia army could be mobilized quickly in the event of a German threat or incursion. Rudi Tschan, a boy at the time, remembers the outbreak of the war in 1939. "My father and five uncles were all called up. The schools closed down because most male teachers had to join their army units. The marching orders came over the radio, and every soldier knew where to go to join his unit. Each man already had his uniform and carried his personal carbine and food for the first two days. Units (companies of 100 to 120 men) assembled rapidly in villages or mustering grounds and picked up their heavy weapons and gear from local arsenals.

"Except for units assigned to fortifications, there was far too little space in existing barracks to lodge the whole army. Each company was assigned to a village or small town for shelter. It was the responsibility of the company quartermaster to organize lodgings. By law, he could requisition space in hotels, restaurants, or schools where his men could be bivouacked on straw bedding. The dance hall or the school gym were the most often used locations. Very rarely did the quartermaster have to refer to the requisition law, because the population did everything they could to support the army. For food as well, the company quartermaster (with rank of sergeant) was on his own. By tradition, the army relied on food available in the area. Very little was centrally provided. The quartermaster would buy from the local butcher, baker and green grocer. This kind of decentralization down to the company level proved to be efficient, and occasionally the odd difficulties could be taken care of without the need for a top-heavy staff."[4] Such mobilizations, however, must have exacerbated local shortages of the two-day-old potato bread which was standard fare for everyone and of foods (such as meat) which were already strictly rationed.

"In spring 1940, after the debacle in Western Europe, 43,000 French and Polish troops crossed into Switzerland from France, laid down their arms, and were interned in several villages and guarded by the army. They were actually allowed a great deal of freedom and enjoyed good relations with the local population. However, I was surprised to learn how poorly the French Army was equipped. Often, a single unit had to make do with several different gun calibers!

"We were lucky to have weekly comments on the progress of the war over the national radio network by the Swiss commentators—J.R. von Salis in German and René Payot (of Geneva) in French. Payot was also a beacon of hope to the French, many of whom continued to listen to the Swiss station even after France was totally occupied, despite a Nazi ban. We regularly glued our ears to the radio for the BBC evening broadcast (which the Germans constantly tried to jam) to keep up with news from the war zones.

"Before the Allied victory in 1945, POW workers from Russia and other East European countries fled from Germany to Switzerland. Some two hundred were housed for several weeks in our village. It made me aware how many different kinds of Russians there were and the difficulty the USSR must have to keep these different groups together. From discussions I had with some of these POW workers, I learned how soldiers were brutalized within the Soviet armed forces. When the war ended, the Allied command supported the Soviet government's demands that all these men be returned to Russia. Many had promised to write after their return. To my knowledge no mail ever came."

The following oral and written recollections present additional insights and panoramas of the war years from the point of view of Swiss citizens.

Max Salm, born in 1922, was one of a group that went to the 1937 Boy Scout International Jamboree in the Netherlands. On the way to Holland, "We spent a day in Köln, Germany, where we were put up for the night in the home of a member of the Hitler Youth. That evening we went out and were sitting at a station when a demonstration of several hundred socialists carrying flags passed by in the street. Suddenly, uniformed Nazis wearing swastikas swooped down on them, beat them with clubs and took them away in lorries. There were five or six of us Swiss. We were shocked to see that violence and went back to our room frightened. I never went to Germany again until after the war, and then only for business.[5]

"When I went to college, we read a book published in Zurich by Wolfgang Langhoff entitled *Die Moorsoldaten: 13 Monate Konzentrationslager* (The Swamp Soldiers: 13 Months in a Concentration Camp).[6] A stage actor, Langhoff had been imprisoned in one of the first Nazi concentration camps. He later managed to flee to Switzerland, where he became the director of the Zurich Schauspielhaus (Theatre). That book made us aware of the extent of the Nazi terror against free speech and against those declared to be non-Aryans.

"When the war came, our army (which included every healthy man between 20 and 50) was mobilized. Most of the men in our village, which is 15 miles from the German border, served in the *Grenzschutz* (frontier defense). Private companies did not pay salaries for men in the service, and service pay at that time was two francs a day, an amount which would buy two pints of beer. This posed big financial problems, especially for families. In 1940 an insurance scheme was created to reimburse 80 percent of a soldier's normal income. Still today, every man pays two percent of his salary for this insurance in order to receive a substitute income while in military service." From medieval times, militia service in Switzerland has been compulsory. Only in recent years have employers been required to continue paying salaries and wages while militiamen are on duty.

"My father served even at age 46. He was stationed in one of the narrow valleys running from the industrial zone of Switzerland down to the Rhine. Having no weapons against armored vehicles, his *Grenzschutz* unit built tank obstacles to cause delays and force crews to leave their tanks so snipers could pick them off. Everyone knew how difficult such a defense would be without heavy weapons. We were angry but not discouraged. Later when we got antitank guns morale went up.

"Like my father, most local farmers were called up. When it came time to harvest potatoes, everyone at our college had to spend three weeks of our holiday in service. I was sent with four friends to an infantry unit near the German border. That was only about a mile from my father's unit. During the day we dug potatoes on nearby farms, and at night we slept with the soldiers on straw bedding. We shared the evening meal with the soldiers, and afterward their captain explained to us how his men built tank traps and trained to use their weapons. Then he bought us rounds of beer.

"After the fall of Poland, the Russian attack on Finland became the talk of the Swiss people. After all, Finland was a small neutral state like Switzerland with a strong spirit of independence. Communism attracted far more Swiss citizens than Nazism. Communists were even represented in Parliament, something the Nazis never achieved, and continued to present a danger within our country. However, the Soviet attack on Finland changed everything. Communism lost favor. The two Communists in our village renounced the party.

"The news on the radio and in the press described the bravery of the Finns, the efficient military leadership of Marshal Mannerheim, and the courageous work of the Finnish women's auxiliary army, the so-called Lottas. We admired the ability of the Finns, how they used their knowledge of the land to resist the huge Russian army. The Finns could move swiftly on skis in the woods and on the frozen lakes, while the Russians had big problems with their trucks and armored vehicles. We admired their courage all the more because they had no help whatsoever from other states.

"The effects of the Finnish war in Switzerland were manifold. First, it boosted our belief that a small country like Switzerland could indeed defend herself against an aggressor. Second, it gave more Swiss incentive to learn to ski, which was promoted by all sorts of organizations. Third, the Alpine units of our army were strengthened. The war in Finland later encouraged the populace to accept the idea of the Réduit. We had heard how a small army was able to resist an overwhelming foe if it takes advantage of favorable terrain. As in Finland, our natural defenses were not situated right at the frontier. We recognized that we might have to give up part of our country, as the Finns had in the peace treaty of 1940. However, we believed that by withdrawing into the Réduit we could survive a long war as an independent state and rebuild after the war.

"In 1940 young and old civilians were encouraged to join the *Ortswehr*. I was in the second year at college in Aarau, and our entire class decided to join. We all had been in the pre-military shooting courses from age 15. We were issued old Model 1889 rifles and a red armband with the white cross to wear on the left arm, to identify us as members of the armed forces. Our instructions were that we should always be alert for parachutists and for people behaving suspiciously. We wanted to shoot as many '*Sauschwaben*' [German pigs] as possible.

"We were encouraged to take our rifles and armbands everywhere, including to college. Since it was tiring to carry a heavy rifle, we were allowed to carry a revolver or pistol instead. I did not own such a weapon, so my uncle gave me his Browning 6.5-mm pistol, which I still have in a cupboard today.

"In addition to our daily lookout, we also had night duty. I was detailed to guard the hospital for two hours every night. At 2:00 a.m. one night, a driver appeared, claiming he had a woman about to have a baby. I thought it might be a trick, but decided to let them in. About twenty minutes later I was relieved to hear the cries of a newborn.

"Before the end of 1940, my father reported that they now had support from a real anti-tank unit and that civil contractors were building concrete shelters for their anti-tank weapons. The soldiers also welcomed the idea of the Réduit. No one knew better than they that they had no chance to defeat the German army. The plan to delay the aggressor near the frontier, gain time for the destruction of factories and bridges, and then to have an unconquerable position in the mountains made sense to all of them.

"Preparations to destroy important bridges were real enough. Our house was situated about 200 meters from a railway viaduct over the river Aare for the main line between Basel and Chiasso. I watched while caches were made in the bridge's pylons and a special unit loaded them with explosives. The bridge was then guarded day and night by an infantry platoon to prevent anyone from getting close to those charges.

"In 1941, I started my military training with the air force at Payene. From now on my mother was left alone at home for weeks at a time to look after the house and garden. The small meat rations had induced my father to keep rabbits. My mother now had to look after them."

The Swiss militia army entailed regular service at specific intervals, which allowed men to work or pursue education when not on duty, but required universal mobilization in times of great danger. Salm recalls: "When my friends and I entered the university in October 1942, we knew that some of us had to drop out of class to do military service in the midst of the term. So we worked out a plan. Anyone currently not in service made his lecture notes with a carbon copy, which he sent off once a week to a buddy who had been called up. Our system worked well.

"There was always a big throng at the ETH Zurich (Swiss Federal

Institute of Technology) for the evening lectures of the historian Karl Meyer. The topic was 'Basic International Politics.' He analyzed contradictions in Nazi policy and took apart Hitler's theories. The largest ETH auditorium was never large enough to hold all the students wishing to hear his lectures. Students stood in the corridors and on the staircases to hear him.

"Colonel R[oger] Masson, the Chief of Swiss Intelligence, spoke on Tuesday evenings about what was happening on the various fronts. We were impressed with his comprehensive knowledge of the progress of the war. He showed us charts that we would see in the papers the following week, and he ventured forecasts which invariably came true." Thanks to the analyses of people like Masson, some Swiss were probably better informed than the populations of the combatant countries. Censorship never extended to Swiss universities. In contrast, the Nazis forbade discussion of the war in German universities, and violators paid a terrible price.

"We had a number of Polish students who had been in the Polish army which fought the Germans in 1940. They were now interned in Switzerland. Those with adequate education were allowed to study. They lived in a camp in Winterthur and came by train to Zurich every day. In one aspect they fared better than we Swiss: they could study full-time, with no interruption for military service. Three of these Poles became life-long friends of mine.

"I did my first service term in a fighter squadron during the winter of 1942. We were stationed at the Buochs Airbase. In July, our routine work at the base was abruptly stopped. A corporal in another unit had betrayed the location of our airbase's ammunition depot, located in the woods above Kerns, to the Germans. So for about one week we were detailed to the woods to load the ammunition on trucks. Another party went to the railway station of Hergiswil to unload the trucks and load the ammunition into railway carriages for a new, unknown destination. Since we could not use any motorized transport in this dense wood, the entire move had to be done manually. We cursed that corporal and were quite satisfied to hear later that he had been sentenced to death and executed by soldiers of his own unit.

"Although the death penalty had long been abolished in Switzerland, no one in my family or among my friends found anything wrong with the death penalty being reintroduced for traitors. Nearly all of the executed men spied for Germany. I think it took quite a lot of courage for our authorities to pass these death sentences, which could not be kept secret from Hitler." Indeed, of 33 death sentences for treason or espionage pronounced during the war, 15 Swiss were actually executed for treason. Once the appeal was denied, the traitor would be immediately shot by a firing squad composed of his own army unit.[7] Salm continues:

"I was again called up for military service from June through August of 1943. This time our squadron was based at Interlaken airfield. The airfields were guarded by infantry and anti-aircraft units. Each member of the air force had his personal 7.5-mm rifle with 48 rounds, and each platoon had a light machine gun and a double-barreled machine gun, mounted on a swivel for use against low-flying aircraft.

"On July 9, we were just setting out for our evening meal in the nearby village of Bönigen when an officer arrived with orders to put us on the highest state of readiness to protect the aircraft. After a while, a truck arrived, traveling from platoon to platoon unloading ammunition for our machine guns. I have never in my life seen such a mass of ammunition. We were convinced that Hitler must have started to invade Switzerland. The evening news, however, did not mention anything. Perhaps some high-ranking officer had a bad day and wanted us to share his misery.

"On the following day we listened again to the news and were overwhelmed to hear that the Allies had landed in Sicily at dawn on July 10. Apparently the invasion was a complete surprise to Italy and Germany. Our esteem for our high command was boosted, as this news showed that our intelligence was better than that of the German Army. Having seen Hitler's eccentricities, which led to the loss of a whole army at Stalingrad a few months before, we all believed that Hitler might now try to seize the north–south rail connections through Switzerland to Italy. It was obvious for us that we must be ready for anything. Knowing about the Réduit, our preparations to blow up the rail tunnels, and being confident that it would be a very difficult task to invade an airbase like Interlaken in the midst of mountains, none of us despaired. 'Let him come' was our thought."

While Hitler never came, some American airmen did. Max Salm recalls: "In late summer 1944 Fighter Squadron 7 served one of its usual ten-week duties at Interlaken airbase. During this time, heavy daylight bombing raids were flown by the American air force against industrial plants in southern Germany. These day raids caused heavy losses to the Americans, and many damaged bombers flew to Switzerland to escape either being killed by German antiaircraft defenses or taken prisoner in Germany.[8]

"The numbers of damaged planes heading for Switzerland had increased considerably during the last few days, and therefore our squadron was transferred to Dübendorf near Zurich at short notice so that these damaged planes could be intercepted when crossing the border and be escorted to the nearest air base for an emergency landing.

"On September 5th a bomber, damaged when raiding the Mercedes plant in Stuttgart, crossed into Switzerland and was detected and escorted to Dübendorf by four of our Messerschmitt fighters. Our planes were surprised by two American Mustang P-51 fighters, which opened fire on two of our Messerschmitts flying behind the bomber. Paul Treu was evidently killed instantly, and his plane crashed in Affoltern. The engine of the second plane, piloted by Robert Heiniger, was knocked out, but he managed to land at the Dübendorf airbase. This was the last action in which Swiss planes were involved during World War II."

The attitude of defiance to the Nazi regime expressed above was apparently universal. Ernst Jenny remembers: "In 1939, at age 16, I was in Luzern High School. We listened to the radio each evening. It was depressing to hear about Hitler's attacks and his successes. This was the first time I experienced powerlessness against injustice. We got some hope from the weekly Swiss radio programs by Professor von Salis.[9]

"In spring 1940, we expected to be attacked by Germany. We lived three kilometers from a military airport. Beginning at dawn fighter planes took off and landed without pause. Capitulation to Germany was never an option. No one ever suggested it. There was general enmity to Hitler and sympathy to Jews." Jenny continued about his military experiences beginning in 1943:

"Service in wartime was quite hard, with little sleep and limited food. We had to get up at 0500 and be ready at 0505 for the *Kampfbahn*, an obstacle course to be run with equipment and arms. The drill was similar to that of the German Army, which was the most efficient army at that time. Those who survived the winter maneuvers had a Russian-like experience!

"By the time I entered service, we had anti-tank rifles and better equipment than before. We had shooting practice once or twice per week. It was always 300 meters prone. Standing position was for the time of Napoleon. Lying down, you are less of a target. We certainly would have had a chance—not against the full German army, but in a fight with a similar number of troops.

"We knew that our equipment was not the most modern. But we were convinced that our armament, fortifications, optimal use of our territory, and our determination would give us a chance. More recently, with much more modern arms, the wars in Indochina or Yugoslavia show that this was not merely wishful thinking."

The enemy was not only without but also within, and Nazis in Switzerland were closely watched. Recalls Hans Kleiner: "In Baden we had German members of the *Nationalsozialistische Deutsche Arbeiter Partei* (NSDAP, or National Socialist German Workers Party). Police had them listed. After the war, they were expelled from Switzerland to Germany and handed over to the French."[10]

Hans Widmer remembers: "I was 13 in 1939. I grew up in Orlikon near the major railroad station. I was a Boy Scout and a messenger in Kommando 6. Boy Scouts went to every yard to measure how much ground could be used for planting. As an incentive, you could keep the potatoes you planted on the playground. We always had enough potatoes. My mother was in a patriotic organization. There is no doubt that we would have fought Germany tooth and nail. I swiped Father's Browning pistol.

"I had a Communist friend who was pro-Nazi until the attack on the Soviet Union. We always had arguments. All pro-Nazi Germans were listed by the police. If Germany attacked, they would be arrested. My mother was German, and she went to the German consulate to get a visa. When she left, the Swiss police stopped us and required us to register. Everyone who went to the German consulate in Zurich got registered. This was before June 1941, because she would not have gone to the German consulate after the attack on Russia."[11]

The Nazis, both foreign and domestic, from the first sought to identify and attack their enemies. Lucie Schaad-Denner of Basel remembers: "Father was a Freemason, and was listed in the Zurich address book as the head of the Masonic Lodge. Like Hitler, the National Frontists [Swiss Nazis] were against Freemasons. Father once noticed that a car was following him. When he was opening the garage gate, a pursuer got out of his car and seized Father's briefcase from his car. Father chased the robber, who fired two shots at him. I heard the shots. The robber got away. Father believed that the Frontists wanted information on the Freemasons, and hoped perhaps to find a membership list.[12]

"Father offered a reward for information about who shot at him. A week later a man appeared at his office seeking employment—there was much unemployment then—and stated that he wished to collect the reward. Father told him to go to the police. He did so, and informed on the shooter. The police searched the office of the Front and found the stolen folder, but the assailant, a German, had fled to Germany." This was still before the war, and while Swiss police monitored the Frontists and their foreign sponsors, the assailant would have been able to slip across the border with a valid passport. Lucie Schaad-Denner continues:

"Later, police were called to a scene where a man had been thrown into a well. It was believed that Frontists had discovered the informant who betrayed their associate and pushed him down the well. The story was published in the *Neue Zürcher Zeitung.*

"Father was the Swiss agent for a sugar refinery and a malt factory in Czechoslovakia. Business was very good until 1938 when Czechoslovakia fell to the Nazis. The owners of these companies were Jews who vanished into the concentration camps, and the companies were taken over by the Germans. Papa refused to work together with the Nazis and so lost his business."

When the war began, Lucie Schaad-Denner joined the *Frauenhilfsdienst* (FHD, or Women's Auxiliary Service). "We were sworn in wearing civilian clothes and the armband with the Swiss cross." She helped care for the military internees, including the allocation of warm-meal ration coupons and *Schokoladecoupons*—chocolate coupons. Most long-term internees were Poles, but they also helped Russians who escaped over the Rhine from German prisoner-of-war camps.

Werner P. Auer was born in 1921. "My father came from Germany in 1895. He was anti-Nazi and had brothers still in Germany. My mother was Swiss and religious. When the war started, Father was 70 but still joined the *Ortswehr*. At my school, I had a Jewish teacher and two Jewish classmates. There was not one Nazi. We did not learn of the Holocaust until after the war." Indeed, most ordinary people in the neutral and Allied countries and even in Germany did not know about the extremes of the Holocaust until the war ended. What political elites may or may not have known about systematic extermination is the subject of numerous studies, but the fact of widespread Nazi persecution of Jews was no secret to the public. Switzerland faced a flood of refugees, and accepted the vast majority.

"In 1939 my school closed and I was sent to guard the Landi, the Swiss National Exposition—a patriotic cultural exposition visited by most Swiss. I was 18 and in the fire brigade. In 1940 people thought Germany might use Switzerland as a back door [into France]. I was a Boy Scout and lived five kilometers from the Rhine. We sensed that something would happen. The road signs were removed. The military used us as messenger boys for the army. Since we had no insignia, we could have been shot had there been a war and we were captured! Later we got armbands. The Boy Scouts organized camps for French orphans. It was a great experience.[13]

"I was in the army from September 1941 through the end of the war and later, in all 2,500 days of service. At the borders with France and Italy, the Germans had fences with bells. The Swiss would ring the bells as a prank, and the Germans would come running.

"In the army we discussed German preparations. We did not distinguish the Germans and the Nazis—they were the same enemy. I never met anyone who would consider abandoning Switzerland. Passive cooperation was excluded. People would have disappeared into the woods and waged guerrilla warfare. The Réduit decision was not opposed and did not lead to discouragement. People never complained that they would be abandoned."

Konstanz is a border town, part of which is in Switzerland and part in Germany. In 1938, Peter Baumgartner-Jost's mother took him across the border at Konstanz into Germany to see what it was like. He remembers: "Everyone was saying 'Heil Hitler!' We were on the train, and everyone looked at us when we did not 'Heil' in return. Their looks were as if to say, 'You're not with us? Who are these people?!' We felt very uncomfortable."[14]

Col. Rudolf Ursprung remembers: "In 1939 I was studying law at the University of Bern. When the war began, I was staying in Grenoble for four weeks studying French so that I could continue my studies in Dijon or Geneva. But my active duty intervened. From 1939 to 1945, the year of my graduation, I served a total of about 23 months on duty.[15]

"I spent most of my time as a lieutenant with a border protection unit in Etzgen, a small village on the Rhine. The company was composed of soldiers from the Mettau Valley and Bötzberg. Our quarters and sanitary installations were extremely primitive, and the local population was poor but willing to sacrifice to accommodate us. Every noncommissioned officer was given a bed, and the company office was for a time set up in a living room.

"Most soldiers belonging to our company were farmers on the side, others were full-time farmers. Those who lived in the area were able to work at their farms in the evening, and those from outside the area had to be given leave so they could go home and help out. When harvest time came around, we had to set up a leave system for the farmers. At the same time we had to work with other self-employed soldiers, bakers, butchers and craftsmen who felt that they were at a disadvantage compared to the farmers." Military units were typically from the same locales since they were a militia army composed of civilians who, when mobilized, grabbed their rifles and assembled at a nearby rendezvous. Once mobilized, however, they could be sent anywhere in Switzerland. Colonel Ursprung continues:

"We didn't really see what a dangerous situation we would be in if we were attacked from across the Rhine. We were calm. We would have fired at any German that we saw. Only the young platoon leader and the young company commander were concerned. They bought *Signal* [a German military periodical], which described things such as combat patrols, at the newspaper stand. I bought all of the German training materials I could find at the Stämpfli bookstore in Bern. We, the young leaders, recognized very early on that the border protection unit and the army in general had inferior training, and we did our best to improve the situation.

"We were also very nervous, especially in 1940. Once a patrol unit in Rheinsulz heard noise on the other side of the Rhine where the embankment consisted of gravel. The patrol thought that the Germans might be crossing the river and immediately informed the brigade commander. Observers were sent over, but the next morning we saw that the noise was only some loose gravel sliding into the river.

"In the summer of 1941 our young cadre conducted five training courses of about three to five weeks each for noncommissioned officers, and later conducted similar courses for privates. We trained in combat techniques our commanders had gotten from books. We practiced throwing live hand grenades and shooting over obstacles. Finally we began to feel more combat-ready, and that was an important psychological gain.

"Being preoccupied with our daily work, we knew little about political events. We subscribed to a paper, but barely had time to read it. We listened to the radio news to follow the overall progress of the war, but at our place on the border we didn't really know much. We recognized the problems connected to Switzerland's neutrality. But in our border area we had confidence." While not reflected in these comments, border troops were under orders to hold to the last cartridge without retreat to give chosen units in the interior time to assemble in the Réduit, where they could resist almost indefinitely.

Felix P. Bentz was a member of the 500-strong delegation of Swiss Boy Scouts heading for the 5th World Scouting Jamboree in Vogelenzang,

Holland, in 1937. Passing through Germany, they saw large red banners with black swastikas everywhere, in the streets, on the buildings, and even inside the immense youth hostel where they stayed. "In Köln [Cologne] we were the overnight guests of the Hitler Youth, presuming that they were nothing more than a German version of the Scouts. They did dress in shorts and brown shirts, not unlike our own uniforms. But that was where the similarity ended. They wore black neckties and swastika arm-bands, and gave the 'Heil Hitler' salute at every opportunity. And the way they acted, one had the uneasy feeling they thought their misplaced 'German brothers' in Switzerland would greatly benefit from an 'Anschluss,' the way they just had annexed the Rhineland."[16]

Bentz also recalled how, in 1938, the leaders of England and France signed the Munich agreement, sacrificing Czechoslovakia to Hitler. Mussolini acted as intermediary. "How little the Swiss trusted Adolf Hitler's solemn promises may have been expressed in my own skeptical reaction. The world events had inspired me to draw a cartoon showing the four European leaders gathered in a palace, pen in hand. The sign over the door read: 'Treaties and Peace Agreements prepared here— CHEAP!'"[17]

In late August 1939, a couple of days before the war broke out, Bentz participated in a tribute to the medieval battle at St. Jakob, where out-numbered Swiss fought to the death against invaders. "Dressed in my Boy Scout uniform, I was beating the drum loudly as we marched down the tree-shaded avenue toward a small chapel on the outskirts of Basel. There must have been hundreds of citizens in the parade . . . and there were thousands of people lining the streets, applauding and waving to friends they knew."

Five hundred years before, some 1,500 Swiss peasant warriors all per-ished in a bloody battle as they resisted the invasion of 15,000 knights and mercenaries from France. The Swiss defense was so fierce and costly that the French retreated and gave up their invasion.

"Two days after our memorial march to St. Jakob, the President of the Swiss Confederation ordered a partial mobilization of the army. One could but wonder whether the example we had just celebrated, of a vastly outnumbered force trying to defend its freedom, would repeat itself in the near future."[18]

When the blitzkrieg hit Western Europe in 1940, young Felix Bentz noted in his diary: "We are neutral, we don't care who is clobbering the Krauts." "But," he said, "our actions betrayed our anxiety. As soon as I left our apartment and turned the corner into one of the main arteries leading to the German border, only a mile away, I could notice the feverish activities. Pilings were driven into the pavement, and heavy chains stretched across the streets."[19]

The Boy Scouts were mobilized and issued armbands to identify them officially as auxiliaries. "I was assigned to one of the border crossings with France to assist with a stream of last-minute refugees. They came through a narrow gap in the rolls of barbed wire strung across the street, guarded by soldiers, while customs agents were scrutinizing these poor folks and their few belongings, piled on pushcarts."

Bentz found himself rushing across town on his bike, "delivering instructions and materials to blacked-out office buildings and hospitals. Preparations to minimize the effects of air attacks were high on the list for everybody. I was made a block warden in our street, which meant that, after just a few hours of instructions, I would be empowered to check on the air defense preparations of our neighbors.

"One of the key requirements was to clear all of the accumulated junk and clutter from the typically vast attics. The only items that were required up there were a shovel and a box of sand, which, in theory, would be used to extinguish fires caused by incendiary bombs. During one of my lectures a lady asked me how one could be so sure that such a bomb would fall into the box? Actually, she was not too far off the mark concerning the usefulness of quite a few of our improvised preparations.[20]

"Just to be on the safe side, we left the north-facing windows open as Mother began fixing breakfast. It was the morning of May 15, 1940. . . . The population of Basel had been advised that there could be an attack by the divisions the German High Command had been massing north of the border. This 'leaked' warning by the well-informed Swiss General Staff had triggered a panic in town." Holland had collapsed the day before, France was routed at Sedan on the 15th, and Wehrmacht concentrations near the border convinced the Swiss that they were next. Bentz continues:

"We had devised our own plan. Yesterday afternoon each one of us had stuffed a backpack with a few clothes, our passports, some money and a few imperishable food items. Then we carried this essential baggage across the bridge to Helli's apartment on the left bank of the Rhine where, presumably, we could retrieve it leisurely in case of an attack. We then returned home, ate dinner, and listened to a recording of Johann Sebastian Bach's 'Air.' The irony of trying to calm our nerves with this sublime German masterpiece, while waiting for a devastating German attack, was not lost on us."[21]

The attack did not come at that time, but the Swiss continued to prepare to resist as the tense hours turned into days, which became months, then years. Bentz's memoirs fast-forward two years. "A motley crew gathered in the barrack square of the basic training facilities in Thun on July 13, 1942. It was the beginning of boot camp for the Cannoneers of the Motorized Anti-Tank troops. Not only did we come from all walks of life, we came from the whole spectrum of languages and dialects spoken in Switzerland. One could hear the genteel idiom of Basel, the guttural sounds from Zurich, the slow spoken words of the Bernese, the French of the Vaudois and Genevois, and the melodic Italian dialect from Ticino.

"Fortunately, most of us could understand the other's language to some degree, and even speak it a little, but the commands given by the Captain of this mixed company, whenever we exercised as a unit, were given in all three languages: German, French and Italian. And it sounded like this:

Zwanzig Taktschritte — Vingt pas cadancés — Venti passi cadenzati
(Twenty goose steps)
Vorwaerts — En avant — Avanti — Marsch!
(Forward, march!)"

While this might sound like the Tower of Babel brigade, it reflected Switzerland's linguistic diversity. The militia army was a primary institution that unified Swiss speaking different languages and a force for social cohesion. Indeed, the Swiss Confederation for centuries had been defended by warriors who learned each other's languages sufficiently to fight together. Bentz continues:

"One of the stunts a few of us excelled at was to somersault over a pyramid of rifles with fixed bayonets into a steep gravel pit. We were called on several times to perform for visiting brass, giving them the impression that all recruits nonchalantly did these aerial acrobatics. But the more interesting phase of our training started when we hit the road and began traveling the highways and byways of Switzerland. We learned to spend endless hours next to our guns exposed to the hot sun or torrential rains, and spent uncomfortable nights on straw, spread out on the classroom floors of commandeered school houses.

"The main purpose of this exercise was to practice detaching our anti-tank cannons from the vehicles at a moment's notice, and placing them into a firing position within seconds in any imaginable situation or location. We learned quickly that whenever the signal 'Tank Attack' sounded in the middle of a village, by far the most strategic location for our position was as close as possible to a café or bakery.

"But seriously, we loved these action-packed days, particularly, when we drove way up to a remote Alp to lob some live shells into the snow fields across the valley. It was easy to determine the accuracy of our aim by the black smudges which each impact made in the pristine snow. After all the days of dismantling, lugging around and reassembling these monsters, it was good to see them work and to hear the ear-shattering booms echoing from peak to peak. For the first time we felt like real cannoneers."[22]

D-Day was launched on June 6, 1944, and is frozen in Bentz's memory as if it were yesterday. "Overnight the posters had appeared all over town, glued to walls and fences; their trilingual headlines called for mobilization! I had expected this would happen as soon as I heard the radio confirm that there had been a major landing by the Allied forces in Normandy. But I first had to scrutinize the long columns of fine print to find out which units were being called and which had been spared. My motorized anti-tank gun company was on the list. We were to assemble at 7 a.m. on June 15, 1944, in Liestal, a small town which was a 20-minute train ride from Basel." Unlike the overnight mobilizations of 1939 and 1940, when Switzerland might have been imminently attacked, this order allowed some soldiers a week to mobilize.

"It was a strange column that drove through those low hills. Led by Captain Greub in his Mercedes convertible, there followed Cadillacs, Buicks and Lincolns pulling anti-tank guns. In between there were Fords and Chevys of lesser power which carried the other crew members, and at the tail end of the column were trucks full of ammunition and supplies. All of these vehicles had been commandeered early in the war. Their owners had to promise to make them available any time, at a moment's notice." Within the Nazi stranglehold, Switzerland had no sources from which to purchase military vehicles. Bentz continued:

"We were still wondering what was happening in France. At the beginning of the invasion the situation was rather confused. The Allies certainly did not announce what they were up to, and the Germans were told to say they were winning. And our unit up in the mountains was told nothing. But then General Guisan, the leader of the Swiss Army, made an announcement. The gist was that very likely this was the last phase of the

European war, and potentially the most dangerous period for Switzerland. We should be prepared to stay on the alert as long as was necessary, possibly till the war was over. But it turned out that, for a while at least, we would be spared, as the battle continued to rage in Normandy.

"Our outfit was moved to another location, where we stayed about a month. During that time I was selected to be part of the squad which was to represent our company at the Division Games in Luzern. This contest between all the units within the Division consisted of a 300-meter swim in the cold lake, a four-kilometer cross country run, shooting at targets, and finally a monstrous obstacle course ending in a ditch, from which one had to hit a target with hand grenades. Our squad did not do too badly, winding up in fifth place." Such endurance races were also excellent military training.

"The next alert came in September 1944, when U.S. troops reached the Alsace. . . . One always had to contend with the irrational orders a desperate Hitler might give to his army. Our unit had been on leave for a month when this sudden call to arms sounded. My squad was one of the first on the scene, and as soon as we were equipped with our anti-tank gun and lots of ammunition, we hightailed it to the border as fast as we could drive. Our orders were to find a suitable position along the half-mile of road which led out of Riehen to the German frontier, to install and camouflage our gun and then wait for further orders, or German tanks, whichever came first."[23]

Such were the experiences of one Swiss soldier. While the varieties of experiences were endless, their common thread was the determination to resist the threat, which remained for the duration of the war.

In July 1934, Bruno Capol attended Boy Scout summer camp in the Grisons. "The Swiss Scout uniform consisted of a brown shirt and black Manchester shorts. As members of a Scout Troop of Lucerne, we wore black scarves. We did not know yet that the uniform of the German Hitler Youth was identical to our uniform. On a hike, when we took a rest along the road from Zizers to Chur, a German car with opened canopy arrived and stopped. The five passengers got out, made the Hitler salute, and enthusiastically called out 'Heil Hitler!' Shocked, we picked up pieces of dirt and bombarded the Germans.[24]

"In 1938, a Nazi office with a Hitler Youth section opened in Lucerne. It leaked out that a German student who attended our school was a member. During a school sports event he was pummeled by his classmates."

On September 1, 1939, when Hitler launched World War II, Switzerland mobilized not just her militia army but also her Boy Scouts. Capol recalls: "In Lucerne, the 16- to 19-year-old Scouts entered the auxiliary services. The school was closed. To our Scout uniform we added a red armband with the Swiss cross and were sworn in! On our bikes day and night, we provided runner services, delivering orders for requisition of food and motor vehicles. At railway stations and crossroads, my Scout group removed all signs which gave any geographic information, such as the name of a village or town."

Capol entered military service and by 1942 was a second lieutenant in the air force, the youngest officer in the Swiss military. "In the evening we used to sit around the radio and listen to war news of the German Wehrmacht and the Allied forces. Still today I hear the noise of the German marching boots on gravel and the sound of their soldiers' songs, *'denn wir fahren,—denn wir fahren,—denn wir fahren gegen Engelland!'* [then we march against England] or their favorite, 'Lili Marlene.' I remember a German soldiers' song which ended with the refrain *'und die Schweiz, das Stachelschwein, nehmen wir am Heimweg ein!'* [and Switzerland, the porcupine, we'll conquer her on our way home!]. The Nazis called Switzerland a porcupine because our borders were protected all around with heavy barbed wire obstacles." Actually, that term went back to medieval times, describing the appearance of concentrated bodies of Swiss foot soldiers with pikes protruding in the air, an impregnable barrier to knights on horseback.

The Swiss porcupine awaited a Nazi attack. As Capol adds: "It was never an option to win, but to sell our skin dear. We knew our territory, we were farmers and knew every tree." This determination is further illustrated in the following account.

Combat Engineer von Schroeder of Radio Signal Company 1 penned a dramatic recollection of taking the oath of allegiance at the time of the Swiss mobilization when Hitler attacked Poland on September 1, 1939.[25] "Late in the afternoon we marched out of the boarding school where we had assembled in our steel helmets and with fixed bayonets. We walked up the hill to a place above the town where we were to be sworn in together with members of a French-speaking telegraph company.

"The Swiss flag was blowing in the evening breeze. We were lined up in ranks looking over the land, our homeland. In the distance we saw the Freiburg mountains, and behind them the Alps. A few clouds were in the sky, and everything around us was very peaceful.

"The radio signal companies at the time were half-battalion size and were mixed units with men of all ages and from almost all Swiss cantons. We were standing there as a symbol of the Swiss army: young drafted soldiers, experienced *Landwehr* soldiers, gray-haired *Landsturm* soldiers who had participated in the last border occupation (veterans of the World War I mobilization)." The Swiss militia army was divided into these three classes based on age. Von Schroeder continued:

"Besides our French-speaking comrades from Vaud, Neuchâtel and Geneva, we had men from Zurich, Basel, Berne, Schaffhausen, Ticino, St. Gall, the Grisons and many others. All had joined the army here to protect our beautiful, common homeland in a crisis, and we were not separated either by age or by language.

"The captain read the articles of war in German and French. A representative of the Freiburg government took our oath: 'We officers, noncommissioned officers, and soldiers swear to be loyal to the Swiss Confederation, to give our life and limb for the defense of our Fatherland and its Constitution; never to desert the flag; to follow the military laws faithfully; to follow the orders of our superiors exactly and timely; to uphold discipline and to do everything required to preserve the honor and freedom of our Fatherland.' We were holding our rifles and steel helmets in the left hand while we raised our right hand for the oath. 'I swear' went over the meadow like a whisper of the wind. Then the whole ceremony was repeated in French. We went back to our quarters. The ceremony made a great impression on me which made my heart beat with renewed and perpetual love for Switzerland."

Heinz Häsler, who would later become the Chief of the General Staff of the Swiss Army, has a vivid memory of the mobilization of September 1, 1939. "That day my father was working with a few other men from the village to construct new barriers to channel mountain torrents into a gorge below the Schynige Platte. Shortly before noon a railroad worker called down to them that things were starting to happen. This information was not a great surprise. We had all been in fear that this would happen sooner or later. In those days the daily talk even in the most remote mountain valleys was about the political situation in Europe and the inflammatory speeches coming from the north.[26]

"My father returned home around 4 p.m. My mother had already readied his uniform, backpack, and other gear, and with tears in her eyes was now gathering underwear and putting a large piece of mountain cheese into a bag. My grandmother was crying, but I was a school-age boy and felt defiance, pride and admiration. From the conversations of the adults I had learned what a dangerous man the 'Führer' in far-away Germany was and how much damage he could inflict with his armies if nobody stopped him. Grandfather had even said that he would shoot him if he ever saw him. So I had formed a view of the world in a simple child-ish way. Now this monster was going to be fought.

"And then father was in uniform. He was a private first class with the field artillery. I had known that for a long time because he often talked about the service. The gold-threaded, green-black cord on his coat was the highest honor for a marksman, and the small yellow chevron in metal on his red arm sleeves was the insignia of a judge. He had explained all of this to me.

"I followed Father to his room where he took the carbine and a pack-age of ammunition from the closet. We always kept rifle ammunition in the house (and still do). Father opened the package and took out six car-tridges which he inserted into the weapon. 'Everything will be all right,' he said when he left with his carbine. The goodbyes were simple and serious.

"Down on the street Father waited for two neighbors. More men came from side streets in uniform, with backpacks and rifles. They disappeared into the woods and into uncertainty."

Resistance to a Nazi invasion and potential occupation was a topic of constant discussion among the Swiss armed forces. Ambassador Heinz Langenbacher remembers it well. "As young air force lieutenants, we often discussed—sometimes all night—what we would have to do if the Germans attacked and invaded Switzerland. We agreed that we would not flee abroad, but go underground to organize a resistance movement. Our models were the Finns whose fight for independence we admired and the French Maquis of whose successful operations against the Germans we kept getting breathless reports from across the border."[27] While the Réduit in the Alps offered the most favorable terrain to engage the Wehrmacht, resistance would take place throughout the entire country. Langenbacher continues:

"We discussed how we would form resistance cells in the mountains, set up resistance groups at universities, conduct covert operations with farmers, and obtain weapons caches from army supplies. We also agreed that we would have to do everything possible to convince our fellow citizens that flight would weaken the spirit of the people. We had learned in particular from the French that mothers and daughters were playing an important role in the resistance movement. We therefore agreed that the women would have to be integrated into our movement from the beginning.

"There was also agreement among us that it would be of great importance for the future of our country to fight to the last, to die honorably. We were convinced that each country is only worth as much as that country is willing to fight for its ideals."

Langenbacher wrote these lines in his diary on December 11, 1942: "It is difficult to resist a nagging depression. Each time I think I am dropping into a black hole, one thought keeps me above the water: the knowledge that, if we were attacked, hundreds of our politicians and journalists, who show such an admirable courage every day, would be slaughtered by the Nazis and tens of thousands of young men deported to Germany for hard labor and our houses plundered, and our women raped and we, the diplomats, thrown into concentration camps. These pictures always give me a new courage to resist."[28]

Hans Hug served in the Swiss Army from 1942 to 1945. "I was stationed most of the time in an area stretching from Schaffhausen to Stein am Rhein. Time was spent in building fortifications, getting acquainted with flamethrowers, shaped charges, and anti-tank weapons, and watching the activities on the German side of the Rhein from observation towers.[29]

"The Swiss soldier, myself included, had no illusions about the long-term outcome of a battle with the German armies. However, it was felt that we could put up a good fight with hit-and-run tactics and hold out several months until our food and ammunition were depleted. We also knew that Hitler and Mussolini were eager to get hold of the north–south railway connections, specifically the Gotthard and the Simplon tunnel complexes. Both tunnels were double track and were served by very powerful electric locomotives. The tunnel under the Brenner Pass into Italy was single track and employed steam locomotives, which limited the movements of heavy freight trains.

"Consequently, the Swiss Army Command expected that an attack on either or both tunnels would be launched by a combination of parachute troops and/or glider formations. Hence, when mobilized, we stood guard and slept near the tracks in haystacks ready to set off the charges which would destroy the tunnels and bridges. It was cold, miserable and no fun. No army barracks here with bunk beds! After two weeks, we were moved out and another detachment took over."

In recent years, Switzerland has been criticized because some refugees were housed in rustic work camps. Hug compared those camps with the living conditions of the Swiss military: In addition, "Refugees in Switzerland in labor camps planted potatoes and vegetables, as all Swiss, young and old, were required to do. These camps were made up of standard army barracks and provided blankets, a stove and cold running water. For us, when returning from several weeks of field duty, this was an unheard-of luxury!"

American airmen who found refuge in Switzerland after bombing missions in southern Germany left lasting impressions on the Swiss who encountered them. In 1944, Hug witnessed the crash landing of a B-24 between Diessenhofen and Schaffhausen. "We were most impressed with the youth of the crews. An aircraft commander I interviewed was 23 years of age and his crew of seven or eight was even younger! Most impressive was their equipment. Fleece-lined jackets with sewn-in first-aid kits! And the airplanes: What marvels they were! Here we met young airmen from the other side of the Atlantic who sought refuge in Switzerland."

While numerous damaged American aircraft came down in Switzerland, a unique incident occurred in spring 1944 when a futuristic Luftwaffe nightfighter got lost and landed by mistake at Dübendorf near Zurich. "Hitler threatened to send a commando outfit to destroy the plane. The Swiss military managed to delay this effort for a day and had Dr. Ackeret—a professor of aerodynamics at the Federal Institute of Technology in Zurich—go over the plane to inspect and photograph it in detail. The next day, in the presence of the German ambassador to Switzerland, the plane was burned and destroyed by the Swiss military. The rumor had it that all photos ended up in Allen Dulles' hands in Bern." Dulles headed the Bern operations of the Office of Strategic Services (OSS), the intelligence agency of the United States.

The Swiss already had a deep-seated attachment to American culture. As Hug relates: "What music did we listen to? The best the BBC had to offer on the long-wave band: Glenn Miller, Tommy Dorsey, etc."

Henry Guggenbühl was a senior sergeant on General Guisan's personal staff. He recalls: "I was concerned with the mentality of the German army. German soldiers were well informed about conditions in Switzerland. In 1946, I had business in Germany and interviewed ex-Wehrmacht members, who told me that they were afraid to attack Switzerland primarily because every Swiss had a rifle at home and shot well; there would have been a *Heckenschütze* (sniper) behind every bush. Further, it was difficult to send spies into the villages, since *Ortswehr* members knew their towns and every face in them. Finally, fortresses such as the Swiss had could not be seen in all of Europe; there were said to be 2,000 fortresses in Switzerland."[30]

These personal observations tell tales not found in the history books. Guggenbühl offers one more: "Two blind people were in my unit. Their hearing was more sensitive, so they listened for aircraft." The Swiss never knew if the Luftwaffe would initiate a blitzkrieg against their country, and every person could play a role in defending the Confederation.

The Reverend Peter Vogelsanger was a Protestant minister in Schaffhausen, which is on the border with Germany. He was once asked to conduct a funeral for a German man whom he did not know. When he entered the chapel, there stood a man in Nazi Party uniform, and a gigantic swastika flag was spread on the coffin. Rev. Vogelsanger declared, "As long as this anti-Christian flag is displayed here, I will hold no Christian burial!" Angry gazes and a deadly tension filled the air. Vogelsanger stood firm until the man at the head of the coffin withdrew the Nazi flag. Later, there were furious, threatening protests from the German colony, and the German newspaper *Stuttgarter Zeitung* denounced the Swiss minister.[31]

As a known critic of National Socialism, Rev. Vogelsanger was a natural enemy of the pro-Nazi National Front. He taught at a school and clashed with another teacher named Carl Meyer. Meyer, who had Nazi sympathies, was fired from his job and blamed Vogelsanger for his dismissal.[32] Vogelsanger had reason to believe that he was put on the list of Swiss to be liquidated when the Nazis invaded.

Rev. Vogelsanger, like all other Swiss men, served in the militia army. The minister was armed, trained, and ready to join in resistance to any Nazi invasion. Ironically, his saddest sermon during the war was delivered at the funeral of the scores of Swiss who died in the accidental American bombing of Schaffhausen in 1944.

Paul Rothenhäusler was in grammar school when the war came. "I had the choice of working on a farm or joining the *Fliegerbeobachtungsdienst* (Aircraft Observation Service), which watched for foreign airplanes. I chose the latter, and spent six months in mountain hotels. We worked in teams of two. One would stand and watch the sky and the other would sit with paper and a phone. There would be three hours of watching followed by six hours of leave.[33]

"In 1940 I biked from Zurich to Geneva, where I stayed as a Red Cross worker. I read letters from prisoners of war on both sides and made summaries." A primary mission of the International Committee of the Red Cross, based in Switzerland, was to facilitate communication between prisoners of war and their families. Letters from POWs had to be sanitized to remove facts of potential military use while leaving information of personal significance to families. Rothenhäusler remarked as follows on the Swiss military training he experienced:

"In 1943 I went to recruit school for infantry training, Prussian style. In the morning, we did gymnastic exercises, maneuvers, marching and walking. Our shoes with nail cleats were the best in the world. We did shooting at a range of 300 meters using the A (bullseye) and B (silhouette) targets. If you did not do your obligatory shooting or if you did not score enough points, you did two days of additional training. I had to do it once. The others there were anarchists and leftists." Such persons, Rothenhäusler opined, were averse to military duty.

"I became a journalist and published an article in *Neue Zürcher Zeitung*, Switzerland's leading newspaper, in early 1944. I wrote on the French Resistance literature, especially new books published in the French part of Switzerland. My articles were not censored. I was in contact with August Lindt and other members of the Swiss Resistance." Lindt was a leading Swiss journalist who advocated the most extreme measures to resist an invasion.

"In 1944 I served in the Jura, where we trained and awaited an attack from the *Sauschwaben* [German pigs]. In April 1945 I guarded Russian civilians. They were laborers who had escaped into Switzerland from German factories. I knew some of the Russians, and invited one for a drink. He filled my beer glass with potato schnapps! I got drunk. One Russian took my rifle and another helped me to bed." Who was guarding whom?

The Swiss Army knife was as ubiquitous then as now. In 1890, Karl Elsener, owner of the Victorinox knife factory in the Canton of Schwyz, founded the Association of Swiss Master Cutlers to promote cooperation between producers to supply knives for the Swiss Army. At that time, the Army knives were purchased from Solingen, the center of the German cutlery industry. The first Swiss-made knives for the Swiss Army were delivered in 1891. The soldier's knife included a blade, punch, tin opener and screwdriver. The officer's knife, patented in 1897, also included an eraser blade (used to scrape ink from paper) and, most important of all, a corkscrew.[34]

The universally known Swiss Army knife has been produced by Victorinox ever since. The only other maker is Wenger of the French Jura region, which also has produced the knife since that era. Karl Elsener, Sr., born in 1922, would inherit the family business. His recollections of the war period in an interview with this author are intriguing.[35] He began:

"Victorinox was founded in 1884. The officer's and sport knives began to be produced in 1897. The army was not buying them yet, so officers and soldiers bought them in shops, including models with the corkscrew. After the army knife began to be issued, many kept the issue knife spotless and unused for inspections, and used daily knives that were personally purchased.

"Beginning in 1934, Father went by train to Leipzig every year to examine new machine products. He saw factories working all night. He said: 'Hitler is dangerous—we'll have a war!' That year, across the street from the Victorinox factory, Father built the first air raid shelter in Switzerland. Before the war, Solingen, with 1,000 firms, was the biggest competitor for cutlery. When Hitler came, these German firms got a 15 percent export premium. The German subsidization of exports hurt our business. During the war, Victorinox made pocketknives, bayonets, and officers' daggers for the army.

"In 1940 I was 18 years old and had heard discussions at school and in my family about the Saarland, Austria, the Sudetenland and Czechoslovakia. We feared an Anschluss because we were German-speaking. Any pro-Hitler person was called a *Verräter* [traitor]. I knew one such person, a Mr. Kundig, who was from the village of Brunnen. He thought Hitler would win and that we should be friends with Germany. This angered my father, and Kundig's business was boycotted and failed.

"Also in 1940 we heard that Nazis met at an old farm house—actually a *Sennhütte* [a building where cheese is made]—on the Fronalpstock mountain. At the foot of the mountain is the village of Stoos, which today is a ski resort. My father told military authorities to post soldiers there. We feared paratroopers and hoped to shoot them.

"There was a munitions factory at Altdorf. The military had storage buildings in the mountains and magazines in Schwyz. In 1935 a German Zeppelin blimp came here. It flew just over the army magazines and was suspected to have taken pictures." That was in the heyday of the great Zeppelins—a well-known photograph shows one, swastikas on its fins, flying over New York City—which ended with the crash of the Hindenburg at Lakehurst, New Jersey, in 1936. Elsener continued:

"Like almost all other Swiss factories, Victorinox established a *Betriebswehr* [factory defense] consisting of males 15 to 19 and over 50 years of age to resist a German invasion. Those aged 20 to 50 were in military service. We had rifles, especially the model 1911 long rifle, and took part enthusiastically in the defense. We saved ammunition and had enough for target practice. Older officers trained the *Betriebswehr*. We did exercises around the Victorinox factory. Those of us under 20 years old found it very interesting—to fight German *soldiers*, and not just saboteurs!

"The border of the Réduit, the Alpine fortified area, started at the two mountains out from here, the Rigi and the Rossberg. Tank obstacles and fortifications were built.

"In 1941, instructions from Bern directed that plans be made to destroy all machines to render them unusable if the Germans invaded. The plan was to remove important pieces of the machines—parts that could be taken quickly—and to hide them in the mountains. This was part of our psychological war: Germans must know that our factories will not fall to them, and there will be few fruits of an invasion. The Swiss did not need to publicize this, for the German spies knew the Swiss would resist and would sabotage their own factories.

"A new factory was built in 1943. Iron and cement for construction were unavailable because large amounts were being used to make bunkers for the army. However, the *Waffenfabrik* [arms factory] in Bern helped Victorinox get a little cement and iron because our factory was located in the Réduit. Natural stones were used instead of cement for the foundation. Stones are not as strong, and heavy machines could not be used in this building.

"During the war, the entire Swiss population was required to grow potatoes, corn and wheat. Our company had to plant a barren piece of land with corn. Due to the poor soil, the yield was only 10 to 20 percent of a normal yield. Workers not in military service were required to help."

While the end of the war ended production of bayonets and army knives for the Swiss military, it opened up a new market: American GIs who were sent to Switzerland for rest and recreation bought as many knives and watches as they could afford. Ever since, the Swiss Army knife has been the most prominent Swiss cultural icon in the United States—a tool for every purpose.

Arthur Bill, who would become a colonel in the Swiss Air Force, went to Germany in 1935. "I knew a German in college who proposed that we bike through Holland and then Germany. At the Dutch–German border, I put the Swiss flag on my bike. I did not know that the Frontist Party (Swiss Nazis) used a similar flag, a white cross with red background, albeit triangular instead of square. We stayed at a youth hostel where other Swiss

stayed. They demanded, 'Why are you with Nazis?' I did not understand.[36] Then my German companion told me that I would have difficulties in Germany unless I gave the 'Heil' salute! I refused. In Germany, I
saw signs with the names of villages and underneath, "*Dieses Dorf ist
Judenfrei*" (This village is free of Jews). I then knew that Switzerland must
resist German influence. This was a warning to Switzerland well before
Kristallnacht [the Night of Broken Glass] in 1938."

When the war came in 1939, recalls Bill, "there were not enough
pilots. General Guisan wrote a letter to the infantry and artillery: Do you
have young officers who want to be pilots? Hundreds said yes. Only 200
were accepted for consideration, of which 24 were selected. I was one.

"In pilot school in 1940, we had 26 young lieutenants, one of whom
was pro-German. He told us that 'if the Germans come, I will work with
them.' We told him our consensus: 'If they come, you will be the first to
be shot!' His career ended." This pilot was weeded out none too soon, for
Swiss fighters shot down several Luftwaffe planes intruding on Swiss air
space during the French campaign that year. Colonel Bill recalls, "Radio
was ineffective, so Swiss planes were not used at night. At night, antiaircraft batteries shot at intruding planes." After Allied bombers began for-
ays over Swiss air space en route to Germany, the Axis protested that the
Swiss were not protecting their supposed neutrality by shooting them
down. While the Swiss pointed out that Axis flak was also remiss, it was
suspected that the Swiss intentionally did not hit Allied bombers. A joke
emerged that an Allied bomber radioed to Swiss antiaircraft gunners,
"You are shooting too low!" The Swiss responded, "We know!" Colonel
Bill points out that this "is not factual, for there was no real radio communication with planes." The oft-repeated joke was one more expression
of Swiss support for an Allied victory.

Regarding damaged American bombers seeking refuge that were intercepted by Swiss fighters, Bill recalls, "The warning order to land, based
on a diplomatic understanding, consisted of Swiss planes on each side of
the intruding aircraft waving or swiveling left and right. Two more fighters followed the intruder from behind to shoot it down if it did not obey.

"U.S. flyers were confused about the Swiss Air Force because we flew
the Messerschmitt. I had a friend who was shot down in a dogfight with a
Mustang. I myself had dogfights with Mustangs." For instance, on September 10, 1944, Bill's C-36 Grenzüberwachungs Patrouille was involved
in a 15-minute dogfight over the Jura mountains with an attacking
Mustang fighter.

"I decided when flying away that I must resolve not just to participate in defense but also in reconstruction. When I got back I read the appeal by the Zurich philosopher Walter Robert Cortis in the August issue of *Du* entitled *"Ein Dorf für die leidenden Kinder"* [A village for the suffering children]. The plan was realized in 1946 with the founding of the Pestalozzi Children's Village in Trogen. Dedicated to war orphans, it educated children against war. I became a housefather for Polish, French, and German children. I served 26 years as the director of the village."

Dr. Florian E. Davatz is an attorney living in Ticino, Switzerland's Italian-speaking canton. He recalls: "During World War II, some people in Ticino sympathized with fascism, but on the whole fascists were hated because Mussolini thought that the Italian part of Switzerland ought to be a part of Italy. I did some military service at the Magadino air base as a temporary instructor of Morse telegraphy, navigation and military geography in pilot training schools. We were warned that there were Nazi spies in Ascona, were told to keep our mouths shut and were ordered to remove our unit numbers from our epaulets. The Germans had bought quite a bit of real estate in the Ticino resort areas, and a joke circulated that the Swiss were about to close down all their military establishments in Ticino 'because the Germans did not like to have foreign troops in their country.'[37]

"A schoolmate of mine, the son of my Latin teacher (Dr. Virgilio Gilardoni, author of *Art Treasures in Ticino*), was tossed out of a university in Italy because he had punched a fascist in the face who said that the Swiss were a nation of hotel keepers. An Italian family who owned one of the best cafés in Locarno was said to be a bunch of fascists, and at the end of the war, some local people smashed all the chairs and tables of the outdoor café. The owner's wife, a stately matron, was known as '*Petacci*,' the name of Mussolini's last paramour.

"There was a time in May 1940 when we thought the Nazis would come. I was on duty during the night at Payerne near Lake Neuchâtel. Someone said he heard shots in the direction of the lake. Indeed, you could hear some 'boom boom.' When someone went across the airfield where a fighter squadron was stationed, he found out that the 'boom boom' came from crews playing soccer on the tarmac." The grim prospect of a possible attack must have given rise to countless false alarms.

"The Nazis did not come, but during those days some saboteurs were caught with weapons and explosives and who were supposed to cause damage among the squadrons stationed in various areas." Indeed, after the Swiss shot down several Luftwaffe fighters in 1940, Hermann Goering

sent nine agents—seven Germans and two Swiss—to blow up two air-
bases and a munitions plant. The Swiss apprehended the terrorists, explosives in hand.[38] Davatz continues:

"I learned how to open the valves of the subterranean gasoline tanks
and was ready to ignite the fuel if need be. I was armed with my Luger
pistol, a Walther PP pistol, a dagger stuck in my boot, and a rifle. On
another night patrol near the Payerne cemetery with one of our student
pilots, we heard a 'whoosh' in the shrubbery, but when we approached the
'threat' we found that it was just a dog on its own 'night patrol'. Great
relief for all concerned!

"There were fifth columnists, Swiss who sold the Nazis military
secrets. Several were executed. The minister who officiated at my first
wedding had to be present at the executions, and he told me it was a terrible experience. The traitors were shot by riflemen from their own units.

"During those days, we air observers called ourselves 'Saint Bernard
dogs' and our motto was '*ach was*!?' [So what?]. Our pilots, whom we
called 'chauffeurs' or 'heaters,' called us, the backseat drivers, 'maggot
sacks,' 'club feet,' or 'lead rolls.' When a pilot of a two-seater had to fly
without an observer, some pretty heavy lead rolls were fastened on the outside of the rear seat to balance the bird.

"In the early stages of the war, officers were equipped with swords
which we also had to take along when flying. Although later we were
issued daggers, I managed to hang on to my 40-inch sword. These swords
had a way of slipping back in the fuselage, and to retrieve them was quite
an operation."

The foregoing descriptions present intimate views of the wartime lives
of individual Swiss who resisted the fifth column and prepared to meet a
Nazi invasion. These accounts, based on oral interviews and unpublished
written statements or letters, add another dimension to previous accounts
of Switzerland's behavior during World War II. The voices of the wartime
generation—the great Swiss generation which successfully resisted
Nazism—should not be forgotten.

CHAPTER 5

BLITZKRIEG 1940

On April 9, 1940, Hitler, claiming "provocations," ordered his Wehrmacht to attack two strategically important neutral states—Denmark and Norway.

Denmark was key to German control of the Baltic and the choking off of shipments of supplies to Russia. Directly on the German border (like Switzerland), Denmark is flat and exposed to both naval and air bombardment. With no natural terrain defenses, no place to hide and little hope against onrushing German panzers, Denmark surrendered rather than risk substantial losses and the destruction of its cities. Unarmed neutrality was no help.

For the Germans, Norway was strategically significant as an outpost for naval and air power. Just as important was to deny the vast territory and coastline to the British. The Germans expected that the English themselves would have few qualms about violating Norway's neutrality. Norway also had metals and other raw materials critical to German war production. Though mountainous and more remote from the Reich, Norway paid a swift and terrible price for not having invested in its military. The armed forces put up a heroic but short-lived resistance primarily along its coastal seaports before capitulating, although—as Swiss reports noted with interest—guerilla sharpshooters continued to harass the invaders thereafter.[1]

The lessons of sudden and unprovoked Nazi attacks on useful neutrals were not lost on Switzerland. The Swiss had ample reason to believe they would be next. However, the Swiss had been threatened through the centuries by powerful neighbors and remembered as well the recent hard lessons of the First World War. They had made it a national priority to maintain a military force credible enough to give pause to any potential invader. With good planning and preparation, Swiss terrain, while not uniform or ideal, was suited to a vigorous defense. The independence and discipline nurtured by Swiss culture and traditions boosted the will to fight. The Swiss considered themselves different from the other neutrals. When it came to defending their homeland, they were little affected by the defeatism that had sapped the spirit of so much of the rest of Europe. Like the English, the Swiss were realistic about the dangers, but were not intimidated. They were determined to resist as the Finns had resisted the Soviet Goliath. They knew the cost would be high and were determined to pay it rather than surrender.

At the policy level—and certainly in the streets—there was precious little accommodation to or respect for the emerging German colossus. Anyone who even brought up the subject of a "realistic" policy toward Germany, publicly at least, came under immediate attack or was removed from authority in the military or the government. In the military sphere, the Swiss built fortifications, improved weapons systems and increased the pace of training.

The Germans thought the Swiss reaction ludicrous, given the country's small size, exposed border and economic dependence on the Reich. More specifically, Nazi ideologues saw this Swiss impudence as the maneuverings of Swiss and Jewish international capital. But as much as they threatened and complained, the Nazis could neither suppress Swiss reactions nor make inroads into the Swiss policy establishment. Since Switzerland was neutral, all they could do was demand that the Swiss live up to the letter of their historic political neutrality under international law. In the streets, the Swiss Nazis were never a significant force. They held rallies, issued manifestos, and spied for the Germans, but were generally ostracized, closely watched. Their efforts came to nothing.

In mid-April 1940, the *Oberkommando der Wehrmacht* (OKW) reported that "rabble-rousing propaganda against the Reich continues" in Switzerland. The Germans claimed to see a pattern in this "hostile propaganda" and believed it was being coordinated from a single source.[2] How the events of the rest of 1940 vis-à-vis Switzerland looked through the eyes of the Wehrmacht and its intelligence branches is the subject of this chapter.

Militarily and diplomatically, the Swiss maintained a carefully choreographed cover of official neutrality. Federal President Marcel Pilet-Golaz explained to German emissaries that the Swiss army would oppose a

French invasion as vigorously as it would resist invasion by German troops.[3] Such statements—and the military dispositions that in fact backed them up—were intended to convince the Germans that their southern flank was secure. The subtext was that Germany had no need to drive into Switzerland in a blocking move should it become involved in hostilities with France or England. But the Swiss knew perfectly well that the only real threat came from Germany, and despite the shadow plays, they had been preparing to resist German aggression for years. Nonetheless, defensive positions against France had to be substantial enough to convince the Germans—and their numerous spies and observers—that the Swiss flatland connection between France and Germany posed no threat.

The underlying Swiss strategic assumptions were, however, suddenly and dramatically overturned with the unexpected collapse of France. On May 10, Germany launched concerted attacks against France, Belgium, and the Netherlands. In the first days, neither the German battle plan nor the French response was clear. But anticipating a German attack, the Swiss had already entered into a secret accord with the French military. If Germany were to attack France through Switzerland, Switzerland was prepared to allow French forces to meet that German assault on Swiss soil.

In those first anxious weeks of May the Swiss were treading on eggshells so as not to trigger a German assault on the basis of Wehrmacht misapprehension or false intelligence. They knew the German army had contingency plans for just such a move. The Swiss army was immediately mobilized, but as the OKW reported, Federal President Pilet-Golaz announced that the mobilization took place "only as a precaution for the protection of our neutrality and is not directed against anyone." He repeated the Swiss mantra that "the Swiss army would repulse an attack from whichever side it comes." In a war zone, neutrality is a tricky business. A more distant neutral—the United States—was also careful not to be drawn inadvertently into the conflict. It was reported that "Roosevelt wants to keep the American appearance of neutrality intact."[4]

As news flooded in of battered French forces reeling back toward Paris, the Swiss expected invasion. Intelligence reported a buildup of Wehrmacht forces along the border from Lörrach to Lake Constance. Rumors were flying, and Switzerland braced for the expected onslaught. No one knew what the French could or would do. To the Federal Council, the French ambassador reiterated his country's policy of neutrality toward Switzerland. Meanwhile, the British legation in Bern loaded up four panel trucks with archives and the luggage of its personnel to evacuate. Family members of the French mission departed. Both the French and British consulate generals in Zurich burned files and left the city, seeking safety in western Switzerland.[5]

In Basel, directly on the German border, there was chaos. Most foreigners fled the city, including the English consul. The Bank for International Settlements closed down when its foreign customers withdrew their deposits. Rumors of German troop movements swirled around the city. Looking up, one could see and hear the war as German air sorties against French targets rolled into Swiss airspace. Swiss air force fighters were constantly in the sky with the tricky task of defending Swiss borders against all comers. But the Germans, far more numerous and aggressive, were the first priority.

In the course of these initial French-German hostilities, Swiss aircraft, mostly Me-109 fighters purchased from Germany, shot down 11 Luftwaffe aircraft. Describing one such incident, the OKW reported that on the evening of May 16 Radio Lausanne broadcast that Swiss fighter patrols and antiaircraft guns had attacked a German Heinkel III bomber. The bomber caught fire and made an emergency landing in Switzerland. Two wounded crew members were arrested and two others fled. The same OKW report also noted:

> Rumors are circulating in Switzerland about an alleged German intent to attack Switzerland. Supposedly Radio London is the source of these rumors. The Zurich correspondent of *Petit Dauphinois* alleges that 25 German divisions are concentrated at the Swiss border.[6]

OKW's intelligence agency, the Abwehr, remained surprisingly candid on conditions in occupied countries throughout the war. To the German occupiers, peoples' attitudes—including their will to either resist or collaborate—were simply military facts. For instance, a report of May 17 had this to say about occupied, previously neutral, Denmark: "Those who are 100 percent Danish make no secret of the fact that they hate Germans. They resent the German attitude and, in a concealed or sometimes open manner, threaten to take revenge later. Their hatred is fueled because of our German demand that even children salute Hitler." The Abwehr was no less blunt about Switzerland:

> The entire population is against us; there is no doubt about that.

Condemnation has become even stronger since the recent events in the north. The Swiss press has a hard time maintaining even a front of objective neutrality. Anyone who reads between the lines sees immediately that the hearts of the Swiss are on the other side.

Abwehr agents further reported: "Reich Germans [in Switzerland] are worried about the continuing [Swiss press] propaganda against Germany and the ugly mood of the people. Jews in particular are instigating inflammatory reports."[7]

How deeply German intelligence moles penetrated into high-level Swiss military and government circles remains unknown. But routine German wartime intelligence was methodical and comprehensive. On a day-to-day level, the OKW continuously summarized and passed on public records, including both Swiss and foreign newspaper reports. No item of news was too small if it pointed to something larger. An example was a Swiss telegraph agency report that the Zurich Cantonal Police had arrested several persons and charged them with spreading false rumors. German intelligence reported British newspaper accounts that the British and French foreign offices in Bern had destroyed documents that could be helpful to Germany and had moved their staffs to Geneva. The Swiss News Service provided the Germans with a handy and detailed account about the Swiss downing of the German bomber, mentioned above, in the vicinity of Dübendorf:

> During the air fight, the force of the projectiles of the fast-firing, wing-mounted canons on the Swiss fighter planes and of the anti-aircraft guns ripped apart the fuselage and the engines and tore off part of the rudder of the German bomber. Two of the crew members were seriously injured and left the plane by parachute. Since the bomber was disabled, the two crew members still in the plane also wanted to parachute out, but one of the parachutes got entangled inside the plane. Both crew members therefore stayed in the nacelle and landed the bomber in hilly terrain, where it immediately burst into flames.[8]

The Swiss, for their part, were also watching, particularly what was happening in the small states to the north, which had been bowled over by the German assault. The Netherlands capitulated just five days after the blitzkrieg was launched. German intelligence reported that the efforts of

Dutch National Socialists seemed to have paid off in reducing Dutch resistance. The Dutch were bitter and disappointed, but on the whole the population of this neutral country behaved very quietly toward the occupying German troops. Most Dutchmen felt betrayed both by England and by the Dutch government. The flight of the Royal House—especially of Prince Bernhard, an officer—was regarded as scandalous. What would happen if Switzerland were tested in that fire? What could be done to prevent such an ignominious rout and surrender?

German intelligence gave this account of attitudes and activities in Switzerland:

> We have reports that the Swiss government has ordered the arming of the civilian population and the drafting of those not fit for military service into an auxiliary. In Basel, barricades and bunkers have been set up everywhere. Requests for leave are being denied. There is fear that Germans will loot Swiss banks, and it is reported that banks have taken measures to move and safeguard assets.[9]

The Swiss had organized and armed their local defense forces, the *Ortswehr*,[10] and removed gold reserves from the cities to hidden locations. Fears of systematic looting were justified as Germany in fact soon began seizing gold and other assets from the central banks of the countries it had conquered.

War seemed imminent and German military intelligence was everywhere in Switzerland. Thousands of German nationals—"Reich Germans"—remained in the country as long-term residents, in commercial ventures, or at Swiss sanitaria and spas. Many were ready and willing to aid the Reich. On June 1, Iwan von Ilsemann, the German military attaché in Bern, reported that intelligence activities had been greatly expanded, with two intelligence officers being added in Geneva. However, he added that gathering information from both Switzerland and France was becoming more difficult and less productive because both nations had enhanced their countermeasures. He recommended additional agents for the consulates in Zurich and Basel.[11]

OKH responded that further increases in the intelligence service in Switzerland were unnecessary for the moment since it appeared that German military operations in France were coming to a successful conclusion. "We are curious to see whether the French will fight to the last man."[12] However, the opening of a second front against France through Switzerland, or a French counterblow via Switzerland, no longer seemed likely.

German intelligence did continue to report accounts in the French press that Germany was concentrating troops on the Swiss border. The Swiss were still on high alert, as trip-wire incursions continued. The Swiss command reported: "On Saturday afternoon foreign airplanes entered Swiss territory in the Jura area. A Swiss air patrol immediately pursued and engaged them, shooting down a bomber in the vicinity of Tessenberg (Canton Bern). The bomber was German."[13] The fact that the bomber was German appears almost as an afterthought.

This setback for the all-powerful Luftwaffe enraged Hitler. He looked down on the Swiss and ordered immediate retaliation, curiously in the form of a clandestine raid rather than a full-fledged military assault. A June 3 directive stated: "At the request of Field Marshal Göring, Abwehr II (Military Intelligence) has been ordered to attack Swiss fighter airplanes on Swiss airfields. . . . L.2 is in charge of executing this order."[14] The raid failed. Swiss authorities managed to apprehend the German saboteurs, who were laden with explosives and carried plans to demolish Swiss fighter bases.[15]

The chaotic retreat of the French army gave the Germans one extraordinary intelligence coup offering an extensive overview of Swiss defensive preparations. The Germans regarded the Swiss Army as outmoded and locked into a World War I mindset, though OKW closely followed its efforts to devise new combat tactics.[16] Then Wehrmacht units racing through France came upon a trainload of secret documents inadvertently abandoned by the French on a siding at La Charité near Dijon. Those documents, quickly processed by the Germans, were a Realpolitik bombshell. They detailed Swiss-French agreements for joint military resistance—in blatant violation of Swiss neutrality! Moreover, Swiss defensive plans were laid out in detail for the German high command. The Swiss, at least at first, were not aware of the break in their security.

Hitler once more flew into a rage. Now he had proof and, potentially, a powerful propaganda justification for attacking a clearly duplicitous neutral. The Swiss-French plans for joint resistance were transmitted to Berlin on June 10 by the intelligence office of the 1st Mountain Division. The transmission included:

> 1) 2 code charts. One of them (top secret!) shows that preparations are under way for armed actions on Swiss territory, Plan H, Helvetia.

2) 1 code book (secret) for lower charges. The note attached to it shows which code is valid "immediately."[17]

Soon, the contents of the seized documents were summarized in a memorandum entitled "Conclusions drawn from correspondence of French command authorities concerning relations between Switzerland and France, from October 1939 to February 1940." [18] The memorandum, which would be archived with Wehrmacht plans to invade Switzerland, stated as follows:

1.) It will take the 5 large [Swiss] units in the sector between Lake Constance and Basel about 1 to 2 days to fully occupy their defense positions. The deployment of large units on the west and south front (1st, 2nd and 9th Infantry Divisions) will take about 5 days.

This means that the Swiss will deploy their major units to defense positions close to the (German) border. The Germans could plan a stunning assault, which could bypass these units or destroy them before they were fully in place. The memorandum continued:

2.) The connection to the French defense position runs on Swiss territory from Hegenheim (5 kilometers west of Basel) via Allschwil to Oberwill. This line will be lightly defended by frontier guard units.
3.) The city of Basel is to be defended by its own troops.
4.) The French recommend that the Swiss strengthen the defensive line from Lützel to Les Rangiers and on to St. Ursanne, as a continuation of the French positions of the Glasenberg and the Jura, with the front facing east, and to defend this position with local units of the 3rd Front Guard Brigade.

This meant that Switzerland had done little or nothing before the end of 1939 to strengthen its border to France, concentrating its efforts primarily along its border with Germany.

5.) Urgent strengthening of defense position between Gempen and Zurich.
6.) Defense against tanks and dive-bombers is very weak. Switz-

erland requested assistance from the French army.

7.) Switzerland requested artillery support with 3 artillery regiments for its main position between Constance and Basel.

8.) Reference was made to deficiencies in Swiss anti-aircraft defenses in crucial zones.

9.) At the time of mobilization or assault, the Swiss air force was assessed to be capable only of "protecting assembling troops and maybe a few observation tasks."

10.) A defense in depth—at least the preparation for destruction [of bridges and roads]—is in place, for example in the Aare section, for the most part behind frontline positions.

These concerns showed that the Swiss were still planning to put up their primary stand at the border.

11.) The French requested urgent strengthening of strongpoints between the Ergolz Tal and Basel to prevent a separation of Swiss and French troops in case of a German attack.[19]

While the Germans were digesting this new information, Wehrmacht units, particularly Guderian's Panzers, were pushing demoralized French and Polish units toward the Swiss border.[20] On June 18 a report to the German General Staff of a meeting in Versailles noted: "12th Army [German] at Swiss border. It is necessary for this army to assemble [to prepare for a move against Switzerland] soon."[21]

To put this report in context, Swiss intelligence obtained information that on June 24, the day France capitulated, Hitler discussed Switzerland with Göring, Keitel, Ribbentrop, Hess and Goebbels. Foreign Minister Ribbentrop favored an immediate occupation of Switzerland, while General Keitel was of the opinion that German goals could be reached through the mere threat of a massive buildup, "without risking the sacrifice of some hundred thousand German soldiers."[22]

An attack plan was clearly on the table. It would be led by General Wilhelm Ritter von Leeb, whom Hitler would shortly promote to Field Marshal. General Leeb personally reconnoitered the terrain and gave the command for the "*Sonderaufgabe Schweiz*" (Special Task Switzerland) to Army Group C, which would take up assault positions along the entire western border of Switzerland. Field Marshal Walter von Brauchitsch, Commander-in-Chief of the German Army, allotted the 1st, 2nd, and

12th armies to Army Group C for the attack. Various deployments proceeded near the border in the following two weeks, including the return of two mountain divisions from northern France.[23]

Because of the unsettled situation in France, neither final deployments nor a final date were fixed. On June 28, Leeb noted in his diary that "the 12th Army now includes additional mobile units and two mountain divisions. Should all my resources be aimed at Switzerland?" In the ensuing days, he continued to prepare the attack. At the July 11 general staff meeting, Leeb expressed concern that some of the preparations might be visible to Swiss customs officials, and worried that the destroyed railroad bridges on the Swiss border had not been restored. In a revealing passage, he added that these two points must be rectified "if the special task for Army Group C, in whatever time frame, is still being considered." The "special task" was, of course, the invasion of Switzerland.[24]

On June 25, the effective date of the armistice with France, a detailed invasion plan was submitted by Captain Otto Wilhelm von Menges of the German General Staff to the Army High Command, the *Oberkommando des Heeres* (OKH). It was entitled "*Vortragsnotiz über Angriff gegen die Schweiz*" (Presentation Notes for Attack Against Switzerland).[25] It laid out a surprise attack on Switzerland by Wehrmacht troops from both Germany and France supported by Italian troops from the south. A coordinated knock-out punch would be delivered to fragment the Swiss army and preclude it from falling back and regrouping for further resistance in mountainous terrain. The plan also outlined a speedy occupation of the economic resources of the country, and the arms industry around Solothurn, and included assaults to prevent the destruction of railroads, roads, and bridges by Swiss defenders. Menges' plan detailed the German units to be involved and specified their objectives. The plan took note of the weakness of the Swiss forces near the French border (there were German troops near Geneva and Lyon) and that any Swiss attempts to reinforce them would only weaken Swiss positions along the German border.

The plan was thorough. It included a document entitled the "Reorganization of the Swiss Army," which described the positions and strengths of the Swiss divisions.[26] "Fortifications at the Swiss Border and in the Interior," a study with map references of fortified positions, was also prepared.[27] It was divided into sections on the north and northeast border with Germany, from Basel to Sargans; the northwest border with France, from Geneva to Basel; and the southern border, from Lake Geneva all the way back to Sargans. Also available was a study on the construction of the Swiss fortifications.[28] Nothing was left to chance.

The machinery to isolate Switzerland and prepare for the offensive swung into place. On July 3, 1940, the 12th Army was ordered to move troops to seal the Swiss border from the Geneva-Bellegarde road to Delle. The 18th and 25th Corps would support Guderian's motorized units on that front. "The task of the border protection is to stop all border traffic to and from Switzerland."[29] On July 5, after the demarcation line was fixed, the 1st Mountain Division was transferred to the heights of the Swiss Jura to enforce the closing of the French border.[30] The Swiss protested against German border violations.[31] The OKH General Staff considered the border to be sealed.[32]

The Germans were now in a position to close the ring. Captain von Menges was informed on July 13 about the revelations of the La Charité documents establishing that Switzerland had been coordinating its defense with the French. That communication further noted: "There will be a meeting at the quarters of the Führer where the issue in question will be discussed."[33]

As the pursuing Germans moved to close the French-Swiss border, the Swiss were giving sanctuary to large numbers of French and Polish soldiers fleeing the Wehrmacht panzers. These military refugees were detained, disarmed and interned. The Germans, although they sought to seal the border, in fact welcomed what they realized was a distraction of Swiss troops. OKH intelligence noted on July 20 that the entire Swiss 3rd Division and part of the 7th Division were involved in securing French soldiers.[34]

The final collapse of French resistance—the endless lines of broken and bleeding soldiers—was an enormous blow to Swiss morale. The situation seemed hopeless. Militarily, the Swiss flank was now openly hostile, occupied by aggressive, battle-hardened and triumphant Germans. If ever there were a time for loss of heart, it was during July of 1940 when the Nazis seemed undisputed masters of the whole of Europe. England might not be able to hold, and the Americans showed no desire to enter the war.

It was General Henri Guisan, the head of the army, who saw the danger most clearly. When, for the first time, voices started to be raised about an accommodation with Germany, he took matters into his own hands. Bypassing the civilian government, he went directly to the army and, through the army, directly to the Swiss people. On July 25, the general electrified the nation with a clarion call for absolute, uncompromising resistance. He made a dramatic speech with religious overtones to his officers standing assembled at the Rütli meadow, the almost sacred place where the Swiss Confederation had been formed in 1291.[35] His speech set the mood and steeled the will for the rest of the war years by appealing to the deepest springs of Swiss patriotism. He cut off potential factional splits and perhaps even the possibility of a move toward accommodation within the army itself. The German envoy in Bern reported the event in an OKW intelligence report:

> General Guisan's call to arms, delivered at the Rütli before his assembled troop commanders, contains surprising declarations. He said Swiss neutrality had been respected by Switzerland's neighbors until today and would be defended to the death. "As long as millions of men are under arms in Europe and as long as important groups could attack us at any time, the army must and will resist." The order warned against the dangers of defeatism and reminded those in the audience to believe in their own strength with which Switzerland, with an iron will, would successfully offer resistance. "On August 1 the new positions that I assign to you are where your weapons and your courage will serve your country best under these new circumstances." There was no obvious reason for this startling manifestation. The Envoy suggests that the Axis powers register a complaint with the Swiss government.[36]

On July 31 the German High Command again discussed closing off the Nazi-occupied border between France and Switzerland. The Swiss border from Basel to the intersection of the demarcation line southwest of Geneva was considered locked up. From this point on, the Army Command and customs personnel enforced a virtually complete prohibition on border traffic and trade, at least along this line.[37] Switzerland was almost completely surrounded.

OKH intelligence continued its reports on Swiss attitudes and defensive preparations. At the end of July 1940, it estimated Swiss troop strength at 220,000 mobilized soldiers. Troops who were released from active duty but remained unemployed were now summoned back into service to construct fortifications. The Germans alleged that, because of the stunning defeat of the British Expeditionary Force culminating in the near-catastrophe at Dunkirk, the attitude in the Swiss army had become increasingly hostile to England, but had not as a result become friendly to

Germany.[38] Reports show the Swiss continuing to construct and expand fortifications at the northwest border, i.e., across from French territory now occupied by the German Army.[39]

In its August 1 report, the OKW gave faint hope for a decisive change of attitude in Switzerland. "Where there is border traffic into Germany, the mood of the Swiss border population is slowly changing in our favor, but not on any large scale." The report continued:

> As for the rest, views in Switzerland remain divided over the term "renewal" (*Erneuerung*). According to our sources, the Swiss are not yet seriously considering giving up their traditional [pro-Allied] allegiances. They do not think that the war has been decided yet. The influential core of the well educated and the industrialists expect England will ultimately come through, even if it takes years. That core still contains many working for remaining French and British interests in the Swiss war industry. They supervise the export to their countries. Some say these agents have nothing to do, but they are very interested in keeping the faith in England and its forces alive in Switzerland. In addition to spreading propaganda for England, these agents are also doing their best to transfer news of all kind back to the Allies. Jewish businessmen in Switzerland have perhaps more foresight. They believe the time has come to try at least to salvage their investments by selling out now.[40]

As the summer of 1940 wore on, the Swiss realized their fate would most likely be decided by events elsewhere in Europe and by Hitler's grand strategies. However, the reality of sudden invasion was never far from their minds. One group of Swiss officers, those most radically committed to total resistance, formed a secret association. In event of an invasion, they planned to arrest or kill any Swiss officers who might attempt a pro-German coup or sabotage the resistance. In early August, Commander-in-Chief Guisan learned of this group. He gave its members a slap on the wrist for insubordination but was in tacit sympathy with their views.[41] Guisan knew the temptation to surrender to end the inevitably heavy losses and destruction of the country—or even to link Switzerland with a triumphant Reich—would be a deadly fault line. OKW intelligence describes the following factually inaccurate but telling rumor about this episode:

We have been told that at the beginning of August there was a revolt of a battalion of Swiss soldiers in Zurich. Apparently it was directed against officers, and the soldiers demanded that the officers be shot [for pro-German sympathies]. There is noticeable hatred against the authorities and superiors [who counsel "realism" toward Germany]. Apparently commanders are very pessimistic [about the Swiss Army's chances], and government circles are observing this development nervously. They are said to believe that nihilism and defeatism will spread across Europe.[42]

With the ending of the war in France, the immediate threat of further hostilities seemed to diminish. By August 3rd, a partial demobilization of the Swiss army was ordered. Keeping men at the front was expensive and disrupted domestic farm and factory production. Older men were dismissed first, and the army was brought down to an active duty strength of 200,000. The Germans noted: "Switzerland has interned Polish and French troops, who possibly will fight on the Swiss side against us, reinforcing the Swiss line. But if the interned troops do not fight, then guarding them takes men away from Swiss combat units." One and a half Swiss divisions were involved in the task of guarding internees. The Germans were also fully aware that the Swiss-French border south of Lake Geneva was still in the hands of the Vichy regime, and must be closed as soon as possible, to block French volunteer forces from moving back into France to harass German troops.[43]

The Germans continued to play chess with troop movements designed to keep the Swiss off-balance. Every time the Germans could get the Swiss to move units to counter a German feint, they gave away strengths and positions. The Germans kept up this exhausting pressure week after week. An agent from the German Counterintelligence Office in Salzburg gained access to a Swiss lieutenant colonel's report:

The assembling of troops in the German border area is camouflaged. Trains of soldiers at the border are supposed to be troops on leave, but are in fact troop transports. We have reports that a German army is moving toward the Swiss border, mainly through Burgundy. Switzerland is keeping a very close eye on these troop movements, especially since the extent of these movements is much larger than at any time before.[44]

In early August, fresh, more detailed, plans to attack Switzerland were prepared again by the same Captain von Menges who did the planning in July. He made a first draft dated August 8 and a final version dated August 12. The plans were divided into two parts: "*Der Deutsche Angriff Gegen die Schweiz*" (the German attack against Switzerland) and "*Der Italienische Angriff*" (the Italian attack).[45] The plans included detailed maps showing attacks by infantry, border, motorized and panzer divisions.[46] The maps include: Swiss troop positions and fortifications, some with question marks;[47] the Swiss defensive line along the French border, from Geneva to Basel;[48] available German forces and the German attack plan from Geneva to Lake Constance;[49] and the Italian attack plan, including what would become the German-Italian demarcation line splitting up Switzerland.[50] This last map of an irredentist redrawing of national boundaries is reminiscent of the carving up of Poland by Hitler and Stalin.

The von Menges blitzkrieg aimed to isolate major Swiss units, preventing them from reinforcing one another or escaping to a fortified stronghold in the Alps. Once more, his plan detailed lightning moves to seize crucial industrial centers and arms production facilities around Solothurn and Zurich (Orlikon weapons facilities) and to prevent the Swiss from blowing up or otherwise destroying the transportation system. Menges described the Swiss army as having a strength of 220,000 soldiers divided into six infantry divisions, three mountain divisions, three mountain brigades, one border brigade and a border battalion. He knew the Swiss had a weak air force, virtually no anti-tank defense and no panzer troops. Internal politics and civilian unemployment problems were driving an ongoing demobilization and rotation. However, remobilization could take place quickly—in just five hours for the border troops. Menges gave a shorthand assessment of the Swiss army as follows:

> Armed forces are functionally organized and capable of quick mobilization. The level of training will have been raised by the long time they have been mobilized. Leaders only theoretically schooled. Inflexible leadership. Shortcomings in weaponry (artillery, tanks, anti-tank defenses, air force, antiaircraft guns). The individual soldier is a tough fighter and a good sharpshooter. The mountain troops are said to be better than those of their southern neighbor. The fighting value of the western Swiss (French type) is limited, while those living south of Constance will

be bitter enemies. Summary: an army suitable only for defensive purposes and completely inferior to its German counterpart.

The OKH General Staff regular report for August 16 noted that interned French and Polish troops had been moved to eastern Switzerland and parts of several divisions were involved in guarding them. The report notes that the Swiss Federal Council had prohibited the Communist party.[51] That was significant to the Nazi planners. Germany was, for the moment, still allied with the Soviet Union, and the Germans were well aware of the role the Communists had played in weakening the French army's will to fight, contributing to its defeat by the Wehrmacht. The Communists would not play a similar role in the Swiss army.

As conditions stabilized in France, a blitzkrieg against Switzerland came more and more into planning focus. On August 26, General Franz Halder of the OKH High Command ordered preparation of a revised invasion plan to be executed by Army Group C. He knew that "Switzerland is determined to resist any invasion by exerting all her strength." There had clearly been discussion between Hitler and Mussolini. Halder wrote: "Italy demands the Swiss territory south of the Bernese and Glarus Alps as being in its sphere of interest. Italy is ready to invade this territory if German forces march into northern Switzerland at the same time." Each army would operate independently, although the usual assumption applied that Italy may request German help, in this case by the advance of shock troops from the Rhone valley to the Gotthard to support Italy's invasion of southern Switzerland.[52]

Blitzkrieg rules would apply. "The operation must be built on *surprise* and *speed*. We must avoid attracting attention by massing troops at the northern and eastern borders of Switzerland." The assault must "shatter the forces of the Confederation and occupy as fast as possible the capital Bern with its surrounding industrial area, the armament centers near Solothurn and Lucerne, the industrial area around Zurich, and then the remaining territory in the German sphere of interest." Most important of all, "the operations must be conducted in such a way that the armed forces of Switzerland are unable to withdraw to the high Alps." General Halder clearly recognized that, otherwise, Swiss resistance could continue indefinitely.

Reports discussed an ever-increasing Swiss food shortage, and brought up the possibility that Switzerland was considering expelling French internees into unoccupied France.[53] Six Swiss infantry regiments were required to guard them, and the drain, combined with the granting of leave to over 30 percent of Swiss soldiers, had sunk Swiss troop strength to 120,000. Intelligence detailed the whereabouts of the border brigades, mountain brigades, and various other units. "In the border areas in many cases the road signs and the signs with town names have been removed."[54] Maps were prepared showing the positions of Swiss troops.[55] Specially marked were "divisions whose strength was about to be reduced by leaves."

The intelligence was highly detailed as to troop positions, types, and armaments. It pinpointed mined bridges, camouflaged bunkers and machine-gun nests.[56] Rumors were flying about the Réduit or central redoubt, the Alpine region in which Swiss Commander-in-Chief Henri Guisan decided to concentrate his forces to meet a German attack. The actual boundaries of the Réduit extended to the fortified areas of Sargans in the east, St. Maurice in the west, and the Gotthard in the south. In the north, there were a series of fortified areas roughly beginning with the mountains near the Lake of Lucerne. However, German intelligence was greatly mistaken about the Réduit's boundaries, describing them as follows:

> According to some reports, the earlier planned *"central redoubt"* is supposed to be strengthened for defense. Its borders are generally as follows: course of the Limmat and Aare rivers to the mountain chains of Weissenstein, Chasseral, and Chaumont to Lake Neuchâtel, then between Lake Neuchâtel and Thun and maybe along the Aare River, then along the chain of Lakes of Thun, Brienz, Sarnen, Lucerne, Zug, and Zurich.[57]

The above mistakenly described what was known as the Army Position along the Limmat and Aare rivers which was abandoned to a large extent after the fall of France, and also incorrectly included areas near the lakes of Neuchâtel and Zurich, when in fact those areas were outside the Réduit. Swiss shock troops were positioned in those locations, but the Réduit was actually centered in the more rugged, inaccessible Alps. A German invasion based on the foregoing faulty intelligence would not have confronted the main body of the Swiss forces.

Attitudes of the Swiss population remained a persistent theme of German intelligence. The OKW report of September 13 noted that "the Swiss considered the German air offensive against England a failure" and that "a British victory was thought to be best for Europe and Switzerland in particular." It added: "It was also said that public opinion was against Germany with regard to the resistance movements in the French colonies. The Swiss saw these movements as signs of new resistance against Germany, a weakening of the Axis and an increase of England's chances to win the war."[58]

German military attaché Iwan von Ilsemann echoed these conclusions in his report from Bern to the OKH on September 23:

> The General may be interested in my impressions about the political developments here in the past three weeks. . . . The fact that the Germans have not yet tried to land in England has strengthened the hope that England will after all be invincible. In addition, reports from England published in the papers here, which emphasized the strong will to hold out despite considerable damage suffered at the hands of the German Luftwaffe, have apparently had their effect on the Swiss population. Accordingly, the opposition to Germany has increased again, after decreasing considerably following the collapse of France.[59]

Every major city in Switzerland had pockets of resident Germans, many long-term inhabitants and some openly pro-Nazi. Swiss who spoke the Swiss-German dialect were most attuned to the Nazi threat. The German consul in Lugano wrote that, although Italian-speaking Swiss in Ticino had previously appeared neutral to Germans there, "Germans known to be National Socialists are boycotted or even harassed" now that German-speaking Swiss troops have appeared in the area. As another example, the report cited "the harsh reaction after the reception by the Federal Council of a representative of the Swiss National Socialists." The report mentioned recent "important visitors—Admirals C[anaris] and P[?]." Canaris was chief of the *Abwehr* (German Military Intelligence).

The OKW information brief for September 24 noted: "The police have published new regulations directed against National Socialists: All Nazi cells are to be eradicated from Switzerland, and Switzerland is to have no relationship with Germany except for commercial connections." Strangely, the German reports combined sharp factual observation with bizarre, theory-driven analysis. Reports—perhaps with an eye to their potential readers—attributed Swiss hopes for an English victory to the influence of the Freemasons.[60]

By the fall of 1940, the secret documents captured from the French outlining the defense arrangements between the Swiss and French armies gradually became known. The reactions were duly summarized in German intelligence reports:

> The General may be interested in learning that it has apparently become known here that certain documents about French-Swiss general staff meetings in France were found. At least Lieutenant General Wille, invited to our house a few days ago with the Envoy and Professor Sauerbruch, mentioned to the Envoy that he had received information from several people, but not officially, according to which we had seized documents in France. He said that these documents showed that the Swiss general staff had extensive contacts with the French general staff, constituting a potential violation of Swiss neutrality against the Germans. Wille added that such agreements could only have been made without the knowledge of the Federal Council.[61]

Since these captured documents could easily be used by the Nazis as an excuse for attacking Switzerland, Wille's motive appeared to be in part to exonerate the Federal Council by implying that the Swiss general staff acted alone in planning mutual defense with France.

Switzerland was a plum, and German staff officers seemed almost to compete with one another to come up with the winning invasion plan. In fact, however, Hitler typically instructed different operations branches to plan different tasks without informing the branches of competing assignments. At least two plans were prepared in this period quite independently of each other. The first would have utilized Army Group C, while the second utilized the German First Army.

The first plan was *Operationsentwurf Schweiz—Tannenbaum* (Draft Operations Plan Switzerland—Christmas Tree). It was submitted for consideration by General Wilhelm Ritter von Leeb of Army Group C on October 4 in response to the August 26 directive from General Halder of the General Staff's Operations Section.[62]

The objectives of Operation Tannenbaum are clear in the plan's Map 1, reproduced in this book (see photo section).[63] Another map shows the positions in France and Germany of motorized and panzer forces and their routes from these positions to get to the Swiss border.[64]

The essence of the attack was succinctly worded: "Concentrated surprise penetration from Lake Geneva to Lake Constance toward the center of the country with strong and fast outer wings. . . . We must force the quick subjugation of Switzerland by using extremely superior forces." The offensive would sweep over all the entire borders with Germany and France. However, the plan began by warning of the defensible terrain even in the non-Alpine areas:

> The shortest way into the politically and militarily vital area of the country (region encompassing Bern, Lucerne, Zurich, Solothurn) leads from the Waldshut area in the north to [the east of] Lake Neuchâtel. What speaks *against* putting the emphasis on this front are (1) the Jura, which offers difficult access and can be defended with weak forces, (2) the existence of the Aare stronghold position between Lake Neuchâtel and Aarau behind it, (3) the difficulties of concentrating and striking through the Black Forest between Basel and Waldshut, and finally (4) the potential of driving the enemy toward the south and the high Alps.

Of course, the "shortest way" as the crow flies was directly from Germany. It was not the easiest way for Wehrmacht troops because it led through the treacherous Jura mountains and across the steep-banked Aare River. The takeoff area on the German side was hilly as well. The approaches from newly occupied France in the west, however, were a different story. From the west, there would be swift breakthrough attacks by panzers, motorized and mountain divisions, and infantry on all roads between Geneva and Basel. The timetable depended on "whether the surprise element succeeds and on the fights in mountainous terrain that we must expect."

Coordinated assaults through the upper Rhone and Rhine valleys would sow panic, hitting the Swiss on their exposed flanks as they attempted to withdraw back from the northern plain toward the high Alps. A simultaneous Italian assault was proposed. "To tie up enemy forces, an Italian attack on all mountain passes to the upper Rhone and Rhine valleys will be desirable. Most important, however, strong Italian forces must advance over the St. Bernhard and Simplon passes to support our own advances through the upper Rhone Valley."

Stiff resistance was expected. "Individual task forces will get involved in many battles. Our horse-drawn medium artillery will be necessary but in many cases will find it hard to get through the difficult terrain." In preparation for the attack, the entire Swiss border must be sealed to prevent communications and cross-border movements. Disinformation and subterfuge were to be used, so as to "deceive the Swiss with friendly reports about Switzerland in the German press and with economic concessions." To minimize Swiss alarm over buildups of Wehrmacht troops close to the border, "aggravate relations with France, either in connection with the noncompliance with armistice conditions or for other appropriate reasons, as a way of explaining the assembly of motorized units."

After review, Operations Division IIa directed a revision of the plan on October 9. The General Staff added the following comments:

1.) The allocation of forces is very high and probably exceeds the required forces considerably.

The 21 German divisions planned are opposed by the following on the Swiss side:

         9 infantry divisions

         3 mountain brigades

         1 combined light division.

2.) Despite division of the attack into two prongs, the surprise element is at risk

    a) because of the large allocation of troops

    b) in particular because of Group E, the assembly of which in Vorarlberg cannot be hidden.

3.) The deployment of two army headquarters is a consequence of the high allocation of forces. It is not desirable because the operation can be led by one army headquarters. . . .

4.) The Operational Division is of the opinion that

    a) Group E (Vorarlberg) should be eliminated. An effective feint can be accomplished with far fewer troops.

    b) The second prong is to be eliminated entirely.

    c) In Group D (Waldshut–Lake Constance) the following will suffice:

         1 panzer division

         1 motorized infantry division

         1 infantry division.[65]

From the above, the initial revisions of this plan reduced the number of divisions deployed from 21 to 11. There were many uncertainties, and German resources were not infinite. No further documents on Operation

Tannenbaum could be found. Hitler had made the fateful decision to attack Russia in the spring. This may have been part of the reason the whole Tannenbaum operation was cancelled abruptly on November 11, 1940, by a telephone call by Captain Worgtzky of the General Staff: "The Operations Division is reporting to the Army Group that plan 'Tannen-baum' is no longer relevant because it has been overtaken by events." This was relayed to the head of the General Staff.[66] The detailed planning, however, provides clear evidence that an invasion of Switzerland came within a hair's breadth of execution. Had the order been given, the course of the war in 1941 and after might have been significantly different.

Also, combat planning inevitably contains an element of chance, in part because both sides cloak their preparations in secrecy, in part because of the unpredictable impact of events. In any case, a second invasion plan, independent of Tannenbaum, was presented on the same date as the orig-inal Tannenbaum, October 4. General Staff Major Bobo Zimmermann submitted a detailed battle plan to *Armeeoberkommando 1* (OAK 1, the High Command of the First Army) entitled "*Studie über einen Aufmarsch gegen die Schweiz aus dem Raume der 1. Armee*" (Study over a Deployment Against Switzerland from the Zone of the First Army).[67]

The opening line of the Zimmerman plan stated the obvious: "The defeat of France has fundamentally changed the military-political situa-tion of Switzerland." Swiss defenses anticipated an attack from the north and northeast—i.e., Germany and Austria—and therefore were concen-trated on the general front of Basel–Bodensee–Sargans where they were buttressed with strong permanent fortifications. The border with France, the Geneva–Jura–Basel Line, was poorly fortified since the Swiss felt no threat from France. As a result of the strategic change, the whole north-ern front of Swiss defenses was now exposed and vulnerable from the west and the rear.

Zimmerman knew the Swiss realized their predicament and were busy attempting to fortify the western and northwestern fronts. He also referred to a map purporting to show the Central Redoubt, the very defensible Alpine terrain, but noted that "details are still missing." The Germans of course were well aware that an Alpine redoubt would likely be the main focus of any last stand by Swiss forces. The fact that they had not obtained the specifics is a compliment to Swiss military secrecy. They did see that defenses in the Jura mountains were being reinforced, and also knew the Swiss were prepared to destroy bridges, tunnels, and highway choke points.

In Zimmerman's plan, the First Army would be deployed against Switzerland's northwest border. It would break through to cut off any retreat to the Alpine Redoubt. The basic thrust of the operation would be to split the mass of the Swiss army in such manner as to block the important valleys which lead from the northwest and north up into the Alps. It warned emphatically: "No operation into the Alps!" German troops would only be tied down and wasted there—as they would soon be in the Balkans, owing to the Yugoslav and Greek resistance continuing even after a formal surrender.

The operation would be difficult and require extensive preparation, utmost secrecy and assaults with maximum speed. It would be launched from two starting points, the southern one being the main thrust. The lightning strike must overcome the difficulties of the Jura barriers and terrain, seize the land bridge between the lakes of Geneva and Neuenburg, and push through the narrow passage between the Neuenburg and Biel lakes.

The Zimmerman plan included and examined a French military-geographical description of Switzerland, apparently one of the many documents that fell into German hands at La Charité.[68] The plan notes that over the 200-kilometer French-Swiss border from Geneva to Basel there were only 6 railroads and 14 major roads, which if destroyed could not be quickly rebuilt. The plan, relying on Michelin maps and observations from reconnaissance, went into great detail about the hazards of breaking through the Jura, which was also entirely dependent on the season—the Jura's summer is short. Attack from May through October was best. Winter would be possible but dangerously slow, although the report notes that snowplows were available in France. Zimmerman seemed to have no inkling of Hitler's designs on Russia.

The whole operation was based on current Wehrmacht troop dispositions and transportation resources, showing that it was very much an "active" plan, not just a theoretical study. The buildup would be carefully camouflaged, with troops being moved to their attack lines via several circuitous routes over two and a half days.

Current Swiss force levels were estimated at 125,000 on active duty, but the plan noted: "There is no doubt that the entire Swiss Army could be under arms in these days of tension. We should therefore expect to face the entire Swiss Army."[69] After analyzing specific Swiss units which the Wehrmacht would encounter, Zimmermann wrote:

The Swiss Army has fighting power and spirit, especially in that they are defending their own country. The army makes good use of terrain and is very skilled in guerrilla warfare. Swiss soldiers have considerable technical skills. We would therefore run into tough resistance, though we would probably not have to worry about major coordinated counterattacks.

The key to success was lightning-fast operations. The breakthrough in the Jura must take place before the roads could be destroyed, and panzers must push through between the lakes of Geneva and Neuenburg. The Luftwaffe was obviously superior to the Swiss Air Force and could be, if necessary, supplemented with units of the Italian Air Force. With control of the air, paratroopers could be dropped behind Swiss lines to seize bridges, tunnels, and other critical points.

In a cover letter Zimmermann listed several attachments—maps of roads over Switzerland's northwest border, Swiss fortifications, details of the areas around Lake of Geneva and the Rhone valley, and specified Michelin maps.[70] Of special interest was a study by General Staff Captain Reinhardt focusing on sabotage of the Swiss railway system to prevent its use for troop movements. Since many Swiss trains were no longer powered by steam but by electricity, destruction of the power stations and grid components could prevent the Swiss from using their railroads to meet a German attack or to pull back into the Swiss Alps. The study details the specific rail lines to be disrupted consistent with the Wehrmacht attack points.[71]

By the second week of October, Zimmerman's plans seemed to have support at high levels. The Swiss clearly were worried. An October 11 intelligence report indicated: "Because of a successful sabotage attack on the railroad tracks between Annecy and La Roche, the Swiss government has now prohibited the export of Orlikon weapons as a concession to the Germans in hopes of avoiding invasion. They had been shipped to England via Lisbon."[72]

Actually, Hitler had ordered the destruction of the La Roche-Annecy rail line in unoccupied France—a critical rail connection between Switzerland and Upper Savoy—in June, just after France capitulated, but the order could not be carried out then.[73] The Swiss firm Orlikon-Bührle had exported thousands of 20-mm antiaircraft cannon to France and England as long as it could. After France fell, the firm managed to smuggle the blueprints to England, which would produce 35,000 cannon; the United

States would make 150,000 of them for her navy. Once Switzerland was encircled, the government entered into agreements to export the cannon to Germany[74]— as with all such exports, in exchange for goods necessary to survive and defend against Germany.

Despite the danger, German agents continued to report that the Swiss favored the Allies. "Propaganda against the Reich" was the subject of an OKW analysis which explained Swiss "neutrality" as follows:

> We have reports that a brigade commander of the Swiss Army made the following statement to his officers: "It is our task to remain steadfast and firm as a rock. We must hope that England will do the same. Then Nazi Germany will certainly be defeated. You must meet any defeatism with vigor. You must make it clear to our officers and troops that the Swiss Army can absolutely hold its ground against the German Army. Only dive-bombers and tanks of the German Army are highly developed, and both are instruments of combat which are useless in the high Alps. Switzerland today is so well armed that we are absolutely capable of victoriously opposing the Nazis on our territory. The only tool that we are missing is airplanes. But I am certain that in case of need we would get those immediately from the Royal Air Force."

The common opinion was that Switzerland would fiercely resist any attack by German troops, even to the point of destroying its own infrastructure. In the event of an invasion, bridges, roads and tunnels in the Alps would be blown up to prevent the Axis from using them.[75] Even the Germans realized they could do little to stop such events.

The possibility of getting air support from the RAF was about as likely as the Poles getting RAF fighters to save Warsaw in 1939. Yet, the determination expressed above was more than just bracing talk for the troops. The Germans knew they would have to suffer heavy losses for an uncertain prize. An OKW report noted that "the general attitude of the population remains the same. The population's hopes are winter and America. People are purposely trying to downplay German successes and war actions." The Swiss went so far as to eliminate the screaming sounds of Luftwaffe dive-bombers in German newsreels "so as to avoid undermining the population's will of resistance."[76]

The United States was far away. While the Swiss knew the Germans would not likely risk an attack during the treacherous winter months, in those dark days in the late fall of 1940 there was hardly a glimmer of hope for American intervention in Europe.

Elsewhere forces of the Reich were overwhelmingly successful. As Hitler was digesting his triumphs, the OKW griped on November 15 that "lately the mood in Zurich is more anti-German." The Swiss believed that the Italians would be a moderating influence on German demands. In fact an article in an Italian newspaper had "suggested that Switzerland should remain an independent country. People are also of the opinion that Mussolini would not allow Germany to attack Switzerland."[77] However, Mussolini had already discussed the carving up of Switzerland with Hitler,[78] not to mention that the bombastic but ineffectual Duce was in no position to dispute German strategy.

The Axis was in a position to put Switzerland in an economic stranglehold. Switzerland had no coal or fuel resources. Germany was rich in coal—in fact one of the few materials of war which it possessed internally and used as leverage. The Reich declined Switzerland's proposal to pay for coal deliveries in gold and demanded a barter exchange. Germany was able to set the terms, since Switzerland had no alternative. Despite the cold, hotels were limited to using small electric heaters. Some Swiss either left the country or moved south. According to a November 1940 OKW report:

> Many rich Jews are said to be departing Switzerland or trying to sell their real estate at any price. The result is that real estate prices have been sinking drastically. There are apparently Swiss citizens who are moving their companies and their residence to southern Switzerland. They prefer to be annexed by Italy instead of Germany in case Switzerland is divided up.[79]

OKW intelligence further reported that "in order to be prepared for all eventualities, the Swiss government has ordered all families to obtain supplies that will allow them to completely support themselves for two months." Such officially sanctioned hoarding ensured that supplies would be adequate and would discourage panic buying. There was a rumor, spread by a business, that soap would run out, but there was no run on soap because everyone already had sufficient supplies. "Some people apparently have sufficient supplies of everything for three years." The German report continued:

The government stores large amounts of supplies. Apparently wheat and gasoline are stored by putting huge tanks filled with wheat or gasoline into Swiss lakes (Lake Lucerne) to protect them from bombs. It is said that these tanks are lifted from time to time and their contents checked. The import of goods from abroad, in particular from overseas, has apparently been halted almost completely. All ships loaded with goods for Switzerland are said to be stopped now in Gibraltar.[80]

These preparations by the population were factors the Germans needed to consider in assessing the extent to which the Swiss could withstand an invasion. Under the heading "Swiss Views about the Possibility of a German Attack," an agent reported on December 2 that the Swiss people knew the Germans did not want to risk the crucial rail links to Italy:

> There are roadblocks, barbed wire entanglements and bunkers all along the line between Basel and Zurich. But currently there is no fear that the Germans will attack. The Swiss are saying that Germany absolutely needs the Gotthard and Simplon tunnels to provide Italy with supplies. In the case of a German attack, the Swiss hope that they would be able to either hold or destroy those two tunnels. They believe that the damage inflicted on the Axis by this act would be greater than any gain from an occupation of the country. However, the Swiss also think that Germany could cause great economic difficulties for Switzerland and that Switzerland therefore must show consideration for Germany.[81]

A small segment of the Swiss military was not immune to the siren song of Wehrmacht successes. A subordinate sent to German General Staff Major Ritter von Iylander an article published in a Swiss periodical, by Dr. Gustav Däniker, Colonel of the Swiss General Staff, entitled "Qualification of an Army." Colonel Däniker had communicated to the [German] Military Attaché in Bern: "If my essay can contribute to show that the exceptional achievements of the German Army are recognized and admired in Switzerland, then it will achieve more than it normally would, given its modest content."[82] General Guisan stripped Däniker of his position and replaced him with Herbert Constam.

Faced with its own blitz in 1940, England remained unbowed. The OKW continued to describe pervasive "English propaganda in Switzerland." English was often spoken in Geneva, where English men and women of all age groups frequented hotels, restaurants, cafes and bars. A few hardy Americans were also present. A striking red, white, and blue scarf was noted by a German agent in a Geneva bar. Great sympathy for Poland was evident throughout all of Switzerland, which hosted many Polish internees. The Polish legation in Bern and Polish consulates elsewhere—all financed by England—remained open, and an exclusively Polish technical college operated in Winterthur.[83]

In a Christmas Eve report, the OKW castigated the Swiss for their rejection of the "New European Order."[84] There would be four more years of such reports. While the year 1940, so fraught with threats of invasion, was now passing, the Axis encirclement of Switzerland would tighten even more.

CHAPTER 6

SWITZERLAND IS
A PORCUPINE

While Nazi blitzkriegs battered Europe, a popular Wehrmacht song made fun of the Swiss:

Die Schweiz die ist ein Stachelschwein,	Switzerland is a porcupine,
Die nehmen wir zum Dessert ein.	We will take her as dessert;
Dann geh'n wir in die weite Welt	Then we'll go to the wide world
Und holen uns den Roosevelt.	And get us Roosevelt.[1]

The Swiss themselves, listening to German radio, joked that only Germans would eat porcupine. However, the image of a bristling hedgehog was apt. At the Swiss border, German soldiers saw concertina wire raised like the sharp quills of a porcupine, intermixed with tank traps and machine gun bunkers, erected to slow a Wehrmacht onslaught. After France fell in 1940, leaving Switzerland surrounded by the Axis, Swiss forces were concentrated in the Alpine Redoubt, or *Réduit*, the oval outline of which resembled a porcupine.

The hedgehog also relates to the traditional Swiss battle array of massed warriors with pikes, halberds, and other long-reach pole arms. Swiss pikemen used these virtually impenetrable formations to defeat German knights and infantry in the Swabian War of 1499.[2] The victories of Swiss peasants against overwhelming odds—far larger numbers of enemy warriors in elaborate armor—were constantly recalled to inspire resistance to Hitler's armies.

Within a year of Hitler's seizure of power in Germany, a Swiss military journal made a pointed reference to a late-medieval invasion that ended with the Battle of Sempach in 1386.[3] Some 1,300 poorly armed

135

Swiss faced 6,000 overconfident Austrian knights. In the battle that followed, the Swiss hero Arnold Winkelreid singlehandedly created a hole in the Austrian lines by drawing an armful of enemy pikes into his own body. His comrades succeeded in breaking through the Austrian ranks, and the Swiss overwhelmed the heavily armed invaders. A sculpture of Winkelreid in the act of catching the spears stands in the central cupola of the Swiss Parliament building today.

Other such episodes from Swiss history were recalled and analyzed to remind the Swiss that they could turn the tables on a numerically superior enemy. One such morale booster distributed to Swiss militia soldiers by the army high command in the second quarter of 1940 was entitled "The Fighting Spirit of the Swiss Confederation."[4] It retold the stories of small but determined groups of Confederates who defeated the great armies of Europe. Significantly, the booklet also stressed the Swiss tradition of individual initiative and personal daring in battle. Everyone knew a concerted German assault would aim to cripple or destroy the formal Swiss command structure, leaving units, or even individuals, to act on their own.

The Swiss also followed closely—and gained confidence from—the resistance tiny Finland put up against invasion by the Soviet Union, which at the time had become Nazi Germany's tacit ally. During the Winter War of 1939–40, the Finnish army, only half as numerous as Switzerland's, held out for almost three and a half months against overwhelming Soviet forces. The Finns had only 100 airplanes and 60 ancient tanks but, like the Swiss, they had few equals in rifle marksmanship.[5] Russian paratroopers were shot in the air, and those that were missed were shot when they hit the ground.[6] Even after suing for peace, the Finns managed to keep most of their territory.

In those few months, Finnish sharpshooters killed or wounded astonishing numbers of Russian troops. In one battle only three Finns died as against 1,000 Russians.[7] A single Finn, Simo Häyhä, who previously had won numerous marksmanship trophies, is said to have killed over 500 Russian soldiers.[8] Overall, *one million Russians* perished in the invasion, versus just 25,000 Finns, according to Nikita Khrushchev.[9]

As with the Finns, marksmanship was a national obsession for the Swiss. The Germans were well aware of the risks posed by sharpshooters. After the war, at the Nürnberg war crimes trials, U.S. prosecutor (later Senator) Thomas J. Dodd examined the defendant Baldur von Schirach, Reich Youth Leader, about prewar military training among German youth. The following exchange occurred:

von Schirach: Switzerland gave her young men much more intensive rifle training than we did and so did many other countries.
Mr. Dodd: Yes, I know.
von Schirach: I do not deny that our young men were trained in shooting.
Mr. Dodd: I hope you're not comparing yourself to Switzerland, either.
von Schirach: No.[10]

Indeed not. While von Schirach was suggesting that pre-war Germany was not militaristic simply because it trained young men to shoot, he obviously could not compare shooting programs within the Third Reich with those of Switzerland. In radically democratic Switzerland, every male on reaching the age of 19 was enrolled in the militia army and issued a military rifle to keep at home. The national sport was not skiing but shooting, and everyone, from teenagers to the elderly, was encouraged to participate.

In Switzerland, not only was every able-bodied man enrolled in the militia army, even youngsters and old men were issued rifles. These latter were also encouraged to join *Ortswehr* units and wear an armband so that, under the terms of the Hague Convention, they would have rights as uniformed combatants if an invasion occurred. When the war broke out, as *Ortswehr* member Max Jufer remembers, older men and young boys alike shook their fists and exclaimed, "We shall hit them. We will kill seven before we are killed." If paratroopers came, Jufer was sure *Ortswehr* members would have picked them off in the air.[11]

Switzerland's landscape offered many advantages for defending forces. Even the relatively flat Plateau has sharp inclines, defiles, gorges, and other natural obstacles. Roads and bridges were mined and ready to be destroyed. The Plateau would no doubt have fallen to a Wehrmacht invasion, but at a high cost. The Alpine Réduit was a different story. Panzers and the Luftwaffe would have been ineffective among the narrow passes, steep slopes, high winds, and snow. The natural cover was a sniper's dream and would have allowed Swiss sharpshooters to resist German infantry attacks almost indefinitely.

With the outbreak of war, Swiss border troops dug in across the Rhine River from Germany and made ready to bear the initial onslaught. Most Swiss forces, however, were concentrated well behind the border along the Limmat River. This line featured numerous interconnected fortifications in addition to natural strongpoints. Blockhouses for machine guns, positions for artillery, tank traps, and underground tunnels and quarters for troops may still be seen today—many in woods, and some in residential areas. A few are now open to the public as museums.

The fortifications in northern Switzerland had been actively under construction since 1934, when the Swiss Parliament recognized the potential threat of German invasion. After Austria's Anschluss in 1938, major fortifications were also built in the mountainous vicinity of Sargans to protect Switzerland's eastern entrance at the Rhine valley. By 1940, fortifications extended both along the frontier with Germany and along what was called the "Army Position," or Limmat Line, which stretched from Sargans to the Lake of Zurich, along the Limmat River, and through the northern Jura mountains.[12]

The defenses of the Limmat Line around the city of Baden exemplify Swiss defenses before the fall of France in 1940, when a Wehrmacht attack was still expected to come from Germany. This author was shown the remaining fortifications by Dr. Walter Lüem, the leading expert on the subject today.[13] The Divisionär (Major General) of the 8th Mountain Division had prevailed on General Guisan to position the defenses on the south side of the Limmat, where steep banks rise up against a precipitous mountainside. The Germans would have had to cross the river and face murderous fire from artillery, machine guns, and rifles hidden throughout those commanding heights.

Before reaching the Limmat, the Wehrmacht would first have to cross the Rhine, where Swiss pillboxes with machine guns swept virtually every inch of ground. The road and railroad bridges across the river were mined and could have been destroyed in 30 seconds. Every soldier had permission to blow up any bridge. The 8th Division was responsible for the area between the Rhine and the top of the steep mountain range on the south bank of the Limmat.

Near the top of the slope on the Limmat's south bank, the pillboxes are linked by extensive underground tunnels protected on top by two meters of concrete. Today, though the locations are overgrown, they are still accessible to the determined hiker. The underground passages have numerous openings for machine guns. On the surface of the mountain, the steps and paths that were cut into the hill for patrols are still used by hikers. There were also forward observation posts for artillery pieces that were located eight kilometers to the rear. The Swiss had 7.5 cm guns with a range of 11 kilometers, 12 and 15 cm howitzers with 8–9 kilometer range, and 10.5 cm Bofors guns with 18–19 kilometer range.

Most of the field artillery was horse-drawn and otherwise adapted to the rough terrain. Those units included 2,500 men and 1,700 horses, which had to be stabled in the mountains. The only motorized artillery was the Bofors cannon. (A Swiss Bofors, manufactured in Thun, could fire 10 rounds per minute.) During World War II, even the highly mechanized Wehrmacht depended in part on horse-drawn artillery. In fact, such artillery played a major role in the Eastern campaigns, especially when motorized units bogged down in mud. Swiss military horses served many purposes in the mountains. Besides pulling heavy weapons, they brought in materials and supplies to defensive positions inaccessible to other kinds of transport.

Within a standard 200-man Swiss infantry company, 66 men were assigned to light artillery squads using 12-cm and 10.5-cm field cannon. The remainder were infantry, whose weapons included three Model 1911 heavy machine guns—similar to the venerable Maxim, which continued in use by all of the warring parties. The company would field roughly 130 riflemen armed with Karabiner 31 (K31 or Model 1931 carbine) service rifles. Most Swiss males were highly skilled riflemen. Further, the K31 rifle was considered superior to the standard German service rifle, the Mauser Karbiner 98k (Model 98k carbine, "k" meaning *kurz*, or short).[14]

Both were bolt-action rifles, but the Swiss rifle could be fired more rapidly because its six-shot magazine could be loaded from above the action with a stripper clip or removed and replaced with another charged magazine. The German rifle's five-round non-detachable magazine could be loaded only from above. More importantly, the Swiss rifle was better adapted to long-distance precision firing—i.e., sniping—due to its lighter trigger pull, better-contoured grip, more easily focused sights, and more accurate cartridge. The Swiss K31 continues to be widely used in 300-meter rifle matches today.

Swiss strategy for an attack in the vicinity of Baden took advantage of natural bottlenecks through which German forces would be forced to proceed. Three rivers converge there—the Aare, the Limmat, and the Ruess, each carving its way through impassable mountain terrain, leaving the roads in the narrow valleys as the only passage for an army. At the end of the bottleneck is Reuenthal, which was heavily fortified with camouflaged cannon emplacements, extensive underground tunnels and quarters, and antitank and machine-gun nests. Although there were only 600 heavy cannon in the entire country, 124 were positioned in this area.

Since Switzerland depended on its part-time militia and had a mini-mal standing, or professional, army, its few crew-served weapons were inadequately supplied and trained, at least at the beginning of the war. The 3rd Light Infantry stationed near Baden used the obsolete Model 1882 12-cm field cannon, which fired only 1–2 shots per minute. These weapons had first been replaced way back in 1903 with the German-designed Krupp 7.5-cm cannon, which fired 6 shots per minute. Luckily, scrap dealers would not buy the obsolete 1882 models, so they could be salvaged from storage and put back into service in 1939. German observers certainly must have laughed at the archaic Swiss. But finally Swiss guns were replaced in 1942–43 with a newer Krupp design. While acquisition of modern artillery lagged during the interwar years, the Swiss military did obtain a respectable supply of advanced designs by the mid-war period. Some armaments were imported, but domestic manufacture was greatly encouraged.

From positions in the rolling hills outside Baden, one can easily see 17 kilometers through the valley to the German town of Waldshut, the nat-ural geographical position from which the Wehrmacht would have launched an attack. It is the point where the heaviest crossfire could be concentrated. Regardless of which side of the Reuss River the Wehrmacht attacked, it would have been squeezed between the river and sharp bluffs to a narrow passage of only 200 meters. This would have been the ulti-mate murderous bottleneck into which would be poured massive artillery, antitank, and rifle fire.

These defensive dispositions explain why many considered Switzer-land to be an extension of France's Maginot Line, which the German command was reluctant to assault frontally. To avoid the massive French fortifications, the Germans had the choice of two indirect invasion routes into France: the northern route through Belgium and Holland, and the southern route through Switzerland. In view of the Swiss terrain and Swiss preparations, the decision was easy to make. The Wehrmacht went through neutral Belgium and Luxemburg around the northern end of the Maginot Line, bypassing Switzerland's defenses altogether.

The Limmat Line fortifications were primary defenses only until July 1940, when the strategic situation abruptly changed. At that point, the Wehrmacht could attack Switzerland from occupied France in the west. Fascist Italy had also entered the war, threatening Switzerland from its southern border. Surrounded on all sides, the Swiss command decided to pull the bulk of Swiss forces into the Alpine Réduit. It was only after D-

Day in 1944 that the Limmat Line defenses were made ready again, when the Swiss had reason to believe that counterattacking or retreating German forces might spill over into Switzerland.

Today, in the vicinity of Baden and in numerous other places in Switzerland, one can still see rows of tank traps as well as bunkers, block-houses, and positions for machine guns, antitank guns and artillery. These structures may be found in residential neighborhoods, cow pastures, dense forests and mountains. Many remain camouflaged and almost as invisible as they were during the war.

As noted, an outline of the Réduit—the Alpine positions where the Swiss forces were concentrated—resembled a porcupine. Its nose sticks out with the Sargans fortifications in the east, its underbelly lies in the south with the Gotthard fortifications, and its tail is in the west with the St. Maurice fortifications. All entrances into the Réduit area were strongly fortified with large numbers of interconnected positions for infantry, anti-tank defense, and artillery, some in subterranean battery locations and others above ground with fields of fire facing out in all directions.

The major fortifications—Sargans, Gotthard and St. Maurice—pro-tected the main valleys extending into the Alpine Réduit. Its northern entrances were defended in the gaps where the Plateau gives way to the Alps. One such strong point was the Fortress Fürigen, located on a lake near Lucerne. It is open to visitors today and, then as now, from the out-side one sees nothing but rocky vertical bluffs. The fortress is completely camouflaged and hidden from view.[15]

One entrance appears to be rock but is actually plaster on screen wire over a heavy metal door. There is a cannon just inside the door, and a sign: "Warning! Before you shoot, open the camouflage door!" One can only imagine the dismay of any Swiss artilleryman who forgot. At first the plan was to open for each firing and then close for the reload. But the plaster disintegrated with constant use; so the door was kept open and, apparent-ly, closed at the conclusion of bombardments. Such are the design prob-lems of new installations. In any case, ventilation was inadequate; gun smoke would fill the room, and each soldier had to wear a mask with a tube attached to pipes which brought in fresh air. With the noise and the smoke, it would be easy to become disoriented and, perhaps, forget the door!

The position consisted of two 7.5-cm Model 1940 cannon made by "W+F" (the *Waffenfabrik,* or arms factory in Bern), supplied with 1,000 rounds. This weapon could fire 16 rounds per minute to a distance of 12 kilometers. Charts showed preset fire coordinates to hit specific locations, and live fire was practiced against targets in the mountains. Observers stationed up the mountain would phone the cannoneers to make fire corrections.

Three heavy machine guns were hidden above the position in the rocky bluffs at different angles from ground level. If the enemy managed to get inside one cannon position, the tunnels to the other weapons were protected by a machine gun behind a heavy metal wall with a small opening to throw hand grenades. Machine gun bullets and shrapnel would have ricocheted off the tunnel walls to increase the deadly effects. Assaulting these dug-in positions would not have been an attractive proposition, even for the most battle-hardened German commandos and paratroopers.

Sleeping quarters with straw mattresses accommodated three shifts of soldiers for each 24-hour period. Infantry normally slept in quarters inside the mountain, but in times of high alert stayed outside in cold and windy foxholes. It goes without saying that male refugees and internees who also slept on straw mattresses down in the valleys had it far better than such soldiers guarding the Réduit.

Fortress Fürigen was one of many such strongpoints that protected the Réduit during World War II. Many continued in use through the Cold War, and Fürigen was not finally closed as a military outpost until 1986. Its reopening as a public museum presents an opportunity to observe a well-preserved example of a small Réduit fortification.

As previously mentioned, the Réduit was located between three major fortified areas at the valleys entering the Alps: in the east, Sargans, where the Rhine cuts a valley from the Alps near the border with Austria; in the south, the Gotthard, which faced Italy; and in the west, St. Maurice, the narrowest point of the valley where the Rhone empties into the Lake of Geneva facing France. After the Germans suddenly appeared on Switzerland's western border in 1940, this front assumed additional importance.[16]

The St. Maurice fortifications were carefully conceived for maximum effect. The Rhone valley resembles a giant "V" lying on its left side. The Lake of Geneva to the west opens the "V," and the sides are towering mountains. St. Maurice lies at the base of the mountains on the eastern side. After the town, the valley continues to widen, but the narrow passage at the town makes St. Maurice the ideal place to meet the enemy. Any invading force would be funneled into the narrow end of this "V," where death and destruction would rain from hidden enclaves in the mountains on each side. The greatest concentrations of defensive positions are in the heights above St. Maurice.

The Rhone flowing past St. Maurice divides the cantons of Valais and Vaud. Nineteenth-century fortifications lie in ruins among vineyards running up from the river's banks.[17] Today, as during the war, cattle graze among rows of tank traps called Toblerones because they are shaped like the Swiss chocolate of that name. The surrounding mountains are likened to Emmental cheese because they are so full of fortified holes and tunnels.

Colonel Alexandre Morisod, Commandant of the Fortifications Corps at St. Maurice-Lavey, guided this author on a tour of the St. Maurice stronghold, a tour which would have been a top-secret briefing until recently.[18] Ascending the mountains, one is immediately struck by breathtaking Alpine scenery and, if lucky, by the sighting of a Chamois. You can make out observation points way up on the tops of mountains which served to identify targets and direct artillery fire.

Camouflaged doors conceal entrances into the fortifications. Once inside, there is a vast underground maze of tunnels leading to gun positions, communications facilities, mess halls and sleeping quarters. Underground funiculars carried men and supplies. There are whole rooms filled with power and ventilation equipment and every other facility necessary for this town within the mountain. Stretches of hallways of hollowed-out stone are broken at intervals by enormous steel doors and other interior defenses designed to thwart enemy intrusion.

Cannon with bores ranging from 5.3 cm to 12 cm were able suddenly to appear from and immediately disappear back into the mountain positions. The most common cannon used during the war were the BK 7.5 cm and the PzT 10.5 cm with an armored turret. One specimen examined by the author had a barrel six meters in length. It received ammunition from an elevator which extended 50 meters further underground. At the bottom, shell components were assembled by a machine according to the desired load. The shells are about a meter and a half long and weigh 75 kilograms, of which 45 kilograms is the projectile. From the highest point, one can shoot all the way to Lake Geneva or to the French border.

Still present is "Big Fritz," a gigantic though slow-firing gun originally put in service during World War I. A later 1942-model cannon had a 15-cm bore, 18-kilometer range, and fired 7 or 8 rounds per minute. The 1958 15-cm model shoots 25 rounds per minute for a distance of 25 kilometers. At least until recently, troops continued to practice long-distance live fire at targets in desolate, uninhabited places high in the mountains. Accuracy is pinpoint and the reverberating boom is unmistakable.

While there were 48 antiaircraft positions in the vicinity, Luftwaffe bomber attacks would have been ineffective because defenses were hidden in bluffs and steep mountainsides rather than on flat land. The valley was too narrow for a massive panzer attack, and any tanks that ventured here would have been hit with a terrible fire from all sides. Infantry would have fared even worse. The soldiers would have been trapped in narrow passages and caught in a crossfire from above.

This description is only partial. It covers just some salient aspects of the St. Maurice fortified area, a critical component of the Alpine Réduit. It does, however, illuminate why the Swiss chose to concentrate their forces in the Réduit as the best location to resist a German attack. Engagement of the main Swiss Army with German forces at the border or on the Plateau would have been suicidal, turning the more populated areas into battlegrounds and the cities into bombing targets. It is clear that German strategists had sufficient wartime intelligence to know that an attack on the body of the Swiss forces in the Réduit would have entailed enormous casualties.

Aside from its advantage in terrain, Switzerland held another edge over the Nazis: its commitment to employ every able-bodied male citizen in the country's armed forces. In Switzerland, the practice of marksmanship was not only a constitutional right but a civic duty. No one was excluded for having the "wrong" ethnicity, religion or political preference. In Nazi Germany, by contrast, selected groups were forbidden to bear arms, and even denied citizenship itself. Possession of any kind of firearm, even by Aryan Germans, was closely controlled by the state.

By the start of World War II the Nazis' virulent ethnocentric nature was well known, particularly to German-speaking Swiss who could follow Hitler's propaganda over the radio. Even so, few imagined the depths of depravity to which the regime would sink. In 1940, after the fall of France, Germany initially had treated its hundreds of thousands of French and British POWs according to the Geneva Conventions. It was not until the following year's invasion of the Soviet Union that the horrific racial nature of Hitler's military ambitions became manifest. Whereas the victory in the West had been won by the traditional German Army, with SS units playing a minor (often ridiculed) role,[19] the war in the East quickly became marked by atrocities. Regular formations were followed into Russia by SS

Einsatzgruppen (Special Groups, or more accurately, murder squads) who committed widespread massacres of the civilian population, particularly Jews. By the fall of 1941, reports had begun to emerge from the East about this new, more sinister, phase of the war. Unfortunately, it was only to get worse, as the Germans decided to systematize their brutality.

On January 20, 1942, at a special meeting in the Berlin suburb of Wannsee, a committee of about twenty leaders from Nazi military, diplomatic, and economic circles adopted the so-called Wannsee Protocol, a document chilling in its bureaucratic detachment, which outlined steps to be taken to accomplish the "final solution of the Jewish question."[20] The conference was directed by Chief of the Police and the Security Service (*Sicherheintsdienst*, or SD), SS-Obergruppenführer Reinhard Heydrich, acting under the authority of Reichsmarschal Herman Göring, and covered disposition of the Jews in all of German-occupied Europe.

Detailed minutes were taken. "Approximately 11 million Jews will be involved . . . distributed as follows among the individual countries. . . ." The listing included "Switzerland 18,000." The Wannsee Nazis, however, did not control all of Europe. They still did not control Switzerland, nor the Jews who lived or found refuge there. These people, some of the very few who not only survived but were protected by a national government, would escape the Holocaust because Switzerland remained unoccupied. Every citizen, including every Jewish man, was issued a military rifle for defense of the country. Within other countries listed in the minutes, including former "neutrals," it was already too late for most. Jewish populations were to be methodically eliminated by deportations that would culminate in genocide.

All of the intricate machinery of Nazi brutality would have come down on Switzerland had the country surrendered to the Germans. But the country did not surrender or yield to the most outrageous of German demands. Although isolated in Axis-held Europe, Switzerland managed to avoid the horrors which everywhere else became the symbol of Nazi oppression. Neither Swiss Jews nor Jewish refugees in Switzerland would be deported by the Nazis to the death camps.

A small group of Swiss known as "Frontists" supported Nazism. In October 1940, Frontist leader Robert Tobler in a speech and a pamphlet attacked Swiss Jews as being anti-military and demanded that they be expelled from the Swiss militia army. Saly Mayer, president of the Federation of Swiss Jewish Communities (*Schweizerischer Israelitischer Gemeindebund*, or

SIG), wrote to Lieutenant Colonel Isidor Nordmann, emphasizing that Swiss Jews served in the military with enthusiasm. A copy of the letter went to General Guisan, who replied firmly:[21] *"L'armée est en dehors de toutes questions de confession!"* ("The army is outside of all questions of religion!"). In the military forces, Swiss Jews were no different than Swiss Protestants or Catholics. Guisan referred the matter to the civilian authorities.

In December 1940, Federal Councilor Rudolf Minger—the tough anti-Nazi head of the Military Department—met with Rabbi Eugen Messinger in Bern. Minger reaffirmed that "no anti-Jewish legislation would be adopted for as long as Switzerland was Switzerland." Minger added that this was not "because of a particular affinity for the Jews, but because of democratic principles that were the basis of [Swiss] democracy." Indeed, the military had no affinity for any ethnic or religious group. Minger condemned Tobler's Frontist agitation. Rabbi Messinger recorded that "Federal Councilor Minger expressed his high regard for the work of Jewish officers and soldiers." In a letter to a Jewish soldier, SIG head Saly Mayer endorsed General Guisan's statement that the army is "outside of all issues of religion." Mayer added: "We will consider this our guideline for this and future cases."[22]

In February 1941, Heinrich Rothmund, the head of the Federal Police for Foreigners, wrote to SIG as follows: "The Swiss population, from the worker to the intellectual, considers Jews foreign elements until they have become fully integrated." This could have been said about any group migrating to Switzerland. More importantly, Rothmund firmly rejected the assertion that Jews could not be assimilated:

There are numerous Jewish soldiers and officers in the army. . . . Yet, besides public schools, the army, beginning with basic training of recruits, is the best integrator there is. In addition, army service is an honor. Whoever wears the honorable uniform and does his duty has the right to be treated with due esteem.[23]

In short, by bearing arms in defense of Switzerland, any person could demonstrate loyalty and entitlement to all the rights of citizenship in the Confederation. The service of Swiss Jews in arms, Rothmund made clear, made them every bit as much a part of the Swiss polity as anyone else.

Swiss Jews themselves are most suited to tell the story. It is noteworthy that the fact of their being Jewish is hardly mentioned. They were Swiss.

The late Robert Simon Braunschweig, a prominent military figure who would become head of the Federation of Swiss Jewish Communities, was born in 1914. His family had members in both the Orthodox and Reformed branches of the Jewish faith.[24] Braunschweig remembered that, at age five, "I saw a parade of two army brigades and decided at once to become a Swiss soldier. In the same year, I saw my first automobile, a taxi. I felt that I had found my future profession." That profession would be performance testing of military vehicles and racecars.

"I entered service in 1934. I was in the 9th Division, and later the 3rd Army Corps. I served in all cantons of Switzerland, for a total of 7,000 days, primarily with motorized units, including light combat vehicles with machine guns and motorized artillery. We had only seven Czech tanks but got more by 1939." Braunschweig's rank as first lieutenant is listed in the 1938 Swiss Army's guide to military officers.[25]

"Mobilization Day—September 1, 1939—was chaotic. I assembled my unit for road transport, and we drove to Bellinzona in the Canton of Ticino. I was assigned to planning in the staff of the Frontier Brigade, part of the 9th Division.

"At the second mobilization (in May 1940), we thought the Germans would attack. Motor officers were scarce, and I was reassigned to the 4th Division in Baden, an old communications hub on the Limmat River. My motorized light gun company was to survey the north bank of the Rhine where German tanks had been spotted. We anticipated that they were poised to attack us, but in fact they were preparing to attack the French Maginot Line.

"France fell, leaving Switzerland with an open and not very defensible flank. I had a conversation with one of my commanding officers, asking him: 'What will you do with your Jewish lieutenant?' He answered: 'The two of us will die together.' We both had heard the German song with the words 'When we go back [from France] through Switzerland. . . .'

"The day France fell, a few Swiss officers and soldiers disappeared and were never seen again. They were pro-Nazi. Were they killed by Swiss?" Braunschweig did not elaborate further on this intriguing suggestion, which is not mentioned in the historical literature. He clearly thought this possible.

"I later returned to my post in the staff of the 9th Division and led my unit to the south, to the Gotthard sector where the heights provided a solid barrier against an attack. The Réduit was just about finished. We were in a mountain of very hard stone, could not be seen, and had artillery positions with very good guns. It was just below Andermatt, and was constructed partly by Polish military internees. They were marvelous—more Swiss than the Swiss. The girls did not like it when they left! By October 1940, construction was complete.

"There was a dam close by. We did not know if Germany would bomb it, which would have flooded the canton of Uri. Germany did not have many mountain troops and would have had a hard time coping with the mountain terrain. We were certain ours would do their best. Our motorized troops were effective in the Alps.

"My duties were to check the road networks for visibility from the north and from the air, prepare for winter problems, keep vehicles in repair, school drivers for access to our new mountain artillery positions, and monitor reserves for fuel, oil, and anti-freeze ethyl alcohol. There were shortages. We had more ethyl alcohol than fuel, but knew that they could be mixed together. In the fall of 1940, we experimented mixing diesel fuel with ethyl alcohol and got good results.

"These were times of great fear. I had many friends in France, the United States, and England, and I gathered intelligence through my unofficial contacts. My uncle was president of the Jewish Society, and we both had contacts in Germany. He brought back information. I knew young men who organized trade with Germany. These trade contacts saved Switzerland. We did not know what was happening at first. I knew the Nazis were against Jews, so it made me want to resist all the more. The whole army was the same. We thought the Germans were coming to Switzerland and prepared for invasion.

"I knew an officer, with whom I did not get along, who was shot for treason. Swiss counterintelligence tricked him by feeding him false information, and he told the Germans."

During the entire period of the war, Braunschweig recalls hearing only a single anti-Semitic comment. He was stationed in the Gotthard part of the Réduit, assigned to the staff of the 9th Division. "It was the summer of 1942. I sat in our office with my major. I was a lieutenant. He said: 'I have bad news for you. I just went to the Division Staff Chief and proposed to make you First Lieutenant at the end of the year. But the Chief said: 'Is this necessary? Just now?'" While the reason was not stated, Braunschweig continued:

"I was flabbergasted. 'And now?' 'Don't worry. Our own boss will be back in a few days, and this guy will be gone.' I was elated. He went on: 'May I ask a very personal question?' 'Yes, of course.' 'Why don't you Jews like your kids to marry Christians? If a decent Jewish chap wants to marry one of ours, we are very happy.' But then he roared: 'But a Catholic will never cross our door!' He ended up laughing at himself, a bit ashamed."

If the Major was slightly bigoted, it had no effect on Braunschweig's promotion. "At the end of the year I had my two stars."

The Swiss government and the military, as a matter of policy, defended its Jews. The country had long been known as a haven for political and religious dissenters, and its multilingual population came from different faiths. The military branch known as *Heer und Haus* (Army and Home) published its Defense Letter No. 26 under the title *Die Judenfrage (The Jewish Question)* on May 29, 1943. These publications were distributed to civilians as well as to military personnel.[26] Letter No. 26 stated:

> Article 4 of the Federal Constitution states that every Swiss is equal before the law. Democracy is based on the principle of tolerance, tolerance of different views, but also—and to be sure, nowhere like in Switzerland—vis-à-vis different races, different languages and different religions. Mass, race, and class hatred are fundamentally undemocratic principles. Anti-Semitism is simply intolerance, it is therefore undemocratic and tears at the roots of our democratic way of thinking.[27]

The pamphlet's conclusion was "Anti-Semitism is an invasion of foreign propaganda."[28]

Braunschweig describes his own reflections about *Die Judenfrage* as follows: "I thought it was not bad. I never had any problem. There were group discussions about such military publications, but they were really not necessary. All in all, people behaved well. They did what they had to do." In short, no significant anti-Semitism existed in the Swiss military, the members of which engaged in voluntary dialogues and did their duty to defend the homeland.

For many, this duty included guarding the border and escorting civilian and military refugees into Switzerland. "My father and grandfather knew French internees from the Franco-Prussian War in 1871. Those memories fade, but some things repeat again and again. My parents hosted Viennese refugees in World War I. In fact, there were always refugees around in my family, from Vienna, Paris, and Germany."

Braunschweig made a life-long career in military transport. He participated in mountain auto races and contributed to safer race car designs. In 1965, he was a colonel in the Transportation Service[29] and later wrote about his experiences.[30] After retiring, he became President of the Federation of Swiss Jewish Communities (*Schweizerischer Israelitischer Gemeindebund*, or SIG) for 1980–88.

The experiences of this one man were in their way typical of Swiss Jews in arms during World War II. He stood side by side with his compatriots ready to fight. He did not face significant anti-Semitism, and in fact advanced through the ranks through his abilities. He remained a stalwart defender of his country and its role in the Second World War.

Braunschweig's wife worked at one point for *Korpskommandant* (Lieutenant General) Herbert Constam, the highest-ranking Jewish officer in the Swiss Army—and perhaps at that time in any army. Her recollection that "he was loved by the soldiers and hated by his officers" expressed his democratic tendencies so atypical in a military force. Constam's leadership position was an affront to the Nazis and a symbol of Switzerland's refusal to submit to Germany's anti-Semitic policy.

Herbert Constam (1885–1973) was born in Switzerland and received his law degree in 1909. His grandfather, Joseph Kohnstamm, had immigrated to America and fought in the American Civil War. Herbert's father, Emil Joseph Constam, was born in New York in 1858,[31] but returned to Switzerland and became a professor at a Swiss technical high school. Herbert first practiced law in Zurich, then entered the army, rising through the ranks to colonel and serving as the Commander of the Walenstadt Shooting School from 1934 to 1937. He then was named Commander of the 6th Division (1938–43) and afterward Commander of Mountain Army Corps 3 (1944–50).[32] His 1944 wartime promotion made Constam one of only four corps commanders, the highest rank next to the Commander-in-Chief.

Constam remains a legend today. He is portrayed during the war years in the historical fiction series *The Frey Family* by Sigmund Widmer, a historian, journalist, and former mayor of Zurich.[33] Considered by General Guisan to be his best corps commander, Constam was notorious for insisting on the very best shooting skills. If a soldier did not shoot well, Constam would stand between two targets and order the shooting to continue. When soldiers were ill treated, he punished their officers.[34] This kind of interaction within the Swiss militia was the polar opposite of what was so often practiced within the German Wehrmacht.

The late Georges-André Chevallaz, who would become President of the Swiss Confederation, went through basic training in 1935 in Walenstadt, Constam's shooting school, and served 2,000 days in the military during the war. He recalled: "I had Jewish friends, and there was no anti-Semitism. Jews in the army were fellow soldiers."[35]

He further said, "Officers were afraid of Constam. Once one of his officers asked to be promoted to the General Staff. His company consisted of reservists who had not yet completed their training and had problems with discipline. Constam shot back sarcastically: 'I congratulate you. You just mocked me!' The officer was not promoted."[36]

Constam stood with the hardest of the hard core in a military force determined to defend Switzerland. At the command level, he had significant influence on plans for resistance. In January 1941, Constam presented a series of innovative operations, based on what he had learned from studying German campaigns, to Commander-in-Chief Guisan to enhance defenses within the Réduit.[37] Bernard Barbey, chief of Guisan's personal staff, wrote that Constam's "Instructions on Combat Tactics" were well received. Guisan incorporated Constam's proposals in his Plan of Operations, including the following:

> A people who had to fight to become independent must not relinquish this independence without fighting. Those who are cowards and renounce their freedom will not find the strength to gain it back under more favorable circumstances. Those who are brave never think that a war is hopeless. Being brave is not only a matter of an individual's courage when he faces danger but to the same extent a matter of the expertise that he has gained through hard work, pain, and sacrifices that boost his self-confidence. We must acquire this expertise by working constantly and consistently. We lack combat experience. Hence, we shall hold our own against a battle-tried opponent only if we learn what is relevant from developments [in the war abroad] and then apply our insights with intensive training.

Referring to the Réduit, Constam noted that we must "do everything to defend the central area. . . . The Gotthard, Grimsel, and Lötschberg are the most important routes across the Alps, and the pawns that have been entrusted to us, the last refuges that we shall protect and never surrender. In our mountains tenacious and well-trained troops, even if they are outnumbered, are able to hold their own even against an enemy who uses modern weapons and combat methods." The Swiss could not wait for assaults from behind their fixed fortifications but had to counterattack aggressively at close range, denying the enemy the use of heavy guns and opportunities for dive bomber attacks.

Constam's tactics were put on display in maneuvers by the 3rd and 6th Divisions in October 1941 before unit commanders and their chiefs of staff, chief engineers, and chief instructors. Military Department Head and Federal Councilor Karl Kobelt attended. As recorded by Barbey, General Guisan turned the program over to Constam, who lectured from a map. Barbey described parts of the action:

> During one exercise pitting one unit against another, everyone could see how the sector was turned into a zone with an aggressive defense; the attacker was granted only enough freedom of movement so that counterattacks could be launched against him from multiple points. In the afternoon, we attended exercises involving sharpshooters and tanks in a demonstration of aggressive battle tactics within the Morgarten sector.

Morgarten was the narrow mountain defile where in 1315 a small number of Swiss peasant warriors swept down from the heights in a surprise attack on thousands of Austrian knights, killing many and routing the rest. During World War II, the Swiss military reached back to legendary victories like these—victories against what seemed then to be hopeless odds—to keep spirits high.

There were, however, naysayers. In mid-1941, Colonel Gustav Däniker, then commander of the Shooting School of Walenstadt, was overheard criticizing army tactics and training orders which had been issued by General Guisan himself.[38] Däniker had long advocated accommodation with the "New Europe," i.e., Germany, and opposed Guisan's anti-German initiatives. Guisan's—and Constam's—battle tactics made it clear that resistance, not negotiation or accommodation, was to be the heart of Swiss strategy. Guisan consulted Constam and then called Däniker on the carpet for insubordination and abruptly expelled him from the Swiss military. Berlin considered Däniker's dismissal yet another Swiss affront to good relations with Germany. Nazi propagandists would view this incident as another indication of "Jewish influence." In fact, it was a clear example of how the Swiss military, which consisted of both Christian and Jewish citizens, succeeded in maintaining a uniform front against the monolithic Nazi state.

Constam continued to play a major role in Swiss tactical planning as the war progressed. In the second half of 1942, German-Italian forces, including the panzers of Field Marshal Erwin Rommel, suffered crushing defeats in the desert war in North Africa. Anti-tank troops engaging the enemy in close combat in coordination with mine specialists and infantry played a decisive role in the British victory at El Alamein. Since a Wehrmacht attack on Switzerland would include major tank strikes, the Swiss studied these encounters carefully.[39]

General Guisan put Constam in charge of anti-tank strategy. His recommendations, based in part on the lessons of El Alamein, were to integrate special grenadier forces into the infantry. In the spring of 1943 Guisan ordered Constam's plan to be implemented. Barbey reflected: "It was without a doubt a good omen that this matter was put in the hands of a strong personality such as Constam instead of the bureaucracy. That is why we could take lessons learned on desert sands and adapt them so quickly and effectively to the heart of the Alps."

Constam was also very conscious of the contribution of women to the Swiss military. He recognized how useful the Woman's Auxiliary Service (FHD) could be in releasing men for active duty. FHD member Alice Renold-Asper remembers: "I was Constam's secretary from 1943 to 1945. He was considered to be severe. Indeed, some of my officer friends asked, 'Will she come out alive?' Once I put flowers on my desk even though an officer warned me Constam would throw them out. He did not, but he was a stickler. A member of his staff used to follow me to the WC to make sure I did not take any secret documents." Security was tight because the stakes were high, and some of her work involved Swiss intelligence.[40]

After the end of the war, Herbert Constam played an important role in military strategy, becoming an influential member of the National Defense Commission.[41] The Federal Council named him the head of the new office of Army Inspector. Reflecting traditional Swiss egalitarianism, Constam thought generals were not necessary in times of peace.[42]

An intelligence report of the German Army's General Staff entitled *Kleines Orientierungsheft Schweiz* (Concise Reference Work Switzerland), which was issued in September 1942 and revised in December 1944, included an analysis of the top 34 members of the Swiss military leadership.[43] It described General Guisan as "Intelligent, very cautious. Behind his overt correctness stands his sympathy with the Western powers."

The German report described several of the top Swiss officers as friends of France and enemies of Germany. Corps Commander Constam was described as *"Sehr tüchtig. Nicht-Arier. Deutschfeindlich"* (Very capable.

Non-Aryan. Enemy of Germany). It is noteworthy that several other high officers were described as *"Tüchtig"* (capable), but only Constam—the "non-Aryan"—was "s*ehr tüchtig*" (very capable).

If General Guisan assigned some of the most critical military tasks to Corps Commander Constam, he also confided in and strongly relied on Major Albert R. Mayer, another Jewish citizen-soldier. Mayer was the commander-in-chief's adjutant during 1939–41. Anticipating a Nazi invasion, Mayer sent his wife to New York while there was still time to get out. Mayer himself remained in Switzerland.

Although Mayer retired in 1941 for health reasons, he continued to serve General Guisan, who oddly enough remained the official Swiss delegate for the International Olympic Committee, receiving mailings from an organization that somehow continued to function, at least nominally, during the war. Guisan did not want the duty and delegated it to Mayer. An envelope dated January 30, 1942, remains in the Swiss Federal Military Library. It was mailed from Germany and bore the Nazi swastika.[44] On it, Guisan scribbled a note assigning the reply to Mayer as follows: "Would you please inform them that you have replaced me at the International Olympic Committee, and that they should then send *La Revue Olympique* [the Olympic magazine] directly to you. Best regards."

Henri Guisan and his wife Mary were personal friends of the Mayers, and a volume has been published of the letters of General and Madam Guisan to Albert Mayer and his wife. They corresponded regularly during and after the war.[45] The most moving parts of these letters are the Guisans' constant expressions of concern about the well-being of Frau Mayer and their obvious efforts to keep Albert's spirits up while his wife was across the Atlantic. In view of the situation in Europe, neither the Guisans nor Albert Mayer knew if they would survive a Nazi invasion.

On New Year's Day 1943, Guisan wrote to Mayer regretting that the latter could communicate with his wife only by telegraph. The war had disrupted postal communications between Nazi-surrounded Switzerland and the free world. The General added: "Let's hope that 1943 will bring us the end of this horrible war and that God protects us here in our small homeland, as He so clearly has done thus far. When the Axis powers are expelled from North Africa and the second campaign comes closer to us, the dangers will increase, because our Alpine rails will be tempting to the Axis! It is necessary therefore that we are all in the Réduit in time! . . . So long as I have a drop of blood in my veins, I will carry on according to my convictions and will not give up."[46]

The general's last comment reflected the attitude of most Swiss. When the war broke out in 1939, young David Kirchgraber was training as a cadet. "As the times demanded, cadet training was dominated by a military esprit de corps and athletic prowess. . . . We learned sharpshooting. They told us to 'imagine that you are aiming at a SS man, and then you will hit your target.'"[47]

Target practice was a family affair. "Pistol shooting took place at the Roggenhausen quarry near Solothurn. I still have the weapon. My sister, born in 1927, was the best shooter."

David came from a family that had originally been Jewish but had later converted to Christianity. To the Germans, people like David were still "non-Aryans."

While he and countless other Swiss practiced shooting at SS men, Switzerland by necessity had to trade with Germany. His father, a businessman, once received a request from the German Consul to meet to discuss his company. "My father went with a heavy heart. . . . With unspeakable fear, we waited in an old restaurant for two hours. 'What will we do, if they keep Dad!' cried my young sister." His father eventually returned rather shaken and recounted the following conversation:

"Behind the Consul's desk, under a picture of the Führer, sat a seemingly polite man. He introduced himself in a sharp tone of voice and declared 'You are not our friend.'

"'No,' said my father. 'What do you want from us?' . . .

"'In addition, you are not of Aryan descent, and several Jews are part of the management,' the Consul continued in a menacing manner.

"Father regained his composure and became assertive: 'The Consul might be interested in knowing that, first, we are in Switzerland where such categories do not apply and, second, we have been Protestants for a long time.' Father wanted to know where the Consul had obtained his information. There was a stack of folders on the desk. As a Swiss, Father became angry and defiant. He mentioned a relative from Württemberg, Germany, whose family history was investigated when she married. We had been shocked that such an investigation would take place."

The Consul was taken aback and changed the subject to trade agreements, but he issued instructions, "as if we were already living in a *Gau*." He added: "Sir, after the final victory, Germany will know how to distinguish between its friends and enemies!"

David's father immediately went to the commander of the cantonal police, who said that "this was not the first known case of denunciation, intimidation and coercion. He reassuringly explained that the authorities were keeping a close eye on most agitators and potential traitors and at the relevant moment would suppress them relentlessly." As it turned out, the Consul was on the long list of Germans who would be expelled from Switzerland at the end of the war.

Many Swiss worked to help refugees. Hans Köfer-Richner, whose experiences are noted elsewhere in this book, had Jewish relatives and worked with his father to assist in the escape of Jews from Germany and Austria. His father hated the Nazis: "We are surrounded by mass murderers, criminals, pigs! . . . What will happen to us when these criminals march into Switzerland? Hitler has his mercenaries even here. They are already planning a concentration camp on Swiss soil and have appointed people who will execute their orders. We even know the name of the Gauleiter-to-be. The worst is, however, that many of those whose names have become known are Swiss!"

Köfer's father remained adamant: "We will not capitulate without resistance, the way the Frontists want us to. We will fight, even if we have to do so from the underground!" Documents found after the war revealed that, had a German invasion occurred, he was on a list to be captured "dead or alive."[48]

The message of resistance was also delivered from the pulpits of Swiss churches. Köfer recalled a Catholic mass during the fourth Christmas of the war. Referring to Nazi antipathy toward traditional Christianity and Judaism and to the deportations of Jews from the occupied countries, the priest intoned: "May our heartfelt prayers save us from this war of Satan. Millions of our fellow men have already been killed, thousands of Jews have been expelled, delivered to their German henchmen and killed. Thousands of Jews who are living with us and our neighbors would face the same fate, if the Germans invaded our country. The deportations from the occupied territories in Europe have clearly shown it. Rise and pray."[49]

PART III

STRUGGLE FOR SURVIVAL:
Food, Fuel, and Fear

CHAPTER 7

THE SPIRIT OF RESISTANCE[1]

"Tell me what you and your closest friends actually said about Hitler and the Nazis . . ."

Oral histories have become common today, but huge gaps remain in the systematic recording of cultural memories. Standard histories seldom dwell on the attitudes or offhand speech of ordinary men and women. But ordinary people are the actual players in the drama of history, and they remember their parts vividly. The worker, the farmer, the housewife, the journalist all live through and react viscerally to the history that swirls around them. They respond to and argue about issues. They contribute their "two bits"—often with considerable wit and a trenchant humor that gives more insight into actual human predicaments than many a telescopic account that emerges years later.

Of course, freedom of expression was not available everywhere. Among oppressed populations, as in Nazi Germany and Communist Russia, the slightest hint of resistance was forbidden and systematically rooted out. With censors and party enforcers lurking on every corner and public news nothing but a party line, words had to be ambiguous. Praise of the existing system was expected, and speaking one's mind on any topic, however trivial or innocuous, was dangerous, even fatal. No one was safe from state censors. So there was a long, spiritually enervating conspiracy of silence.

Switzerland, on the other hand, is the oldest democracy in the world, and its traditions of freedom—of speech and of the press—were firmly established ages ago. Swiss at every level of society have always taken great pride in debating issues publicly. While a limited press censorship was deemed necessary during the war, the man on the street could say anything he wished. As a result, the oral history of Switzerland before and during the Second World War is both lively and informative. Switzerland was "open" at a time when Germany, Russia, France, Italy and other nations were closed societies.

So what were the Swiss saying as the Nazi colossus closed in around them? Switzerland's *geistige Landesverteidigung* (spiritual national defense) against Nazism was as important as actual military preparations, and extended through all levels of Swiss society. Moreover, the vocabulary of *Widerstand* (resistance) was anything but polite. The Swiss used many insulting terms in reference to Nazi Germany, even as the military odds grew more dangerous and the Swiss found themselves the last remaining democracy on the continent.

Repeating those terms today should by no means reflect on Swiss attitudes toward modern Germans. Though rooted in history, they also do not accurately reflect Swiss sentiment prior to the Nazi period. During the Great War, for example, much of the population was philosophically as well as politically neutral, at least at the start. Unfortunately, pejorative terms about any national group often fail to distinguish between the leaders and the led, and when Hitler rose to power in Germany it became a delicate if not impossible task to distinguish between Nazis and the broader mass of German people who supported or tolerated Nazi rule. But one thing is clear: the derogatory language used by many Swiss to describe the Germans under Hitler reflected a widespread rejection of National Socialism. Hitler's racist, expansionist credo, driven by personality-cult politics, was anathema to everything the Swiss had stood for since the founding of their independent confederation in 1291.

Children picked up their parents' attitudes. For instance, the earliest memory of Hitler's assumption of power in 1933 by then eleven-year old Bruno Capol of Windisch is characteristic. Like graffiti spray-painted on buildings today, "so at the very beginning of Hitler's takeover we found chalk-cartoons showing a man hanging at the gallows with a swastika and the following words:"

Heil, heil, heil!	Hail, hail, hail!
Hitler soll an's Seil!	Hang Hitler on a nail!
Und es tönt an allen Ecke,	Shout it loudly to the sky,
Adolf Hitler soll verrecke![2]	Adolf Hitler's going to die!

This singsong schoolboy rhyme uses the vulgar term "*verrecke*," which means to die miserably.[3] In English the term "croak" approximates the insulting meaning of the German. The Nazis used the term against Jews.[4] Swiss graffiti turned this insult upside down to say: Let Hitler croak!

Of course, at first Hitler was just another voice out of the raging anarchy that was Germany. Ruling coalitions were formed and almost as quickly fell. For all anyone knew the so-called "Führer's" government would be just as chaotic and short-lived. The following "Joke of Little Hansli,"[5] which circulated in Switzerland during this early period, expressed in Swiss dialect the strong possibility of a quick change:

Eusi Katz het Kaetzli kha,	Our cats had kittens,
Sieben a der Zahl.	seven in the count.
Sechs sind fuer d'Hitler g'sie,	Six are for Hitler,
Und Eis isch Radikal.	and one is a Radical.

A few weeks later, Hansli was asked to repeat his verse, but he recited a revised version as follows:

Eusi Katz het Kaetzli kha	Our cats had kittens,
Sieben a der Zahl.	seven in the count.
Eis isch fuer d'Hitler g'sie,	One is for Hitler,
Und sechs sind Radikal.	and six are Radicals.

"But Hansli," the joke continued, "you told it differently before!" He replied: *"Inzwischen sind ihre Augen uf g'ange."* ("Meantime, their eyes have opened.") So there was clearly a "before" and an "after." Germans recognized Hitler's real agenda too late, and by then even "radical" solutions were no longer possible. Hitler's regime would not fall, and those who opposed it were rapidly silenced or disappeared into the camps. The Nazi consolidation of power moved with whirlwind speed, and the implications were recognized as ominous, as expressed in the following anecdote.

At the 1934 federal shooting competition in Freiburg, Peter Voser's father was firing when suddenly a "Special Edition" of the newspaper arrived. "Hindenburg is dead, Hitler is Reichspräsident!" screamed the headlines. Voser recalls: "The men dropped their pistols, went over to the tent and discussed the event, saying 'Hitler, this *Sau* (pig), now he is fully in power, now there will be war, there will be war . . . .'"[6]

In German "*Sau*" is a very strong term, akin to "*cochon*" in French or "*bastard*" in English. It carries the meaning of "dirty swine" or "son-of-abitch."[7] And it is frequently used as a prefix to convey disgust. But the whole Swiss vocabulary of revulsion and disgust rapidly came into play. Consider the following. "*Schabe*," which means "cockroach,"[8] sounds similar to "*Schwabe*," which means "Swabian,"[9] a person from southern Germany. "*Schwaben*" (Swabia in English) is the region and medieval principality in southwestern Germany chiefly in the area comprising modern Baden, Wurttemberg, and West Bavaria.[10] So the wordplay was not long in coming, wordplay that moved easily through the mountains that separate high German from the Swiss German dialects.

A recollection by Swiss Füsilier (Infantryman) Wenk, Stabskp. (Headquarters Company), Füsilier Battallion 69, entitled "*D'Schwabe chöme!*" ("The Swabians are coming!")[11] contains the following:

> In January 1940 we were set up in Höri near Bülach. Our headquarters were in a small, old farmhouse. The bedroom was on the upper floor. We had to leave our backpacks, clothes, shoes and everything else in the farmer's small living room. But we always had our weapons with us because at that time the situation was dangerous.

In the next paragraph in Wenk's Swiss German account, "Swabian" is used both as a contemptuous word for Germans and for cockroaches. "*Nun, eines frühen Morgens wird Alarm geschlagen, und einer ruft: 'D'Schwabe sind ibroche!'*" This passage reads in English:

> Early one morning, someone sounded the alarm by calling: "The Swabians have broken in!" It was pitch dark, and we all grabbed our weapons and ran downstairs. A soldier was standing there, laughing as he turned on the light. In fact, the Swabians had broken in, but the "Swabians" were only "cockroach" Swabians. And I think there were more of these "invaders" than there ever were Germans. Cockroaches were everywhere, in shoes, backpacks, pants, socks. It took us more than an hour to throw out the enemy. We had been lucky once again.

Behind lighthearted wordplays like these, of course, was a very serious threat. Whether humorous or dead serious, derogatory slang expressions were increasingly directed against the Nazi regime and its supporters. Colonel Rudolf Ursprung explained:

In 1939 I was studying law at the University of Berne. From 1939 to 1945, the year of my graduation, I served a total of about 23 months on active duty. I spent most of my active duty as lieutenant with the border protection unit in Etzgen, a small village on the Rhine.

The soldiers were forced to dig trenches not far from home, to cut trees to build positions, to sleep on straw instead of working and living on their farms, and all this because the damned "dirty Swabians" were terrorizing the world from across the Rhine. In our area we called the Germans "Swabians," and the Swabians were put at the same level as Hitler and the National Socialists. The anger against Hitler knew no bounds, and we cursed the situation created by him and the hardship in which we found ourselves because of him.[12]

Germans were often called "*Sauschwabe*"[13] or in Swiss German "*Sauschwob*," meaning "Swabian pig." A Swiss soldier recalled that they clipped off the ends of bullets issued for their rifles to make the bullets create deadlier wounds against the expected Wehrmacht invaders. His uncle stationed at Lake Constance quipped, "We have no chance, but we would rather die than fall in the hands of the Schwabe."

Dr. Ramon Meier, a 12-year-old boy at the time, recalled the time of the Nazi blitzkrieg against France and Western Europe:[14]

During the second general mobilization [May 1940] the cadets and students serving in the auxiliary service were given a room at the local headquarters in Glarus. While we were waiting for new orders in the room, we were looking out of the window and noticed a German Nazi that we knew walking by. We cried "*Sauschwab*" [German pig] which caused the insulted man to head back into the headquarters. But we had already left through the back door. We were in the vicinity of the train station when an auxiliary service soldier in a car stopped us and ordered us to go back to the headquarters. He said that if we did not do as ordered he would call the police. He then reported us to the commander and we anxiously awaited our punishment. To our surprise and that of the "*Häschers*" [bloodhound] (the German having left in the meantime), the major only said: "Boys, you were right, just don't say it out loud in the street."

Max Salm, a teenager at the time, remembers: "In 1940, to counter any potential fifth column, the young were encouraged to join the *Ortswehr* [Local Defense]. We had no training except shooting courses from age 15. We were given old Model 1889 rifles. We wanted to shoot as many Germans as possible. '*Sauswabian*' was a generally used term for Germans."[15]

Verena Rothenhäusler lived 10 kilometers from the Rhine, heard alarms at night, and lived in almost constant fear of hostilities. She was in the *Landsdienst*, helped farmers after school and during holidays, and had been trained by her father to shoot a rifle—which she would do if the Nazis came. "My mother called a German '*Saunazi*' [Nazi pig], a term which could also apply to a Swiss with Nazi sympathies."[16]

Right across the border in Germany, any speech or writing which could be interpreted, however indirectly, as opposition to the Nazis brought immediate arrest and punishment. University student Sophie Scholl was beheaded in 1943 because she and her White Rose cell of resisters in Munich had "most vulgarly defamed the Führer, thereby giving aid to the enemy of the Reich and weakening the armed security of the nation."[17] They had distributed flyers questioning the war in Russia after Stalingrad, at a time when most Germans knew virtually nothing of the full extent of the disaster there.

And what about the Germans and German sympathizers in Switzerland? Peter Voser recollects of daily life in Baden, Switzerland, in those days:

> The Jews were not being harassed, but the Swabians had to pay attention. It was not good to be a German in Switzerland at the time. A German who was criticizing Hitler was okay, but a German who was speaking in support of Hitler would get harassed. At the Gymnasium we had a German who was an ardent Nazi. We irritated him constantly because of that.[18]

"I was 13 in 1939," remembers Dr. Hans Widmer. "I grew up in Orlikon near the railroad station. Father called Germans '*Boche*,' a derogatory French word.[19] He never called them Germans."[20] Other sources note use of the term "*Sal Boche*" (dirty German), which was used by French-speaking persons in Switzerland.[21]

Georges-André Chevallaz, who would later become the President of the Swiss Confederation, recalled: "I was born in 1915. My father was a teacher at Verdu near Lake Neuchâtel at the border with France. Everyone was against Hitler. A Nazi was called a 'boche.' I had no fear about the Germans coming, because I was young and I hated Germany. I remember the April 1940 order that any surrender announcement must be regarded as enemy propaganda. This was the policy for the entire war."[22]

Swiss resistance to potential tyrants from the north was not new. It went back hundreds of years, and traces of a colorful vocabulary can be found in Swiss writings dating to the First Reich. In 1493 the Imperial Diet of Worms attempted to impose a common penny tax on the Swiss and to subject them to the jurisdiction of an Imperial Chamber of Justice. This sparked a conflict, known as the Swabian War, that would result in the Swiss winning their independence from the Holy Roman Empire.

The enmity was mutual. Professor Luck writes: "In south Germany, pamphlets and poems insulting to the Swiss appeared, and the name *Schwabe* (cockroach), with contemptuous overtones, found its way about."[23] In the Swabian War of 1499, the Swiss fought the German and Austrian *Landsknechte* (heavy infantry) of Maximilian I, a Habsburg and emperor of the Holy Roman Empire. Just as in World War II, the Swiss built fortifications all along the Rhine River and stayed armed and ready for immediate mobilization.[24]

In the winter of 1498–99, soldiers shouted insults back and forth across the Rhine. Albert Winkler explains the incident that sparked the first fighting as follows:

> At Gutenberg, the *Landsknechte* mocked the Swiss by composing unchristian songs that offended the pious Confederates. The final affront came when the German mercenaries offended the Swiss' sexual preferences. The Swabians displayed a cow and called to the Confederates to come over and make love to the animal. The men then mooed like cows and calves. Shortly, the Swiss leader from the state of Uri, Heini Wolleb, took a group of men across the river and burned a house and stall. At this point, the war began in earnest.[25]

Such ancient verbal hostilities came repeatedly into play during the Third Reich. A Wehrmacht veteran states that, during World War II, the Germans called the Swiss *"Kuhschweizer"* (cow Swiss).[26] Indeed, *"Schweizer"* is defined in part as: "(a) Swiss, (b) dairyman."[27] Swiss border residents recollect *"Kuhschweizer"* and *"Schwaben"* being yelled across the Rhine.[28] This had been going on for almost five centuries.

Germans residing in Switzerland used a similar insult. Armin Camen-isch, who was born in 1933, remembers: "The Germans called the Swiss by a very old name: '*Kuhschweizer*' (cow Swiss). In Chur, a man named Ude Kirchmeyer was thought to be the future Gauleiter [governor] when the Germans invaded. His son was always fighting, and I once kicked him in the stomach. When the war ended, the Swiss seized the Nazis and sent them to the border with Austria, turning them over to the French."[29]

The following joke recalled by Gustav and Margot Durrer about a border exchange told during World War II probably had an equivalent in the 1499 war:

> One morning, at the Swiss-German border, a German soldier handed over a package to a Swiss soldier. When the package was opened, it was found to contain cow manure (*Kuh Fladda*). The next morning, at the same border, the Swiss soldier handed over a beautifully wrapped package, containing a big piece of Swiss cheese, and a note: "Each country sends its best!"[30]

Such catcalls and insults often preceded real conflicts. And these were bloody indeed as the feisty and increasingly independent Swiss resisted attempts to bring them into the expansive northern "Reich." Combat in the Swabian war involved the use of the "hedgehog" defense and the "push of pike" between massed forces. At Triboltingen, the Swiss claimed to have killed 1,300 Swabians and sustained casualties of only 20. At Frastanz, the Swiss reported 3,000 enemy dead to only 11 Swiss.[31] At Calven, 4,000 Austrians died to 2,000 Swiss. The battle at Dornach result-ed in 3,000 *Landsknechte* dead to 500 Confederates. "We are the peasants who punish the nobles," bragged the Swiss.[32] These statistics, whether accurate or not, would inspire the Swiss to resist outsiders for centuries to come.

In the Swabian War, the Swiss emerged victorious and established their independence. Beaten on the battlefield, Maximilian agreed in a peace treaty signed at Basel to abrogate the tax and the judicial im-position. The independence of the Helvetic Confederation was recog-nized de facto. There would be no *Grossdeutschland*. However, the existence of this independent Confederation remained a thorn in the side of the rulers to the north. And the Swiss example was not lost on others. At the time of the peasant uprisings against the church and the nobility that swept southern Germany like wildfire after Luther, this song was heard:

The peasants tried to learn
Evil tricks from the Swiss
And become their own lords.[33]

The peasant rebellion was ruthlessly put down, but the Swiss "porcupine" over the years was successful. The image stuck, and put fear into the hearts of many a would-be invader who risked battle in the deadly mountain passes. The almost mythic horde of Swiss pike men resembling a porcupine took on a new meaning during World War II, as the whole country bristled with armaments, fortifications, and barbed wire.

The Führer himself was well aware of how the Swiss used the derogatory term "*Schwaben.*" At their June 2, 1941, conference in the Brenner Pass, Hitler and Mussolini discussed carving up Switzerland. "The Führer characterized Switzerland as the most despicable, wretched people and national entity. The Swiss were the mortal enemies of the new Germany, but . . . *Die Schwaben am Ende den Krieg doch noch gewinnen würden*" [the Swabians would win the war]."[34] Then, if not before, the "*Schwaben*" would pay the Swiss back in kind.

The thousand-year Reich, of course, lasted only a dozen years. The contempt for this Reich and its Führer is expressed in the following joke which the Durrers remember being told in Switzerland:

Hitler was taken for his first ride in an airplane, and became very nervous, to the point that he had diarrhea. Having no bathroom facilities on board, he used his hat to relieve himself and then tossed it out of the window. Later, when landing at the airport, everyone was singing and dancing, but paid no attention to Hitler. "What is being celebrated here?" he asked. "Well, Hitler is dead! His hat has been found with all that remains of him!"[35]

The Swiss viewed the 1939 Hitler-Stalin alliance with scorn. When Germany attacked Soviet Russia in June 1941, the Swiss rooted for mutual destruction. The following incident recalled by Dr. David Kirchgraber captures the emotions of the time:

Herr P, an affable German-born businessman, loved to talk about growing up in Switzerland. He spoke Swiss-German without accent and up until about 1940 pretended to give full support to the red and white flag. Anybody calling him by the common

"*Sauschwob*" [German pig] would have been in trouble. I did not even realize that he was from across the border until I noticed that he took a more and more neutral stance. He was one of those emphasizing that Nazism and the German people were not the same. In the beginning, some Swiss citizens also tried to make us believe this. However, during the "*Siege*" [victories] under the very regime they pretended to disapprove of, the majority of Germans living among us showed this to be a rash conclusion.

When the news of the attack on Russia came over the radio on June 22, 1941, we were all standing with our friend P. in the most popular modern swimming pool of the area, in a romantic little valley away from the hustle and bustle of the city. Everybody became quiet, everybody was thunderstruck. Then Herr P's baritone voice sounded across the glistening water: "Yes, in a month we will be in Moscow!" He said "we" and everybody looked even more bewildered. Someone said "hopefully, many of them will die" ("*verräble*" [croak] in the original Swiss-German dialect), and another called out "Nazi!" My father, beside himself, struck the water with his fist and shouted "*Jawoll!*" (yes!) into the bitter applause triggered by the response against Herr P. . . . A young man collected his uniform and called up to the loudspeaker: "Let them devour each other!"[36]

No one attempted to drown "Herr P," but an incident of resistance in Davos could have resulted in a drowning. A large number of Germans resided in Davos, which offered several sanatoria for tuberculosis patients. Cornelia Rogger, a teenager at the time, remembers:

The war was raging in Russia. A 15-year-old German schoolboy said to me: "We will invade Switzerland and we will take your fur coat for our army!" I replied: "You murderers. I'll burn my coat before I give it to you!" I saw him a few days later at the swimming pool. He said: "I hope you're not mad at me." I knew he could not swim, but I pushed him into the pool anyway and ran away. Someone rescued him. The German consulate telephoned me to come and answer for my act. I refused.[37]

Everyday resistance in Davos took other forms. In 1999, I interviewed 99-year-old Anton Bueler-Smulders and his son, who was six years old at the time of the following. They both remembered Dr. Becker, a Dutchman who worked at the Dutch Sanatorium in Davos, who regularly walked Tanky, his well-trained dark brown poodle. When a Prussian-talking German would pass, Dr. Becker would snap "Heil Hitler!" Whereupon the dog would raise his leg and pee![38]

Everyone in Davos knew about it and thought it was funny. The German Nazis objected, but the police refused to do anything. They warned Dr. Becker to watch out, as the Germans could shoot him, but he paid no attention. In fact, he became a local hero!

Other dogs were used to express anti-Nazi sentiments. One informant recalls: "I saw a man who had his dog trained in a special way. He would put a dog biscuit on his nose and say, 'This is from Hitler.' The dog stayed still. Then he would say, 'This is from Churchill.' The dog jumped and swallowed it."[39]

Switzerland was forced by necessity to trade with Germany for fuel and food. Karl Elsener, Sr., whose father headed the Victorinox factory— maker of the famous Swiss Army knives—recalls: "We got raw material from Solingen, Germany. Letters from German suppliers would have National Socialist propaganda. Father always said: "*Jemand, der einem Deutschen etwas glaubt, ist ein fertiger Esel!*" (Anyone who believes a German is a complete ass!)[40] Elsener adds: "Speeches by Hitler and Goebbels made the Swiss angry. Hitler was openly denounced. The Swiss and all of Europe heard Prof. Jean Rudolf von Salis on the radio. Everyone spoke what he thought."

Heinz Langenbacher, a pilot during the war who would later become the Swiss Secretary of State, remembers a common rhyme: "*Wo der Deutsche hindenkt, wächst kein Gras mehr.*" (Where a German thinks, there will be no more grass growing.)[41]

The Swiss are serious about their wine. Indeed the Swiss Army knife which everyone uses contains a corkscrew (although the knife the army actually issues does not). The following was related by Alice Renold-Asper, who served in the Women's Auxiliary Service. In 1940, a military parson from Solothurn left home, admonishing his mother: "If the Germans come, start a fire under my wine cellar! No Germans shall drink my wine!"[42]

Dr. Peter Voser related his own experience as follows:

We knew war would come. I was 17 and lived in Baden, the mid-point of the Limmat Line, the main defensive position of the Swiss Army. The authorities requested that the population invite soldiers for coffee in the winter of 1939. My father and brother were in the army, and soldiers visited every evening. They spoke about whether we could resist Germany.

Champagne was very expensive, and Father had six bottles in the cellar which he got from a client. As spring approached, we thought the Germans would attack and that it would be a pity if the Germans got our champagne. So we drank them all! That summer, Father returned from the army and said, "Now I will have a bottle of champagne. Peter, fetch me one!" I responded: "I thought the Germans were coming. It was better that Swiss drink the champagne than Germans!" At first Father was angry, but then said that it was all right.[43]

When the Nazis conquered France, they decreed the death penalty for any person who failed to surrender firearms. This would have had special significance in Switzerland, where every man had been issued a rifle for militia service. While the Nazis may not have decreed the death penalty for failure to surrender the fruit of the vine, they certainly seized all they could. A typical bottle from occupied France had the label "Henri Abelé Reims Champagne" and was stamped in red: "*Réservé à la Wehrmacht – Achat et revente interdits.*"[44] (Reserved for the German Army—purchase and resale forbidden).

Peter Voser's uncle, a doctor who was too old for military service, planned a special wine tasting for the Nazis. He had a beautiful home with a garden, and was sure the Germans would come and take it over. He prepared for his guests by putting poison into three bottles of his best French wine. He planned to invite them in and to drink the poisoned wine with his guests. He waited until the war ended to discard the wine.[45]

On April 28, 1945, Mussolini was executed and strung up by his heels from a lamppost. The news was received by Corps Commander Herbert Constam, who was the highest-ranking Jewish officer in the Swiss military and one of General Guisan's most trusted officers. Constam telephoned his wife and sang out "Mussolini is dead. *Ciao!*" and then hung up. He was saying "so long" both to his wife and to Il Duce. This was related to the author by Constam's secretary and phone operator, who overheard the remark.[46]

At the end of the war, someone broke into the German Consulate's house in Davos, ripped a picture of Hitler off the wall, and threw it out by the road. There was one policeman for all of Davos, and he said dryly,

"This person is not to my taste." He had no interest in catching whoever broke into the house.[47]

The Nazi leadership—Hitler, Göring and Himmler—committed suicide rather than face punishment for their actions. The Swiss made fun of them even in death:

> When Göring died and went to Hell, he was brought before the throne of Satan, who stood up and heartily welcomed him. Himmler was also given the same cordial welcome when he arrived in Hell. Finally, when Hitler arrived and was brought before the throne, the Devil did not rise to greet him. When questioned by his subjects regarding this, he replied: "Oh, I know that fellow. If I were to get up, he would immediately steal my seat."[48]

As these stories and anecdotes indicate, the vast majority of Swiss, at all levels of society, were deeply opposed to virtually everything the Nazis stood for. Their democratic traditions and fierce independence for centuries had opposed a centralized state and above all the rule of a single all-powerful leader. They were prepared to defend their homeland with their lives. It will never be known what would have happened if German armies had in fact invaded Switzerland, but it is certain that the war would have been bitter, and that the price in blood would have been exceptionally high.

CHAPTER 8

GAS MASKS & POTATO BREAD:
An Oral History

A woman went up to the General and exclaimed, "I must have them back!"

The General, who had heard this many times, answered: "I know, you want your husband and son back."

The woman responded: "I want my two horses back!"[1]

Horses were critical for plowing and harvesting crops—especially to the women who were left to do the farm work—but they were also needed by the army for pulling artillery and hauling supplies in rugged Alpine terrain. This wartime witticism was recalled by Walter Schmid, who was in his teens during the war. A Boy Scout and member of a shooting society, "At 17 I took the oath to defend the country to the last. In 1940, Swiss teenage boys joined the *Ortswehr* (Local Defense) with their grandfathers. Our motto was 'Every one of us takes seven Germans!'"

Besides becoming the backbone of economic production to release the men for military service, women played a major role as military auxiliaries, in civil defense and in assistance to refugees. Women and children also grew and processed food for the nation.

Fritz Wille was a retired corps commander of mountain troops whose grandfather was the Swiss commander-in-chief during World War I. Fritz, who commanded a cavalry squadron during World War II, remembered how "the soldiers complained that no one was at home working the farms and the horses were with us—'we have to go.' I replied that it was the same with all the other units. They quieted down and continued their duties."[2]

His wife, Martina Wille von Erlach, an elderly but strong-willed lady whom this author interviewed six decades after the war, remembers May

1940 like it was yesterday. "My father, Rudolf von Erlach, commanding officer of the Grisons mountain brigade, told his officers one evening that Holland had surrendered after a brief resistance in which fewer than 2,000 soldiers were killed. A young lieutenant exclaimed: 'That's shameful! We would have more casualties in the Grisons alone!'"[3]

Units of the French army found refuge in Switzerland. Frau Wille recalls: "I remember a remark of a French internee—they had come in large numbers to Switzerland during Hitler's campaign in France. The man disparaged the tiny little fields of potatoes or beans on the very steep slopes in our valleys. He said that in France nobody would ever do such a thing. But the Swiss people at that time were adapted to hardship. This was one of the reasons we were able to resist Hitler's ambitions.

"Food and fuel were in short supply. Our government did its best to organize a just apportionment by points and rations. 100 grams of butter once a month; hot water once a week! We shared the short stocks with 300,000 refugees. . . . Of course it was not for us to complain, being spared the terrible suffering these people had to endure.

"I was a secretary and library helper at my uncle's estate. But since my boss was commander of a battalion guarding the frontier and was absent for months, I worked on a farm with a peasant family at Maienfeld, a little town near the frontier with Liechtenstein. There were vineyards and cattle, though the peasants had no barns in which to store the grain harvest.

"The farmer had to leave for military service, and so we had to work extremely hard. Often we had to do threshing and load carts with corn sheaves during the night so they would be free the next day for further harvesting. Maienfeld had only one threshing machine. The harvest was enormous. Our government ordered farms to grow as much corn as possible so we wouldn't be so economically dependent on Hitler's Germany.

"In the summer of 1941, I lived for a few weeks with a peasant family in Oberhalbstein, a wonderful mountain valley in the Grisons. We harvested hay. The father and his three sons belonged to the 93rd Battalion and had to report for duty. How would the mother and sisters manage now with a stable full of cows and a bull? This situation was not extraordinary at all, but the men made countless petitions for leave. My father, commander of the Grisons brigade, granted leave for one of the sons. But for a great number of other farmer families, the difficulties continued. These are the problems of a country where every civilian is at the same time a soldier.

"My brother, a young law student, ploughed up our lawn to make a garden to grow potatoes and vegetables. As he was an excellent hobby gardener, we had not only beautiful harvests, but far too much for our own family. The manager of the Grand Hotel Bellevue Palace in Bern was glad to have our fresh vegetables, so my brother went with an old hand cart the five kilometers to Bern with the surplus from our garden. (Motorcars were requisitioned for military service and were largely unavailable, and gasoline was reserved only for medical emergencies or other special cases.)

"In 1955, the village of Bevaix on the lake of Neuchâtel celebrated the tenth anniversary of the end of the war. Everybody who had contributed to national defense was to take part in a parade through the village. Everyone from school children to grandparents was in the parade. So there were hardly any spectators. Every person had made an extraordinary effort during the war to ease the hardships of his neighbors. Children had sent little parcels and written letters to the men in military service. Women had taken over as much as possible the jobs and responsibilities of their absent husbands. Men beyond military age helped them, and the grandmas knitted stockings for the soldiers."

Despite all the gardening and extra cultivation, food was short in Switzerland during the war. The American airmen who found refuge there were in for a rude awakening.

Heinz Langenbacher of the Swiss Air Force, today a retired ambassador, recalled helping damaged American bombers land: "I remember a cartoon: 'Where can we land our plane?' So many American Liberators were on the runways that the Swiss planes could hardly land." He recorded in his diary: "On July 13, 1944, a double patrol of the flight squadron had to intercept an American Liberator bomber that was entering our neutral space from Basel in the direction of Lucerne. We gave the bomber the agreed-upon signals, to which the U.S. crew responded immediately. Half an hour later we landed in Payerne. One of the American crew members told us that they had been instructed at the base in England: 'If you have any problems, fly in the direction of the Alps and the "Swiss taxi service" will pick you up!'[4]

"We ran into problems the next morning when the Americans were served cocoa, old bread and a small piece of cheese for breakfast. They spit 'the muck' out, exclaiming, 'We are not pigs and we will not eat it!' They wanted ham and eggs. We explained the rationing system and said, 'Look, we are eating it too!' In long discussions we explained to them that foodstuffs had been rationed in Switzerland for years and that we had not eaten fresh bread for a long time (because bread could only be sold two days after baking). We told them that our monthly rations were very small. Luckily, for breakfast that day we did not have 'federal bricks,' that hard kind of zwieback that almost breaks your teeth."

Before and during the war, one of every three Swiss was a farmer (today it is only three percent). Robert Gasser-Hänni is a farmer today. He gave an interview for this book at his old farmhouse in the rolling hills near Bern. He was born in 1926 in a village in Canton Freiburg, the youngest of a family of three brothers and three sisters. The family farm consisted of ten acres of fields and five acres of forest, all of it very steep land, requiring grueling manual labor. Area families were large, one having 22 children. The depression decade between 1929 and the war had left farmers extremely poor. Mr. Gasser remembers: "At the beginning of winter we would get a pair of clogs which often left us with frostbitten feet. There was no device to check whether the clogs fit, but if they did not we were so happy to get a new pair that we forgot how much they hurt. The shoemaker was a neighbor who secretly made potato liquor when he did not have enough work.[5]

"In the morning we ate *Rösti* (hash brown potatoes), at lunch boiled potatoes, and in the evening potato soup. We ate bread sparingly, old cheese, and butter—but only on Sunday. In the winter we slaughtered an old sow and that was that. Often we had people eating with us who were even poorer. We let them sleep in the straw. We slept on bags of straw too and in the winter covered ourselves with horse blankets.

"I was a schoolboy in 1939 when, while harvesting wheat, father came up the hill with the bad news that general mobilization had been declared. We children were all close to tears and mother was crying. We had to be courageous and clench our teeth. My oldest brother, a corporal, took one of our two horses into the army with him. To get our wheat home, we had to borrow a neighbor's frisky three-year-old horse, which bit my hand and left it practically unusable for a long time. Then my second-oldest brother was drafted to the army, and we got further behind with our work.

"The fall was wet and cold. The potatoes were still in the soil when the first snow fell. We had to collect the potatoes from soil that was mixed with snow and partially frozen. We had no gloves to protect our hands and keep them warm. In the evening, even though we were very tired, we had to unload the potatoes and take them to the basement.

"We had practically no machinery and no automated mower to cut the grass. We got up at 4:30 a.m. To feed our 10 to 12 cows, Mother cut grass with an old McCormick mower, after which we turned the hay by hand and loaded it on carts with iron wheels. We were unloading hay or wheat until late at night.

"To this day we are grateful to my teacher. He was my brother's captain and often sent him home on leave to work in the fields. We were plowing with a steer, a horse, and a cow (but only for a half-day so she would still yield milk). Two of my sisters had to help. We also had many soldiers staying with us; they would work some and we shared our food with them.

"In the winter of 1942–43, we had to cut wood to replace coal, which was no longer available. Even in bad weather or a snowstorm we went to the forest with our axes and saws, in worn shoes because shoes were rationed, with cloth wrapped around the lower legs to keep the snow from getting into the shoes. I was not a very strong boy and sweated profusely while doing this hard work, so I caught pneumonia. We did not go to the doctor because health insurance did not exist. I ended up staying at a sanatorium for 18 months and had pneumothorax for seven years. This creeping illness in my lungs was luckily discovered in January 1944 when I was being x-rayed in recruit school. Otherwise those bugs would have gotten me.

"We had many American planes flying over at night on their way back to Italy after bombing southern Germany. Not far from our house searchlights beamed at the airplanes, and the antiaircraft battery in Bümpliz would go into action. One night there was a violent thunderstorm. The planes had to drop their bombs to gain altitude. This caused several windows to be broken. We were often very afraid.

"We had no money to put in the bank, but we helped our neighbors and refugees, regardless of whether they were Jewish or Christian. Our family hosted children from Holland, France, Hungary, Germany and some Swiss from abroad. Some of the children were skin and bones. We shared our bread with all of them."

That would have been the infamous wartime two-day-old potato bread. When we concluded the above interview, Frau Gasser-Hänni served her own homemade bread, traditional country style. One can only imagine the difference.

Verena Rothenhäusler is a soft-spoken but determined woman who told her story with fire in her eyes. She was 12 in 1940 and lived at Rapperswil, near Aarau, between Bern and Zurich. "My father had polio, which paralyzed his right side. He could not join the army, but he could still shoot. Father bought a rifle, I think from a soldier, and kept it at home.

We practiced in the garden, using a special cartridge and target set-up. I was a good shot. My three cousins had a small Flobert [ball cap] rifle. We all practiced with it. Later one cousin was trained as a grenadier.[6]

"Both of my parents had lived in Germany. During World War I, my father, who was Swiss, moved from Germany to Switzerland. So I knew something about the Nazis. I went to my grandparents at Singen for Christmas and vacation. In 1934, when I was six, Father took me over the border to see a Nazi parade. He became more and more angry. 'It will not be good for Germany,' he said.

"Everyone in the family was against the Nazis except for a German uncle, who said, 'We have work again.' That was true. Grandfather's house in Germany was near a printing press where before Hitler long lines of unemployed had appeared every morning.

"When I was 6 or 7, we took a taxi from the Swiss border to a train station in Germany. We had 50 grams of tea in my handbag. German border guards searched the bag and found the tea. You were forbidden to take tea or coffee to Germany. The guards took my parents out of the taxi and conducted a complete search. We never went that way again.

"I did farm duty three weeks a year. This was in summer vacation, and I would live at the farm. Women had too much work to do. There were always cows to milk. I helped in the garden and picked cherries. You get tired of eating them quickly! The farmer's name was Keller. Mrs. Keller and her four children were there together with one 20-year-old employee. Mr. Keller was away in the army. We gave the Keller children clothes, so they gave us extra rationing coupons. Farmers did not need all of their coupons." Sale of coupons was prohibited, but this kind of informal mutual aid was probably widespread.

Frau Rothenhäusler talked about the wartime bread: "The potatoes in it kept it fresher. Every day we had bread for breakfast and took a sandwich to school. We went two days a week without meat. Meat was more controlled in town but not so much in the village. Later, there were three meatless days every week.

"We had many alarms from German and American airplanes. At night there was blackout, requiring that we keep the shutters closed. The blackout was very strict in the beginning. Later, many times I was in bed and the night guard saw that I had a light on, but he did not bother me.

"We heard the radio news every day at 12:30 during our mid-day break from school. On Friday night after the news, there would be a political report from Prof. Jean Rudolf von Salis. These were broadcasts on

Radio Switzerland which could be heard in Germany." Germans caught listening to foreign radio broadcasts were subject to severe penalties, because hearing outside perspectives would have only encouraged doubts about the Nazi regime. German broadcasts heard by the Swiss, by contrast, could be terrifying. Verena Rothenhäusler remembers:

"I heard German radio, including Hitler speeches. I get freezing cold when I remember it! Those speeches made us afraid.

"Father was in the *Ortswehr* and the *Luftschutz* (Air Defense), and protected the factory. He had supplies of cotton and a spinning mill. Had the Germans come, he would have set fire to his factory.

"One did not talk about details [of defense]. Posters admonished against talking too much. There were Germans and even Nazis in Switzerland. At school in Aarau, there was a German girl. I once saw her on the street on a Saturday afternoon shopping, and she was wearing the uniform of the *Bund Deutscher Mädel* [League of German Girls], which meant that she was an active Nazi. She tried to communicate with me (my grandparents were still in Germany). Did she perhaps want to know about the factory? Later, her family had to leave Switzerland." This last statement was uttered with a sigh of relief, but the following came with a cringe:

"I first heard about concentration camps in 1944. A visiting aunt told us about terrible things in the East, including awful camps for Jews. My uncle was editor of a Protestant paper and got secret information from the Protestant church in Germany."

The Women's Auxiliary Service, known as the FHD (*Frauenhilfsdienst*), was a popular organization formed to assist the Swiss Armed Forces.[7] Their activities, which ran the gamut from nursing to watching for aircraft, included services traditionally provided by women as well as activities meant to free the men for armed service. An FHD recruiting poster read: "*Schweizer Frauen meldet Euch zum FHD. Jede FHD Macht Einen Soldaten für die Front Frei*" (Swiss women, join the FHD. Every FHD enlistment frees a soldier for the front).

In a 1999 interview, FHD member Esther Terrier recalled: "I was in Girl Scouts. My family was patriotic. My father and brother were called up in the general mobilization of 1939. I was 18 in December and joined the FHD Army Hospital administration. Everyone thought that the FHD represented solidarity and showed you had a positive attitude. We learned to march and wore Scout uniforms. Those who were not Scouts before the war wore aprons. Those who were 20 or older wore the Swiss arm band and had a service book."[8] The armband identified them as members of the Armed Forces, and the service book recorded their military training and service.

"There was also an organization consisting of nuns from hospitals and cloisters. Nuns who were nurses were incorporated into the Army.

"In March 1940, I was drafted into a unit as secretary for the director of the Military Health Service. We were in a central facility for all of Switzerland located in Luzern.

"After Hitler attacked Belgium, Holland and France, the Swiss could observe the Germans over the border. On the highways we saw people fleeing Zurich and Basel. It was very emotional. Switzerland remobilized and we were sworn in as FHD members.

"We cared for French and Polish military internees. I selected those who qualified as being sick—many were not sick but were faking to get comfortable quarters. They were taken by rail to an internee center in Lausanne.

"I was later sent back to Luzern and worked in administration until 1942. I was training to be a nurse and finished as the war ended, becoming an assistant to a surgeon."

Like male soldiers, FHD members wore IDs called "death tags"—Americans preferred to lighten the topic by calling them dog tags. The tag of one FHD veteran, which this author examined, reads: "Alice Renold-Asper, 22.12.19 [birth date] Prot[estant], Dättwil AG [address], D [*Dienst* or service], *Chef* [commander]." The tag is oval shaped and can be broken in the middle. Half stays with the dead body; the other goes to the family.[9]

Frau Renold-Asper, whose neck the tag had once adorned, recalled some prewar events: "A Jewish lady who was a family friend invited me to Berlin in 1937. We sat on yellow benches for Jews and spoke in French so we would not be understood. Her family frequently came to Baden and owned a factory. She later escaped from Germany with her family and sailed on the *Simon Bolivar*, the last ship full of Jews leaving Holland. It went to England.

"In September 1939 I finished school and, like thousands of other women, volunteered for the FHD. There was no pay. I was placed in the Zurich State House to work in Soldiers' Assistance. I did typing and administration, including applications from wives for financial help. A committee considered the financial situation and the children's needs. A favorable decision would bring two Swiss francs per day in aid.

"In May 1940," she continued, "things were dangerous. There was panic and flight from the border. At the train station in Zurich you saw ladies with bird cages and walking sticks."

What were members of the FHD instructed to do if the Germans invaded? Alice explained: "I learned how to use a pistol. Our order was to stay in place and keep working unless we received new directives. Some lost their nerve and needed psychological counseling by clergy. We were attached to troops, so we would also have become prisoners of war if the Germans came and captured them. We knew we were not to cooperate. We were prepared for the worst.

"In August a professional gymnast who had trained in Finland designed a 13-day physical training course for the FHD. Our instruction also included how to behave correctly, keep written records, and use the telephone. After we were examined and entered the program, we got our armband and service book. Then we were put in a service group, which included pigeon courier service and air defense. At another time I was the secretary of a commandant for a recruiting and training school.

"Nuns did military service, including marching! It was a funny sight. But they did not get military uniforms and received no training with weapons.

"The FHD served in refugee camps. Hundreds of Italian women and children would arrive at the same time. Once, instead of the expected 160 women and children, 160 partisans arrived." The Italian partisans were no doubt escaping from the Nazi occupation forces in northern Italy. Countless such occurrences are now lost to history. They are only personal memories.

The oldest daughter in a family which had been devastated by the Depression, Alice Schelbert, was another FHD recruit. She was fifteen when the war erupted and remembers: "Each family was obligated to cultivate a plot of land to grow vegetables, potatoes, and Indian corn. I hated working in the fields and gardens, but luckily my younger sister enjoyed such tasks. So I did the household chores, mending clothes and undoing the runs in stockings with a special hair-thin hook.[10]

"In the Linth plain not too far from the village, we cut peat. Old and young were brought there by tractor or truck to labor in the bog for hours. It was quite strenuous work, but we earned a few cents that would buy bread. Peat bricks for heating were cheaper than coal, which was scarce."

Alice eventually joined the Women's Auxiliary Service. "I was assigned to antiaircraft defense as part of the medical service. A lazaret, a provisional hospital and air raid shelters had been established in basements of community centers and churches. We conducted obligatory courses in first aid. I was also called up to do a month of basic military training in Vevey, a beautiful town in the French-speaking part of Switzerland."

The training was no vacation. "We had to climb walls and trees and take care of those designated as wounded and even make temporary bandages from grain stalks. We had to haul in our food and drink in heavy containers and had to march, often singing." She remembers "The Gas Mask Song," which the German-speaking Swiss sang in their own dialect below. The refrain went:

Maskedienscht, dä tuät allne imponiere,	Gasmask duty is everyone's duty,
stundelang muäsch der Glich griff träniere!	On and off—again and again and again!

Of the main stanzas, Schelbert remembers these lines:

Passet uuf, ihr Soldate, gänd schön acht,	Attention, soldiers, take care,
Luäget guet, dass dä Schluuch es Achti macht;	That your hose makes an eight,
Ja keis Siebni söll es si, keis Nüni darf es gä,	Not a seven, not a nine…
Müänd d'Sach numä rächt i d'Finger nä!	Do it right or you're done for.

The war did not put an end to the events of everyday life. Alice well remembers a special Saturday in 1940. "My mother was pregnant, about to give birth to her eleventh child. She asked me to come home early, as she thought the child would be born before noon. When I asked permission from my supervisor, he wanted to know the reason. 'Because my mother is expecting a child!' I answered. 'From whom,' he inquired. 'From my father, of course!' He was dumbfounded and at once gave me permission. At that time many refugee children were arriving in Switzerland, and he assumed that my mother was expecting one of them. . . . Unfortunately I did not make it home in time. When I arrived, the midwife put my new little brother into my arms. Later, when he grew bigger, I took him to the swimming pool. He was unusually thin, and someone there asked: 'Is he a refugee child?' Tuberculosis was still quite common, and you had to have a check-up every year. When I took my brother to the physician, he removed layer after layer of clothing from the boy and finally sighed: 'By God, little fellow, is there anything left of you?!'

"After some time, I chose to serve in the central air alarm station.

There were three of us, one at a table with an ear set to receive orders and, on order, to trigger the air raid alarm; another was to keep the logs; the third rested, since we switched jobs every two hours. The office was small, in a cellar, and with only a tiny window near the ceiling. Normally it was dead quiet, but every so often someone making the rounds would knock at the window and receive our answer: 'All in order!' Sometimes we would sing softly, but mostly the atmosphere was tense with unspoken questions: 'Will there be an air raid alarm again? Will they bomb again somewhere? What if they hit us? What if they should bomb the dam in the Wäggital (which would then mean dangerous flooding all the way to Zurich)? Do we still remember all the things we need to do in case things get really bad? Did everyone remember to darken their windows so that the pilots recognize Swiss territory as a dark area?' Nevertheless Schaffhausen was bombed; paralyzed with horror, I triggered the air raid alarm. We three remained totally quiet even after the alarm was over."

The issue of bombing dams and causing floods is intriguing. The Swiss military itself planned to flood the Linth plain in the event of a German attack, which would have made the eastern invasion route into Switzerland impassable. The known German invasion plans do not mention bombing dams, perhaps for that very reason.

Many women not in the FHD served in occupations related to defense. The following account illustrates some of the ways women were used by Swiss intelligence to reduce the spread of Nazi propaganda and intimidation:

Madame Denise Lecoultre was a young woman in 1939 when she began employment with the Station-des-amplificateurs, Telephon-Central, a division of the Post, Telephone and Telegraph (PTT), on the rue du Mont-Blanc in Geneva. "My office was on the top floor, behind the row of gigantic statues, the ethnic representatives of the various continents of the world, the grandiose symbols of 'international communications.'[11]

"On the night the Germans attacked the French Maginot Line, I was on duty. We knew that if 'the Line' resisted the German thrust, Hitler's armies would choose to pass via Basel and invade Switzerland. Some inhabitants of Basel and the adjoining Cantons had begun their exodus and were telephoning their families and friends who were expecting them. As the interurban network was not yet automatic, the lines were overloaded. We chatted with the callers awaiting a connection to keep them patient. What a memorable night of anguish and terror! Early in the morning, we were amazed and saddened when we learned that our friendly neighbor France had been occupied.

"The Telephone Exchange had been supplied by the Army with officers charged with the supervision and censorship of suspect communications. This was partly carried out at the amplification station through monitoring telephone lines suspected of re-transmitting the messages, speeches and propaganda of the totalitarian countries. I was one of the small team entrusted with the interruption of these unwelcome utterances.

"My very humble role was part of a 'censorship' organized by the military. In the Telephone Exchange of Geneva, we saw officers in uniform discreetly passing through the large telephone center. They had a hidden office where they probably listened to foreign conversations and decoded messages.

"We were three 'girls' in this station, and I was the youngest at 20 years old. Broadcast radio programs were difficult to receive in Switzerland, not only because of the mountains but also because the belligerents jammed radio programs with 'parasites.' As a result many radio programs in Switzerland were transmitted via cable. We called this '*Telédiffusion*.' With a special subscription, Swiss people could receive speeches, news and very good concerts with no 'parasites.' The 'deletions' were part of our neutrality and were strictly observed: no Nazi or Fascist speakers were allowed, and we could delete propaganda simply by pressing keys.

"For 24 hours a day, we three 'girls' with complementary work schedules monitored Axis programs, reporting to our supervisors what we cut and why. Of course, *we* could listen to what we cut! We performed our duty conscientiously without really being aware of its importance." This reference to "neutrality" is revealing, for it illustrates how Switzerland could be "neutral" in a formal political sense but not morally neutral. She did not allow her citizens to be barraged with totalitarian propaganda.

Denise Lecoultre was also involved in helping refugees. She recalls: "The first refugees were those who had the courage and the means to flee, such as those from the professions who arrived with their families, sometimes with their savings. They dispersed in various Cantons and, for the most part, integrated there, their children attending schools and universities. The Swiss Quaker Association provided considerable help and care for these immigrants. Thanks to a family I knew, I was able to attend their meetings and so became aware of the growing dangers of the Nazi dictatorship.

"Courses on postwar mutual aid were organized so that the young of all nationalities would go to the aid of the populations of the devastated countries as soon as the war was over. In 1944, after taking such a course at the School of Social Assistance at Zurich, I spent a period of probation for a few months at the Hôtel des Terrasses in Territet-Montreux, where women refugees were lodged. They were Russians, Yugoslavs, French and Italians who had been 'utilized' by the invaders and had managed to escape, pregnant or with their babies. There were some thirty to forty refugees, mostly women, and about twenty babies. I assisted the principal by accompanying the future mothers to the maternity ward and back to the hotel, and by being available to help them resolve their problems. The organization of this home was simple. The atmosphere was full of conviviality and tolerance.

"Early in the morning, all the refugees and those responsible for them gathered together on the ground floor for roll call and the distribution of duties, allocated according to the varied qualifications of our refugees. For example, two Jewish Italian doctors looked after the health of the mothers and children; a Jewish Italian woman supervised the preparation of meals for the babies. She knew a good deal about infant nutrition and gave advice to the inexperienced foster mothers who helped her; her husband (a former bank director) helped the principal with administrative matters.

"The mothers cleaned their rooms or dormitory, then helped with the care of the children; everybody could come and go in accordance with a prescribed rotation for meal times. All of us, Swiss and refugees, took our meals in the same dining room. The menus of the adults were somewhat monotonous. The staple was boiled potatoes, sometimes with a little jam or cheese. The babies received minced veal liver, high-quality milk products and fruit."

As soon as the war ended, arrangements were made for the refugees to return home. "At Montreux station, when a train was departing for Italy, I was saying goodbye when suddenly a young woman whom I had accompanied to the maternity ward during my training period handed me her baby as she got on the train . . . and vanished. Other Italian refugees on the train took the baby back through the open window, promising they would find its mother. I still often think about that child."

For Swiss children, mobilization meant the sudden departure of fathers and brothers. Gertrud Seiler has a vivid memory of the day the war began in September 1939: "General mobilization! What an unforgettable day! I was only 14. When Father got orders to report to the army, he was in the middle of a delicate process at the factory. He dropped everything, dashed home and immediately packed to leave. We stood around him, deeply depressed and full of anguish. Father hardly spoke and refused to be seen off by any of us. I disregarded his wish and tagged along with him for a short distance. I clung to his hand and felt his fingers tightening around mine. I said more than a thousand words! His features were tense and twitching as he bent down to kiss me farewell. The only words he was able to utter were '*Bhüet Di Gott!*' [God bless you]. His blessing accompanied me all my life! He then went off . . . *alone.* Would we ever see him again? What would become of our country? How was Mother going to manage with her four children and with the family business losing most of its male employees? Tears, anguish and prayers swept through our whole country.[12]

"In the spring of 1940, when the threat seemed greatest, our government ordered civilians from border areas to prepare a backpack with strictly indispensable gear and emergency food rations. So each of us had, by our bedside, a backpack for a possible evacuation, should we be attacked by the Germans." While it is unclear exactly where such civilians would have been directed, obviously it would be south, away from the front. In France, there was a massive civilian exodus away from the advancing German armies.

As the war dragged on, shortages of all kinds worsened. Gertrud Seiler recalls: "Most private homes were equipped with little cast-iron stoves. Only one room could be heated. We made paper briquettes out of old newspapers. Bedrooms were cold. It took hours to fall asleep. Electric stoves were not allowed.

"School children from the age of 14 on were compelled to contribute at least two weeks of their vacation to help farmers. I ended up on a farm that had 40 cherry trees. While at first it seemed great fun to pick cherries, we soon ached all over from standing on a ladder the whole day. We had to whistle while picking cherries, in order not to eat too many!

"I know of hardly any Swiss families who did not take in children from occupied countries to give them a period of recovery. In the war years, we had at least five children. They were supposed to stay three months. Most stayed much longer. It was good to see them gradually losing their fear, putting on weight and becoming normal children again."

Snow was falling as this author interviewed Rita de Quervain at Davos in 2000. "I was 14 when the war broke out. Father was in the army most of the time. Fascist Italy built roads on the Italian side to Switzerland. Father was stationed near the Gotthard, the first time in 1939 and the second time when Germany retreated from northern Italy."[13] That is

The founding of the Swiss Confederation at the Rütli meadow in 1291.

The union was intended to be a perpetual alliance against invaders.

Image: Otto Schön, *Die Schweitzergeschicte in Bildern*, Verlag der J. Dalp'schen Buch und Kunsthandlung in Bern (K. Schmidl), 1872

The Battle of Dornach, 1499.

Switzerland defeated the First Reich in the Swabian War.

Image: Otto Schön *Die Schweitzergeschicte in Bildern*, Verlag der J. Dalp'schen Buch und Kunsthandlung in Bern (K. Schmid), 1872

The Swiss wielded the pike and halberd with a thirst for blood.

To the insult "Sauschwob" (German pig), which already existed as a term as far back as 1499, "Saunazi" (Nazi pig) was added to the Swiss sneers for the Third Reich.

Image: Otto Schön *Die Schweitzergeschicte in Bildern*, Verlag der J. Dalp'schen Buch und Kunsthandlung in Bern (K. Schmid), 1872

General Henri Guisan assembled the officers at the Rütli on July 25, 1940, after France fell, exhorting them to resist any invader at all costs.   Photo: Swiss Mililtary Department.

Corps Commander Herbert Constam, former head of the Swiss military shooting school and the highest-level Jewish officer. German intelligence's assessment: "Very capable. Non-Aryan. Enemy of Germany."

Photo: Swiss Military Department

General Henri Guisan, Commander in Chief of the Swiss armed forces, reviews Alpine sniper exercises.

German intelligence said of Guisan: "Intelligent, very cautious. Behind his overt correctness stands his sympathy with the Western Powers."

Photo: Swiss Military Department

Jewish refugee boys at the Rütli on Swiss National Day 1945, from the Hôme de la Forêt, which cared for young survivors from Buchenwald.

Photo: United States Holocaust Memorial Museum, courtesy of Norbert Bikales

This wing of a Swiss fighter aircraft has been peppered with German machine gun fire in a dogfight, but Swiss planes shot down 11 Luftwaffe aircraft.

Photo: Swiss Military Department

German panzers were another new threat in 1940. The author amid rows of tank barriers still standing at St. Maurice, where the Swiss hoped to ambush the Germans between narrow mountain passes.

Photo: Author

▲ Ski troop maneuvers in the Reduit, the Alpine redoubt which would have been Switzerland's main defensive area in the event of an invasion.

German panzers and the Luftwaffe would not have been effective in the Swiss Alps.

Photos: Swiss Military Department ▼

▲ Rifle with tank mortar shell. Constam drafted tactics combining sharpshooters with anti-tank grenadiers which General Guisan ordered to be implemented in operational plans.

Photo: *Die Schweitz in Waffen: Ein Erinnerungsbuch über den Aktivdienst 1939/45 für Volk und Armee.* (Vaterländischer Verlag A.G., Murten und Zürich, 1945), p. 80

▲ Carrier pigeons are released by Swiss soldiers to send messages in the Reduit. Switzerland ended its carrier pigeon service in the 1990s, the last country to do so.

Photo: Swiss Military Department

The Women's Auxilliary Service (Frauenhilfsdienst or FHD) played a key role in the Swiss Military.

Above: FHD members observe and chart intrusions into Swiss airspace by foreign aircraft.

Below: A military encampment with typical straw bedding. The woman on the left makes sure a gas mask is in proper order while the other two examine the contents of a backpack.

In this training exercise filmed by the Swiss weekly newsreels of the "Ortswehr" (Local Defense Force), a boy scout speeds by on his bicycle to spread news of an invasion. Note his M1889 rifle.

As the newsreel continues, snipers take their positions ready to ambush the invaders and fifth columnists.

Above left, center and right: stills from Swiss Newsreel *(Wochenschau), Landesverteidigung und Ortswehren,* August 1943

"Ortswehr" partisans prepare to throw Molotov cocktails at an approaching enemy vehicle.

"Total war requires total defense," admonishes the news-reel.

War mobilization, September 1939.

In minutes, this farmer dropped his scythe, donned his uniform and grabbed his rifle, said his goodbyes, then left to join his militia unit.

Still from Swiss Newsreel

◄

Women and children were left to do all of the farm work when the men were mobilized.

The workload increased as the economic stranglehold tightened.

Switzerland was forced to grow far more of her own crops.

Image: *La Suisse en Armes: Mobilisation 1939.* (Éditions Patriotiques, Morat, 1940), p. 170

▼

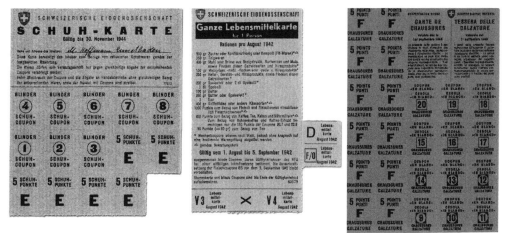

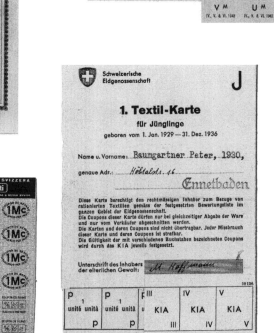

*Food and consumer goods were heavily rationed. Above are ration coupons for shoes,
hot meals, food and clothing.* Original coupons courtesy of Peter Baumgartner-Jost

After the fall of France on June 24, 1940, Hitler's General Staff ordered attack plans to be drawn up against Switzerland. Several were submitted, including the one to the right dated August 12, 1940, under the title "Der Deutsche Angriff Gegen Schweiz."

Image: Bundesärchiv/Militärchiv, Freiburg am Breisgau, Germany

Operationsentwurf Schweiz - Tannenbaum (Draft Operations Plan Switzerland - Chrismas Tree), October 1940.

Bearing the signature of General von Leeb, this was the cover letter for the Tannenbaum attack plan against Switzerland.

Image: Bundesärchiv/Militärchiv, Freiburg am Breisgau, Germany

General Wilhelm Ritter von Leeb, who planned the invasion of Switzerland in 1940.

He assigned the task of "Sonderaufgabe Schweiz" to Army Group C, which was positioned along the western border of Switzerland.

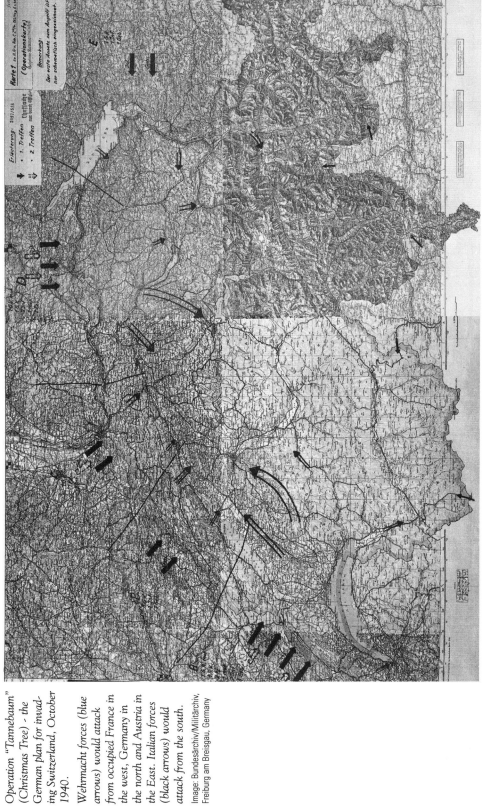

Operation "Tannebaum" (Christmas Tree) – the German plan for invading Switzerland, October 1940.

Wehrmacht forces (blue arrows) would attack from occupied France in the west, Germany in the north and Austria in the East. Italian forces (black arrows) would attack from the south.

Image: Bundesärchiv/Militärchiv, Freiburg am Breisgau, Germany

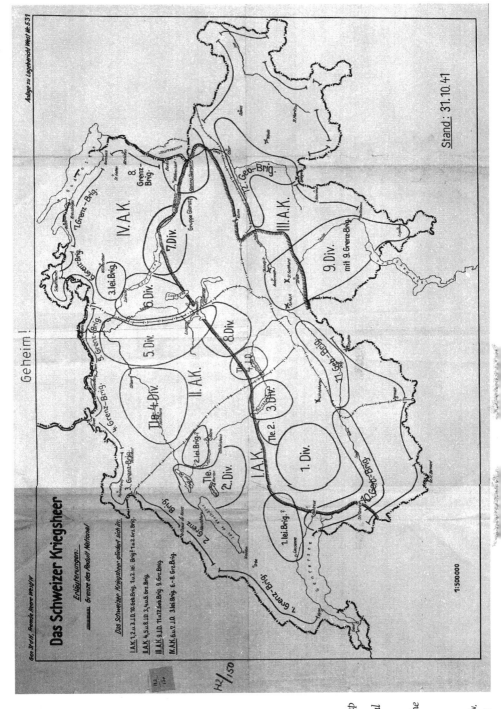

German intelligence map of Swiss troop positions prepared for the General Staff in October 1941. Swiss divisions and brigades are shown at the borders, in the plateau and especially in the Alpine Réduit.

Image: Bundesärchiv/Militärchiv, Freiburg am Breisgau, Germany

"So Würd's bessere!"

Kicking the foreign dogs out. From Switzerland's leading satirical magazine, Nebelspalter, May 1938.

Image: *Gegen Rote und Braune Fäuste*
(Nebelspalter Verlag, Rorschach, 1949)

Shooting the Nazis in the butt with a crossbow. Satire at the Caberet Cornichon. "The Rat Catcher," 1939.

Image: Elsie Attenhofer, *Caberet Cornichon* (Benteli Verlag, Bern, 1975), p. 158

"Die Allerletze Zusammenkunft"

The final reunion - the dead Hitler and Mussolini ascend over the ruins of cities and piles of corpses (Nebelspalter, May 1945).

Image: *Gegen Rote und Braune Fäuste* (Nebelspalter Verlag, Rorschach 1949)

"Die neuen Freunde."

The new friends - Nazi Germany and Communist Russia drip with blood after partitioning Poland (Nebelspalter, September 1939).

Image: *Gegen Rote und Braune Fäuste* (Nebelspalter Verlag, Rorschach, 1949)

Switzerland arranged the rescue of 1200 Jews from Theresienstadt in February 1945. Here they enjoy a warm meal at a school in St. Gallen.

Helping the victims of war. Needy children, mostly from France, were cared for by Swiss families for several months at a time to recuperate. The tags shown here identified each child at train stations.

Swiss soldiers - who protected everyone, including refugees - slept on straw. Some refugees who were able-bodied men did the same. Refugee women and children stayed in hotels and private houses.

Photo: Swiss Military Department.

Many American B-17 Flying Fortresses flying bombing missions over Germany were shot up or ran out of gas. The lucky ones were able to crash-land in Switzerland, which provided safety to over 1,700 American airmen.

Photo: USAAF

General Henri Guisan, the Swiss Commander in Chief, met with American intelligence operative Allen Dulles, who assigned the code number '839' to Guisan.

Guisan passed on intelligence about Nazi preparations for bacteriological warfare to Dulles.

Photo: Swiss Military Department

Allen Dulles, head of the American OSS (Office of Strategic Services), stationed in Bern, Switzerland, which became America's window on the Third Reich.

Images: Allen W. Dulles Papers, Princeton University Seeley G. Mudd Manuscript Library

*Boys at arms in World War II.
Young Swiss train as cadets with
service rifles*

Photo: Gottlieb H. Heer & E. A. Geßler,
*Armee und Volk: Sechs Jahre
Landesverteidigung* (Verkehrsverlag A.G.,
Zürich, 1946)

◀

*The man on the left skates by on a
mini-scooter with a 1911 bolt action
rifle, while the boy on the right carries
the assault rifle 1990, the current
Swiss military service rifle.*

*These scenes from the parade at the
Swiss Federal Shooting Festival in
Morgues, July 2000, show the continuing Swiss tradition of allowing citizens to bear arms, ready at any time
to defend the country.*

Photos: Author

◀   ▶

*The annual Rütli
Schützenfest (shooting festival) takes place annually at
the historic meadow where the
Swiss Confederation was
born.*

November 2002.

Photo: Author

▶

a rugged Alpine region where an attack would have been stoutly resisted.

"Father was a chemical engineer for manufacturers who traded with firms in Germany and Italy before the war. He went to Germany and found some for, and some against, the Nazis. After he returned, he reported what he saw in Germany to Swiss intelligence. Anti-Nazism was strongest in German-speaking Switzerland because they understood Nazism the best. Had the Nazis attacked Switzerland, Father would have been eliminated." The author heard similar comments from many Swiss, who knew that opponents of the Third Reich in occupied countries were executed.

"The son of a German family living in Switzerland went to the Gymnasium with my future husband. The boy later studied theology in Germany and then joined the Wehrmacht. His mother was the head of an organization—German Women of Zurich. Her sister was the Secretary of the German Consulate in Zurich. They acted against Switzerland by sending information and preparing the organization in the event Germany took over.

"We were frightened in 1940 after the fall of Belgium and Holland. I was in a program organized by the Girl Scouts in Zurich to help elderly people. I would go to the old-people's home at 5:00 a.m. every morning and look into the sky to see if the Germans were attacking. Everyone knew the Luftwaffe always began its attacks in the early morning. Later, when Germany became too engaged elsewhere, the fear subsided, and I no longer had to wake up at 5:00."

Rita de Quervain had the typical experiences of helping farm families where the husband was often away on military duty. As a Girl Scout, she was sent to the army near the end of the war for hospital training. She commented: "The standard of living of the ordinary person was low. Some refugees had a higher standard of living, which led to resentment." However, she recounted how public opinion favored letting in more refugees:

"I personally knew Gertrud Kurz, known as 'the mother of refugees.' She was outspoken when the border closed to refugees, and even approached Federal Councilor von Steiger, head of the Federal Department of Justice and Police, in the Valais when he was on holiday there in August 1942. She kept going back to see him every single day, with phone calls coming in to her from border guards asking, 'Can we let them in now?' At the middle of the week she told them, 'Yes, von Steiger agreed.' The guards responded: 'Thank God we can let them in!' Von

Steiger agreed at the end of the week!" The formal decisions to close the border and then to reopen it are described in the next chapter of this volume. This anecdote exemplifies the desire of humanitarians and soldiers alike to rescue refugees. Rita de Quervain continues:

"I graduated from the Gymnasium in 1944. I went to Geneva to study and worked for several months as the cook in a camp for 30 refugee children, some Christian and some Jewish. The children were from Italy, Poland, France and Germany.

"Some children did not have enough meat. Orthodox rabbis would not allow them to eat non-Kosher meat, but kosher slaughter methods were not allowed under Swiss animal protection laws. Rabbis came regularly to the camp to give instruction, teach religion and for festivities. We had very good relations with the rabbis and did not try to convert anyone."

The above accounts come from ordinary young people during the war. The following, however, is by a woman who was in the top echelon and an official responsible for finding housing for refugee women and children.

Hedwig Stamm, whom this author interviewed when she was a very alert 92 years old, worked for *Heimat und Lager* from the late fall of 1942 until 1948. More precisely, the organization was called *Eidgenössische Zentralleitung der Heimat und Lager/Direction fédérale des homes et camps*—Federal Administration for Home and Camp. She acted as the right hand for Dr. Heinrich Rothmund, Director of the Police Division in the Federal Department of Justice and Police, administering over 50 "homes" (tourist hotels) for refugee women and children, the majority of whom were Jewish. The men stayed in camps nearby. The first to open was the Hotel Bellevue in Schaffhausen. The network of refugee hotels eventually reached from northern Switzerland down to Interlaken and west to the Lake of Geneva, and to the south in Ticino. For military security reasons, hotels in the Réduit were not used for refugees.[14]

"I began on November 15, 1942, as *Helfsleiterin* (assistant manager) of the Home Management Department. By December I was in charge of all of the refugee homes. The owner had to agree to rent the hotel. I had to get permission from the local and cantonal authorities and, in areas where refugees were disallowed, I had to get special permission." The disallowed locations were in militarily sensitive areas.

"Some persons coming over the border had valid papers, others had false papers. Others no papers at all. The first stop after crossing the border was the *Auffanglager*, a primitive screening camp where identities were checked and verified. They were like military camps; refugees did not sleep directly on straw, but on bags filled with straw for mattresses. One took a shower and had a medical examination before proceeding to the camp. A band would be playing music. If there was a difficulty, a refugee might be detained in the *Auffanglager*. Soldiers stood guard because there might be spies. Otherwise the military had nothing to do with the camps.

"Once cleared, women, children, doctors, other professionals, musicians and members of theatrical groups went to the *Flüchtlingsheime*, refugee homes. Able-bodied men were placed in *Arbeitslager*, work camps near the hotels where the women and children stayed. The men were required to work. They were not allowed simply to stay in the hotels with the women and children. Jewish organizations helped place some Jewish refugees in private homes.

"Refugees were paid 2.80 Swiss francs per day. However, the pay of people placed in homes depended on what work they did. Many did kitchen duties and sanitation. Men in camps were paid for work such as drainage projects for farmers.

"Some work was 'make work' which nonetheless enabled them to learn a trade and get paid. There were some large workshops where they could choose carpentry, shoemaking or tailoring. Girls learned housekeeping and were trained as in a kind of finishing school. Special places were set up for the elderly. Pregnant women went to designated shelters with medical services. There was even a home for intellectuals in Geneva, where many attended the university.

"There were more refugees than residents in the resorts of Canton Valais. The tourist hotels had, of course, no tourists.

"Emigrants were distinguished from refugees. By and large, the Jewish emigrants had papers and came to Switzerland before the war. Many German Jews came to Switzerland during 1934–35. Some of these went on to England. Most of the emigrants were educated Jews from Austria. Many were professionals.

"Jewish emigrants played a key role in helping to administer and care for the Jewish refugees who followed them. You could rely on the emigrants. Homes for the elderly included Swiss nurses and an emigrant staff. Swiss dentists assisted by emigrants went to the camps and hotels. Without the emigrants, there would have been chaos in many places.

"Behavior problems existed in refugee camps. Some refugees destroyed furniture. You could tell the class of people by the damage they did. Some were opposed to any authority and did not clean the WC, requiring refugee doctors and assistant managers to clean up. In one incident, some women kept stealing the cook's pans. I ordered that only soup would be served until they were returned. The pans were returned. No angels, those refugees!" Hedwig Stamm's remarks are plainspoken, but they reflect the true experiences of a person who helped to rescue the victims of Nazi Germany. She continued:

"In fall 1942, the first Dutch refugees came to Chexbres. The Dutch Jews abided by kosher rules. That led to conflicts. After the war, Queen Juliana visited Luzern and asked for the bill for giving sanctuary to the Dutch Jews, but Switzerland forgave the debt.

"I located over 50 hotels for refugees. I rejected some hotels as unsuitable due to problems with water, chimneys, and other defects. There were extra expenses for transportation, food, and other items when the hotels were located in the mountains.

"The hotel in Luzern had a large, modern facility which laundered clothes for refugee camps all over Switzerland. Occupants kept busy with mending, ironing and running the steamrollers. The refugees had enough clothes to send some off to this laundry."

As noted, Swiss refugee policy was administered by Heinrich Rothmund of the Federal Department of Justice and Police. Hedwig Stamm recalls: "Dr. Rothmund was tall and imposing. Annual conventions of managers of homes and camps were held at the Congress House in Zurich to hear complaints and resolve problems. About 700 people attended. I sat next to Dr. Rothmund, who said, 'I'm the most criticized man in Switzerland.'"

Head of the Department was Federal Councilor Eduard von Steiger, who was also severely criticized. Hedwig Stamm recalled that von Steiger attended one of the above meetings and said, "'Every refugee has a right to write me personally, and every one will be answered.' Yet a Swiss private in the army could not write and get an answer. Von Steiger heard complaints about that." It seems that those in charge of refugee policy could satisfy no one. While Swiss refugee policy is analyzed in detail in the next chapter, Stamm's observations give a close-up view of the realities of refugee life. She continued:

"Movement was restricted by the police. The authorities set hours and boundaries [for travel]. They could leave during the day and did not have to sign out.

"I knew emigrants personally, but not refugees. Associating with refugees would have led to jealousy." Although emigrants were originally foreigners, they had become permanent residents and were active in assisting Swiss officials and professionals in caring for refugees. Refugees were persons who were taken in for humanitarian reasons but were not permanent residents.

"Rations were the same for refugees as for Swiss people in retirement homes. Salad dressing was made from butter-making residue. A soup was made that tasted so good it was named after Hürlimann beer! Potatoes were mixed with the bread, which could not be consumed until it was two days old. It got gooky. Refugees from the Eastern countries were accustomed to large amounts of cheap, non-nutritious food, and had enlarged stomachs. Under rationing, there was a sufficient amount of nutritious food." Potato bread was the only bread available in Switzerland to everyone, citizens and refugees alike. Potatoes were needed to make large quantities of this bread, and the potatoes were cultivated in every arable piece of land in the country. The two-day rule was devised to make the bread harder, more filling, and less desirable so it would not be eaten quickly.

It was Hedwig Stamm's job to care for refugees, but police were concerned with security and were not as sympathetic to their concerns. Stamm relates: "Signs were posted throughout Switzerland: 'Whoever cannot hold his tongue, harms his homeland!' Police wanted to restrict refugees for security reasons. The mayor of Luzern was in favor of taking in more refugees, but police chief Walter Strebi opposed it. Strebi imposed restrictions on refugees. I proposed a liberal plan, which he rejected. After all these years I still have fire in my heart. He made me mad!

"I also quarreled with Colonel Hauptmann in Zermatt, who said that 'for military reasons I cannot give permission for that hotel.' I got him on the phone, expressed my anger and got the permit. I would not tolerate interference with helping refugees, despite the military threat from Germany."

92-year old Hedwig Stamm concluded our interview: "I never heard of any anti-Semitism in Switzerland. Swiss were preoccupied with daily food. Women had to keep things running when husbands were mobilized. Regarding charges in the late 1990s about the work camps, I feel exasperation that we only hear from men complaining about the camps. We hear nothing about the women and children—they lived in hotels."

The above aside about economic difficulties could be illustrated in countless ways. The following segment concerns a factory that processed rubber products.

Fifty-one-year-old Andreas Capol, a veteran of the World War I mobilization, was called up again on August 28, 1939, into a border protection company. Since he was president of the rubber factory Gummi-Werke Richterswil AG, he was granted a short leave in September. Returning, he found great unrest and dissatisfaction at the factory.[15]

It seems that Dr. H.J. von Fischer, a 40-year-old chemist from Austria, was plant manager. "While Fischer had opposed Hitler after the Anschluss, he later married a Sudeten German girl named Ritter who turned him to Nazism. The Fischers became aggressively vocal, creating tension in the factory and village, where people were anti-Nazi. Mrs. Fischer criticized Swiss soldiers and members of the Home Defense, and Mr. Fischer complained when soldiers practiced near the plant or trampled on flowers. It was reported that on Sundays the Fischers received Nazi visitors. The authorities began to monitor the Fischers' telephone conversations."

It was learned that Mr. Fischer was a leader of the Nazi *Partei-Genossen*. He became increasingly unpopular at the factory, and his performance went downhill. At last he suffered a nervous breakdown, blaming Mr. Capol, who remembered: "He was arrogant about it, saying: 'The Führer takes notice of everything, he will forget nothing and will call you to account in due course!' Apparently my fault was that I had reprimanded him for greeting the office staff in the morning with the '*Hitler-Gruss*' [Hitler greeting]." When Fischer continued his Nazi activities, the company fired him and then, in 1941, the Swiss government banished the couple from the country. For this too he blamed Capol. As Fischer took leave of his few friends, he said, "Till we meet again."

Fischer also filed a report, later shown to be false, alleging that the company violated gasoline-rationing restrictions. This could have caused the company's export business to collapse, since gasoline was essential as a solvent for the fabrication of certain rubber products. Capol had to intervene with the authorities in Bern to restore the allotment.

Raw materials were increasingly hard to come by. The authorities controlled the small stocks of crude rubber. Capol heard from the Swiss Military Department about the waste of large amounts of scrap rubber in the manufacture of army gas masks. The company was able to obtain worn tires and other discarded materials and transform it into tons of high-quality rubber.

As coal supplies dwindled as well, the company turned to tree trunks and low-calorie domestic brown coal for fuel. Capol remembers: "With an electric wood saw and a cutting machine, we sawed the tree trunks into small blocks, storing them by the boiler house. We also purchased pine cones and even sent unoccupied workers into the forest to collect them. Storage of the pine cones close to the boiler house caused problems. Thousands of insects swarmed out and harassed us."

Switzerland's struggle for economic survival took some strange turns. Despite the fact that Switzerland is totally landlocked, ocean-going vessels flying the Swiss flag played an important role in furnishing the country with necessities and in aiding humanitarian efforts for the Allies.

Albert Vogel remembers: "Not many Swiss worked with our seagoing vessels, and only a few are still alive. I happen to be one of them. Switzerland had 14 ships, of which 3 were used exclusively by the International Committee of the Red Cross (ICRC) carrying POW food parcels from Philadelphia to the Mediterranean ports of Genoa, Toulon, Marseille, and Barcelona. From autumn 1944 onward, trucks and trailers were also shipped by sea, so that the parcels could be transported to the POW camps. Since railroads by then had been largely destroyed, truck drivers were sent out by bus from Switzerland.[16]

"The remaining eleven vessels under the Swiss flag could not sail without a Navigation Certificate, or 'Navicert.' Navicerts were issued by the Allied Naval Command when the loading papers had been forwarded and they had assured themselves with inspections that the papers matched the cargo actually on board. All vessels had to pass Gibraltar. There the daily positions, transmitted by wireless, could be compared with the logbook and charts whenever the slightest doubt existed as to any delay during the sea voyage which could have been used to supply a German patrol boat or a U-boat. Upon arrival in Switzerland the cargo was cleared by customs. It must have been very easy for Allen Dulles (head of U.S. intelligence in Bern) to compare the customs papers with the original manifests. The Swiss seagoing vessels did not supply the Axis powers.

"I made about six voyages from the United States to Spain to ship parcels to U.S. and Canadian POWs. The packets contained food, chewing gum, cigarettes and other items. These Swiss flagships also carried raw materials from Africa and elsewhere to Switzerland. I was on a Swiss flagship which a submarine torpedoed and sank." Albert Vogel obviously survived, but sea lanes were always dangerous in wartime and mistakes almost inevitable.

With imported goods cut off by both the Allies and the Germans, Switzerland promoted makeshift production at home. Peter Voser, who was born in Baden in 1923, recalls:

"Owning a garden was extremely important during the Depression and then later during the wartime cultivation effort known as the Wahlen plan. Many workers got into fights to get a garden plot. People were using wood and coal to heat. Poor people were collecting wood in the forest. Wood collection cards cost five Swiss francs and permitted the owner to collect wood in the entire forest. With the cultivation battle starting in 1939, every family had to work a plot. Since we had left our large house with garden for a small roof apartment, an acquaintance gave us a small field in Birmensdorf where we had to grow potatoes. It was hard manual labor, especially since he seemed to have given us the piece of land with the most clay. Accordingly, we were poorly motivated and the yield was poor too. We abandoned our contribution to the Wahlen plan soon.[17]

"Bread was the most important basic foodstuff, while today it is more of a side food. In the military, men received one pound of bread a day. During the war we could not buy fresh bread. There was only dark bread, and the flour was supplemented with potato starch. We had to make certain that the bread was not kept in too warm a room because it would turn sour and become inedible very fast. The flip side was that the Swiss population was never as healthy as during the war. There were only slim people.

"Today everybody eats meat, but meat was scarce then. During the war I took a bicycle trip to Appenzell. We decided to rest in Trogen. We went to a restaurant and ordered spaghetti because it was cheap. When we were served the large plates and were digging into the spaghetti, we discovered a small piece of meat which the generous host had smuggled in. That was strictly forbidden on meatless days (there were three per week, and we were traveling on one of them). You can imagine with how much pleasure we ate our meal.

"Blue-collar workers lived outside Baden in Wettingen and rode bicycles to work. At the beginning and end of work, there were masses of bikes like you see today in China! The people rode their bikes through the city and below the narrow city tower. At the railroad crossing on Bruggerstrasse there was a traffic jam."

Whether the day was meatless or not, a ration card was required. A meal at a restaurant required a *Mahlzeitencoupon*, a coupon with either "1 Mc" (a full meal) or "1/2 Mc" (half a meal, such as a sandwich). To purchase food, one needed a *Berechtigungs-Ausweis* just to get food coupons and a *Ganze Lebensmittel Karte*, the monthly food card. Purchase of clothing required the *Textil-Karte*, and for shoes the *Schuh-Karte*. The *Seifenkarte*, the ration card for men's soap, was printed with the exhortations "save soap—do not use hard water" and "before washing, put soda in the water with the soap." Numerous other ration cards were in use. Misuse or sale of a coupon was penalized.[18]

Finding adequate shelter was not an easy task for many. Arthur Oberle, who was born in 1921, described living conditions during the Depression. "Our family lived in a block of six apartments, each consisting of 3 rooms. Two of the three rooms had a heating stove for wood and coal. In order to save money we used to collect fir cones. Each apartment had one WC (water closet or toilet), and there was one cold-water faucet in the kitchen. The basement of each block was equipped with two laundry rooms and a bathtub. Each person in the block was entitled to a full bath every third week. The water had to be heated in a wood-fired stove. My father was a pattern maker at the Brown Boveri Company. There was insufficient work, so he worked two-weeks-on, two-weeks-off for many years, earning just half a normal wage. The majority of people living in these workers' quarters (a total of 100 families) were on the Left politically, but one thing was clear: there was not a single Nazi among them.[19]

"We moved to a two-family house shortly before World War II broke out in 1939. This meant exceptional comfort for us: a full bathroom and central heating with a boiler right in the apartment!

"I was a machinist apprentice at Brown Boveri, did my basic military training in 1941, and completed vocational education with exams during a three-day break from military service. I spent the remaining war years either in the army or at college and later at the Federal Institute of Technology (ETH), where I graduated in 1946.

"During all these years I never came in close contact with a Nazi. They did not exist in the social environment where I grew up. We knew they were there, but Nazi sympathizers amounted to only a small percentage of the population.

"There were many who were scared, believing that too vigorous and open opposition to Germany could provoke Hitler to attack. For very good reasons, many Jews in Switzerland belonged to this group, since they would have had to suffer most under German occupation."

Hedi Köppel was born in 1922 and lived at Rorschach on Lake Constance, the north shore of which is part of Germany. She remembers: "In 1935 we heard about the concentration camps. From then on I had refugee classmates in every grade in school right through upper-level. Refugee children went to school like any Swiss. My graduating class in

1941 had six Jewish girls, one of whom was the daughter of a well-known German conductor, Klaiber. These girls received their diplomas with us, and several of them stayed in Switzerland to take jobs.[20]

"In 1938, we heard about the Night of the Broken Glass (*Kristallnacht*) on the radio. My father was horrified. I didn't associate Jewish names with being Jewish then; it never occurred to me. Jews did not segregate themselves. They participated in community life like everyone else. They served in the army and became officers if they chose. They might be lawyers, doctors, teachers or workers. They were Swiss first, then Jewish, just as the rest of us were Swiss first, then Catholic or Protestant."

In the years after Hitler came to power in 1933, "we Swiss worked hard to develop fortifications and beef up our infantry, artillery and even our little air force. This put an enormous strain on the national treasury." The continuing Depression made it difficult. "We tried to keep our sense of humor, and there were jokes about the Swiss military. A story goes that when Mussolini invaded Abyssinia in 1935, he called our Defense Minister, demanding to borrow Swiss tanks. The councilor replied, 'Did you want one, or both?'

"In 1937 I joined a girl scout program which trained us to help neighbors in the event of a disaster. We were encouraged to join the Red Cross as junior members. We worked with kids, served in soup kitchens for the very poor, and practiced first aid. We knew that if there were a German attack, all kinds of community services would be desperately needed.

"When the war started in 1939, our Red Cross group was integrated into the army with the first mobilization. I was still 16 years old when I suddenly found myself, with my best friend Susi, a member of the army's Women's Auxiliary Service, the FHD (*Frauenhilfsdienst*). We were packed off to a military hospital in the interior. When it was discovered after a couple of weeks that we were underage, we were sent back to school, much to our disappointment. But we were not out of the army. Once we had our diplomas, we were called up every year for 3–4 months' duty.

"We took the oath and they read us the Articles of War. You could be executed for so many acts of assisting the enemy—passing messages, giving information, providing material help, and on and on. Susi asked me, 'Are you sure you want to stay?'

"In uniform, we wore the FHD armband. Other auxiliary services were also organized to free male soldiers for the hard part—fighting an invading enemy. The Red Cross had many nurses on duty in field hospitals. I did clerical work.

"I never had official firearms training, but I had gone often with my father to the shooting range where every male was required to practice. Father would occasionally have me shoot. I still remember the kick of the gun on my shoulder. No bulls-eyes! The army instructed us only how to handle a loaded gun. We were not to be treated as combatants.

"Living on the border we knew that if there was a German invasion, our whole region would be sacrificed. Our retreating army would blow up every bridge (they were all mined), every rail terminal, main roads—everything that would help the enemy move.

"My father, a schoolteacher, went on active duty for four months at a time. My mother didn't handle this well—she got panicky and depressed; with five dependent children (aside from me) she could never take her situation calmly.

"In 1940, the Germans sealed the border and amassed huge numbers of men and equipment facing Switzerland. We mounted our second total mobilization. Everything inside the country was under military control—railways, roads, bridges, power plants. We quickly learned that the German threat to us was a feint—they invaded France through Belgium. It wasn't as though they couldn't have taken Switzerland rather quickly, but they must have known we would put up a savage fight and leave them only ruins.

"Once the air war started in earnest, the British and the Americans flew high-altitude bombers over Switzerland, knowing they were safe from our guns. The German Embassy complained repeatedly, but we told them we could not stop Allied planes flying over our territory. If a German plane crossed our border, our fighters attacked instantly. In my hometown I saw two German fighters pursued by four Swiss fighters which were firing in earnest. One of the German planes was hit and crashed in Lake Constance.

"For a time during the war, I worked in a machine tool factory in Rorschach belonging to an old Jewish family named Levy. The company bore their name. The Germans still placed huge orders with us to replace equipment lost in the bombings. Our company needed permission from the Swiss government for these exports, which they issued only with long delays and dragging of feet. German representatives came to do business. We hated them; they greeted us with "Heil Hitler" in the halls. If we replied with a reluctant "*grüezi*" (Swiss German dialect for "hello"), we really wanted to slug them in their faces. Behind their backs we called them '*Sauschwabe*' (Swabian pigs), our name for all Germans."

Hedi Köppel told an interesting anecdote that well illustrates the curious ways of Swiss democracy. In Switzerland the Federal President and other officials are treated like anyone else. Many people would not even know the name of the President or recognize him on the street. Marcel Pilet-Golaz was Federal President in 1940 and thereafter became the Foreign Minister. In 1943, Hedi went to work for the Foreign Office in Bern. "One evening I was waiting to sign out of the building when Pilet-Golaz arrived. He swept past the sentry, who sternly called him back. He protested, 'I am Pilet-Golaz!' The sentry said only, 'Anyone can say that!' Pilet-Golaz was required to sign in. No one knew who he was because he did not arrive in a limousine with flags—he took the streetcar to work.

"We had a fairly large German population living in Switzerland. During the war there seemed to be more of them. It was known that German residents were organized by the German embassy into a fifth column. They held open rallies wearing green pants and white socks, sang Nazi songs, and raised their arms to 'Heil Hitler.' A fifteen-year-old German boy I knew told me that one day his father would be the boss of Rorschach." Hedi anticipated a full-scale war: "If the Germans came, the Swiss would have no way to make prisoner camps, so they would just have to get rid of them." She continues: "Willi Wohlgennant, a Swiss Jewish businessman and soldier colleague who became a lifelong friend, told me that Jews in Switzerland got a lot of moral support, and they in turn made great efforts to help refugees, both Jewish and others. He also told me of the fear Swiss Jews felt—his sister had already fled to America.

"My father was stationed right on the border when he was on active duty. Often he told us of the refugees who tried to enter Switzerland. They would first have to pass the German border guards. If they had the right documents, they were allowed through. Those who didn't pass were almost certainly Jewish. They were sent back. This enraged my father. He saw it happen day after day. As the war went on, the German guards became more brutal. But once a refugee reached the Swiss border, he usually made it.

"Two to three hundred refugees—Jews, gypsies, political fugitives— were staying in my hometown. Nobody asked them why they were there; we knew only too well. Many had a chance to work at regular jobs—in wartime, everyone is needed. The hardships they faced were the hardships every Swiss had to bear. Housing was difficult and scarce. We all had poor food. The whole army slept on straw mattresses or just plain straw.

"As an industrial country, Switzerland was not self-sufficient in food.

We imported alot. During the war our devil's bargain with the enemy allowed some food in (never enough) in exchange for manufactures. Every bit of land that could be spared was planted with potatoes, grain and vegetables. No geraniums in Swiss parks! We even had our own fleet of chartered freighters bring food from South America—the 'Swiss Navy.' I later came to America on one of these.

"Cooking gas was rationed. Cooking became a nightmare for many housewives. Often two or three families in a building would cook one joint meal for everybody—a soup or a stew to make one warm meal a day. My family, with five young children, often went to the soup kitchen for a hot meal.

"Everybody in Switzerland was cold. Coal, too, came from Germany. For every briquette there were conditions—all repugnant. In winter I could see my breath when I woke up in my room. In school, we wore mittens to avoid frostbite. When we were at home in the evening, a small stove heated a single room. We went to the public bath because there wasn't gas to heat enough water at home.

"Of course, we were not unique. The Swiss knew quite well that nearly all the rest of Europe suffered these hardships routinely and, in countries at war, much worse ones. We were grateful we were not under the bombs or the tanks. We were still, uneasily, free.

"When Germany surrendered in 1945, there were huge celebrations in Switzerland just as in all liberated Europe. Church bells rang, and thanksgiving services were held in every church and every synagogue.

"Switzerland officially represented both Allied and German interests in negotiations between the two sides. After the surrender, I was sent to the German embassy in Bern with a Swiss foreign office team to conduct an inventory. The embassy chimneys had been pouring out smoke for days. German domestic workers were still there, keeping the premises tidy. They couldn't help themselves—they still clicked their heels and almost bowed when they announced, 'Coffee is ready.' But they did not say, 'Heil Hitler.'

"I was next assigned to work for the Swiss Foreign Service in the United States. Off to my first foreign post aboard a ship of the 'Swiss Navy,' I landed in Philadelphia in June, in time to see American troops— and a crowd of their anxious dependents—at the time of their massive movement by rail to the Pacific coast. I reported to the Swiss consulate in Los Angeles. Fortunately, the passengers on those trains had only a few weeks to wait for a second mammoth celebration, the surrender of Japan."

These recollections of Hedi Köppel and others represent only a small part of experiences in wartime Switzerland. The individuals this author interviewed were young when the war started. Hopefully more oral history from that heroic generation will be recorded before these memories are lost forever in the passage of time.

CHAPTER 9

THE "J" STAMP, THE LIFEBOAT, AND REFUGEES

The Goldstein family was among the group of nearly 1,000 Jewish refugees who sailed across the Atlantic on the ill-fated S.S. *St. Louis* in May of 1939. Denied entry to Cuba, the United States, and elsewhere in the Americas, the ship was finally forced to return to Europe. The Goldsteins managed to disembark in France, where they lived until 1942, when Herr Goldstein was seized and deported to Auschwitz. Frau Goldstein and young Heinz hid in an attic until they were able to acquire false papers and a guide to the Swiss border. They walked over pastures to Geneva. Although they entered Switzerland illegally, they were not turned back.

At first, both mother and son were taken to a reception camp in the countryside. It was Spartan but certainly adequate. Heinz spent Christmas with the family of a Swiss staff sergeant who welcomed the young German boy into his home. Heinz eventually was able to move in with a Swiss Jewish family. He enrolled in the local high school and joined the Swiss boy scouts. His mother was moved to a more permanent internment facility in a former resort hotel in Luzern which had been converted to house refugees. Later in the war, she was reunited with her son, who by that time was attending a school near Zurich. In 1947, both Goldsteins immigrated to the United States. Heinz—now Henry—would recall: "I never encountered any act of anti-Semitism in six years living in Switzerland!"[1]

Despite hundreds of personal recollections like these, in recent years persistent allegations have arisen that Swiss refugee policy was anti-Semitic. The charge is made that in 1938 it was the Swiss who suggested to German officials that passports of German Jews be stamped with a "J" so they could be readily identified—and denied access. It was certainly true that some Swiss officials asked whether "the Swiss lifeboat was full," in view of the fact that Switzerland, with its limited food supplies, resources, high unemployment and fragile social order, could not absorb every refugee who came to her borders. As was typical of the lively Swiss democracy, such officials were sharply criticized by Swiss who wanted to do more for refugees.

In fact, Switzerland, with a 1940 population of 4.2 million, accepted a proportionately larger number of refugees—particularly Jews—than did the great democracies, including the United States. The border rules changed again and again as the war progressed, and were in any case made by a handful of assigned bureaucrats. Due to the wartime empowerment of the executive branch of government, they were not subject to the local or national referenda that frequently established Swiss policy as per the practice of direct democracy. The general Swiss population neither participated in—nor was in many cases aware of—ongoing decisions about refugee policy. Segments of Swiss society that were more aware—the press, religious bodies, and many other concerned individuals and groups—openly denounced certain of these policies. Moreover, "official" rules about refugees were widely ignored—effectively nullified—by many border guards, local officials, and whole communities in the border areas.

During the wartime period, the senior bureaucrat who made and enforced controversial immigration decisions was Heinrich Rothmund, Director of the Police Division of the Federal Department of Justice and Police (*Eidgenössisches Justiz- und Polizeidepartement*, EJPD). He had headed the Federal Police for Foreigners since 1919.[2] During critical wartime years, Federal Councilor Eduard von Steiger was head of the EJPD and politically responsible for refugee policy.

Wartime decisions on the subject of refugees were exhaustively reviewed in a 1957 report commissioned by the Federal Council and authored by Professor Carl Ludwig.[3] The Ludwig report included the full text of most of the important documents that became the basis for Alfred Häsler's *The Lifeboat Is Full*, an excellent, albeit critical, account.[4]

Numerous firsthand accounts written by Jewish refugees are readily available. Ken Newman, himself a refugee, has produced a compilation of eyewitness testimony of refugees in Swiss wartime work camps.[5] In addition, Swiss author Meir Wagner has assembled moving accounts of Swiss who saved the lives of Jewish refugees and who were later named by Yad Vashem as "Righteous Among the Nations."[6]

Before and during the war, virtually all countries followed extremely restrictive immigration policies, and enforced special restrictions concerning the classification of refugee. Widespread poverty, shifting geopolitical boundaries following World War I, the Russian Revolution, the Spanish Civil War, and the flotsam and jetsam of European empires created waves of people seeking to escape, cross borders and resettle. With the advent of the Depression in the 1930s, social orders were hard-pressed to deal with their own restless unemployed. Amidst factory strikes, pitched battles in the streets, and the collapse of currencies and public order, few countries were eager to take on more "huddled masses yearning to be free." There was great fear of social chaos.

As the situation in Europe deteriorated, Switzerland, a small country surrounded by the political and social disruption in Germany, France, Italy and Austria, feared being overrun and losing its identity through "inundation by foreigners" (*Überfremdung* in German). Also, during the Depression the Swiss, like most others, wanted to protect the country's dwindling number of jobs for Swiss citizens. Fear of massive unemployment was a constant theme.[7] The traditional role of Switzerland as a refugee haven was not forgotten, however. The Swiss were reluctant to refuse refugees, and initially adopted a compromise based on residency. After Hitler seized power in Germany in early 1933, the EJPD issued regulations, approved by the Federal Council (the head of the Swiss executive branch), under which the borders were to be kept open, but refugees in most cases were to be granted only temporary residence. They had to move on in due course. Political refugees, a definition which evolved over time, were given special consideration.[8]

The Nazi regime quickly moved toward a totalitarian reorganization of German society. With compulsive efficiency, it declared whole classes of people enemies of the state, and started the process of rooting them out of the German Volk. Political opponents, Jews, Masons, Jehovah's Witnesses, gypsies, the disabled, the mentally ill, many Catholic priests, homosexuals and other "undesirables" were encouraged to leave Germany minus their property and possessions, deprived of their livelihoods and subjected to increasing intimidation and physical violence. Those who resisted or could be labeled as criminals or traitors began to be placed in concentration camps. Wolfgang Langhoff's *Die Moorsoldaten* (*The Swamp Soldiers*), published in Zurich as early as 1935, was the first major exposé of Nazi concentration camps.[9]

Prompted by the authorities in Nazi Germany, the flight began. But where could refugees go? Virtually every European country plus the United States had restrictive quotas. Because Switzerland, like Holland and Belgium, had a direct border with Germany, the Swiss feared they would be overrun with refugees, who would complicate their already tense relations with the Nazi state and swell the ranks of the unemployed. The Nazis dubbed Switzerland—an open, tolerant society with a free press— a "liberal Jew-state" and a "Freemasons' democracy."[10] The Swiss were also characterized as "*Bergsemiten*," mountain Semites.

There was also the rising military threat. Swiss policymakers knew how dependent their own economy was on Germany for foodstuffs, coal and raw materials. Without German imports, the Swiss economic situation, already battered by the worldwide Depression, would be grim. The Germans knew they had a stranglehold, and were quick to use it against the Swiss. Any decisions the Swiss made regarding borders also risked German tit-for-tat reprisals against Swiss living in or traveling to Germany. The fairly large contingent of Germans resident in Switzerland posed the danger of a German fifth column.[11] The employment situation was tense, and newcomers had to be supported. They could not be immediately put to work. Throughout this period there was a fear of skilled foreign workers displacing Swiss in the labor market. Unemployment and displacement continued to be boiling hot political issues. Therefore refugees—at least in large numbers—created mounting political pressure.

So-called illegals, people without permission to enter (visas were not required of Germans or Austrians) or without travel documents, were a special problem. However, lack of documentation did not disqualify a refugee's entry into Switzerland, and refugees were to be returned to Germany only in exceptional cases. Flexibility was urged in dealing with illegal entrants.[12] Swiss policymakers gradually began to resist the flood. In early 1938, Rothmund explained that "because of our geographical location, the foreign overpopulation, and the many foreigners living on our land, as well as because of the state of our job market, Switzerland can only be a country of transit for new refugees."[13]

Germany began an ominous—and under international law, illegal— one-way visa policy. For "undesirables," visas would be granted only for departure, not for return. Then, in January 1938, a Swiss citizen living in Leipzig noticed, on renewing his traveler's identity card required by the Germans, that a red stamp "Jew" had been added. German authorities informed him that "this stamp was being used for all 'non-Aryans' regardless of whether native or foreign, and that exceptions could not be made for Swiss citizens."[14] This was a harbinger of what would become the notorious "J" stamp which identified Jews.

Events were overtaking policy. Germany's Anschluss of Austria on March 12, 1938, precipitated an immediate refugee crisis as thousands of Austrian Jews, under Nazi pressure, were forced to flee. European countries would not, with few exceptions, admit these refugees.[15] The Swiss Federal Council ordered the reinstitution of visa requirements for holders of Austrian passports. However, Switzerland at first readily granted visas and accepted refugees. Roughly 4,000 Austrians thus legally entered Switzerland by April 1.[16]

This small flood occasioned by the issuance of visas for citizens of—and refugees from—the new Grossdeutschland rapidly became problematic. Was there to be a "visa barrier" and, if so, what kind? Initially, Swiss authorities considered mandatory visas for all German passport holders residing in Austria.[17] Germany immediately threatened retaliation. On May 16, Privy Councilor Roediger of the German Foreign Ministry told Paul Dinichert, Swiss minister to Germany, that if Switzerland started requiring visas for German-Austrians and extended that requirement to all Germans, Germany would demand that all Swiss have German visas to enter Germany. This would have severely curtailed all cross border traffic and effectively cut Switzerland's "lifeline" by vastly complicating the import of foodstuffs and fuel. Using visas across the board to restrict immigration thus became dangerous. However, Dinichert did report to the Federal Council: "The simplest solution, of course, would be to restrict the visa requirement to non-Aryan German citizens. This is admittedly repugnant to our principles, but it could easily be justified in that it is also in the interest of Swiss Jews to be protected against any further influx of foreign Jews."[18] This "simple solution" was not taken by the Swiss.

Entry permits were a painful problem throughout the world. Right after the Anschluss, U.S. President Franklin Roosevelt proposed an international conference to establish a permanent agency to assist the primarily Jewish refugees emigrating from Germany and Austria. Thirty-two governments participated in the resulting Evian conference, which was held in July 1938. It soon emerged that the conferees were more interested in getting rid of, rather than accepting, refugees.[19]

Switzerland shared a border with Austria and offered at least a relatively easy, if not necessarily secure, escape. Soon the Swiss government saw that the number of refugees was already overwhelming support services. Switzerland needed and demanded help. Swiss representative Rothmund told the Evian conferees that the German and Austrian refugees admitted since March already posed a large burden, exacerbated by the Depression, on the country's public and private relief agencies. Switzerland could not be expected to be the only lifeboat, and henceforward its acceptance of refugees would depend on the ability of those refugees to gain and demonstrate legal admission to other countries.[20] Switzerland would provide transit, not permanent residence. Other countries must open their doors.

Rothmund's pleas fell on deaf ears. American delegate Myron C. Taylor indicated that the United States would not increase its own small immigration quota. Lord Winterton, head of the British delegation, insisted: "The U.K. is not an immigration country. It is fully peopled and suffers from unemployment."[21] The London *Times* had opined on July 6 that "the presence of a large number of Jews within the state creates grave problems in certain countries, especially when they attain an importance there that is out of proportion to their number."[22] France and other European countries announced that they had no room for emigrants, nor did Canada, Australia, or Latin America. Only the tiny Dominican Republic agreed to accept refugees.

Despite the front-door rules, refugees were admitted through a variety of side doors. By early summer of 1938, according to the Council of German Jewry, the 150,000 Jews who had fled Germany were dispersed as follows: Britain 52,000, France 30,000, Poland 25,000, Belgium 12,000, Switzerland 10,000, and the Scandinavian countries 5,000.[23] Those entering the United States were so statistically insignificant that they were not mentioned by the Council. In August, Lord Duncannon of the High Commission for Refugees from Germany stated that Switzerland had done everything possible for refugees and that other members of the League of Nations should give the Swiss some relief by agreeing to accept some refugees.[24]

Meanwhile, the Federal Council was on the point of ordering that only persons with Swiss visas could enter Switzerland and that issuance of such visas required proof of entitlement to return to one's own or some other country. That draconian proposal led to protests by the Swiss population.[25] On August 22, Rothmund broached the possible solution to Franz Kappeler, Swiss Legation counselor in Berlin, that in order to avoid adoption of a general visa requirement, "Aryan individuals whose return to Germany is prohibited, as well as all non-Aryans, should receive

German travel passports only after a duly qualified German passport official has stamped the first page with the following restriction: 'Valid for travel into Switzerland; visa of Swiss Consulate required.'"[26] In other words, Swiss authorities would decide who could enter her borders, particularly Germans who could not return to Germany.

The Swiss Jewish community itself was concerned about the influx. During this period, Rothmund met on refugee policies with Saly Mayer, president of the Federation of Swiss Jewish Communities (*Schweizerischer Israelitischer Gemeindebund*, or SIG). In accord with the policy worked out at Evian, refugees were cared for in part by the religious or ethnic communities of the host countries. The number of unauthorized refugees was overwhelming the resources of the SIG and its Association of Jewish Support for the Poor (*Verband Schweizerischer Israelitischer Armenpfleger*, or VSIA). Thus, on August 19, the VSIA asked the Jewish community in Vienna "to suppress and prevent all attempts of illegal entries into Switzerland."[27]

During this period, negotiations via the Swiss Legation in Berlin were taking place under the growing war clouds over Europe. German-Swiss relations were strained. Refugees were only one of the thorny issues. Hitler was outraged at the killing of German Nazi leader Wilhelm Gustloff in Davos, Switzerland, by David Frankfurter, a Jewish medical student, and by the Federal Council's subsequent prohibition of Nazi party activities in Switzerland. Nazi officials thundered against open attacks on Nazism by the Swiss press, harassed Swiss citizens within Germany, and connived in illegal border violations.[28]

On August 30, 1938, the Federal Council moved ahead by deciding to abrogate the 1926 accord with Germany that eliminated visa requirements.[29] Rothmund wrote that "Germany persists in a ruthless deportation policy."[30]

On September 2, Dr. Otto Köcher, German minister in Bern, asked Rothmund if a general Swiss visa requirement could be waived if German passport holders who were Jews were identified as such. Rothmund replied that it was "technically" possible, but made clear "that we could not follow the course provided by Mr. Köcher."[31] In other words, the Swiss would never agree to identify "their" Jews.

Despite this apparent rejection of a "J" stamp by the Swiss, Privy Councilor Roediger of the German Foreign Office informed Swiss Legation counselor Kappeler that Germany was preparing "to mark German passports issued to Jews," and would require a similar mark on

Swiss passports issued to Swiss Jews. Kappeler responded that "special identification of the passports of Swiss Jews was impossible on both practical and constitutional grounds."[32]

At the time, Swiss Jews in Germany were subject to the same restrictions as German Jews—including limitations on professional activity and the requirement to register property. On September 8, Rothmund telephoned Kappeler that any such [passport] discrimination "against Swiss Jews is *out of the question*." "What is to be avoided if at all possible is express consent to special treatment of our Jews," Kappeler insisted. However, he warned, Germany might require Swiss Jews to obtain visas if the Swiss required visas for German Jews.[33]

Rothmund rejected any such concession in a report to the Federal Department of Justice and Police on September 15. "An arrangement with another nation under which Swiss Jews would be dealt with differently from Swiss non-Jews seems unacceptable to me." He added: "It is more than enough that we must submit to the special treatment of Swiss Jews who live in Germany. In my opinion, the German proposal must be rejected at once insofar as it calls for reciprocity." Even without reciprocity, the proposal was considered a Nazi ruse, since the Swiss believed that, whatever the official agreement, Germany would continue to expel selected groups without regard to legalities.[34]

Rothmund foresaw new waves of unauthorized refugees as Nazi Germany sought to expel other unpopular groups. He wrote:

> The National Socialist Party's campaign against its enemies will steadily intensify. As soon as the emigration of Jews is resolved, the struggle against the Church will be revived; the repression of German nationals may well take many other forms. We will find ourselves defenseless against other categories of emigrants if we accept the German proposal; in short, we would be left with no control over the entry of refugees. The number of refugees with the stamp "political" would likely far outnumber the Jewish refugees.[35]

In Rothmund's view, a general visa for all Germans, not just Jews, was necessary. Otherwise, the German press would assert that "such measures proved the virulent anti-Semitism of the democracies, and they would display it as evidence of our adherence to the racial axis." The German proposal is an "effort to draw us into anti-Semitism, or at least to make it appear to other countries that such is the case." He continued:

> The Jews figure with all the other foreigners as a factor in the excessive influx of foreigners. Now we have assumed our share of the general obligation toward emigrants, and we intend to fulfill it humanely but with the utmost discipline through the Alien Police. The Swiss Jews are helping us and also see our policy as being in their own interests. If now we come up with special measures that discriminate against them, we are simply alienating them. If they begin to protest internationally, instead of exerting their influence in their international circles on behalf of the measures that we have adopted, as they are doing today, then we risk having the whole civilized world turn against us.[36]

A general visa policy would have been complicated. Requiring a visa for all Germans meant examining each applicant to determine whether he or she would be allowed to return to Germany. Certification as an Aryan meant that one would be readmitted, while status as a Jew meant that one would not.[37]

While Switzerland was powerless to require Germany to rescind its racist policies, it is remarkable that Switzerland stood up for equal treatment of every one of its citizens, including every Swiss Jew. Switzerland did in fact attempt to limit the deluge of refugees. But its border controls had less to do with the fact that most of the refugees were Jewish than with the fear that the country would soon be overwhelmed by a large flood of refugees from Nazi repression. Switzerland should not be condemned for failing to admit unlimited refugees when the great democracies—England, France, and the United States—served notice that they would not accept any significant number of refugees. From the Swiss perspective, the argument continued to revolve around the overall *number* of refugees, not their religious or ethnic identity.

The Germans opposed Rothmund's insistence on a general visa requirement. On September 17, 1938, in Bern, he had a stormy meeting with Köcher and Hans Globke, the German legation counselor, who withdrew the German demand for reciprocity with respect to Swiss Jews but announced that Germany would *unilaterally* place a mark on the German passports of non-Aryans. Rothmund shot back the query of "how other categories of emigrants would be singled out if the struggle against the churches should be revived," and stated that Germany's past activities and her campaign to get rid of her Jews gave no confidence that she would abide by her agreements to restrict illegal emigration.[38]

The peace of all Europe seemed to hang in the balance in that fall of 1938. Europe was in the midst of the Sudeten crisis. It was just days before the infamous Munich conference. No one knew what might trigger an explosion. Swiss Minister Hans Frölicher in Berlin warned Rothmund that "in today's tense situation, our country must avoid anything that could be interpreted as one-sided," and it would "be seen as both unfriendly and non-neutral if . . . the visa is introduced only for Germany and not for other neighboring states, which, like Italy, also have a problem with Jews."[39] Rothmund disagreed on this issue, adding: "I believe this would be interpreted as us bowing before Germany again and participating in the racial axis between Berlin and Rome. I fear that this would result in enormous damage for us."[40]

Rothmund then reluctantly journeyed to Berlin to negotiate what would become the German-Swiss Protocol of September 29, 1938. The German representatives began with the announcement: "For the execution of its laws and regulations against those Germans defined by the Nürnberg laws as non-Aryan, for domestic and foreign purposes, the German government needs an identity document designating them expressly as such. Domestically an identity card will be introduced which is compulsory for non-Aryans, and German consulates abroad will identify non-Aryans on passports." Regarding the latter, "All passports issued in Germany for traveling abroad will have on the left top of the first page a special mark for Jews in the form of a circle with a diameter of two centimeters and an inserted 'J'."[41]

Rothmund later stated that this disclosure by Germany's chief delegate—characteristically, Dr. Werner Best of the Gestapo—about this "special marking of the passports delivered to Jews" was "the greatest surprise for him."[42] He should have expected it, in view of the previous German statements. At any rate, the "J" stamp on German Jewish passports was instigated as part of a broader enforcement by the Nazi government of the Nürnberg laws, which purported to define Jews and enact discriminatory policies against them. Identification of Jews on passports paralleled their identification on domestic identity cards.

Faced with the fait accompli of the "J" stamp on German passports, the Swiss delegation insisted that Swiss Jews must suffer no discrimination. Rothmund "emphasized vigorously that an agreement would be unacceptable if it made a distinction between Swiss Aryans and Swiss non-

Aryans. He said Switzerland did not make such a distinction and would not allow it. Rather, it treated Swiss Jews as full citizens. He said that we did not practice anti-Semitism and would prevent it from arising."[43] The 1999 Bergier report, which appears to imply that Swiss policy was anti-Semitic, does not discuss this statement or its implications.

During the 1938 Berlin negotiations, Rothmund visited the concentration camp in Oranienburg, where he found "incorrigible criminals, Jews, political offenders, anti-militarist Bible students, foreigners subject to labor service who have evaded it—all jumbled together."[44] At lunch in the camp, Rothmund declared to the German negotiators that in Switzerland "Jews are useful members of the community" and that "I have found outstanding persons among the Jews who had fled to Switzerland from Germany." He admonished: "The Jewish race has been tempered by the ordeal of history, made strong and stubborn against all persecutions. Thus far it has resisted all attempts at extermination and always comes out of persecution stronger than ever before." Rothmund told the Germans point-blank that "the present German method is wrong and dangerous."[45]

The Swiss delegation's report of those negotiations concluded with the following:

> In his previous reports to you on the control of the entry of refugees from Germany, the first undersigned (the Director of the Police Division [Rothmund]) has many times expressed his misgivings about a measure directed only against the Jews. The present report only deals with the technical side of such control. The Federal Council will have to determine whether the said misgivings will permit its approval of the steps proposed in Berlin.[46]

As adopted, the Protocol provided that Germany would stamp the passports of German Jews with a symbol identifying them as Jews. Switzerland would authorize entry to such German Jews provided that the passport was endorsed with a Swiss assurance of permission to reside in or travel through Switzerland. Germany reserved the right, in agreement with Switzerland, to require a similar assurance for Swiss Jews—a dead letter, in that Switzerland would not agree to such treatment of her citizens.

The Federal Council acceded to the Protocol, but kept the negotiations secret from the Swiss Parliament and people.[47] A circular letter informing the Swiss legations and consulates about the new rules noted that 3,000–4,000 Austrian Jews entered Switzerland before April 1 without visas, in addition to over 2,000 penniless refugees and several thousand more with visas. They became trapped in Switzerland "because all other countries have also introduced very strict controls over emigrants." While illegal entrants should be returned to Germany, such measures should be "confined to exceptional cases."[48]

The policy was fully enforced only at major checkpoints, and often not even there. At that time as well as throughout the war, many border guards bent the rules and allowed illegal refugees to slip into Switzerland. It was easy for soldiers and guards charged with enforcing the rules to keep refugees hidden until the path was clear. When Swiss border guards felt compelled to reject illegal entrants, they frequently did so when the German border guards were out of sight.[49]

The SIG, Switzerland's Jewish organization, expressed reservations about Germany's "J" stamp, but the SIG executive committee agreed that "something had to be done to avoid an invasion similar to that of August 1938. . . ." "We do not dispute that for financial reasons and because of the proportionately large size of the Jewish population compared to that of the country and given the thousands of refugees present, the desire to prevent more Jews from entering is understandable." VSIA, the Jewish relief association, with the support of Switzerland's Jewish population of about 19,000, was caring for 3,000 destitute refugees. SIG president Saly Mayer expressed the dilemma: "Even if one is personally inclined to take in more refugees, this inclination is counteracted by financial concerns, concerns over the workload, the danger of growing anti-Semitism and the number of refugees who will refuse to leave."[50]

The Nazi government continued to enforce discriminatory regulations against German Jews and encouraged them to leave their country. Systematic deportations to extermination camps would not begin for several years. No one foresaw the Holocaust—the Nazis would not adopt their top-secret Wannsee Protocol for the "final solution of the Jewish question" until early 1942, and even then would keep a veil of secrecy over their crimes.[51] Meanwhile, Switzerland did what it could, which was more than most.

Nonetheless, long after the above events, Switzerland would become subject to criticism regarding refugee policy. In 1954, the Swiss periodical *Beobachter (Observer)* published the untrue assertion that Rothmund originated the "J" stamp.[52] The author misidentified German minister Köcher's earlier cited mention on September 2, 1938, of marking the passports of German Jews as being that of Rothmund, who instead had strongly rejected the idea.[53] The uproar from the accusation prompted the Swiss Parliament to order a full report on refugee policy during the war. The subsequent report by Professor Carl Ludwig—which remains the primary source on the subject—provided all of the relevant documents and established Rothmund's repeated rejection of the "J" stamp. This scholarly report attracted little media attention at the time and remains obscure even today.

The myth that the Swiss originated the "J" stamp has persisted. In 1995, Swiss Federal President Villiger apologized for "our too cautious policy on persecuted Jews," such as "the stamp in the passports of Jews."[54] However, the facts were set straight in a 1998 exposé when the author of the 1954 *Beobachter* article conceded that he had reversed the roles of the German and Swiss representatives.[55] Nonetheless, the allegation continued to be widely circulated.

Toward the end of 1938, the refugee situation deteriorated even further. In October of that year, the Nazis rounded up Polish Jews living in Germany and dumped a mass transport of them on the Polish border. Poland would not accept those without proper Polish passports, and 7,000 were left stranded in wretched conditions between the borders at Zbonszyn. Among them was the family of a 17-year-old Polish Jew, who shortly thereafter took revenge by shooting an official of the German embassy in Paris. This incident gave the Nazis the excuse for the pogrom known as *Kristallnacht* (Night of Broken Glass) on November 8–10, in which Jewish homes and businesses were attacked and twenty to thirty thousand Jews were detained by the Nazi government.[56]

One of the American consulates reported to U.S. Ambassador Hugh R. Wilson in Berlin that his office was flooded with Jews begging for visas or immigration assistance for themselves and their families. He described them as "a mass of seething, panic-stricken humanity."[57] The large democracies recoiled in horror, but did virtually nothing to open their borders.

The flow of refugees into Switzerland placed increasing burdens on the Swiss Jewish community. Minutes of a SIG executive committee and VSIA meeting in mid-December 1938 even recorded criticism of Swiss authorities, who "should show more resistance to Germany regarding illegal entries." The leaders of the SIG noted that "it was not enough to emphasize humanitarian issues; rather the entire situation had to be taken into account," and chastised the machinations of refugee smugglers.[58]

A year later, on September 1, 1939, Hitler attacked Poland, launching

World War II. The Swiss Federal Council ordered an immediate mobilization of the military and finally imposed a universal visa requirement for all foreigners seeking to enter the country. Reflecting security concerns, it also ordered that illegal entrants be expelled, although this policy would be carried out only on a selective basis at the local level. Reflecting centuries of tradition, military refugees and political fugitives were exempt from expulsion even if they had entered unlawfully. There were two categories of lawful entrants, based on whether they had become permanent residents or were recent arrivals. The first, "emigrants," were foreigners who had entered Switzerland since 1929, lost their nationalities, or could not return to their home countries. Emigrants were officially accepted by specific cantons. The second category, "refugees," were persons who fled into Switzerland since the outbreak of the war, and who were the direct responsibility of the Confederation.[59]

Although the border policies and legal distinctions would continue to have practical significance, the coming tumultuous years saw official restrictions more often than not outweighed by humanitarian impulses. There were seemingly heartless expulsions of innocent people, but there was also much good-samaritan nullification of formal requirements by ordinary Swiss and some officials. There were rules on paper, and there were the realities of how much at any given period the besieged democracy could do consistent with its security and survival.

With the outbreak of the war in 1939, national borders everywhere were either sealed or subjected to strict monitoring. Indeed, during the last months of peace Nazi officials themselves concluded that expulsion of the Jews from the Reich would not solve their "problem." The Western powers had suggested various African colonies as a homeland for the Jews, but concrete decisions never materialized. The Nazis established the *Reichvereinigung* (Reich Association of the Jews in Germany) to promote Jewish emigration, but it became instead a network to control the Jews domestically. If they could not emigrate, Jews needed to be organized for compulsory labor.[60] By early 1942, the Final Solution was formulated, under which Jews would either be used for slave labor or killed. In any event, expulsions of Jews from Germany ceased to be a policy issue with the beginning of the war.

When France fell to the Wehrmacht's onslaught in May–June 1940, it was the French-Swiss border that became the new refugee "front." In mid-June, the Federal Justice and Police Department instructed the cantonal police departments that military personnel crossing into Switzerland were to be disarmed and interned by the Swiss army. Civilian fugitives—with the exception of women, children up to the age of sixteen, men over the age of sixty, and invalids—were to be turned back.[61] These exceptions, which would exist in one form or another throughout the war, meant that the only civilian refugees who would not be *automatically* allowed into Switzerland were able-bodied men, i.e., those most likely to be able to fend for themselves and, if they were so inclined, to join or continue the struggle against Nazi occupation.

The effects of the war were soon felt. The Hague Convention of 1907 authorized a neutral country to permit troops of a belligerent to enter its territory.[62] On June 19–20, 1940, 28,000 soldiers of the French 45th Army Corps, including a Polish division, crossed the border into Switzerland to escape annihilation or capture. The total quickly climbed to 42,600 soldiers being admitted from France, as were 7,500 French civilians.[63]

With the armistice, many of the French civilians could return home. When France withdrew from the war, conditions were set for the repatriation of French soldiers to Vichy France in 1941. However, Poland stayed in the Allied camp, and the Polish internees consequently remained in Switzerland for the entire war. They were housed in schools, restaurants, farms, and work camps. A fair number eventually attended Swiss high schools and universities. Had Germany attacked, the Poles would have fought side-by-side with the Swiss.[64]

In the coming years, Switzerland would first stiffen and then eventually liberalize her policies on refugees. While military requirements, security and scarce resources were always important factors, humanitarianism was also a strong consideration, particularly after the second half of the war when reports about the fate of the Jews became known. Switzerland always expected that larger nations would help by accepting refugees. Such help did not materialize. Had the great democracies stepped in, Switzerland could no doubt have accepted far larger numbers of refugees in transit. While greater France was occupied by German forces in 1940, for a time Vichy France remained a possible escape route. Then it too was occupied in late 1942. Refugees could be smuggled out of, as well as into, Switzerland, but where could they run after that?

Legal transit through Spain and Portugal, which temporary refugees in Switzerland might reach, was restricted to holders of visas for "states outside Europe." Immigration regulations in the United States remained restrictive.[65] The Close Relatives Edict of June 1941, which passed when the United States was still neutral, expressly prohibited the immigration of persons with relatives in German-occupied Europe—the status of virtually all refugees.

As an example, Dr. E.M. Landau was a German Jew whose Berlin company published a book criticizing National Socialism in 1934. He eventually fled to France but was arrested in Paris in 1940. Through the intervention of the Thomas Mann Committee in New York, Landau was approved for a "danger visa" for the United States, but it could not be issued because he had close relatives in occupied Europe. Thousands of younger people in the same situation perished. Landau was released in 1941 but remained in danger because he was Jewish and had published an anti-Nazi book. In 1942, on his third attempt to enter, he was admitted into Switzerland as a political refugee. An officer of the Swiss Intelligence Service picked him up at the border. The next day the Gestapo came looking for him in France.[66]

The United States and the other democracies had been extremely cautious in taking in refugees before the war, in large part due to Depression-era measures to protect the domestic labor market. Once these countries entered the war and were fighting for their lives, even less incentive existed to focus on refugees, entry of which could also bring spies and subversives. Winning the war was the paramount objective. Some attribute the Allies' disinterest to open or latent anti-Semitism.[67] Whatever the reasons, Switzerland—herself isolated and encircled by the Axis—had no way to influence the Allies to open their doors to large numbers of refugees.

In 1941, Jews residing in Switzerland numbered 19,429, which was 0.46% of the population, and of that number 10,279 were listed as Swiss and 9,150 foreign.[68] Most of these foreign Jews would have been refugees from countries adjacent to Switzerland, as crossing over the Reich itself or more remote countries would have been difficult with wartime controls.

As the war progressed, the cooperation between the Swiss Jewish organizations and the authorities increased. The head of VSIA was in almost daily contact with the Department for Justice and Police.[69] This was hardly surprising in that VSIA needed to make arrangements to care for newly admitted Jewish refugees and was able to influence the admission process somewhat.

Consistent with this cooperation, in August 1941, Rothmund argued that National Socialism and anti-Semitism were inconsistent with Swiss democracy. He advocated the integration of Jews into the larger society, just as Switzerland's other faiths now coexisted in reasonable harmony. However, he said "a distinction would have to be made between eastern Jews and those who have lived for a long time in western European countries"—the former being more difficult to assimilate. Rothmund continued: "Swiss Jews had understood this and also made considerable effort to explain the Swiss view of the emigrant problem to foreign circles. In these circumstances there was certainly no reason for Switzerland to allow the entry of German anti-Semitism in any form."[70]

The Swiss press continuously campaigned to liberalize standards for entry into Switzerland and attacked the authorities for the restrictions they imposed. However, in April 1942, Zurich delegate Max Sandberg, who was Jewish, denounced attacks on the Swiss Police for Foreigners "by members of the press who have no idea how much this authority has done to help us."[71]

The Geneva office of the World Jewish Congress (WJC) received the first reports of mass murders of deported western European Jews in the summer of 1942. Dr. G.M. Riegner, the director of the WJC office, found the details so dreadful that at first the reports were dismissed as unbelievable even in Jewish circles.[72] Swiss newspapers, however, quickly published credible accounts of the deportation and extermination of Jews.[73] Hundreds of Jewish refugees entered Switzerland during this period.[74]

In Germany and the occupied countries, Nazi policy had changed from expelling Jews to using such Jews as were fit for slave labor and sending the rest to death camps. It was now the Gestapo which rounded up persons who failed to report to labor camps as well as Jews who refused to assemble for deportation.

By July 1942, Dr. R. Jezler, Rothmund's deputy, reported to the EJPD that Swiss police would no longer send any refugees back to France, even though they met none of the criteria for entry. "The unanimous and authentic reports on the methods by which the deportations are being carried out and the conditions in Jewish areas in the East are so ghastly, that it is impossible not to understand the refugees' desperate attempts to escape such a fate and equally impossible to assume any further responsibility for sending them back."[75] However, he foresaw an ever-increasing flow of refugees. Switzerland's food shortages, the lack of any other countries willing to accept refugees, German economic retaliation and internal security still counseled against the admission of "too many" refugees.[76]

Nonetheless, in August 1942 the Federal Council suddenly ordered that foreigners who entered illegally were subject to being sent back "even

if the foreigners who fall within this legislation may have reason to anticipate the most serious consequences (danger to life and limb)."[77] Rothmund ordered the borders hermetically sealed. "Political refugees, that is,
foreigners who declare themselves as such when first questioned and can
also provide evidence of such status, are not to be expelled. Those who
seek refuge on racial grounds, as for example, Jews, are not considered
political refugees."[78] Political refugees—dissident writers, politicians, and
religious leaders—had long found sanctuary in Switzerland; no tradition
existed of accepting refugees based on ethnicity. However, Rothmund forbade the expulsion of refugees at specific places where German border
guards would catch them.[79]

Almost immediately Rothmund's order to turn back civilian refugees
became public knowledge and encountered fierce opposition by the Swiss
people and the press.[80] The official policy was universally derided and as
a result was withdrawn in a matter of days.

On August 20, the central committee of the Swiss Jewish Federation
(SIG) met under Chairman Saly Mayer, who reported bleak news: a new
wave of refugees, deportations from France, and appalling information on
the conditions of Jews in the East. Rothmund appeared at the meeting,
stating that in regard to the refugee question "the determining factor must
be the interests of Switzerland, not those of individual persons or of foreign nations." Primary concerns were preservation of order and peace,
employment opportunities and food supplies. Switzerland could not take
in all the refugees from neighboring countries. "It is better that we take
care of those who are here and try to keep them with us."[81]

SIG committee members strongly opposed Rothmund's restrictive
policy. The rumors, the minutes stated, "were so horrific that one would
prefer not to believe them even though at this point . . . one could no
longer deny as impossible even the most horrific things." Switzerland, it
was decided, should not reject refugees.[82] Having finally learned of the
extermination of the Jews in the East, SIG thenceforth exerted every effort
to save those who could be saved.

Just after that August SIG meeting, Dr. Gertrud Kurz, known as "the
mother of the refugees" and director of the Christian Peace Center, met
with EJPD head and Federal Councilor von Steiger, dramatically detailing
the plight of the refugees. Kurz stressed the Christian obligation to assist
the persecuted and urged him to ameliorate restrictive policies. He immediately ordered a relaxation of the border policy to take "special cases"
—a vague term—into account. This would become, in effect, a carte

blanche for Swiss border officials to use discretion to let in any sympathetic persons.[83] The new restrictive policy had lasted less than a month!

Moreover, some cantons were already tacitly refusing to follow federal regulations and accepting refugees at will. St. Gallen police commander Paul Grüninger saved hundreds, perhaps thousands, of Jewish refugees by falsifying papers, for which he would be severely disciplined. Some border officials categorized almost all refugees as "emergency cases," others warned of German police, and Swiss soldiers sometimes helped refugees climb over barbed wire.[84]

Border controls ran the gauntlet from passport checking bureaus at rail stations and highway border crossings to guard sheds at rural locations suitable for transit. Land mines, tank traps and explosives at bridges were in place to help defend against a German invasion. Barbed wire contributed to that effort as well as deterring illegal entries. It goes without saying that unchecked border crossings would have allowed free entry to Nazi subversives as well as innocent refugees, and the latter needed to be screened to determine whether they were legally acceptable as well as to determine whether they carried infectious diseases.

The oft-cited "lifeboat" characterization, which was later both taken out of context and made to appear as if it were the *only* Swiss response, appeared in Federal Councilor Eduard von Steiger's speech in August 1942 to 8,000 young Swiss at the Youth Church of Zurich-Orlikon. It included the following:

> Under certain conditions one must be absolutely hard and unyielding, one must endure insults and complaints and calumnies and yet be able to resist and not break. . . . When conflict arises between sentiment and reason, when the heart is willing but duty cries "halt," then one begins to understand what it means to resist. . . .Whoever commands a small lifeboat of limited capacity that is already quite full, and with an equally limited amount of provisions, while thousands of victims of a sunken ship scream to be saved, must appear hard when he cannot take everyone. And yet he is still humane when he warns early against false hopes and tries to save at least those he had taken in.[85]

The lifeboat analogy may have been inspired by the still-resonating tragedy, thirty years before, of the Titanic—the image of the broken dreams of fin-de-siècle Europe.

Von Steiger explained the spiritual anguish that the lifeboat captain feels when he must accept some and reject others who have an equal right to live. "Shall he take the women first, or the children, or the ailing, or the married couples, and say to himself: 'Perhaps the young and strong still have a chance to survive in spite of all dangers; but I have to make a choice!'"[86] This was actually official policy at that time, i.e., children under 16, the elderly, and the sick were automatically granted asylum while able-bodied men were not. In view of Switzerland's encirclement and the refusal of the Allies to accept refugees, it was an almost impossible task to distinguish between persons who could be accepted for permanent residence and those who had no other place to go. In mid-1942, it should be remembered, the Germans were still winning victories in Russia and North Africa, and with their U-boats on the high seas. The outcome of the war was not clear.

Nevertheless, more room was always being made in the Swiss lifeboat. Pastor Paul Vogt originated the "free places" campaign in August 1942 in which private citizens welcomed refugees into their homes, particularly children, mothers with small children, the elderly, the handicapped and the ill. Participants provided free room and board or made monthly donations. Some Protestant parishes subsidized institutional homes for Jewish refugees.[87] The Swiss Committee for Aid to Children of Émigrés (SHEK) placed 2,000 children for the most part in private homes for stays of several months. Over 90% of refugee children were Jewish.[88] The Swiss Red Cross formed the Swiss Coalition for Relief to Child War Victims, the members of which found families to host over 60,000 children during the war. The families volunteered to take children from German-occupied areas and keep them for three months.[89]

A raucous debate in the National Council took place in September of 1942. Von Steiger reported that 7,000 new refugees per year could be sustained, but that over 100,000 refugees attempting to cross the border from France might be expected. While the basis of the latter figure was not explained, the following was certain: "It has become almost impossible to pass refugees on. So far, in 1942, we were able to obtain only 30 entry visas from the United States (compared to 566 last year), 31 from Brazil, and 5 from Argentina."[90] Illegal immigration threatened the spread of infectious diseases, food shortages (which were dependent on economic negotiations), security against dangerous elements and the labor market. One farmer plowing a field near a refugee camp reprimanded von Steiger for spending money on refugees but not on unemployed Swiss.[91]

Representatives of the various political parties set forth their positions in the debate, some supporting and some opposing current policy.[92] Independent Walter Muschg suggested that the Federal Council should intervene with the governments "in Vichy and Washington, for the purpose of persuading these governments to make it possible for our Swiss refugees to cross the ocean and at least save their lives, and also, if possible, to initiate measures that would lead to a mass movement of refugees overseas."[93] Unfortunately, American policy precluded the implementation of this suggestion. Not unexpectedly, the major parties supported the position of the Federal Council as explained by von Steiger. Refugees should be accommodated to the extent possible, but there must be limits.

Despite the official rules, in September the Police Section allowed 3,800 unauthorized refugees to remain, even though they had entered illegally. Despite checkpoints and barbed wire at selected places, the border remained by and large patrolled but open. Officials agreed that the churches would submit to the police lists of persons who were not to be turned back in event of border violations. The Swiss consulates in France, from which many refugees came, were authorized to issue a "C" visa (*Visum "C"*) to everyone on these lists so they could cross the border unhindered. The lists included as many as 800 persons, many of them prominent members of the community.[94]

On September 26, 1942, the Police Section once again amplified its instructions to border officials. Refugees "are not political refugees solely by reasons of race." The Swiss had traditionally granted asylum to persons fleeing persecution for political reasons. But there was no precedent for persons being persecuted on the basis of ethnic type or "race," as in the Nazi innovation of distinguishing between Aryans and non-Aryans. The Police Section's order provided that French Jews were to be turned back "because they are in no danger in their own country," a naïve proposition. However, "hardship cases" could enter, including the sick, pregnant women, persons over 65, children under 16 who were alone, and parents with such children.[95] This meant that virtually the only persons who had no automatic right of entry were able-bodied adults without children—a sizable group to be sure, but one with the best chances of survival.

At that time the Swiss Legation in Vichy France protested against anti-Semitic measures, particularly the seizing of Jewish children from Swiss Red Cross children's homes, another Swiss humanitarian initiative. French authorities promised not to bother children under 16. Vichy leader Pierre Laval exclaimed to Swiss representative Walter Stucki: "Have you also come to lecture me about my measures against the Jews?"[96] Nonetheless, humanitarianism was balanced with a motive of self-preservation. Focus on the refugee question *alone* would obscure the fact that Switzerland was itself in very serious danger from Axis forces. Swiss commander-in-chief General Henri Guisan told the Swiss Reformed Pastors' Association that he "fully understands the impulses of the heart that move us, but in the solution of this [refugee] question, too, concern for the security of our country must take the first place."[97]

Few refugees left Switzerland on official convoys (largely through Vichy France) to Allied countries: The totals were 170 at the end of 1940, 1,201 in 1941, and 148 at the beginning of 1942. The United States took in 32 in 1940, 566 in 1941, and 30 in 1942. When Swiss diplomats asked Washington to raise its visa quota in October 1942, the American representative responded that "since Pearl Harbor we had necessarily become very careful in our examination of each individual case; that there was no objection to taking persons because they were from Switzerland but that the examination of each case would determine whether that particular individual should be admitted."[98] Inquiries with the U.S. Legation Secretary in Bern about the emigration of stateless children produced only evasive replies. The United States government was focused on winning the war, the ultimate solution to the refugee issue.

At the end of 1942, the Police Division once more ordered that foreigners seized in unlawful border crossings were to be expelled. Exceptions were to be made for military refugees. According to international law, such refugees included soldiers of any belligerent, including escaped prisoners of war and downed pilots. The majority of those were members of the Allied forces. Exceptions were also made for persons seeking political asylum, which included political leaders, writers, and activists. However, persons who only claimed membership in a political party or being a member of a "racial" group were to be excluded. Hardship cases, including lone children, parents with children under 6, the sick, elderly, and pregnant women were excepted. Further excepted were persons on "C" visas and other listed persons.[99] The rules were tempered with considerable flexibility. To a large extent, the chances of getting through depended on how one presented oneself as well as on the sympathies of the official who was doing the interviewing.

By February 1943 Germany had suffered a disastrous military defeat at Stalingrad. The regime was in need of a quick, morale-boosting victory. That is one reason why in March, Swiss intelligence warned of an imminent German invasion of Switzerland—an attack which fortunately never materialized. The turn of the tide of war, combined with ever-increasing rumors and reports of Nazi death camps, caused official refugee policy to be considerably relaxed. In a dramatic liberalization of policy, directives issued in September recognized "mortal danger" as a reason for granting asylum. Rothmund ordered Jews to be accepted in greater numbers, since "they are undoubtedly in exceptional danger." Border guards and the army allowed many to enter, and local residents helped refugees.[100] Italy's capitulation in September 1943 led to so much border pressure that Switzerland ordered that males over 16 be sent back. As persecutions of Jews in German-occupied Italy increased, Jewish refugees of all categories were admitted. Through the end of 1943, Switzerland took in 20,000 soldiers and 7,800 civilian refugees from Italy.[101]

After having pursued exclusionist policies toward refugees during the Depression and most of the war years, the United States finally created its War Refugee Board (WRB) in January 1944. In April, the WRB sent a representative to the American Legation in Switzerland. Federal Police Department head Pilet-Golaz wrote bitterly of this "belated interest [by the United States] in the remaining members of the Jewish population of Central Europe."[102]

Meanwhile, in March 1944, Germany occupied Hungary and began deporting its Jews to Auschwitz. The Federal Council decided to admit 14,000 Hungarian Jews, although it became impossible to get very many to Switzerland.[103] Swiss diplomacy was, however, effective in preventing many deportations and saving thousands of lives. Specifically, as many as 62,000 Hungarian Jews were saved by Swiss Consul Carl Lutz, who served in Budapest during 1942–45.[104] None other than Adolf Eichmann himself affirmed to Lutz Germany's agreement that 8,000 Jews were under the protection of the Swiss government and would have safe transit to Switzerland. Lutz fraudulently issued certificates to almost eight times this number of Jews in a successful ruse to save their lives. Although the rescue efforts of Swedish diplomat Raoul Wallenberg have been far more widely publicized, Simon Wiesenthal writes that Swiss envoy Lutz actually led the cooperative effort of these and other neutrals to save a total of 100,000 Hungarian Jews.[105] Swiss diplomacy was at the heart of successful efforts to stop the deportation of many Hungarian Jews to Auschwitz.[106]

In Switzerland itself, some Swiss consular employees allowed thousands of refugees to enter contrary to official regulations. Officials and soldiers helped refugees cross illegally, and border residents fed and sheltered them. There were also organized escape routes set up by Jewish and Protestant groups.[107] One such group was the Joint Committee on Behalf of Evacuees, which was thought to be under Swiss government protection. A June 1944 report implied that the military courts "received the impression that 'emigrant smuggling' was taking place with Rothmund's protection."[108]

Rothmund told the American legation in Bern that he was "convinced that the news of Jewish extermination by the Gestapo was consistent with reality."[109] On July 12, 1944, Rothmund published new directives replacing those of December 29, 1942 (which were being enforced leniently) declaring that Jews were in mortal danger.[110] The sentence "refugees on exclusively racial grounds are not political refugees" was conspicuously deleted. The new directive provided that admission shall be granted to "foreigners who for political or other reasons are truly in danger of losing life and limb and who have no way of avoiding this danger other than that of flight to Switzerland." Boys through age 16, girls through age 18, and other categories would also be admitted.[111]

The Police Section immediately informed the SIG that all Jewish refugees would be admitted because they were now deemed to be in danger in all countries bordering Switzerland.[112] Rothmund declared to customs officials: "As a general rule, Jews are to be considered as endangered."[113]

In November 1944, Rothmund directed the Swiss Legation in Berlin to declare that Switzerland would accept the 1,300 Jews who survived a recent transport from Hungary. He ordered the legation to "intervene against deportation and to request food and clothing for all other Jews still remaining in Germany." Rothmund attempted to pressure an official in the German Foreign Ministry to appeal to Gestapo chief Himmler, explaining:

> That we are very much in earnest about saving the Jews who are still alive can be seen from the fact that, when our Legation in Budapest notified us that the Hungarian and German governments had agreed to allow 8,000 Hungarian Jews to travel to Switzerland, we answered by telegraph two days ago saying that in principle we were ready to admit them. . . . If we are now committing ourselves to such positive measures of assistance, surely we have a right to take a stand against further deportations.[114]

These were the same 8,000 Jews Germany had agreed to release to Switzerland and whom the Swiss representative in Hungary, Carl Lutz, multiplied to close to 60,000 by issuing certificates declaring that all were under the protection of the Swiss government. Rail transports of many of these Hungarian Jews arrived in Switzerland—318 in August, and 1,552 in December.[115] Far larger numbers of Jews remaining in Hungary were saved by the Swiss Consul's actions, inasmuch as every Jew with a Swiss certificate was officially protected. Swiss diplomatic protection greatly alleviated, but could not completely halt, deportations and the murder of Jews in the chaotic conditions in Budapest.[116]

Meanwhile, during the fall of 1944, Switzerland took in 17,000 children and mothers from France and Italy, both countries where the Allies were advancing and the Nazis were retreating. In February 1945, the Swiss Federal Council itself attempted via diplomatic channels to stop the killing of Jews. Ex-Federal Councilor Musy led 1,200 Jews wrested from the Theresienstadt concentration camp to Switzerland by rail.[117]

A new "refugee" problem arose at the end of March 1945 when the Police Section issued directives to stop the entry of Germans, particularly Nazis. For the last half decade the Swiss had prepared for a possible Nazi invasion. Now they were certainly not going to allow fleeing Nazi war criminals into the country, hidden within a tide of refugees. The Federal Council ordered parts of the border closed, although thousands, especially escaped foreign workers and prisoners of war, were still allowed to enter Switzerland.[118]

By May 1945, Switzerland was caring for 106,470 refugees and internees, including 46,470 military fugitives. Just before the armistice the total rose to 115,000.[119]

During the entire war, 295,381 persons were documented as finding refuge in Switzerland either for short or long periods of time. They included 103,869 military internees, 55,018 civilian refugees ("unlawful" entrants), 9,909 emigrants (lawful entrants), 251 political refugees (political, religious, and intellectual leaders), 59,785 children (who entered as refugees, or in organized groups for several months of recovery and then returned to their families), and 66,549 border refugees (short-term refugees who came across the border to avoid hostilities). Of the civilian Jews who found refuge, those without permission to enter totaled 21,858—a little less than half of such illegal entrants—and lawful Jewish emigrants totaled 6,654—over two-thirds of the lawful entrants.[120]

The Swiss Confederation expended 128 million Swiss francs for refugees within Switzerland for the period 1936–54. Private sources, including religious and political groups, contributed as much as 87 million francs more. There were countless anonymous acts of individual charity.[121] During 1933–45, the 19,000-member Swiss Jewish community contributed almost 10 million francs to support emigrants and refugees.[122]

Refugee organizations traditionally assisted those in need according to religious, political or social affiliation, although Christian groups also supported Jewish refugees. Relief organizations included the Swiss Central Office for Refugee Relief (*Schweizerische Zentralstelle für Flüchtlingshilfe*, or SZF); the VSIA, which, as described earlier, helped Jewish refugees; the Swiss Churches Relief Committee for Protestant Refugees, with its "pennies for the refugees" collections; Caritas, which aided Catholic refugees; the Committee for the Placement of Refugee Intellectuals; the Social Democratic Swiss Workers Aid; the Crusaders for Peace of Gertrud Kurz; and the Relief Organization for Refugee Children.[123]

The Swiss Confederation also spent over 352 million francs from 1940 to 1950 on refugees abroad through the Swiss Red Cross, the International Committee of the Red Cross, and Swiss charities. Private sources contributed over 631 million francs to such relief agencies.[124]

This account of Swiss refugee policy focuses on official documents collected in the Ludwig report, which traced the orders of a relatively small group of government policymakers. It does not tell the story of the Swiss nongovernmental humanitarian organizations or of the citizenry at large, which did not participate in and was often unaware of the refugee policies adopted by the government. These stories remain untold. Countless acts of generosity in those days were unrecorded and will never be divulged. Yet the history of the official refugee policy itself, the starting point for understanding what happened, has been so neglected and distorted that a close review of the original documents about refugee policy is warranted.

In the late 1990s, publications appeared in the United States criticizing Swiss wartime policies. A monograph published by the Los Angeles-based Simon Wiesenthal Center denounced Switzerland's treatment of refugees who were admitted.[125] None other than Simon Wiesenthal himself, the famed anti-Nazi hunter, was embarrassed by the study and denounced its author as "a historian by hobby."[126] The study in question sought to depict Switzerland as a place where refugees were relegated to slave labor, based on the fact that many refugee men were placed in work camps where they were assigned manual labor and slept on straw bedding. In fact, not only were refugees generally happy to have escaped the Nazis, but such experiences were also shared by a great part of the Swiss population. All Swiss adult males served in the militia army, and when on duty typically slept on straw, as did many poorer Swiss families.

Kurt Schonstein, an Austrian Jew who found refuge in Switzerland in 1938, recollected: "There was no difference in materials used, sanitary equipment or other facilities between the Swiss Army's and refugees' camps." He added: "The soldiers ate somewhat but not much better. They had a hard life, and needed more calories. No refugee would have changed places with a Swiss soldier!"[127] It is evident that Swiss soldiers made great sacrifices to defend their country and everyone within it, including the refugees, who had no such obligations. The influx of refugees varied with the war's current crises and corresponding types of refugees—civilian and military, ethnic and political, male and female, children and adults. As a rule, refugee men either worked or pursued educational opportunities, while women and children resided in hotels set aside for refugees or in private homes.

The much-heralded report by the Bergier Commission—chaired by Professor Jean-François Bergier—entitled *Switzerland and Refugees in the Nazi Era* appeared in 1999. This report is an enigma which contains valuable information but appears to portray Switzerland in a negative light.

The Bergier report fails to present accounts by the large number of people who found refuge in Switzerland. The Commission had access to numerous letters from refugees collected by National Councilor François Loeb, which the report notes "rejected sweeping judgments of the camp system. Letters from Swiss citizens noted that the local population was also subject to many wartime restrictions, including mandatory labor and widespread shortages." The report also states that it had available the refugee letters obtained by Ken Newman, who published them in a book.[128] None of these documents of living history by actual refugees is made a part of, or even summarized in, the Bergier report. In fact, Bergier references these authentic refugee accounts only in a footnote.

Bergier seems to imply that "the army leadership saw every foreigner as a security risk"—not a bad idea for a country surrounded by Nazis. The report does concede: "In everyday life, the Swiss demonstrated solidarity with the refugees." Many took them into their own households and made it possible for them to become part of the intellectual and cultural life.[129]

Not taking note of the dire straits of everyone in Switzerland during the war, Bergier observes that refugees from the white-collar classes found work requiring physical exertion to be difficult. When Swiss farmers chose the strongest men, it was "as if they were bidding at a slave auction." But one might normally expect a farmer to choose those who looked stronger, or more able to do the work. Yet, the eyewitness record suggests that refugees in Switzerland were generally thankful to be there. The jobs to which refugees were assigned were necessary to free Swiss men to perform military service.[130]

The Bergier report concludes with the hypothetical question: What would have happened had Switzerland somehow prevented Germany from adopting the "J" stamp in 1938 or not closed the border in August 1942?[131] In the context of the time, Switzerland was powerless to dictate policy to the Third Reich, then at the height of its power and menacing Swiss borders. In addition, Swiss policy to limit the flow of refugees cannot be judged fairly, many believe, except in its proper context, including the refusal of the United States, England, and the other democracies to accept refugees. One could just as well ask, what would have happened had the large democracies agreed to accept large numbers of refugees emigrating through Switzerland, or had Switzerland not placed every adult male under arms to protect every person, citizen or refugee, within its borders?

The Bergier report dramatically claims that 24,398 refugees were "turned away at the border" and "expelled during the war years."[132] Importantly, this figure reflects not the number of people, but the recorded number of *times* that persons, most of them anonymous, attempted access into Switzerland and were denied. That number is by no means the same as the total who ultimately were denied entry. Bergier made this blatant statistical blunder by counting multiple *attempts* as multiple *persons*, thereby greatly inflating the numbers. As recorded in many refugee accounts, a person might not be successful in entering Switzerland on the first or second try, but often was granted entry later. A sophisticated mathematical study by Prof. Jean-Christian Lambelet estimates the number of *persons* actually rejected at about 5,000.[133]

Moreover, the Bergier report's figure of 24,398 rejections includes 9,703 named persons and 14,695 anonymous rejections, many of whom would have been military personnel, including escapees and deserters.[134] Needless to say, persons attempting to enter included not only legitimate refugees but also subversives, including Nazi spies and fifth columnists. It would be at the least naïve to suggest that Switzerland should not have policed her borders during World War II.

In contradiction to the Bergier thesis, it should be noted that at the critical time when the border was officially closed, the number of refugees admitted sharply increased.[135] From August 1942 through fall 1943, 22,367 refugees were admitted, at a rate of 82% for each attempted entry.[136] During the entire war, 51,129 "illegal" civilian refugees gained entry. On average, their chance of being legally admitted was 68% per attempt. Combining the acceptance rates of persons without prior permission who attempted once and those who attempted twice, there was a 90% chance of being admitted![137] There were an additional 9,909 legal refugees, i.e., persons who were authorized to enter beforehand.[138]

The Bergier report states that 21,304 (42%) of all 51,129 illegal civilian refugees admitted during the war were Jewish. The proportion of Jews was almost certainly higher since Jews frequently did not identify their religion. In Europe at that time, they had good reason.[139] Jews seeking sanctuary had no guarantee that Switzerland itself would not be invaded by Nazi Germany. In the second half of 1942, most refugees were probably Jewish. Between August and December, 7,899 refugees were admitted and 1,949 denied entry, for an acceptance rate of 80% per attempt. The acceptance rate for Jews was over 90% during this period.[140]

In his comprehensive critique of Bergier, Professor Lambelet sharply distinguishes between officially stated policy and actual practice. The official policy was restrictive, sought to discourage more refugees than could be supported with limited Swiss resources and was in part driven by the restrictive policies of larger states. In practice, according to the best estimates from the records, any given refugee had a two-thirds probability of acceptance per attempted entry, and an 85% chance with multiple attempts. Jewish refugees were treated more generously than others. Subversives were a serious issue. Entries were also deterred or prevented by Axis forces at the border, which were a barrier to entry throughout the war. While Switzerland did not accept what she considered an uncontrollable influx, she opened her borders at the times when the need was greatest from a humanitarian perspective.[141] As the reality of the Holocaust became known, her doors opened wider.

The most fundamental duty of any government is to protect its citizens. A small democratic country in a sea of tyranny, Switzerland made great sacrifices to protect herself militarily and to survive economically. By doing so, she successfully defended both her citizens and the refugees within her border from the ravages of war and the Holocaust. In judging

Switzerland, it should be noted that most other European states failed utterly, or, at worst, actively abetted and aided the Nazis' new order.

In prewar negotiations with Germany, Swiss officials went to great lengths to protect the rights of Swiss Jews. Before and during the war, Switzerland took in numerous refugees but would not and could not accept them all. For this, Switzerland has been greatly criticized. These same critics have been strangely silent on the far more restrictive policies of the large democracies, which could have readily accommodated large numbers of refugees. Switzerland's restrictions on refugees did make exceptions for children, families with children, the sick and the elderly. Though able-bodied adults not automatically granted asylum had better chances of fending for themselves, many were nonetheless granted entry. Toward the end of the war, when credible evidence of the Nazi extermination program became firmly established, all Jews became eligible for automatic entry, and Swiss officials did their best to rescue foreign Jews.

Peter Munk, a Hungarian Jew rescued by Switzerland in 1944, would write a half-century later about those dark days:

> At that time, every able-bodied Swiss was serving in the army, protecting the country . . . from the Nazi conquest. Theirs was thus the only country that, with enormous courage, consistently flaunted the directions of the all-powerful Nazi German neighbor not to take in Jewish refugees. Yet, at that time, the four million of this great nation resisted and saved thousands from Auschwitz.[142]

If other democracies had opened their far less threatened frontiers to persecuted Jews in numbers proportional to their populations, the Holocaust would not have consumed six million lives. A 1946 issue of the *Atlantic Monthly* put it in perspective: "America might have taken in 1,225,000 [Jews], since our population is 35 times that of Switzerland; actually, we did not take as many as Switzerland."[143]

head of the Military Department, he will not rest until the Swiss army is so well equipped and trained, and Swiss territory is so well fortified, that even mighty Germany will be afraid of the Swiss armed forces.

Kobelt must have been on the ever-growing list of Swiss leaders to be put in concentration camps or executed when the invasion came. Nazi agents spied on ordinary Swiss as well. One typical Abwehr report from "liaison agent A 2029" reported conditions in Davos, the Alpine health resort in southeastern Switzerland, and went into minute detail. "Dr. Maurer, head physician of Schatzalp Sanatorium in Davos," is "not pro-German." His assistant and friend, Dr. Rossius of Berlin, "associates mainly with foreigners. She keeps making negative and derogatory remarks to these foreigners about the Germans."[2]

A great amount of personal detail went into the German files, with reports focusing on untrustworthy German expatriates as well as Swiss. For example, there was Comtesse Sala from Vienna, living at the Wald-sanatorium Davos. "She attracts attention with her behavior, shows strong interest in military matters and makes herself conspicuous with her questions about political and military issues addressed mainly to members of the German army. She also frequents Jews." Finally, agent 2029 shadowed a German named Hilliges at the Waldsanatorium Davos. "He is considered an informant. It is possible he is working against Germany."

On April 6, 1941, Hitler moved to consolidate control of the eastern Mediterranean by attacking Yugoslavia and Greece. The Swiss immediately denounced the invasions, cheered the resistance mounted by both of these countries and clearly were distressed at the collapse of the resisting armies.[3] German Military Attaché Iwan von Ilsemann reported from Bern to OKH:

In Switzerland, the surprisingly fast collapse of the Serbian and the Greek/English resistance has had a very sobering effect. The conviction is gaining ground among the Swiss that they must find some kind of agreement with Germany. However, as before, they do not want to give up their independence and neutrality. But they are afraid that the [German] request will be made at some point, perhaps soon, and that Switzerland will have to take a decision. Accordingly, the country is under constant pressure. Rumors are circulating that a new general mobilization will be necessary soon.[4]

This was only one of repeated episodes throughout the war in which countries were attacked without warning and subsequently had to endure occupation. Switzerland's location on the very border of Germany left the country exposed to the Führer's whims. Hitler was not pleased to have an independent nation—a fully armed and often intractable nation—directly on his southern flank.

With fascist Italy to the south and Austria to the east, Switzerland was still managing to smuggle war matériel to the Allies through Vichy France. The German Armistice Delegation for Economy pressured France to choke off this transit of goods to and from Switzerland. The delegation's reports stated:

We have repeatedly brought up the demand expressed in the German memorandum of March 15, 1941. The French government has declared itself willing to do all it can to prevent the illegal transit of war matériel and other goods indispensable for the war from Switzerland to enemy countries and agrees in particular to increase the surveillance at the border. However, the French government declines to limit the transit from third countries *to* Switzerland because it is of the opinion that such a demand has no legal basis.[5]

The French delegation pointed to existing agreements with Switzerland stipulating freedom of transit, and expressed concern that the German demands would make French goods and services less competitive compared to those of countries that could freely conduct transit trade with Switzerland. They were referring to the age-old competition between Marseille and Genoa. Meanwhile the Allies had initiated a counter-blockade, cutting off transit of anything useful that might reach Germany if allowed into Switzerland.

The Swiss economy was being hammered by both the Axis and the Allies. Tough German-Swiss economic negotiations were instituted on May 23–24, 1941, to the intense interest of OKW since the discussions concerned the military implications of Swiss smuggling. The Swiss extended credits to Germany in exchange for relief from the Allied counter-blockade by expansion of the free list the Germans would allow to pass. So that critical cross-border traffic could be monitored, the Swiss-French border was closed to persons and goods with the exception of the rail and roadway Geneva-Pougny-Bellegarde. German customs officers in both Geneva and Basel would control goods to be exported and imported through France. This was actually a small concession by the Germans. "A single checkpoint in Basel that the Germans requested would cost Switzerland dearly. England would have considered it an obvious submission to German control. The Germans therefore had to agree that goods would in part be inspected in Geneva."[6] The Swiss would thereby avoid a tightening of the Allied blockade.

It was a complicated dance of demand, concession and counter-concession. Both sides needed what Switzerland produced. If one side—Axis or Allied—seemed to be gaining an advantage, the other would threaten to tighten the screws on Switzerland economically.

The crux of all these negotiated trade-offs lay in the effectiveness of enforcement. The Swiss continually found new ways to evade restrictions. The OKW representative demanded that so-called trade samples in letters be prohibited. Until then hundreds of mailings containing precision-engineered components weighing less than two kilograms had gone out daily, unchecked and unhindered via Portugal to England and overseas. Although controlling all mail—as opposed to export shipments—was a huge undertaking and in violation of international mail agreements, the OKW repeatedly sought to intervene, since Swiss mailed exports were significantly aiding the Allies and undermining German defenses.

The Armament Group of the German Armistice Commission reported from Wiesbaden to the OKW General Staff about the substance of these meetings as follows:

> In the meeting of the Delegation for Economy of the German Armistice Commission (Subcommittee for Currency, Banks and Traffic of Goods) in Paris on May 24, 1941, Dr. Schöne, Senior Executive Officer, informed the French that the Germans wished to close all border crossings to Switzerland with the exception of the Geneva-Bellegarde line, which is to be reopened. All other border crossings are to be closed in both directions except for local frontier traffic. Given the urgency of this matter, he asked that his request be answered as soon as possible. He said that the request was directed solely against Switzerland because according to reports in his possession large quantities of war matériel were being exported from Switzerland by way of unoccupied France.
>
> Dr. Schöne said his intent was to redirect all traffic between Switzerland and France within the occupied territory to the

Geneva-Bellegarde line. German flying columns would provide
assurance that French customs control was diligent even in unoccupied territory. However, he added that concern about illegal
arms traffic was no reason to stop the traffic of persons in both
directions. . . .

Should difficulties arise in the movement of goods, cross-border traffic could be allowed over side railroad lines and by truck
over major roadways into Switzerland from France, but in no case
in the other direction. Germany was particularly intent on stop-
ping the export of fuse parts because these were small and could
be transported in large quantities.[7]

Schöne was aware that Swiss smugglers were mailing these miniature
precision fuse parts via roundabout routes to the British for making bombs
to be dropped over Axis territories. They were so tiny that they could be
mailed in ordinary envelopes or hidden in packages with other innocuous
items. The Wehrmacht intended to stop this traffic. Meanwhile, general
negotiations over an economic treaty continued. The OKW noted the
German position:

> In this area, any concession toward freer export by the Swiss to
> countries hostile to Germany constitutes a German sacrifice, since
> there are no severe bottlenecks in the British and American arma-
> ments production. However, we avoided concessions which could
> increase enemy armaments output and ruled out any and all con-
> cessions on heavy machinery and equipment, as well as other crit-
> ical articles such as current rectifiers and generators from the
> comprehensive customs discussions.[8]

Swiss smuggling of war matériel through Vichy France was the subject of a conference in Wiesbaden, on July 11:

> It has been reported that the watchmaker "Le Coultre" in
> Geneva, which is owned by Jäger, is producing parts for time fuses
> for England. These parts are being shipped via Marseille and
> Lisbon in meat, chocolate or cheese containers or packages. The
> request was made to inform the French customs specifically about
> the shipments made by this company.[9]

German intelligence was hot on the trail of John Lomax of the British embassy, who coordinated a robust smuggling operation from Switzerland, but they may not have known about his relations with Emil Bührle, a German World War I artillery officer who immigrated to Switzerland before World War II and founded a weapons factory. The Oerlikon-Bührle firm supplied the Allies with antiaircraft guns until the fall of France in 1940, then smuggled the blueprints to England and the United States, which produced hundreds of thousands of guns for use against the Axis.[10]

Now surrounded by the Axis, the Swiss government made agreements with Germany requiring Swiss firms, including the weapons industry, to export products to Germany. Paradoxically, Switzerland could thereby obtain raw materials from Germany to produce weapons to use against a potential German attack. The Allies blacklisted such Swiss firms, refusing to trade with them. British operative Lomax, however, needed samples of weapons components. He wrote: "The best source was a Swiss factory: but they were working for the Germans and on the blacklist. With the owner, an ex-German artillery officer, I had already had a stormy interview in which he had protested that his factory had been ordered by the Swiss government to accept a German order; they—not he—should be blacklisted." On one visit, the owner, who was obviously Bührle, responded to Lomax's request for the weapon component:

> "And if I give it will you take me off your blacklist?"
> "No, colonel."
> "And are these the ethics of the British government?"
> "No, colonel, they are the ethics of war."
> But I went out with the sample in my pocket.[11]

Throughout this difficult period, Germany still had a few friends in Switzerland. Some just urged realism in the face of the Nazi threat. Others remained attuned to German culture or admired German military successes. Swiss Colonel Gustav Däniker, the officer who was so impressed by the initially successful strategy and tactics of the Wehrmacht, continued to be sympathetic toward Germany. Däniker and his immediate circle were mistrusted by Swiss hardliners. He would eventually be demoted, but it is possible that officers like him were feeding information to the Germans. Officers with German connections may also have given the Swiss military useful intelligence. Just as the Germans were making lists of potential enemies, the Swiss were watching individuals they deemed untrustworthy.

German Military Attaché Iwan von Ilsemann reported from Bern on May 27, 1941, to OKH that he had met with Däniker after the latter's return from a visit to Germany. Däniker told the German attaché that he would report to the Federal Council his impression that "material is currently being gathered in Germany for a white paper against Switzerland," i.e., an official report indicting the Swiss which could serve propaganda purposes justifying aggression. Däniker believed that "the decisive question—whether and to what extent Switzerland will cooperate with Germany in a new Europe—will come to a head as soon as Germany resolves its issues with the countries to its east. He was of the opinion that Germany intends to find a satisfactory solution with Switzerland without using force." Däniker was invited to return to Berlin to attend the course for foreigners at the Scientific Institute for Foreign Policy, but was "afraid that he will be prevented from going if Germany at the same time invites members of organizations prohibited in Switzerland [Nazi Party groups]."[12]

Däniker's reference to Germany confronting Switzerland after resolution of issues in the East was noteworthy, in that Hitler would launch his attack on the Soviet Union less than a month later, on June 22, 1941. Indeed, two days before the attack, OKH Headquarters sent von Ilsemann its "Instructions for Military Intelligence Organization in Switzerland." The organization's head, while directly subordinate to the Foreign Office/Intelligence, was to work closely with the Military Attaché on all issues affecting Switzerland. Those duties included execution of reconnaissance requests concerning Switzerland made by the Attaché, submission of copies regarding all military reports concerning Switzerland, and close consultation with the Attaché.[13]

The Germans expected that the Eastern question would be resolved quickly. Thus, a new German attack plan against Switzerland was submitted on July 14, 1941, by a Major Wiest to Colonel Adolf Heusinger, Chief of the Operations Division of the German Army General Staff. Heusinger was a key planner of Operation Barbarossa, the attack on the Soviet Union, by now rolling over whole Russian armies. Wiest entitled the plan "*Unternehmen W*" (Operation *Wartegau*). A *Gau* was a Nazi administrative unit, and "*Warte*" means to wait. *Wartegau* was thus a play on words, referring to a "province-in-waiting." Wiest's cover letter stated:

Should it become necessary to invade the Swiss Confederation, I take the liberty of sending you a contribution to the preparation of such an invasion under the key word "*Unternehmen W*" (Operation *Wartegau*).

The plan contains a short discussion of operations to be recommended and a section about how and where the Rhine could best be crossed. A third section proposes an entirely new procedure to break up the Confederation from the inside and possibly to paralyze it militarily within a few hours. Sections 2 and 3 can be executed simultaneously.

My draft does not explain all of the details, but gives an overview of the best approach to achieve the goal with the least resources and losses. Given my knowledge of these details, I would consider it appropriate to be temporarily assigned to the Operations Division with orders to work on the operation and to the Army Headquarters charged with its execution.[14]

In Operation *Wartegau*,[15] Wiest recommended an overwhelmingly rapid conquest of the populated middle section of Switzerland from Lake Geneva to the Rhine and Lake Constance, and the prevention of any retreat to the Réduit in the Alps. "The regions of the Alps and the Jura will then fall on their own because it is impossible for the Swiss army to conduct large operations there." Interestingly, he makes the assumption that "the French will occupy the French parts of western Switzerland." Ominously, just weeks earlier Hitler had met with French Admiral Jean Darlan and invited Vichy France to occupy the French-speaking part of Switzerland.[16]

The *Wartegau* plan designated invasion routes to Swiss cities, with particular attention to areas where weapons industries were located. The "occupation of the power plants located between our thrusts will immobilize Swiss troops and make it impossible for them to maneuver (more than 50% of all Swiss trains operate with electricity!)." Assault boats would transport troops across the Rhine in twilight or fog, and armored or camouflaged troop trains would storm into Switzerland using the railways. Wiest suggested the following innovative tactic:

Since [seizing] the Rhine crossings will not be easy to execute and Switzerland has massed troops along the Rhine, the idea suggests itself to assault Switzerland from the inside. However, our experience in Crete has shown that paratroops have great difficulties in mountainous terrain. Air landing troops can be dropped in large numbers only if paratroops secure airports and other landing areas. But then the element of surprise is lost and even if the airfields themselves are secure, the enemy can prevent the landing of troops by targeting runways with long-range artillery. Given this situation, an air landing operation remains problematic.

In the following I am proposing a completely new surprise attack against the enemy:

Our sea transport planes will be gathered on Lake Constance —if necessary also on the lakes of Upper Bavaria—and loaded with troops, in particular light motorized troops. Those planes can then land—all at the same time—on the numerous lakes which form an almost connected string of waterways bordering the middle section of Switzerland. Such a water landing will be a complete surprise to the enemy. The Swiss will have no means to counter it and, once landed, our troops can seize the operational objectives listed in Section I almost immediately. These troops will then proceed to erect barriers and our most mobile units will begin operations in the reverse order from that described in Section I. These operations will be considerably easier to conduct since Swiss border defenses will be attacked from the rear. Their front-facing border fortifications will be worthless.

Luftwaffe planes would conduct this surprise attack in pre-dawn hours, approaching all lakes simultaneously. Landings near cities such as Zurich, Thun, and Luzern would prevent the enemy from using artillery for defense. The plan concluded: "Given the prevailing weather in the foothills of the Alps, the fall (first half of October) should be particularly appropriate for this operation." Within the German strategic context, this July plan was intended for execution in October, by which time Russia would have been knocked out of the war and troops could be spared to eradicate the irritating Swiss democracy once and for all.

German planning security was not total, and thanks to reports provided by Swiss intelligence, Commander-in-Chief Guisan devised plans to resist such a German lake invasion.[17]

On July 21, Colonel Heusinger of the German General Staff commented on Wiest's plan as follows: "The case discussed by you is not critical at this point, although I have ordered an evaluation of your suggestions."[18] For the moment at least, Heusinger had other fish to fry. The Wehrmacht's advances in Russia were staggering and had become a logistical nightmare. In the short run, Switzerland had little to contribute and no *Lebensraum*. He was willing to let the country continue as a *Wartegau* (waiting to be a Nazi *Gau*) a little longer.

In the first half of August a German informant on a business trip to Switzerland noted that "the military is everywhere." Passengers on trains were mostly soldiers. The Limmat and Jura defensive lines were being extended. There was intensive work on the defensive fortifications leading toward the *Réduit national*—the National Redoubt—particularly the construction of bunkers and field fortifications. Inside the Réduit, massive decentralized reserve depots of ammunition, fuel, and food had been assembled. The general population remained vigorously opposed to a *Grossdeutschland* (Greater Germany) to the point that "people in German-speaking Switzerland abstain from speaking High German in interactions with Reich Germans and speak only Swiss German."[19] This was not only an anti-German "attitude" on the part of the Swiss, it was a way of allowing them to speak more openly without divulging information useful to the enemy, since the Swiss German dialects cannot, for the most part, be understood by Germans.

Meanwhile, Gestapo chief and SS Reichsführer Heinrich Himmler was making detailed plans for a future occupation. He even named specific Nazis he intended to assign to govern the country. SS *Gruppenführer* (Major General) Gottlob Berger was directly under Himmler in the SS hierarchy and reported to him.[20] Himmler named Berger to head the *Schweizer Referat* (Swiss Project).[21]

Himmler trusted Berger, who was a very active Nazi and a stalwart of the SS. He had been involved in recruiting volunteers of Aryan blood throughout Europe for the Waffen SS, Himmler's troops, for the campaign against the Soviet Union.[22] The SS Viking Division, for example, was composed primarily of Scandinavian volunteers. The huge breadth and depth of the Russian front had meanwhile diverted attention and resources away from any plan to attack Switzerland. It had begun to put a heavy strain on German resources and increased the need to find additional manpower and supplies. Perhaps Switzerland could make—or be forced to make—a contribution.

In this context, Berger wrote to Himmler on September 8, 1941, concerning who might become Reich Commissar of a Nazi-occupied

Switzerland. It is apparent from his letter that Nazi officials were already fighting among themselves over who would become leader of the conquered Alpine republic:

> Some people see a ray of hope in Württemberg! Both the mayor of the city of Stuttgart, Dr. Strölin, and Reich Governor Murr think that they will get the post of *"Reichskommissare"* for Switzerland.
>
> Based on personal knowledge, I would not appoint either of them to this post. In particular not Reich Governor Murr. He would attempt to "positively Aryanize" Switzerland, which would delay the country's true integration for at least one generation.
>
> I have made my position clear to SS Oberführer Dr. Behrends, and have asked him and the VDA [*Verein für das Deutschtum im Ausland*, or League for Germandom Abroad] not to provide any funds for "transition organizations" unless the Reichsführer SS [Himmler] has ordered them to do so.
>
> We should set up the leadership of these transition organizations in Berlin, not locally. All Swiss National Socialist leaders currently in Germany should gather in Berlin. This would guarantee control, ensure quality outcomes and avoid clashes of ego.[23]

In short, a police state for Switzerland would have been carefully structured by the SS in Berlin, with German Nazis in command and Swiss puppets to do their bidding. It is noteworthy that at the time no Swiss National Socialist had any influence at all, in stark contrast to Norway's infamous Quisling or France's Laval. The only real contenders were Germans and outsiders—Wilhelm Murr, Gauleiter (district leader appointed by the NSDAP) of Württemberg, and Dr. Karl Strölin, Mayor of Stuttgart. This political squabble over potential spoils is evidence that plans to invade Switzerland were circulating at the highest levels of the Gestapo.

The 1941 offensive against Russia slowed as fall turned into winter, leaving intentions against Switzerland in an uncertain mode. A detailed map of Swiss troop positions dated October 31, prepared for the German Army General Staff, shows the placement of Swiss divisions and brigades at the border, in the Plateau, and in the Alpine stronghold, the Réduit.[24] As with previous maps, the presence of some question marks indicated that Wehrmacht intelligence did not have full information, but that its spies were systematic and diligent.

Indeed, top Nazis made clear their intentions to a member of a Swiss contingent that provided medical services in the campaign against the Soviet Union. A future Federal Councillor obtained the following intelligence and recorded it in his diary:

> Dr. Thönen-Zweisimmen was at the Eastern front with a group of Swiss physicians in the winter of 1941/1942 and stayed at the Führer's headquarters for three days. Hitler himself was not there during those three days. But Göring, Himmler, Goebbels and Heydrich were present. Thönen had the opportunity to speak to all four of them. The four were in agreement that the German Wehrmacht absolutely needed to occupy Switzerland, that Switzerland should not be allowed to remain independent, and needed to be glad if, as a concession, a Swiss national would be appointed Gauleiter.[25]

In December 1941 the Germans were finally stopped at the gates of Moscow, then reeled before a Soviet winter counterattack. Then the blows and counterblows of renewed German offensives—seeking the ever-elusive knockout blow—set the skies aflame through the spring and summer of 1942. From his bunkers, Hitler followed the chaos on the Eastern Front with maniacal intensity. Switzerland was a detail in this struggle of titans, the subject of jokes and asides. Nonetheless Nazi intentions to take the Swiss Confederation continued. In the fall of 1942, Berlin made more plans for an attack against Switzerland. Hitler toyed with knocking down the Swiss throughout the war.[26]

Foreign Minister Ribbentrop directed the German legation in Switzerland to prepare a report estimating how long Swiss food and raw materials would last. The legation responded that, thanks to her foresighted economic policy, Switzerland had stored sufficient raw materials and foodstuffs to sustain its National Réduit in the Alps for approximately two years. Going on to answer the real question behind Ribbentrop's inquiry, legation head Köcher wrote that the Swiss are a hardy mountain people who would resist fiercely. Moreover, they would never allow the Gotthard and Simplon rail tunnels to fall into a conqueror's hands undestroyed. So, no improvement of transportation to and from Italy could be expected after an attack on Switzerland.

Theo Kordt, Counselor at the Embassy, informed Admiral Wilhelm Canaris, chief of the Abwehr, about Ribbentrop's inquiry and the embassy's response. Canaris, in his report to his military superiors, emphasized Switzerland's will to resist and its economic and geographical strengths.

These legation and Abwehr reports may well have discouraged Hitler from moving ahead with an attack. Shortly before his dismissal from the Abwehr, Canaris made his last visit to Bern, where he expressed gratification to Kordt over the success of their common efforts to prevent an attack against Switzerland, which would only have shed more German blood. Canaris would later be executed for his membership in the failed conspiracy to assassinate Hitler in 1944.

In September 1942, the Division for Foreign Armies West of the German Army's General Staff put together a *Kleine Orientierungsheft Schweiz* (Orientation Booklet about Switzerland). It included a brief exposition of the Swiss Army's fighting qualities:

> Under the Swiss militia system, all men fit for duty are registered at relatively low cost. This militia system maintains the martial spirit of the Swiss people and establishes an army that, for such a small country, is strong, well organized, and quickly mobilized.
>
> Swiss soldiers love their country and are hardy and tough. They are excellent marksmen and take good care of their weapons, equipment, uniforms, horses and pack animals. In particular Swiss Germans and soldiers from the Alps are reputed to be good fighters.
>
> However, despite intensive drills and exercises over recent years, soldiers were not trained well enough, at least at the beginning of the war.
>
> Army leadership reflects both German and French influences. However, the lack of real-war experience and the overly bureaucratic organization of the staffs complicate most operations. Also, the Swiss tend to commit their reserves too quickly.
>
> With that said, so far there have been no indications that both the government and the people are not determined to defend Swiss neutrality against any and all attackers.[27]

For their part, Swiss intelligence had a source in the German high command known as the "Wiking Line" (sometimes called in English "Viking"). On March 19, 1943, the Swiss learned from this informant that the Germans, anticipating an Allied attack in Italy, were once more planning to invade Switzerland. The Swiss believed mountain troops were concentrating in Bavaria. The definitive account of this episode, which became known as the *März-Alarm* (March Alarm), has been set forth in a book by noted historian Pierre-Th. Braunschweig.[28]

There was another factor to concern the Swiss. The German general staff had been discussing a strategic retreat from Russia into a Fortress Europe, of which Switzerland could be a pillar but which would include all defensible parts of occupied Europe. The SS had orders to prepare such a Fortress and wished to incorporate Switzerland into the plan. Fortunately for the Swiss, Hitler decided against any voluntary retreat.

According to one account, when "Wiking" warned Swiss intelligence of the Germans' "Case Switzerland," Swiss Colonel Roger Masson naïvely asked SS General Walter Schellenberg if an attack was about to commence. (In the murky world of intelligence operatives, the most unlikely people talk to each other; none other than OSS operative Allen Dulles also had contacts with Schellenberg.[29]) Masson thus tipped Schellenberg off that a leak existed in Hitler's headquarters. The element of surprise was lost for a German attack which the Swiss were now preparing to repulse. Schellenberg—probably to ingratiate himself with the hope of soliciting intelligence—later told Masson that he had persuaded the German command that an invasion was unnecessary.[30]

The existence of independent Switzerland continued to gnaw at Hitler's mind during this period. In a May 8 diary entry, Nazi Propaganda Minister Goebbels described Hitler's address to a conference of Reichsleiters and Gauleiters, Party sub-leaders. "The Fuehrer deduced that all the rubbish of small nations [*Kleinstaaten–Geruempel*] still existing in Europe must be liquidated as fast as possible." Recalling Charlemagne, who was called the "Butcher of the Saxons," Hitler asked:

> Who will guarantee to the Führer that at some later time he will not be attacked as the "Butcher of the Swiss"? Austria, after all, also had to be forced into the Reich. We can be happy that it happened in such a peaceful and enthusiastic manner; but if [Austrian Chancellor] Schuschnigg had offered resistance, it would have been necessary, of course, to overcome this resistance by force.[31]

Meanwhile, in July 1943 the Allies invaded Sicily, and Mussolini was deposed. Hitler immediately dispatched troops to northern Italy to secure

the Alpine passes. The Swiss made it clear that they would fight any invader. The German Luftwaffe Attaché in Bern reported on July 31, 1943,
about a conversation he had had with Lieutenant Colonel von Wattenwyl,
head of the Swiss *Kriegstechnische Abteilung* (KTA, Technical War Unit):

> The development of the war in the Mediterranean region was
> causing growing concerns that the front might after all move clos-
> er to the southern border of Switzerland in the near future. He
> said that Switzerland was preparing to fight unwelcome surprises
> there. He also said that the high command of the Swiss army was
> firmly determined to defend the country's borders *against any*
> *attacker* and under all circumstances.
>
> He stated that this was a firm decision and did not doubt that
> the entire population would defend the country, even against the
> Americans from whom an attack was most feared or against the
> British. In his opinion, the population has an unbending will to
> defend the freedom and independence of the country.
>
> We have also heard that some Swiss army members are of the
> opinion today that the moment might come where it might be
> appropriate to ask certain forces of the German army to provide
> help. We must, however, emphasize that such statements are
> merely private opinions at this point.[32]

Swiss determination to "defend the country's borders *against any*
attacker" applied above all to Germany. The explanation that the Swiss
would defend their country "also" against the Americans was almost certainly an attempt to shore up the Swiss posture of neutrality. It was highly unlikely that Switzerland would be invaded by anyone but Germany.

The above included a report by the Foreign Office/Military Intelligence (*Amt Ausland/Abwehr*) stating the following: "Reliable liaison agent on
June 25. Switzerland has entered into a secret agreement. In case of a
German attack, England would immediately land and put at disposition
2,000 planes in Switzerland." The German Embassy in Buenos Aires
reported that the U.S. government made continued grants of navigation
certificates to Swiss ships traveling there dependent on Switzerland granting "the right to march through the country in case of an invasion of
Italy." The next entry in the intelligence log: "Alleged preparations in
Switzerland for a general mobilization in August. On July 4 the Irish
Envoy in Bern reported to Dublin that he had learned that Swiss author-

ities were preparing for a general mobilization in August." On July 23, a German liaison agent reported:

> Learned today from two independent and reliable sources that Anglo-American acts of sabotage by paratroops on the southern shore of Lake Geneva and the Italian shore of Lake Maggiore and Lake Lugano in the vicinity of the Swiss border are about to take place. Goal: to destroy power plants, transportation hubs, key structures. Paratroops will enter Swiss territory after finishing their tasks. My own opinion: take report seriously.

It was an intelligence shadow game—rumors and counter-rumors, the planting of disinformation for specific ends. For instance, the same German intelligence report noted the following—almost certainly duplicitous—discussion with Swiss intelligence:

> [Swiss Colonel] Masson spoke openly to me about the Allies' plan to march through Switzerland. He said that two factors could save us from such a transit: 1. Should the Allies succeed in invading France, which he doubted, they would have no need to move through Switzerland. 2. Our never-ending watchfulness. He was talking, no doubt, less of the Swiss army's watchfulness than that of the Swiss counterespionage. He said that he had proof that the Allied plan to march through Switzerland was of recent vintage and that Allied espionage rings would have to develop its basis.

By such crafted communications, Masson was actually trying to persuade the Germans not to invade Switzerland. But German intelligence mistrusted the Swiss and saw through these machinations. The following German report depicted Swiss intentions as utterly conniving:

> Reliable liaison agent of the Münster division reported on September 10 that in mid-August the Anglo-American side held negotiations with General Guisan about a potential Allied strike through Switzerland. It would involve an invasion through the southern Alpine passes—St. Gotthard, Maloja, and Bernina—and would follow on a successful landing in upper Italy on the Mediterranean coast between San Remo and Spezia. The Swiss army, it was agreed, would pretend to fight in the first hours to

avoid giving Germany a reason for a counter-invasion into Switzerland. That would allow the Allies to get control of all of the
Alpine passes. The Anglo-Americans were hoping that a rapid
advance through Switzerland would decide the war. That would
be preferable to a long-lasting conflict in the Alps between Ortler
and Trento. As for Switzerland, the Allied passage would not create any new danger since Germany was already too weak to
undertake a precautionary invasion of Switzerland or attempt an
occupation of its Alpine passes.

Both the Anglo-Americans and General Guisan are said to be
of the opinion that the Reich will not be capable of holding Italy,
and that a swift move of the Allies through Switzerland would
decide the war faster.[33]

An Allied incursion through Switzerland in 1943 may or may not have
decided the war faster, but Switzerland was genuinely neutral, and
General Guisan would not have agreed to an invasion of his country by
any belligerent. As with Guisan's 1940 agreement that French troops
could enter Switzerland in the event of a German invasion, it is conceivable that Guisan may have agreed that Allied forces could enter the country in the event of a German invasion. No known Allied documents from
the 1943 period, however, suggest such an agreement. Moreover, Switzerland's centuries-old policy was to protect her inhabitants by staying out of
war, not to become a battleground. By entering the war, the Swiss would
have risked national suicide, would have exposed Jewish citizens and
refugees to the Holocaust and would have compromised humanitarian
activities, including Red Cross assistance to POWs. Among the Allies, only
the Soviet Union recommended an invasion of Switzerland, and only
because Stalin detested the democratic republic. The Nazis were also still
formulating invasion plans.

German military authorities were exasperated that the Swiss refused
to allow the Wehrmacht to transport war booty and to evacuate forces
from Italy through Switzerland.[34] As the situation in Italy turned more
chaotic and the responsibility for defending Italy passed to the German
army, the Italian supply routes became more critical. It was necessary for
Germany to secure those chokepoints. Throughout 1943, the increasing
scale of the war in the Mediterranean contributed to the crisis in north–
south transport, particularly at the Gotthard and Simplon passes through
the Alps.

The German general staff feared a collapse of their position in Italy, suddenly bringing the war to the Alps. It is likely that several Swiss invasion plans were formulated during this period. The only surviving plan was authored in late 1943 by SS General Hermann Böhme, who had become chief of the Austrian military intelligence service after the *Anschluss* and was knowledgeable about Switzerland. His draft plan was entitled "thoughts concerning Swiss defenses in the event of a German armed intervention." The details of his plan, provided in this author's *Target Switzerland*, will only be summarized here.[35]

Böhme was aware that Switzerland was posturing her military forces to demonstrate strength against the German threat. Instead of adapting to the new military-political situation in Europe, Switzerland had been driven by her internal politics into a peculiar defensive posture. "The visible consequence is the Réduit (Alpine fortress): fight, instead of putting herself entirely into the concerns of the new Europe." Having refused to join the crusade against Russia, Switzerland found herself completely surrounded by the Reich's seizure of Vichy France. Böhme pinpointed the following grievances:

1. Swiss defense measures taken against Allied flights over Swiss territory are insufficient considering Swiss defenses.
2. The bulk of news whether broadcast or in the press is anti-German. . . .
3. The granting of asylum to so-called refugees and the presence of large numbers of Allied intelligence services seriously damage German-Swiss relationships.
4. The numerous connections of Swiss capital with foreign countries are increasingly organized in the interests of Allied, not German, interests. German victory in Europe would have disastrous financial consequences for Swiss financial interests.
5. Members of Swiss military who appeared German-friendly always claim to be strictly neutral and have turned against us.

The Allied invasion and the fall of Mussolini led to exclusive German army control in northern Italy, tightening the noose around Switzerland. Switzerland was once more threatened, even as the war seemed to be turning against the Germans on all fronts. Still, the Swiss continued their refusal to revise their defense posture to accommodate increasingly shrill German demands.

Anticipating that Switzerland could now become a stepping-stone to Germany for the Allies, General Böhme addressed the question: "With the present realities, how can Switzerland be quickly subdued with military force?" He proceeded to consider in detail the strength of Swiss national defenses, recognizing the Swiss Army's roots in the populace. There were 470,000 soldiers to contend with in 1939, but there would be 550,000 by the end of 1943. Domestic industry supplied the army with a good quantity and quality of arms—from 34mm machine guns to 120mm cannon—as well as ammunition and motor vehicles. Fortifications both at the borders and in the interior had been significantly strengthened.

On the other side of the equation, the Swiss Army was inexperienced in combat; it possessed insufficient tanks and air power; and the country's industry was concentrated near combat zones. Yet Böhme knew this army should not be underrated. He wrote:

> The *fighting spirit* of Swiss soldiers is very high, at a level with that of the Finns. A people that produces good gymnasts produces good soldiers, and the unconditional patriotism of the Swiss is beyond doubt. As for skills, despite the army's dependence on a militia system, Swiss marksmanship is better than that found in, say, the former Austrian Army. . . .

The goal of a German attack had to be to conquer the country *intact*. An invasion would be profitable only if Swiss industry remained substantially undamaged. The population had to be willing and able to work, and essentials like electric power and railways could not be destroyed. The reprovisioning of German armies had become precarious, and it would not be advisable to undertake military operations that would transform Switzerland into a wasteland.

Swiss national defense was based on a large and strong army. It would be difficult to overcome the stubborn resistance of the Swiss troops defending a steep and geographically advantageous Alpine Réduit. The Germans could not get away with using a limited number of troops, no matter how well trained and aggressive. But Böhme had a plan he thought could succeed.

He detailed two operations to be executed independently of each other. Operation I would focus the main attack against the northern plateau, with swift occupation of the Swiss airfields and the capture of the mass of the Swiss army. Operation II would leapfrog directly into the

Réduit with paratroopers, mountain troops, and ground forces. To succeed, paratroopers would have to split Swiss forces by cutting off the plateau from the Réduit within the first 72 hours. The Luftwaffe would fend off any possible Allied bombing attacks.

Böhme's plan recommended a surprise attack from all sides with 15 divisions. Casualties were expected to be 20 percent. The operation had not only to eliminate the last army of central Europe opposed to Germany, but also to seize numerous stores of arms and take possession of a large number of factories able to serve German war industry. It would secure Swiss railway lines and the links to Italy. After the invasion, a permanent German security force would be required to guarantee the pacification of the country.

Böhme's attack was targeted for the late summer of 1944, preferably in August. Any preparations, however, were abruptly halted with the Allied invasion of Normandy in June 1944. From then on, Nazi battle plans would reel into a cycle of fierce resistance and chaotic, bloody retreats toward the Fatherland.

In the spring of 1944, that was all in the future. In the weeks before D-Day, the everyday war went on. The German Military Attaché in Bern was reporting on illegal traffic at the Swiss-French border, support based in Switzerland for French partisans in the high Savoy Alps, the Swiss attitude in case of an attack by the Allies, the attempts by Polish internees to contact the French resistance and changes in Swiss military dispositions in Ticino ordered by Lieutenant General Herbert Constam.[36] Constam was now preparing to defend the southern border from German forces in Italy being pushed back by the Allies.

Then came D-Day, followed in August by an Allied invasion of southern France, and as the weeks wore on, the success of Allied onslaughts from both France and Italy opened up new dangers of a desperate German move against Switzerland. A report to the Army High Command (OKH) and General Staff on August 22, 1944, included a comprehensive analysis of the military situation vis-à-vis Switzerland:

> The Swiss army has sufficient modern weapons and equipment. Its armored force is weak, but armor won't be a factor in this terrain. The air force is negligible. However, the army is well trained. Its able-bodied men have been mobilized repeatedly since the war began.
>
> Given the indoctrination of the army with the imperative that

the home country must be defended *against any attacker*, we have to expect that the Swiss soldiers will fight well. Against Allied troops, we would, however, expect them to exhibit certain sympathies for the Allies. . . .

The main focus of the current mobilization is directed at the southern border, in particular in the area of the Ticino. Recently, Swiss defenses there have been considerably strengthened and extended further south.

The Swiss plan of operation provides for a vigorous defense of the mass of the field army in the fortified high Alps (National Réduit). Originally, the fortifications along the country's border were designed to be held by weaker forces only until the assembly in the Réduit had been completed. According to newer plans, however, it appears we would have to expect vigorous resistance along the borders too. . . .

There are also some significant fortifications in the area between the border protection zone and the high Alps (the Baden-Zurich defensive line). The accesses to the high Alps are protected in the west by the fortification *St. Maurice* (where the Rhone flows into Lake Geneva), in the south by the *St. Gotthard* fortifications, in the east by the fortification at *Sargans* (north of Chur), and in the north by the fortifications *Glarus* and those along the general line Zug–Luzern–Thun." All roads leading to the high Alps are defended by substantial roadblocks.[37]

Reacting to the Allied campaigns in France and Italy, Switzerland further secured her western and southern borders. After a trip to Bern, a German military intelligence officer reported on September 14, 1944:

We are aware of the partial mobilizations ordered at the western and southern borders. . . . From conversations with leading personalities we may assume that Switzerland will fight any attempt to violate her neutrality by use of arms. The old policy that anybody stepping on Swiss soil bearing arms is an enemy of the country is still valid. Whether all Swiss soldiers would fight with enthusiasm and nerve, even against Anglo-American or French soldiers, remains to be seen. Even some Swiss officers doubt that. It appears certain that the Federal Council and the army staff are determined to fight any violation of neutrality. As for the rest, the

danger of an attempt by Allied forces to march through Switzerland is considered lower than it used to be, since there are no
longer large German units fighting along the Swiss border in the
west and the German left wing is assumed to be near Basel/St.
Louis. In this connection I would like to mention a statement
made to the Envoy by Federal Councilor Pilet-Golaz wherein he
maintained that the Allies do not have any plans to march through
Switzerland.[38]

Minister Pilet-Golaz, now head of the Swiss Foreign Ministry, had
every incentive to make this representation, whether true or not. The
Swiss knew only too well that an allegedly impending Allied occupation
had been used as the pretext for German preemptive invasions of other
neutral nations. Swiss diplomats and military spokesmen thus went out of
their way to assure German envoys that the Allies would not intrude on
Swiss territory. There was to be no justification for a German "preemptive" strike such as occurred against Norway in 1940.

Yet a very real danger existed that Switzerland would become a battle-
ground between the Allies and the Axis in 1944. A clash of foreign armies
in Switzerland and a devastating occupation had occurred during the
Napoleonic wars. Stalin was even urging his Western allies to smash
Germany through Switzerland because, among other things, he had a
strong dislike of the Swiss way of life. Fortunately, the Americans and
British would have none of it. As is now known, the Combined Chiefs Of
Staff in their instructions for the Supreme Headquarters of the Allied
Expeditionary Force (SHAEF) removed the question of breaching Swiss
neutrality entirely from the realm of discussion.[39]

The Germans, however, were unsure of Allied intentions. Thus,
German commanders methodically went ahead with plans for meeting
the enemy on a "Swiss front." General Balck, who headed Army Group
D—including the 19th Army whose left wing extended to the Swiss border—thought an Allied push through Switzerland possible and set about
devising counterstrokes. A September 25, 1944, diary entry of Army
Group D noted that one corps headquarters anticipated an Allied march
through Switzerland into the south Baden area. Army Group D must prepare a surprise advance at Schaffhausen to be supported by Luftwaffe sorties over Swiss territory.

The German high command in the West decided against violating
Swiss neutrality, which was a risky proposition at best given the prospect

of robust Swiss resistance. Field Marshal von Rundstedt, the Commander-in-Chief West, issued an order to secure the left wing of the 19th Army from possible threats to its flank. Strengthening of the left wing along the Swiss border was required, but Swiss neutrality was to be strictly observed, and it was forbidden to cross the border or to communicate with Swiss military personnel or civilians.

Another entry for Army Group D stated: "Daily reports show that the Army Group has taken measures to protect Switzerland from enemy invasion." If true, such measures were indeed protection, but not for Switzerland. The Wehrmacht wanted no Allied attack through Swiss territory to reach the southern border of Germany.

Between November 1944 and April 1945, Army Group D took various jump-off positions along the Swiss border—following the Rhine past Basel to Lake Constance, and also in the Canton of Schaffhausen. That "Case Schaffhausen" and other German strike plans never materialized can be attributed in part to German reluctance to engage the Swiss porcupine—especially when men, transport and planes were desperately needed on other fronts. The Allies also chose to respect Swiss neutrality. Their advances were going well enough elsewhere.

The full extent of Nazi plans for subversion and invasion against Switzerland, from the birth to the death of the Third Reich, will never be known. After the war ended, the Swiss government prepared a report detailing known Nazi subversive activities against Switzerland. The report was introduced as an exhibit by the Allies in the Nürnberg war crimes trials. The Office of Chief of Counsel for War Crimes of the U.S. Army described its import as follows: "Report by the Swiss Federal Council to the Swiss National Assembly on anti-democratic activities during the war years has it that SS-Obergruppenführer Berger knew of a plan, advanced by the SS Main Office, aiming at extending Nazi rule over Switzerland."[40] The report was categorized under "SS" entities and "Preparation for Aggressive War." The summary stated in part:

> This is a report by the Swiss Federal Council (*Bundesrat*) to the Swiss National Assembly (*Bundesversammlung*) on anti-democratic activities of Swiss nationals and foreigners during the war years 1939 to 1945. . . . Disclosed in that report is, especially, the information the Swiss had obtained on German plans aiming at occupying Switzerland and make it another *Gau* of Greater Germany. Particular reference is made to a document contained in Swiss

files, bearing the heading "The Reichsführer SS, SS Hauptamt, Aktion S," in which a detailed plan is set forth for the realization of the German intention to establish Nazi rule in Switzerland.

The Swiss report details Nazi threats to Switzerland throughout the war. In fact, actions to undermine Swiss security were planned and executed without interruption until the very end of the conflict. However, Swiss counterespionage was highly effective. The report notes that from September 1944 through January 1945 a Swiss citizen who worked as a clerk at the SS Main Office's Section for Switzerland regularly made secret reports to the Swiss Embassy about the Section's activities and transmitted important documents.[41] Still another invasion plan was being hatched, this one directed by German SS operatives who would make use of Swiss traitors who had joined the Waffen SS and were fighting for Germany. Section head Paul Benz was certain that Germany would conquer Switzerland by military means at some point and that, even in 1945, he was convinced that Germany would win the war. During 1944, while Benz was an official at SS Main Office D I/3 *h*, preparations were made for the period following the expected conquest and seizure of power. Attempts were made to organize Swiss personnel in the Reich within German *Sturmbanner* (SS battalions) for this purpose.

During the war years, a small contingent of Swiss had volunteered for service in the Wehrmacht. Some were committed National Socialists; others were young, unemployed, and caught up in the martial ardor of the anti-Bolshevik crusade. A Swiss law passed in 1927, which is still in effect, made it a crime for a Swiss citizen to fight in a foreign war. This law was violated by about 700 Swiss who had joined the proto-Communist International Brigades in the Spanish Civil War.[42] It was also violated during World War II by some 870 Swiss who resided in Switzerland and who volunteered to serve in the German forces, as well as by another 1,110 Swiss living abroad, particularly in Germany, who did the same.[43] In view of Switzerland's 4.2 million population at the time, these numbers were insignificant. Far larger numbers volunteered for German service from France, the Netherlands, and other European countries. When it was possible to apprehend them, particularly after the war, such violators were prosecuted and imprisoned under Swiss law.

These were the Swiss on whom the SS planned to rely. In mid-1944, Benz wrote a plan based on previous discussions with his friend, Waffen SS officer Valdo Rodio. Rodio had forsaken Zurich and his homeland to attend the SS-Junker School in Tölz, became an SS *Untersturmführer* (second lieutenant) in a panzer regiment, and had died at age 22 of wounds received in combat earlier that year.[44]

Addressed to "Reichsführer SS, SS Main Office" (Himmler) the Benz plan was entitled *"Aktion-S"* (Action Switzerland). The plan provided:[45]

1. Carefully observe military and political developments. Cooperate with SD [Security Service] and Ministry of Foreign Affairs.
2. Take in Swiss National Socialists and their families. Report by way of Special Commission, Gestapo and Ministry of Foreign Affairs. Prepare shelters for them.
3. Retrieve a number of Swiss SS leaders from the front to deploy them in Switzerland for political purposes.
4. Collect all Swiss SS volunteers. Combine them in a Swiss unit later.
5. Combine all Swiss National Socialists in the Reich and organize them through the *Sturmbanner* [SS battalions].

In Switzerland:
6. Together with the Reich Main Security Office, destroy all enemies of the Reich.
7. Set up a German head office in Switzerland to serve as central political lead agency.
8. Set up an *Ersatzkommando Schweiz* (Swiss replacement command) of the Waffen SS and a Swiss SS unit.
9. Determine all National Socialists (not economic opportunists) and combine them in one organization.
10. Set up a German SS in Switzerland as a pool for all good forces and a political fighting organization.

This last reference to establishing "a *German* SS in Switzerland" had reference to the sizable German fifth column in Switzerland as well as German agents who would be sent there for that purpose.

In addition, *"Aktion-S"* by Benz made lists of the persons who he thought would facilitate the Nazi occupation. The categories of lists included:[46]

a. "List of all National Socialist Swiss living in the Reich who could be used for political action," containing 14 names.

b. "List of SS leaders earmarked for political deployment in Switzerland," containing 11 names.

c. "List of SS leaders stationed at the SS Main Office and earmarked for deployment in Switzerland," containing 3 names.

d. "List of Reich Germans who could be used for political deployment to Switzerland," containing the names of Dr. [Georg] Ashton [former German vice counsel] and Mr. von Chamier, former press attaché in Bern.

e. "Connections in Switzerland," containing 4 names.

f. Hand-written lists of names under the following headings for Divisions: Agriculture, Education, Church, etc., Economy, Army, Justice and Police, *Gauleitung* [head of Nazi administrative unit], Plenipotentiary of the Reich, Higher SS and Police Leader, Leader of the German SS, Head of the *Gau* leadership in Switzerland, Youth, and Culture.

Benz worked with Dr. Max Leo Keller, a Swiss Nazi whose *Nationale Bewegung der Schweiz* (NBS, or National Movement of Switzerland) had been banned by the Swiss government in 1940 as a subversive organization. Keller and other NBS members were tried before a Swiss military tribunal and imprisoned. After his release, Keller moved to Germany for the rest of the war to engage in anti-Swiss activities for Himmler's SS.[47] Dr. Heinrich Rothmund, Director of the Swiss Federal Police Division, referred to Keller as among "the Swiss Lumpen [riffraff] in Germany."[48] After the war, Keller was apprehended by Swiss authorities and sentenced to imprisonment for 14 years.[49]

Urging German occupation of Switzerland, Benz wrote a letter on August 28, 1944, to Keller, informing him that Switzerland had mobilized five days before and "may be approaching war faster than we are aware." He urged Keller to continue exerting his influence with the Ministry of Foreign Affairs and Party Headquarters, noting that "Romania's case has taught us that we can never be careful enough." (In view of the near approach of the Red Army, Romania had just switched sides to the Soviet Union.[50])

Benz continued: "If necessary, we would promote the unification of *der Schweizerbünde* (Swiss groups) in the Reich. We would do that in a way that the German SS would have complete authority to combine all Swiss National Socialists in the Reich and to send them out for political action in Switzerland."[51] While Benz grossly overrated the ability of his tiny number of Swiss to facilitate this ambitious task, both the SS and Wehrmacht were still fully capable of wreaking havoc, as the occupation of Hungary and later the Ardennes offensive demonstrated.

On November 27, 1944, there was a meeting about "Aktion S[witzerland]" at the SS *Bureau des Referates Schweiz* (Office of the Section for Switzerland). A lieutenant colonel from the OKW, German SS Colonel Erich Spaarmann, SS Captain Hans Georg Lindt (previously a Swiss attorney from Bern),[52] SS Lieutenant Colonel Heinrich Hersche (who was Swiss and was later imprisoned by Swiss authorities for his activities),[53] and Benz participated in that meeting. They discussed how the political and police structure would be organized in Switzerland if there were a political upheaval or if war broke out. The plan was to set up an SS police corps of 50 to 100 men per Swiss city. The police organization would be headed by a former German consul in Lausanne (probably Daufeldt, who had been expelled) and a consul working for the German Embassy who dealt with police issues. In addition, the SS group decided to send all Swiss belonging to the Waffen SS and deployed on the Eastern Front to a special training camp in Hallein near Salzburg under the command of SS Captain Wilhelm Knapp, who was Swiss.[54]

In a report dated December 13, 1944, Benz observed that since 1940–41, National Socialists in Switzerland "had been put in prison, jail or security detention or had to find refuge in Germany. Those who stayed in Switzerland . . . were monitored so strictly by the police that it was impossible to conduct any political activity, even insignificant tasks." Thus, Benz argued, it was necessary to start a Swiss National Socialist movement from scratch. "There would be only one way to restart this development, namely with the volunteers of the Waffen SS and the members of the SS Sturmbanner. . . . He thought that the best approach to develop the National Socialist movement in Switzerland further would be to put all of the Swiss National Socialists under the umbrella of the German SS, to educate them in their common view of the world and to prepare them professionally for the tasks they would assume later."[55]

Once again, although Nazi Germany was nearing defeat, just three days after the above report it would launch a devastating attack against the Allies in the Ardennes, leading to the Battle of the Bulge. An alternative plan by Hitler could very well have involved an attack against Switzerland. It would have been a thoroughly German operation, the numbers of Swiss in the Waffen SS being so few; yet, those Swiss were considered essential to any operation. The Wehrmacht could launch a military attack, but persons with intimate knowledge of the country would be necessary to set up the police state that followed.

The head of the SS Main Office, Lieutenant General Berger, must have known about the above attack plans, for Benz reported to him every month. The postwar Swiss report thus noted that not only Berger but also the Reichsführer-SS Himmler must have known about the conspiracy against Switzerland. It was rumored that Benz was called to see Himmler in Salzburg in late fall 1944.[56] Berger was one of Himmler's closest confidants during this period.[57] "Aktion S" was a real option.

This intrigue against Switzerland in the last months of the war indicates the degree to which she was still under threat of Nazi attack. Like the Allies, the Swiss never discounted the Nazi threat. The nightmare for the Swiss, who had been surrounded, isolated and menaced since 1940, ended only with Germany's unconditional surrender on May 8, 1945.

The full extent of the Nazi threat to Switzerland during World War II has never been adequately acknowledged. This study seeks to contribute to a better understanding of a subject that is not mentioned in the studies by the governmental commissions published in the late 1990s and early 2000s in the United States and Switzerland. The reality was that the Swiss citizenry, rifles in hand, stood up to the Nazis, threatening an unacceptable loss of German blood in the event of an invasion. History does not disclose what would have occurred had conditional plans been executed. But Walter Lippmann perhaps said it best when he wrote prior to the end of the war, "We must not forget, now or in the future, how faithfully the Swiss Republic has borne witness to the cause of freedom."[58]

CHAPTER 11

INTRUDERS IN OUR MIDST

On February 4, 1936, just before 8:00 p.m., a young man nervously approached an apartment door in Davos and rang the bell.

David Frankfurter was a Jewish medical student from Yugoslavia. He had an infection in his bone marrow which interfered with his nervous system and had required repeated operations. David had previously studied medicine in Yugoslavia and Germany, but failed his preliminary examinations. He had come to Switzerland to complete his studies. His mother, with whom he was close, had recently died, and her death had further distanced Frankfurter from his father, a rabbi who had an authoritarian nature. Nevertheless, David's friends thought of him as an extrovert and a merry person who enjoyed good times.

Standing outside the apartment in Davos, Frankfurter was not in a talkative mood. He was concealing a 6.35-mm automatic pistol, which he had recently purchased from a gun shop in Bern. "For me and any Nazi," he would later tell authorities.[1] Frankfurter had been practicing to use the firearm—the first he had ever owned—at the shooting range of Ostermundigen, near Bern. The pistol can still be seen today in the *Bündner Polizeimuseum*.

The seconds he waited at the door in Davos must have seemed like hours. Then a woman appeared. The young medical student asked to speak to her husband—Wilhelm Gustloff.

Gustloff was head of the Nazi Party organization for Germans residing in Switzerland. He had come to Davos in 1917 and worked for a private technical institute. In 1923, he joined the NSDAP and helped form a local Swiss Nazi party. He was more of a fanatic than a deep thinker, once telling his doctor, "I would murder my wife if Hitler commanded it." Of course, loyalty to the Führer had its rewards, and Gustloff rose quickly through the ranks.

Gustloff first came to the attention of the Swiss Federal authorities in 1931 when customs officials discovered him to be circulating pro-Hitler propaganda. The Davos police decided that Gustloff's political activity did not comprise a threat, since most resident Germans were against Hitler's party. In 1932, NSDAP organizer Georg Strasser appointed Gustloff leader of the NSDAP Landesgruppe Switzerland. Each foreign country had a local Nazi Party for Germans abroad. Gustloff was now in charge of the Swiss Nazi Party. All local German Nazi groups and individuals in Switzerland were subordinate to him.

Hitler believed in keeping the Nazi message simple to win the greatest number of supporters. Although the Swiss government prohibited public marches in uniform, the NSDAP organized discussions in restaurants, sponsored cultural programs and showed German films. It held a big party on Hitler's birthday.

All of these events were exclusively for Germans. Although Swiss members were originally allowed in the German Nazi Party, they were barred in 1933 with Hitler's ascension. The few Swiss who felt compelled to express Nazi sympathies were forced to join the National Front, an organization that was particularly weak in the Canton of Graubünden, which encompasses Davos.

The Nazi Party in Switzerland was quite small. Davos had a population of around 11,000 in 1933, of which approximately 900 were Germans. Only 300 were members of the NSDAP, and of these only 20 to 30 were actual party activists. Most of the NSDAP members were terrorized into joining—often threatened with loss of their jobs if they did not sign on. Germans with money, however, were able to bribe their way out of membership. The older bourgeois Germans tended to have nothing to do with the NSDAP.

Two elected members of the legislative council in Chur—Moses Silberoth and Gaudenz Canova—cast a jaundiced eye on Gustloff's organization. Silberoth was a Jewish attorney who had come to Davos from western Russia in 1919. Dr. Canova was the leader of the trade unions and a member of the national Parliament. They were both natural enemies of the Nazi movement.

In 1935, Silberoth sought an investigation of National Socialism and, in particular, Gustloff's activities. Canova reiterated Silberoth's request in the Parliament in Bern. Canova pointed out that Gustloff was attempting to organize a state within a state in Switzerland, terrorizing German subjects and forcing them into NSDAP organizations.

"Gustloff has no right here to condemn the socialists, the Jews, and the democrats as inferior people," Canova implored. He denounced "Gustloff's ideological friends in the Third Reich" for suppressing "political and ideological dissenters in a bestial manner . . . torturing and murdering them." Canova and Silberoth demanded that the NSDAP Landesgruppe be dissolved and Gustloff be deported. An inquiry was made; however, the Swiss Federal Council, noting Gustloff's relative insignificance, could not find any unlawful activities.[2]

Gustloff and his Nazi organization remained in Switzerland until, on the evening of February 4, 1936, David Frankfurter was admitted to Gustloff's apartment in Davos. It was just before 8 p.m., and Gustloff was on the phone, so Frankfurter would have to sit in the study and wait.

For the young medical student, it must have been agonizing. He would later tell a psychiatrist that he felt indecisive and wanted to flee. Then he heard something that hardened his resolve. Gustloff was talking on the telephone in the nearby hallway, and Frankfurter could hear snippets of his conversation: *"diesen Schweinehunden . . . diesen Schweinejuden und Kommunisten."*

Frankfurter had personally witnessed the persecution of Jews in Germany. Hearing Gustloff in the hallway casually refer to "these pig dogs . . . these pig Jews and Communists" was more than he could bear. It was exactly what he needed to hear to accomplish his mission. A furious rage erupted inside him. He saw visions of Hitler.

A moment later, Gustloff entered the study. Frankfurter rose, leveled the pistol and pulled the trigger. The weapon did not discharge. He stepped backward and pulled the trigger again—repeatedly. This time it fired. Three or four shots went off, mortally wounding Gustloff. Frankfurter had planned to commit suicide after the deed, but could not bring himself to do it. He instead surrendered to the Swiss police.

The 1936 assassination of Wilhelm Gustloff was a watershed event that would bring Davos to the center stage of Swiss-German relations. The Nazis viewed Frankfurter as a cold-blooded Jewish murderer. The Swiss, by contrast, saw Frankfurter as either a misguided but sympathetic youth or as a modern-day William Tell.

Dr. Paul Müller, who was born in 1913, lived much of his life in Davos and lives there still today. In our interview at his home, Dr. Müller pointed out his window to Gustloff's apartment in an adjacent building. "Gustloff was shot there in 1936. I was a patient with a broken arm in a military hospital in St. Gallen when I heard the news. When I was a boy, Gustloff lived next door and always frightened me. But I was surprised at his murder, because he was not an important Nazi figure.

"A quiet fellow, Gustloff worked for a scientific organization. My father told me that other Germans were afraid of him."[3]

We again looked through Dr. Müller's window at the apartment where Gustloff lived, perhaps 50 meters away. "David Frankfurter rang at Gustloff's apartment. Mrs. Gustloff let him in. Frankfurter asked to see Gustloff. When Gustloff came out, Frankfurter shot him."

Did the Swiss think of Frankfurter as a murderer? Not according to Dr. Müller. "The Swiss people sympathized with Frankfurter. He was probably mentally disturbed. At the time, we didn't even know of concentration camps. After the war, Americans brought photographs of the camps. This created much more sympathy for Frankfurter. He was sentenced to 18 years, but was released early." In fact, when the war ended, he was immediately freed.

Rather than leading to the persecution of Jews, the Gustloff affair led the Swiss to clamp down on Nazi organizations within the country. Germany was outraged. The homicide and ensuing trial dramatically escalated Nazi antipathy toward Switzerland. German officials attended Frankfurter's trial every day. The Nazis elevated Gustloff as National Socialism's first martyr abroad.

"Case Frankfurter/Gustloff" quickly became "Case Switzerland," ready grist for the Nazi propaganda mill and a pretext for anti-Jewish measures. Although Gustloff was a minor figure, his stature was at once elevated for purposes of propaganda. In fact, Adolf Hitler would personally give him a funeral oration. The Germans blamed Switzerland's anti-Nazi press and were livid that the Swiss government refused to censor the Swiss media.

German Emissary von Weizsäcker immediately conferred with the Swiss secretary of state, Federal Councilor Giuseppe Motta, complaining that "the Swiss socialistic and Communist press . . . prepared the groundwork for the crime against Gustloff." This characterization was bogus, in that the mainstream Swiss press was the leading critic of German National Socialism—as well as of Soviet Communism—because of their totalitarian characteristics.

Weizsäcker reprimanded Motta for not imposing censorship. Motta, however, refused to accept that the Swiss press was responsible for the deed, arguing that Frankfurter acted on his own and was not inspired by the stand taken in the past years by the press against the German regime.

Three days after the assassination, the Swiss newspaper *Volksrecht* accused the German envoy of interference with the internal affairs of Switzerland. That opened a press campaign to dissolve the NSDAP in Switzerland. The Swiss Federal Attorney recommended the prohibition to the Federal Council on the basis that National Socialism was a movement that suppressed basic liberties.

The Nazi press responded with its usual propaganda. On February 27, 1936, *Das Schwarze Korps* (the Black Corps)—the official publication of the SS—printed a front-page cartoon depicting the Swiss Federal Council as a marionette in the hands of a Jew. The Swiss figure holds a ribbon stating "Prohibition of Swiss NSDAP Organizations" and stands by a coffin labeled "Gustloff, martyred by Marxist."[4] Rejection of Nazism was often depicted as Communist.

Gustloff's deputy became the new leader of the local Nazi party in Davos. He died in December 1936 and was replaced by the German Vice Consul Böhme, who brought new power into the organization. While the Federal Council prohibited the *Landesgruppe* as constituted, it was allowed to continue as an adjunct of the German embassy. Its chief became Freiherr von Bibra, second in command to embassy chief Weizsäcker.

While Nazi Germany was the closest and most direct threat to Switzerland, it is worth noting that Switzerland did not recognize the Soviet Union and had no diplomatic relations with that country. Domestic Communist parties were allowed to exist, but had no influence. However, in reaction to subversive activities, the Canton of Geneva outlawed the Communist party in 1937, and the Federal Council did so in 1940.

Meanwhile, Frankfurter prepared for trial. The young medical student was now a pawn in a much larger game.

The International Federation of Leagues Against Anti-Semitism in Paris offered Frankfurter moral and material support. However, it pressed his defense to accept responsibility for the homicide. A harsh punishment would turn him into a martyr—a suffering hero who struck a blow against Nazism—in the eyes of international opinion.

The Anti-Semitism Federation indicated that it would act unilaterally if the Swiss-Jewish Federation (SIG) did not become active. However, SIG Secretary Saly Mayer wrote that it would make matters worse if action was taken inconsistent with the Swiss mentality. Moreover, he noted that the locally based SIG was more experienced in dealing with the authorities in Switzerland. The International Federation should not intervene.

Frankfurter's family and the SIG wished to seek a verdict that Frankfurter was not guilty of murder, which would limit his exposure to longer incarceration. Moreover, the SIG did not wish to give the Nazis an excuse to blame the Swiss—and particularly the Swiss Jews—for countenancing political assassination as a rational act.

Before the trial, Dr. Johann Jörger, director of a psychiatric clinic, examined Frankfurter. Dr. Jörger found the young man to have a sensitive nervous system and "inner mental conflicts that exploded when they became untenable and unsolvable." Although the "explosion took place in a tragic manner," Dr. Jörger determined that Frankfurter's deeds had been compelled by "outside events." He was not, according to the doctor, a cold-blooded murderer.

The prosecution argued that the act was indeed premeditated murder, although it conceded, consistent with the psychiatrist's report, that Frankfurter acted with an unsound mind and diminished responsibility.

Frankfurter testified that Gustloff as a person was not the target. He was simply a Nazi agent, a personification of Hitler's oppressive regime. "I like Switzerland, and Germany is trying to destroy Switzerland."

Frankfurter's argument that he was acting against Nazism was not a defense to the crime of murder. In fact, he calmly explained his actions and articulated how he had prepared carefully. He bought a pistol and practiced shooting in Bern. He planned to commit suicide after the murder but could not do it. So he turned himself in to the police. All of the evidence suggests that Frankfurter testified what he believed—that he killed Gustloff to strike a blow against Nazi Germany.

Although not accepted as a defense to be found in law books, this particular political homicide had special relevance in Switzerland. Many Swiss saw Frankfurter as a modern-day William Tell. Tell, better known for shooting an apple off his son's head, also shot the tyrant Gessler through the heart—thus helping to free the country from foreign tyranny. During Frankfurter's trial, the story of William Tell reverberated loudly throughout Switzerland.

The trial itself was a media circus. There were over 30 journalists attending. On one side of the courtroom sat the German journalists, on the other side the Swiss press.

German propaganda blamed an international Jewish conspiracy and accused Frankfurter of membership in the Communist Party. The

National Socialist paper *Weltdienst* (World Service) wrote: "Frankfurter was only the subordinate of a Jewish Bolshevist executive, of which a member apparently sits in Bern." The Swiss Jews were responsible, it asserted, for the "Jewish Murder Headquarters in Switzerland."

The Swiss Federal Council was roundly accused by the Nazis of tolerating Swiss press attacks against "decent German comrades." One Nazi publication claimed that the attacks began in 1933, when "the Jew Moses Silberoth from Galicia instigated the lying attacks in the Marxist press in Davos."

The Nazis found it an opportune event to argue that Jews are dangerous and must be disarmed. An example is the book by Diewerge Wolfgang entitled *Ein Jude hat geschossen . . . Augenzeugenbericht vom Mordprozess David Frankfurter* ("A Jew Has Shot . . . Eyewitness Report of the Murder Trial of David Frankfurter").[5]

The Swiss media, on the other hand, sought mild treatment of Frankfurter by the court, spreading the prevailing opinion of Swiss Jews that the murder was an understandable reaction to anti-Semitism in Germany. Swiss newspapers, without regard to political alignment, still condemned the assassination. They were united in the conclusion that the consequences would adversely affect the Jews. Even so, they attributed responsibility for Gustloff's murder not so much to Frankfurter, but to the rulers of the Third Reich and to National Socialist ideology.

The court itself admitted into evidence documents demonstrating the Nazi persecution of Jews. In light of the trial, the criminal character of Nazism could not be ignored. The episode confirmed the Nazi threat to the Swiss and reinforced the necessity of armed resistance against National Socialism.

In the end, the judges found that Frankfurter was ill and, because of his weak nervous system, not fully responsible for his act. Frankfurter was then sentenced to 18 years. Although some Swiss cantons still had the death penalty, in Graubünden the maximum penalty was 20 years of incarceration. Most Swiss were satisfied with Frankfurter's punishment, though some on the left said it was too harsh.

Frankfurter's assassination of Gustloff exacerbated Nazi Germany's anti-Semitic policies. When a young Polish-German Jew named Herschel Grynszpan shot a staff member of the German embassy in Paris in 1938, he was dubbed "a second Frankfurter," and his act was the excuse to instigate the infamous *Kristallnacht*, a general pogrom against Germany's Jews.

Over the following years, Frankfurter's attorneys and the Swiss press sought his release from prison. On June 1, 1945, Frankfurter was released early and emigrated to Israel, where he worked in the Ministry of Security and Defense. A film about Frankfurter and Gustloff entitled "David and Goliath" appeared in 1969. Frankfurter died in 1982.

In 2000, when this author visited Davos, there was a discussion brewing about whether to erect a monument to Frankfurter, whose deed is still viewed by many as a heroic act.[6]

Less than five years after the 1936 assassination of Wilhelm Gustloff, another watershed event occurred in Graubünden, the mountainous canton which encompasses Davos. The canton's seat of government is in Chur. It was there that on November 18, 1940, Dr. Gaudenz Canova, president of the cantonal legislature, opened the session with a remarkable speech to the deputies.

Canova was the same political leader who in 1935 had called for Gustloff's deportation and the dissolution of his local Nazi party before the Swiss national parliament.

Now, he would speak again before his countrymen, but his characteristic fire-and-brimstone style was never before so well received. Indeed, his speech would have a galvanizing effect in the canton and throughout Switzerland. Newspapers refrained from publishing the speech because it was considered inflammatory and might contribute to provoking a Nazi attack.

While widely known, Canova's speech would not be published in the press until decades after the war.[7] The speech was a formidable indictment of Nazi aggression and its insidious techniques of subversion and conquest. While not naming names, the words of this indictment also included the Soviet Union, with its grisly record of intentional famine, purges, and attacks on Finland and Poland. The following are excerpts from that groundbreaking speech:[8]

"For the third time, you have appeared here in session since the day in which the furies of the most terrible war that the world has ever experienced were unleashed against mankind. It was launched by those whose highest law is their own self-interest, who have elevated power to the highest right, who thoughtlessly lie, slander, murder, and use the most brutal violence to reinforce their power. On their command, their troops attacked peaceful people, murdering, stealing and burning, and threw them into unspeakable sorrow and misery, into abysmal mental and material need. What were yesterday peaceful, happy countries are today gruesome places of devastation, and their inhabitants have fallen into a sea of blood and tears.

"Our country yet persists in the highest danger, and the heaviest fears about our freedom and independence weigh on our people and authorities. Yet we remain saved from the worst. Our soldiers have not undergone the ordeal by fire, and our wives and children have not had to flee as white as ghosts into the air-raid shelters. Our civilian population has not been torn into hundreds and thousands of shreds or beaten into cripples. We also suffer no serious lack of essentials. We are yet privileged by fate. . . .

"A tremendous danger stands before us: The danger of the Fifth Column. By that, I mean not only the traitors, spies and saboteurs. . . . But the real danger is that of self disownment, the danger of accepting our fate (*Anpassung*), letting ourselves be forced into line (*Gleichschaltung*), and accepting annexation (*Anschlussbereitschaft*)—it is the danger of mental treason and defeatism."

Here, much is lost in translation. The terms *"Anpassung," "Gleichschaltung"* and *"Anschlussbereitschaf"* were key Nazi code words that were applied to countries marked for attack and obliteration. While the Nazi threat was the greatest—with the fall of France, they were poised to attack Switzerland from several directions—Canova's following words also applied to Fascist Italy and Soviet Russia:

"We also reject dictatorship in every form and defiantly declare ourselves for democracy. We hate every tyranny, with whatever cover it disguises itself.

"We surely understand military neutrality and are willing to adhere to it. But we know no neutrality of the spirit or of basic convictions. We know to distinguish between good and evil, and our sense leans toward the good. We can distinguish between right and injustice, between freedom and slavery, between humanity and brutal power, between culture and barbarity.

"Above all, we want to accept deprivations of every kind that the economic and military defense of our nation requires, with silence and without complaints and moaning. Perhaps very bad days are in store for us. Whatever may come, however, we desire to await the future with courage and confidence. Our soldiers have done their duty at the border and are resolved to do it further—even if it means sacrificing their lives. Throughout the country we gratefully thank them and remember the manly words of Winkelried: 'Brothers, provide for my wife and children.'"

Again, this last sentence loses something in the translation. When spoken in German, *"Eidgenossen, sorget für meine Frau und meine Kinder"* recalls a moving episode in Swiss military history. A Swiss military communication had recently reminded the soldiers of the battle of Sempach in 1386, where 1,400 Swiss peasants defeated 6,000 of the far better equipped knights of Austrian Duke Leopold III.[9] With both armies pushing each other without an opening, Arnold Winkelried drew an armful of enemy pikes into his torso, allowing his comrades to break through the enemy lines and decimate the invaders. In the moment before Winkelried sacrificed his life for the good of his country, he asked that his brothers-in-arms "provide for my wife and children." Canova's mention of this moving event tapped into powerful feelings of Swiss pride and evoked strong historical memory.

Canova's robust speech brought forth prolonged applause. Although newspapers did not publish it pursuant to the rules of self-censorship set by Federal authorities, his courageous words were widely circulated and inspired the populace. The nominal censorship allowed the delegates to hear the anti-Nazi message and to communicate it to their constituents, while at the same time preventing the open publication that might provoke a German attack.

The Swiss government was afraid to allow the speech to be circulated in public. This strange but understandable mix of anti-Nazism and fear reveals a paradigm that prevailed throughout much of life in Switzerland during World War II.

Today, Davos is best known as the site of a prestigious annual conference of international leaders. Each year, thousands of politicians, business leaders, economists and multinational agency officials descend upon this peaceful ski resort to participate in the World Economic Forum. Before and during World War II, however, Davos was a hotbed of Swiss-German tension. With its hotels and sanitaria filled with well-connected Germans, it was a potential flashpoint for violence and intrigue.

Davos was the center of Nazi fifth column activity in Switzerland and thus a focus of Swiss intelligence operations. It is no surprise that Gustloff was assassinated there. Or that Canova gave his speech in Chur, the capital of the same canton.

Toward the end of the war, American bombers damaged in raids on Germany, some pursued by Luftwaffe fighters, appeared frequently in the skies over Davos. American airmen, particularly officers, who managed to land or to crash without being killed in neutral Switzerland were interned in camps around the town.

Dr. Paul Müller, who was mentioned earlier, knows the interesting story of how Davos became so popular for Jews and Germans seeking a place to convalesce.[10]

"In 1848, a student who had joined the revolution in Germany fled here and finished his studies. He became a doctor and noticed that tuberculosis was very rare in Davos. That is the origin of Davos as a curing place. There was also a Jewish sanitarium here, and Swiss Jews lived here."

Müller remembers what it was like living in Davos as the Nazi influence began to creep in.

"I went to school in Davos in 1921–29, then to the Cantonal College in Chur for two years. The German school in Davos was originally built for German children with tuberculosis. Everyone here went to the German school because our parents thought it had better standards. It had between one and two hundred pupils, 80 percent of whom were German. None of my friends had any sympathy for Hitler. We were strictly anti-Nazi. My friends were all from higher-class families. I knew only one person who was a Nazi Party member.

"The German doctors here did not like Nazism. Others did. My father had a dental office and my mother worked as his receptionist. Mrs. Friese, the wife of the German sanitarium manager, said she would like to have a child by Adolf Hitler. Mother was horrified.

"Some friends had problems with the Germans here. There was a feeling of unease, but not much open trouble. I didn't like the Germans—no one in Switzerland did. There were very few sympathizers."

By 1940, most Swiss expected a Nazi invasion. It was just a question of when. With its large German population, Davos swirled with rumors. Swiss living in Davos in 1940 must have anticipated Wehrmacht paratroopers raining from the sky, as they had done in Holland and France. (The surrounding mountains made a Panzer attack out of the question.)

"In May 1940, I was in the Army in the Medical Corps. My wife and I thought, 'It will soon be our turn.' Locally, we discussed resistance. The Nazis had a blacklist of Swiss and vice versa. Rumors flew around. Shooting ranges were always open for practice. Ammunition was limited, but there was enough. We had rifles, and I also had a Luger pistol. Father was in the Local Defense (*Ortswehr*). Swiss people openly discussed the German threat, although not with Germans. We were well prepared."

Indeed, they were. Today one of the world's leading ski resorts, the

Davos area would have been treacherous for any enemy, particularly during the winter when heavy snow made avalanches an ever-present threat.

Prof. Marcel de Quervain, who was born in 1915, came to Davos in 1942 as a member of the Swiss Federal Commission for Avalanche Research. While the use of avalanches as a weapon to bury large numbers of enemy troops may have been problematic in practice, the Swiss intently studied avalanche control.

De Quervain was a first lieutenant and later a captain in the military's mobile transmission troops—who operated radio, telephone, and teletype—and he well recalls what it was like in Davos preparing for war. His accounts of life in the mountains and, particularly, avalanche control are fascinating.

"In the army, I knew only one soldier who was in favor of the Nazis. All the rest were either pro-Allies or neutral. I was on the staff of a division in 1940. We were really afraid the Germans would come in the spring and summer of 1940 and in 1943 when the Germans were in Italy. The feeling was that our country wouldn't surrender. Those were hard times. In the army we got 1 franc per day, and it was eventually increased to 1.5 or 2 francs per day.[11]

"In Davos, I worked at the station on Weissfluhjoch, which has an elevation of 2,700 meters (8,800 feet). The cable car went up and down once per day. In the lab and outside, we studied the physical relations of snow and ice, along with methods of preventing avalanches. The knowledge of how to release avalanches was well developed long before the war and could be applied for military uses. At times, avalanches were created to make the countryside accessible.

"Planting dynamite was the cheapest method of releasing avalanches. Mortars could also be used, but each shell cost 100 Swiss francs and 10 shells were needed, so it would cost 1,000 Swiss francs to start an avalanche with mortars. One can also bomb from the air if the weather is not too bad. The most primitive method is to send people into the starting zone to release the avalanche under their feet. But it is hard to get to starting areas, and the avalanche could take you with it! You just find the right spot and start jumping. An avalanche might start.

"In World War I, avalanches killed 10,000 soldiers in the Austrian-Italian campaign. They began preventative avalanche shooting and releasing avalanches on the enemy's side. It was not too successful.

"The avalanche service in the Swiss army functioned to warn and to engage in preventative avalanche shooting. Near the end of the war it became a full avalanche service company. It remains so today."

Dr. Christian Schmid, who was born in 1923, also resided in Davos during the pre-war and war years. He too recalls a life in Davos marked by strong sentiments of anti-Nazism and preparation for war. Although he was not in the mountains planning avalanches, the picture he paints is remarkably similar to that of de Quervain and Müller.

"Individuals said anything they wanted against Germany. Organizations had to be more careful. When a local college announced a benefit concert for refugees, the Chur newspaper didn't report it until two days later. Apparently, officers had phoned the newspaper editor and ordered it not to publicize the event. The Swiss military was afraid that Germany would think Switzerland was being too nice to its refugees.[12]

"We used normal radio to communicate. After 1938 or '39, we also had telephone radio, which was required in the mountains. There were clear programs on four or five stations of Swiss radio and some German and English news. BBC had a German-language broadcast. If the English said something against Germany, the censor would turn off the program for about 30 seconds. This was in the period 1940–42. Afterwards, the censors stopped doing it.

"My relatives who were soldiers said that if the Germans came we would form guerrilla bands in specified places in the Alps. I joined the army in 1943. The food was bad. An officer once asked whether anyone had a complaint. I responded: 'I'm hungry. There is not enough food.' The officer replied: 'You're right. I'm hungry too!' We had only potatoes . . . and cheese once a week. All servicemen slept on straw, which was dusty. But the generation of men in the active service endured."

With the German blitzkrieg of 1940, Swiss Jews in particular sensed the danger. Müller remembers:

"We had neighbors, Swiss Jews, who contemplated fleeing. They were members of the same family as Captain Dreyfus, the French officer falsely accused of spying for Germany at the turn of the century. The Dreyfus family of Basel had purchased a Jewish sanatorium in Davos. Two other sanitaria were also used by Jews. They were treated by Swiss, not German, doctors."

Before long, however, many Jews were fleeing *to* Switzerland, as opposed to away from it, to escape the persecution in the rest of Europe which culminated in the Holocaust.

"I often met refugees who came as patients before the war," says Müller. Additionally, "thousands of Jewish refugees were brought over as patients between 1945 and the end of the 1950s. The Americans brought concentration camp victims here."

By 1943, Davos and the surrounding area had also become a "convalescing place" for a different type of guest. Because it was a convenient route for American bombers flying from and to bases in Italy to targets in southern Germany, this path through the Canton of Graubünden saw more than its share of distressed American aircraft.

"We heard bombers frequently," Müller remarks. "Once I saw about five American bombers being pursued by German fighters—at least three Luftwaffe pursuit planes for each bomber. The Germans always came from behind, below, or above, never from the front. The bombers, with crews of eight to 10 airmen, flew slowly and the faster German fighters swarmed them like mosquitoes.

"I had a lot of contact with the American fliers because my commander knew I spoke English well. They even came to Father's dental office to chat with my American wife. The American officers, who stayed in the Palace Hotel, came from either downed aircraft or over the frontier. The people here liked them. The Americans were also free to travel. It was easy to escape, although it was rumored that one was caught by the Germans. Those who did escape successfully would have to sneak through occupied France. They all left in 1945 anyway."

Müller rattles off names of his old American friends, with whom he has had reunions. One acquaintance was Dan Boone, whose B-17 landed in Dübendorf in 1943 and who, in recent years, helped sponsor a monument to the American fliers in Kurpark—a peaceful park area that is, ironically, not far from Gustloff's apartment.

Like Müller, Schmid also recalls Allied bombers crashlanding in the area. "One day, I was on military duty having lunch, and we heard planes," says Schmid with a smile. "An American plane had run out of gas, and the airmen had parachuted out. I rushed to one of them and said, 'You are in Switzerland, not Germany!' He replied, 'I shaved this morning to be here!'"

Armin Camenisch, who was born in 1933, recollects: "We boys in Chur did not go to the air raid shelters, but instead often watched the fleets of American B-17 and B-24 bombers and the attacking German fighters which flew overhead.

"Once I saw a B-17 pursued by German Me-109 fighters, which looked like a swarm of bees. I saw black smoke—the B-17 was hit. The airmen bailed out, and I ran to the crash site. Another boy was watching from a tree and jumped out just in time, as the wing of the downed plane hit the tree, and German planes machine-gunned the area.[13]

"On November 16, 1944, at the town of Malix, I saw a B-24 crash. I later learned that it had originated in Italy, was hit by flak while bombing Munich, and had engine trouble. I saw the crippled plane circling alone over Chur with two engines out. I later met airman John Stevens, who said that none of the crew had ever parachuted before. They were scared, saw beautiful scenery and snow, and crash-landed. All 11 crewmen survived.

"The Swiss Home Guard appeared with rifles. The Americans thought they were dead and cried, 'Please don't shoot!' The Home Guard did not know who the Americans were, but one soldier said 'Schweizer,' and then the Americans knew they were in Switzerland. The only Swiss there who spoke English was a young girl. The pilot gave her his parachute, and her mother later made blouses from it! They were all reunited on a visit in 1998.

"One plane bombed Augsburg, Germany, was hit, and crashlanded in this area. Three of a crew of 10 survived, one of whom was Norris King of Denver, whose parachute opened just as he hit a tree! He still visits here." The plane had been hit again by Swiss antiaircraft guns. While many believe that the Swiss intentionally missed American planes—and that may have been true in some cases—it was official policy to shoot at intruding aircraft that refused orders to land. Eventually the rule was relaxed so that gunners needn't fire on single planes but only formations of three or more—action demanded by the laws of neutrality.

Debris from the many crashes is still scattered throughout this region of Switzerland. Camenisch and this author visited a farm where a B-17 engine had hit behind the barn. The elderly man and woman living in the house told us the story. Anything useful, particularly engines, was retrieved by the locals and used for farm work or other purposes. One scavenger retrieved a Browning machine gun from a B-24 crash site, kept it for 40 years, and gave it to one of this author's interviewees.

Not all the planes that crash-landed in eastern Switzerland were Allied, of course. Camenisch recalls: "A German plane with three deserters landed. I saw them come out. In Chur, there were internee camps of Polish and German soldiers. I once brought a German soldier home for a visit. My parents scolded me, exclaiming: 'Never bring anyone in a German uniform to our home!'"

"The Germans had political party meetings at two or three hotels. There was strict control in the German community. They observed one another. People were intimidated by the Germans. The Nazis had name lists. Father often said not to talk to certain people."

Even while interned, the Germans were viewed by the public as dangerous. It was very different with the American internees.

Between 1943 and 1945, 166 American planes landed or crashed in Switzerland. Allied planes came to Switzerland as a place of refuge after being damaged in battle or because of spent fuel or mechanical failure. Some 1,742 Americans, mostly airmen, would be safely interned in Switzerland during the war.[14]

The circumstances, plight and exploits of the American airmen who crash-landed in Switzerland are beyond the scope of this study. The subject has been exhaustively covered elsewhere, particularly in Stephen Tanner's *Refuge from the Reich: American Airmen and Switzerland during World War II* and Fredy Peter's *Jump Boys, Jump.*[15]

The U.S. airmen were interned and cared for by the Swiss according to international law. Many escaped, often with Swiss connivance, to continue the fight. Others were unable to do so. Today, many of the survivors are members of the Swiss Internees Association. There are less than 600 alive today.

The American airmen who were officers were interned at the Palace Hotel in Davos. This author stayed at this elegant establishment, now renamed the Hotel Europe, in 2000. Given the size of the German colony in Davos, the German Embassy in Switzerland protested that Americans should not be interned there. The Swiss government paid no attention.

An American had only to step out of the Palace Hotel, turn right down Promenade Street, and cross the street to the German Consulate (today, a building advertises *Schmuck*—gold—jewelry on the first floor). This author paced a mere 120 steps between the two buildings, a proximity which could only lead to a certain humorous mischief from the young American servicemen.

July 4, 1944—American Independence Day—was the occasion for the first attack on the German Consulate. A young American internee named Ralph Jackson obtained chemicals from a pharmacy to construct rockets and fuses. Jackson and his American friends aimed the fireworks at the German Consulate and fired. The humorless Germans protested to the Swiss commander, who warned the troublemakers to refrain from future pranks.[16] The rebuke by the Swiss commander had no effect. On a

Sunday morning a month later, some young internees apparently went to work removing the Nazi emblem—a statue of a large eagle with the swastika in its claws—which hung over the entrance to the German Consulate. The work party then left the scene carrying the emblem.

The Germans lodged an official protest in Bern demanding severe penalties for the "criminals" who mocked their Third Reich. The American officers were put under "house arrest"—in their hotel—pending return of the property.

The American commander, Captain Lawrence McGuire, assured the police that such theft would not recur. The Swiss Ministry of Foreign Affairs ignored the German demand that the Americans be relocated out of Davos. It later turned out that some Swiss boys had aided and abetted the Americans in this symbolic attack on the German Consulate.

For the Americans, when war could no longer be waged with bombs, it was waged with pranks. For the Swiss, it meant participating in the antics—but also preparing for the ever-greater possibility of war. This included a straightforward military buildup as well as clandestine preparations against the fifth column—which entailed, among other things, making lists of subversives to arrest or possibly to execute in the event of a Nazi invasion.

Police Sergeant Major Christian Rostetter was stationed at Davos from 1938 through 1945. Back then, the town had only three policemen. They investigated Nazi activities in Davos and observed Nazi meetings. The police tried to cultivate informants who would report on Nazi plans. Rostetter kept many documents from that period, thinking that they might be of public interest one day. He passed away in 1978, but his cache of wartime records throws an interesting light on those years.[17]

There is a "List of Suspicious Foreigners in the Davos Area" compiled by Swiss police on April 5, 1940 (just before Germany attacked Denmark and Norway) and again on May 15, 1940 (just after Germany attacked France). It includes 85 persons, including names, birth dates, nationality (mostly German), addresses, occupations, and in almost all cases the entry "Nazi." A few of the Nazis worked for the German Consulate or the Gestapo, while others worked in the private sector. A very small number are listed as "Fascist" or "Communist."[18]

Throughout the war, the Davos police watched every move of the German colony. Police files include a collection of invitations from the German Consulate to German residents for various events including, as just one example, the invitation to view "the great German film *'Über alles in der Welt'* and a weekly newsreel" on May 26, 1942. All of these invitations ended with the obligatory "Heil Hitler!"[19]

The Film Section of the Swiss Division of Press directed local police to investigate subversive films anywhere in the country. One such directive to Rostetter is dated June 4, 1943, and warns about four films that were to be shown in the movie theatre Vox. He was instructed that only German and Italian nationals were to be admitted. The police unit was also tasked to report the size of attendance, the identities of any Swiss citizens who were present, and the name and nationality of the film operator.[20]

Lists of subversives were drawn up with an explicitly ominous intention. Swiss patriots in the Davos area originated their own secret Local Defense organizations by 1937, three years before the Swiss military created the Confederation-wide *Ortswehr*, in which 120,000 armed volunteers served in more than 2,800 communities. These local organizations made lists so that Nazi sympathizers could be rounded up and imprisoned or executed in the event of a German onslaught. Dr. Peter Bollier, a local historian in Davos, writes:

> The self-confidence of Germans in Davos grew with each new victory of Hitler's armies. The surrounding Swiss population was at first merely aggravated by the National Socialist activists, but increasingly came to perceive them as a real threat. The main question for the Swiss was whether to adopt a policy of defeatism or resistance. Fortunately, Davos had a local military commander who served with prudence and determination. Major Christian Jost personified the Swiss people's will to resist. Before the *Anschluss* of Austria with Germany was completed, Jost had already established a secret organization. The organization—"Assured Mobilization" (*Sicherstellung der Mobilmachung*)—operated independently of the military and civilian authorities. In the event of an emergency, the organization would seek to prevent sabotage and fifth columnists from taking subversive actions. At the beginning of the war, there were about 40 persons who were plainly committed to Jost's mandate. From these beginnings, the organization was reinforced by actual Local Security (*Ortswache*).[21]

In an interview in Davos in 2000, Bollier explained that he had obtained much of his information from Major Jost's Chief of Staff. He stated: "After the war began, the organized Germans were very aggressive. The Swiss police and military tried to ferret out espionage agents but found only about 10 percent of them. The army had a number of troops in the Davos area. Under the militia system, each soldier knew where to go if a rapid mobilization was required. Local commanders were able to make their own plans in the event of an invasion.[22]

"Major Jost, the military commander from Davos Dorf, the smaller sister village of Davos Platz, had perhaps 2,000 people under his command. The authorities in Bern did not know the local Nazis. Jost organized a small special troop in case of invasion which would have eliminated dangerous Germans and Swiss. While the Cantonal Police were to imprison Nazi agents, Major Jost was prepared to shoot them."

Through Bollier, this author sought an interview with Jost's Chief of Staff. However, Bollier replied, "He refuses to be interviewed based on the French saying, 'Serve and then go away.' In 1945–46, he burned the papers with the names of the Nazis to be shot. I cannot give you his name as he wishes to remain anonymous."

Bollier went on to note that "the list of people to eliminate was burned because, once the war was over, it was time to start a new beginning. All members of the NSDAP and other Nazi organizations were expelled from Switzerland."

Indeed, once the war ended, the Swiss were finally able to purge their country of dangerous Germans. Davos police prepared a blacklist dated July 12, 1945, of 100 undesirable foreigners to deport.[23] The blacklist includes the reason for deportation, usually "Nazi fanatic and National Socialist Party member" *(Nazifanatiker & Partigenosse)*. Others are listed as SS member, SA leader, Gestapo agent, spy, or a person who had made remarks against Switzerland. There is even a Nazi Party member targeted because he had received a "decoration from Hitler for the operation in Greece." All were considered subversives.

After the war, the fifth column dissolved. The Swiss soldiers came out of the mountains. The American pilots went home to their families. The internment tents were folded up, and the blacklists were destroyed. Davos became quiet again. And so it remains.

CHAPTER 12

AMERICA'S WINDOW
ON THE REICH:
Allen Dulles in Bern

As the only country in central Europe which was neither Axis nor Axis-occupied, Switzerland was a hotbed of espionage. Neutral Switzerland hosted the embassies of all the combatants, so there were literally hundreds of agents of all stripes. Allied operatives, at times in cahoots with Swiss intelligence, gathered information from German sources and radioed it to Britain or Russia.[1] The Nazis spied on the Swiss,[2] and the Swiss had informants reaching even into Hitler's headquarters.[3] The British not only spied but managed to run sophisticated smuggling rings to supply diamond dies, jewel-bearings, chronographs and other intricate Swiss products needed for RAF fighters and bombers.[4]

The United States remained officially neutral until the Japanese attack on Pearl Harbor on December 7, 1941. Thereafter the American intelligence network was organized as the Office of Strategic Services (OSS), the predecessor to the Central Intelligence Agency.[5] The OSS dispatched Allen Dulles to Bern, posing under the innocuous cover of special assistant to the American Minister to Switzerland, Leland Harrison. He reached the city in November 1942 on the last train through Vichy France before its occupation by German forces. Dulles set up his spy shop in an apartment building at 23 Herrengasse in Bern's old city, a quiet, inconspicuous location which to this day visitors stroll by without knowing its history.

Switzerland quickly became America's window on the Reich, the ideal location to spy on the Axis, support partisan movements in France and Italy, and communicate with the anti-Hitler underground in Germany. After the war, Dulles wrote books detailing his knowledge of German resistance and the conspiracy to kill Hitler, as well as the surrender of

German forces in Italy near the end of the war, a supremely delicate undertaking which was materially assisted by Swiss intelligence.[6] The recent declassification and publication in 1996 of many of Dulles' OSS dispatches from Bern shed new light on the significant role played by Switzerland in the struggle against Nazism.[7] The OSS reports in particular reveal much about Swiss involvement in the war.

Dulles' mission was clear: to gather any and all intelligence that would be useful to the defeat of the Axis powers. Countless informants of every kind and with every motive supplied a steady stream of fact, suspicion, rumor and lies. Dulles sought to distill fact from fiction and to report critical information to Washington, DC. Obviously, the big picture involved not Switzerland but Wehrmacht intentions, German morale and opposition, the occupied countries and psychological warfare. Thus, although the OSS dispatches do not include a comprehensive chronology of Swiss-related developments, individual dispatches on varying topics provide revealing insights into Nazi Germany's threat to Switzerland and the latter's resistance to that threat.

On November 21, 1942, shortly after his arrival in Bern, Dulles wrote that the OSS was trying to persuade the Swiss to set up an air service to Lisbon—a direct flight to neutral Portugal would be most helpful for the spying and smuggling businesses—but he doubted that the Swiss felt strong enough to push through the project against German opposition. He continued:

> Even though the Swiss press is excluded from Germany except for a chosen few, the Germans definitely fear Switzerland as a free news center. A Swiss official who has just returned from Berlin says he expects further drives to try to shackle the freedom of the Swiss press. It has been openly stated by the German press that within the European Fortress all British and American representatives will be treated as "Centers of espionage, blackmail, and subversive activities within countries concerned."[8]

Despite limited censorship, the Swiss press reported news that was in great demand both in the occupied countries and in Germany. Dulles, having unusual access to a wider range of intelligence because of his Swiss vantage point on the Reich, understood through his direct contacts that encouragement of German resistance to Hitler could end the war sooner. Perhaps President Roosevelt did not fully appreciate this opportunity.

At the Casablanca conference in January 1943, Roosevelt announced, without prior consultation with the other Allies, that the goal of the war was to achieve the "unconditional surrender" of the Axis powers. Dulles wrote: "The Swiss were not surprised at unconditional surrender, nor did it cause any particular comment locally." He added, "Although Goebbels may find temporary help in the slogan, it is believed that in the long run, it can be safely stressed as much as you desire since, as psychological warfare, it is absolutely sound." Dulles, however, emphasized the importance of making clear that unconditional surrender by the Nazis did not implicate innocent Germans.[9]

Dulles repeated this moderating advice over the next two years, but it went unheeded, and the Allied refusal to consider an alternate formula might have prolonged the war. By 1944 there were many Germans, including high-ranking army officers, in favor of peace with the Western Allies; however, hardly anyone favored surrender on the Eastern Front, thus allowing a tidal wave of Soviet vengeance and Communist ambition to overrun the country. The unconditional surrender policy may have prevented anti-Hitler Germans from gaining far more support than they could have otherwise.

Fortunately, the American leadership understood the need to support resistance movements in German-occupied territories. After the Wehrmacht occupied Vichy France, the Americans stepped up efforts to supply and encourage French resistance. The Swiss connection in this deadly ballet of ambush and atrocity is illustrated in a March 1943 telegram from Dulles about OSS support of the umbrella organization Forces Françaises Combattantes de La Métropole (FFCM). OSS-FFCM planning would be based in Switzerland and included:

> Secret representation in Lausanne to be established as contact points for the French headquarters England and USA. . . . A summary of financial needs is as follows. (1) Sufficient Swiss funds to cover local representation. This item we have already agreed to meet. (2) To develop the organization as above 25 million francs monthly. (3) An additional amount to cover specific maintenance for guerrillas, sabotage, etc. (4) a reserve capital to take care of releve [relief] personnel. . . . There is an immediate need of materials, arms, explosives and a reserve stock of rations for guerrilla organizations.[10]

Dulles urged planning from London to help organize French guerrilla warfare and resistance programs. "For reasons explain[ed] separately 511 proving cooperative and this greatly facilitates the maintenance of communications across the border with groups."[11] The number 511 was the code for the Swiss intelligence service, headed by Roger Masson, whom Dulles referred to as "Bones."[12] Dulles did not identify specific Swiss agents when using the number 511. What was significant was that "511" cooperated with OSS assistance to the French maquis. Moreover, General Henri Guisan, commander-in-chief of the Swiss armed forces, who had ultimate authority over Swiss intelligence, cooperated with Dulles.

Secrecy was critical, because the threat of invasion was real. Had Nazi spies gained information about Swiss cooperation with the Allies, Germany would have another reason to attack. During the 1943 "March Alarm," discussed earlier in this book, Swiss intelligence was informed by its "Wiking Line," which reached into Hitler's headquarters, that an invasion of Switzerland was imminent.[13] Dulles was privy to Swiss intelligence evidencing that "Germany is commencing a new war of nerves against this country. Detailed invasion plans are being planted, perhaps for the purpose of bolstering economic negotiations which may be pending. Despite the fact that immediate danger is discounted, all possibilities should be considered and plans laid accordingly."[14] This intelligence, even if it proved inaccurate, demanded the highest levels of military preparedness by the Swiss.

To this day, it remains unknown whether the reports about an imminent Nazi attack were real or planted, either to blackmail Switzerland into economic concessions or uncover sources of suspected leaks in the German high command. Both of these scenarios were typical of the insidious intelligence warfare waged by the Hitler regime. Switzerland nevertheless continued to allow herself to be a center of resistance planning.

The OSS was highly active in supporting resistance against the Fascist regime in Italy. Early on, Mussolini saw the writing on the wall and recognized that his days in power were numbered. In an April 1943 telegram to "Victor" (an OSS transmitting and receiving station in England), "Burns" (Dulles) wrote:

The Swiss authorities have been approached by Mussolini with a view to finding out whether they would grant him admission into their country in case of eventualities, as he has fears for his personal safety in the event internal revolution or invasion by the

Allies should take place. It was also reported by this source that consideration of the matter at this time was refused by the Swiss. It may be recalled that a number of years ago when Mussolini was a youthful agitator, he was compelled to leave Switzerland under orders of expulsion, and that later when he came to Switzerland as Prime Minister, the decree of expulsion had to be speedily revoked.[15]

Germany being a far more formidable enemy than Italy, intelligence gathered in Switzerland about the former was more valuable. One of Dulles' most important German sources was Hans Bernd Gisevius, an Abwehr (German military intelligence) agent stationed in Zurich under the cover of Vice Consul. A member of the anti-Hitler German underground and a conservative lawyer, Gisevius rejected Nazism.[16] Although the Abwehr actively spied on Switzerland, its head, Admiral Canaris, discouraged a German invasion there, just as he had previously counteracted Hitler's designs regarding Spain and other neutral countries. Hitler mistrusted Canaris, eventually dismissed him, and finally had him executed as a conspirator in the July 1944 assassination plot, from which Hitler had barely escaped. Gisevius, who had a good relationship with Swiss police authorities, tried to halt the replacement of Abwehr personnel with those of Himmler's SD (*Sicherheitsdienst*) intelligence network. In view of Himmler's increasing power, Dulles knew this was a losing battle.[17]

In a telegram in mid-March 1944, Dulles expressed concern about a meeting between Swiss intelligence chief Roger Masson and Walter Schellenberg of the Gestapo. Without naming any agent or information passed other than the mere fact of the meeting, Dulles described the contact as a "perilously close association" (even though Dulles himself also had contacts with Schellenberg[18]). Dulles believed that "the controlling Swiss authorities have a basic desire for an Allied victory," but others hoped for a compromise peace. Dulles thus presented evidence of possible leaks "in strictest secrecy to the highest Swiss Quarters"—headed by General Henri Guisan, commander of the Swiss armed forces. Guisan, as it turned out, was aware of the meetings between Masson and Schellenberg, considering it the task of any spy agency to obtain intelligence from all sources. Dulles continued:

The disclosure could be made in such a manner as to implicate the Lomax shop [the British spy and smuggling ring in Switzerland],[19] which the Swiss already know to be very leaky. General Guisan has just indicated his wish for a confidential conversation with me, and it is to him, and to him alone, that I would personally submit my evidence. I am convinced that his integrity and devotion to our ideals are unimpeachable, and that the discovery of what is occurring (presumably unbeknownst to him) might move him to act.[20]

Dulles used the code name "Castle" as a general indicator for messages dealing with the German threat to Switzerland. Under this category Dulles sent a telegram recording his March 1944 meeting with General Guisan as follows:

> Recently I talked to General G. [Guisan] and made known to him that the situation in general was causing me some concern. He said that he would begin an investigation on his own. I think that his reason for requesting a talk with me was to try to gain some indication of whether or not it is probable that France will be invaded in the near future. It is evident that he fears the threat to Switzerland present in the fact that the Nazis may wish to use Swiss railroads to transport Nazi forces into safety in the event of a retreat of the Germans from the South in case the attack is carried on simultaneously in the North and South. We have assigned General G. our 839.[21]

Thus, General Guisan became code number "839," a standard OSS practice to protect the identities of contacts in case the message was intercepted. Had Germany intercepted this telegram, it would not have been hard to guess that "General G" was number "839." It was hardly a secret that General Guisan was a bitter enemy of Nazi Germany.

During this same period, Dulles continued to question the demand for "unconditional surrender." He knew that most Germans believed the Allies were set on annihilating German economic power once and for all. "The expression 'unconditional surrender' therefore signifies to most of them total catastrophe for the country and for the individual German, as we ourselves haven't done a thing to offer them any hope of any more optimistic meaning for this expression." The Allies had made no efforts to restrict the term to military and party leaders, and the horrific ongoing air raids seemed evidence enough of Allied intentions.[22]

Nazi propaganda chief Goebbels used the demand for "unconditional surrender" to harden German resistance. Dulles suggested that Churchill, Roosevelt and Stalin should issue harmonizing proclamations that would allow the German people to accept the complete surrender of the Nazi government and war machine without the annihilation of Germany. Through radio broadcasts and other means of propaganda, some Germans had been encouraged (albeit remaining suspicious) by the Free German Committee set up by Moscow.[23] Dulles feared that the West's failure to drive a wedge between the Nazi leadership and the German people was prolonging the war and could turn Germans toward the Soviets.

All the intelligence trails in such matters seemed to lead to Switzerland. Dulles sent a telegram to the head of OSS, General William ("Wild Bill") Donovan, that the group code-named "the Breakers," a pro-Western, anti-Hitler faction within the German military, proposed military operations to help Allied forces enter Germany from the West and to isolate the Nazi leadership, on condition that German forces be allowed to hold the Eastern front. They knew the war was lost and sought to have as much of Europe as possible occupied by the Americans and British to prevent the spread of Communism. Although the West would not agree to the Germans continuing to fight the Soviets, Dulles sought to encourage the Breakers to strike the Nazi leadership. "This group can safely contact Switzerland," as "their contacts here are more secure than anywhere else. . . ."[24] Much of the encouragement and coordination of the July 20, 1944, attempt on Hitler's life took place in Switzerland.

D-Day intervened before this attempt, and emboldened the anti-Hitler conspirators. By a radiotelephone transmission on June 6, 1944, Dulles commented on German reactions to that morning's Allied invasion of Normandy as reported in the evening edition of Switzerland's leading newspaper, the *Neue Zürcher Zeitung* (NZZ). NZZ reported that surprised German authorities waited until afternoon to inform the German people, who were skeptical of Nazi propaganda, that the invasion was ordered by Moscow. Dulles noted that the OSS would now step up its intelligence efforts "from this vantage point behind German lines," concluding: "Undoubtedly, every effort will be made by the Germans to tighten the control of access to Switzerland, but this will require troops, and these they can spare with difficulty. The general impression here is that with the main attack apparently coming from the North, Switzerland itself is not in any immediate danger from the Germans."[25]

Just days into the D-Day invasion, Dulles telegraphed General

Donovan a report on the use of Dulles' German contacts for the postwar organization of Germany. Dulles was concerned that the identity of the German informants communicating with him in Switzerland be kept strictly confidential, noting: "Switzerland, with its literature and newspapers printed for the most part in German and with the majority of its nationals speaking that language, is in a better position to maintain contact with Germany than other countries are, regardless of the fact that the German-speaking Swiss are fundamentally opposed to the Third Reich philosophy." Dulles identified a number of German exiles in Switzerland who were anti-Nazi and could assist in the occupation and reeducation of Germany.[26]

Dulles had another confidential meeting with General Guisan on June 13 and reported in a telegram:

> 1. 839 [Guisan] stated in a private talk which I had with him yesterday that he felt a renewed sense of unrest regarding the local situation, in view of the developments in Italy and the presence of a substantial number of Nazi reserve troops on his northern border. He said that their SI [Swiss Secret Intelligence] services had located 35 Nazi divisions in the general vicinity of Alsace, Vorarlberg, Wurttemberg, Bavaria, Black Forest and Baden; they estimated that the total Nazi strategic reserve amounted to 60 divisions.
> 2. He was aware that the greater part of the 35 divisions were in all probability either recuperating or training and that a majority of them were only two regiments strong. He stated, nevertheless, that they had identified among this group two air divisions and several veteran field divisions. Therefore, in the light of this, he was exercising every possible precaution and was calling up additional troops.
> 3. 839 mentioned that the Brenner Pass was becoming increasingly precarious. . . . He said that if the Italian approaches to Simplon and Gotthard were destroyed, Nazi pressure would be rendered less effective.[27]

Guisan thus all but suggested that the Allies bomb the transportation routes on the Italian side of Switzerland which led to the Simplon and Gotthard passes through the Swiss Alps. Switzerland was bound by long-standing treaties to allow commercial transit through these passes but not to facilitate troop movements of belligerents. The Swiss resisted Axis pressure to use these passes for troops going between Germany and Italy, and were ready to destroy the tunnels immediately upon an Axis invasion. The Swiss never relented on this issue, but as Guisan mentioned, the pressure was increasing because the Brenner Pass between Austria and Italy was becoming insufficient for the Germans.

Dulles reported that no other source had indicated the number of organized German divisions north of the Swiss border as Guisan had asserted, although there were several hundred thousand convalescents or trainees. Knowing the German tactic of disinformation about surprise attacks, the Swiss could hardly afford to take chances. Dulles continued: "We, however, do have reports which state that more and more Nazi deserters are coming over; this, of course, would require larger patrols along the Swiss border." There were also rumors that, "in view of the developments in Italy and France, the Swiss are weighing the possibility of preparing some defense at the frontiers, instead of immediately withdrawing to Réduit in the event of attack, and as a result, are planning that the forces outside of Réduit are to be increased."[28] The Swiss obviously believed Allied campaigns might induce Germany to intrude into Switzerland, and they reacted quickly. Swiss forces which were previously concentrated in the Réduit (the central Alpine redoubt) were relocated to the borders with France and Italy, which had the greatest danger of incursion by German forces.[29]

Dulles later wrote that Guisan's report about "sizable Nazi concentrations in the general region of the northeastern border of Switzerland" were not confirmed by American sources. "The Nazi divisions in that sector seem to be mainly Ersatz divisions which are being established and they have comparatively little strength." Dulles speculated that "the SD [German intelligence] planted this report on our local friends."[30] The Swiss left nothing to chance and prepared for attack whenever threatened.

During the unfolding of the Allied campaigns, Guisan informed Dulles of the following shocking intelligence: "A report concerning Nazi preparations for bacteriological warfare was being carefully checked by 839's SI [Guisan's Secret Intelligence] services. According to rumor, scientific experiments were conducted in laboratories at Lyon; the product was produced then forwarded to Leipzig."[31] This kind of detailed intelligence about the possibility of such a devastating weapon was of critical importance to the Allies, and of course to Switzerland. Whether true or false, such intelligence would have to be met with all due precautions.

Similarly, Swiss intelligence shared with the OSS information on Germany's advances in aerial technology. A German Messershmitt-110 twin-engined fighter, which had been fitted with secret advanced technology, landed in Switzerland by mistake. The Swiss obviously examined the technical features thoroughly. The plane was equipped with a nightfighting mechanism which, Dulles was informed, "the Nazis are vigorously trying to protect." It included 16 dipole antennae on the nose of the airplane which receive and transmit on a wavelength of 60 centimeters. "They produce an extremely narrow beam which makes it possible for the pilot to locate on an oscillograph any hostile bombing planes which are flying on the direct course of his plane."[32]

The above exemplifies the value of Switzerland as America's window on the Reich. Dulles was also as interested in active psychological warfare as he was in simply gathering and reporting intelligence. He repeatedly returned to the need to clarify the "unconditional surrender" slogan in a manner to encourage German resistance to Hitler. In a message transmitted via General Donovan to President Roosevelt on July 15, 1944, Dulles wrote that, since Nazi Germany's end was in sight, the United States should make it clear that "unconditional surrender" applied "to the Nazis and the German war machine, but not to the German people if they took it upon themselves to overthrow their criminal government." Without such clarification, Nazi Propaganda Minister Goebbels would continue to broadcast that an Allied victory would mean "unconditional annihilation" for Germany. Dulles believed fanatical German resistance would only prolong the war and cost the lives of thousands of Allied soldiers.[33]

Dulles' advice again went unheeded, despite the nearly successful assassination attempt against Hitler on July 20. The Führer survived the explosion of the bomb planted by Claus von Stauffenberg and instigated a new reign of terror against any semblance of a German opposition, executing thousands.[34] Some of the conspirators managed to escape to Switzerland. Gisevius, the Abwehr agent who was a chief informant for Dulles, participated in the attempted coup but eluded capture in Berlin when it was crushed. Dodging the Gestapo for several weeks, he slipped over the border into Switzerland, where he would later write a history of the anti-Nazi resistance.[35] Gisevius was assisted by Mary Bancroft, a Dulles aide in Bern who later wrote her own autobiography recounting her espionage adventures in Switzerland.[36]

Within days of the assassination attempt, Dulles noted, the Gestapo knew that Abwehr agents were involved in the "Breakers" action and sought to liquidate the perpetrators and assimilate the whole Abwehr organization into the SD. SD chief Walter Schellenberg went so far as to furnish Swiss intelligence chief Roger Masson with a list of Abwehr agents in Switzerland "with the idea of having them expelled. However, we think it unlikely the Swiss will take any action. . . ."[37] Switzerland continued to be a safe haven for anti-Hitler conspirators.

Safe haven, however, did not translate into a carte blanche for anti-German resistance. Switzerland had to maintain her formal neutrality in order to survive and to protect humanitarian organizations such as the International Committee of the Red Cross which operated out of the country. Dulles wrote in mid-August 1944 about the realities: "Although the Swiss are not particularly concerned about what goes on across French and Italian borders, so long as these are carried out with a certain amount of discretion, they are extremely energetic in seeing that nothing like this takes place on the German border. . . . The Swiss are anxious to avoid border incidents with the Reich and will go to any lengths to prevent them."[38] Secret liaison with the German opposition and informants had to be carried out with the utmost discretion and secrecy. "Switzerland is [the] most incorruptible neutral nation in existence, and we must exercise the greatest tact in getting anything done here."[39]

This neutrality gave Switzerland recognition by all belligerents as a sanctuary for interned military personnel. During this period the number of American airmen arriving in Switzerland—via parachute, crash-landings or aboard crippled bombers escorted by Swiss fighters—reached its height. The American airmen were cared for by the Swiss military and were put in touch with the U.S. Military Attaché, Brigadier General Barnwell Legge. Dulles reported on August 11, 1944:

No case of any nature has come to the attention of myself or 520 [Legge] giving the least credence to the report that American airmen are attempting to evade any more combat by landing here. I believe this is nothing but ill-willed propaganda inspired by Nazis, since I learned in a confidential talk with Gen. Guisan a short time after many U.S. planes landed here, that under his orders each case was thoroughly investigated and it was determined that none of the planes could possibly have returned to its home field. . . . Naturally, the information from Gen. Guisan should not be disseminated.[40]

As the Allied bombers pounded away and Allied forces advanced on all sides, rumors abounded about a Nazi last stand in an Alpine redoubt. Dulles wrote that "511"—General Masson of Swiss Intelligence—"has a rather grave approach to the situation, due to the fact that any such Réduit could be flanked by the Swiss and therefore they are paying close heed to this matter. He seems to feel that there is some leaning towards a concentration of materials in this region." The Swiss believed the German redoubt would include a portion of northern Italy and extend to the sea in the region of Trieste-Venice. There was only inconclusive evidence that a specific plan existed, but some Nazis believed that a million troops on the Vorarlberg, Austrian, and Bavarian Alps with supplies could resist for six months to a year.[41] Both the Allies and the Swiss would continue to monitor intelligence on any such plans.

Meanwhile, Allied forces were advancing. As the German front in Normandy was cracking, the Allies landed another army on the French Mediterranean coast, quickly advancing northward. Luftwaffe incursions and even attacks spilled over into Switzerland. On August 25, 1944, the Swiss Federal Council called up more troops as American armies reached the Swiss border near Geneva.[42] Dulles wrote: "Presumably the arrival of U.S. troops at the Swiss border indicates practical control of the Alpine region from the Mediterranean to Lake Geneva and raises the issue of coordination of our military action with that of Partisan groups across the border in Italy. We have set up many contacts with the Partisans. . . ."[43]

Allied advances, desperate German resistance, and the movements of refugees fleeing across borders offered spying opportunities for both sides. The Germans were driven out of strongholds in the Jura Department before the Belfort Gap on the Swiss border. In October 1944 Dulles noted that "refugees who have been moved from the Belfort region via Switzerland into France offer the Nazis good cover for infiltration of spies, saboteurs and the like." This caused General Jacob L. Devers, who led the U.S. Sixth Army Group from southern France to the Swiss border, to be "apprehensive about the situation on the Franco-Swiss border in the area of Pontarlier." Contrariwise, Dulles anticipated that "a station at Pontarlier might secure valuable information and could be used to dispatch agents to and from Switzerland for German work as well."[44]

On November 3, Dulles met with General Guisan, who passed on intelligence that Hitler appeared to have made a speedy recovery from the July 20 attack, but was later bedridden for three months due to a cerebral hemorrhage caused by shock. Hitler's public appearances during that

period were reportedly faked. For purposes of this study, it is less important whether the reports were true than the fact that General Guisan
shared such intelligence with Dulles—obviously without warranting its
veracity. Guisan ("839") then addressed a different sensitive topic: accidental American bombings of Switzerland:

> 839, who is a good friend of ours, was obviously seriously dis-
> turbed at repetition of our bombing attacks on Swiss towns and
> villages. He indicated this was seriously affecting attitude [of the]
> Swiss people toward USA. While realizing mistakes are inevitable
> he could not understand low level attacks on Swiss territory.
> Personally I believe situation created by attacks makes it more dif-
> ficult to get Swiss cooperation in our present task of penetrating
> Germany. Assume everything being done to prevent recurrence.[45]

General Henry H. ("Hap") Arnold, Commanding General of the U.S.
Army Air Forces, told General Donovan that perhaps Germans using captured American planes had bombed the Swiss towns. Instructed to suggest
this to the Swiss, an annoyed Dulles responded: "Swiss observers state they
clearly identified planes as American, reports indicate 14 to 15 involved.
It will be hard to make Swiss believe that Germans had this number of
American planes with American bombs assigned to apparent task of blowing up power plant in which Germans have joint interest with Swiss."
Evidence gathered by U.S. Brig. Gen. Legge did not support the thesis that
the bombings were committed by the Germans.[46]

In fact, these and other American bombings of Switzerland were tragic accidents.[47] U.S. diplomats and military authorities were well aware that
the benefits to the Allies of Swiss services as a neutral far outweighed Swiss
economic relations with Germany. The above bombings took place in the
vicinity of Basel, where—as the Swiss had just warned the Americans—
there were three marshaling yards, one each in Switzerland, France, and
Germany, all of which appeared indistinguishable from the air.[48] A joint
Swiss-German interest in a power plant in this area where the Rhine flows
through would not have been unusual, and the Americans never intentionally dropped bombs on Switzerland.

Despite the accidental bombings, the Swiss remained staunchly in
favor of the Allies, and cooperation between Swiss and American intelligence agencies continued. Dulles learned the intelligence bombshell from
the "highest Swiss source that [Field Marshal Albert] Kesselring has

received orders to complete German withdrawal from northwest Italy by December 15th." Now that Switzerland was accessible through southern France, Allied experts came to learn the status of Germany's atomic energy program, on which Dulles had been gathering intelligence. In the coming months, German atomic research and development continued to be monitored from Switzerland.[49]

The Swiss were even more insistent than the Americans that no one associated with the Nazis should be able to find refuge in Switzerland. As 1944 ended, Dulles anticipated a "brain drain" either to the West or to the Communist East, and was of the opinion that nonpolitical Germans possessing technical expertise should be allowed into Switzerland. He mentioned that the two Schmidt brothers, German industrialists, sought entry with their families. Reflecting Swiss refugee policy, the Schmidt's minor children were allowed in, but the adult brothers were turned away. The brothers' professed motive was to escape the Russians and the chaos sweeping into Germany from the East. The Swiss official refused entry to the male adults because they had worked with the Nazis. Dulles disagreed with a blanket policy and suggested that non-political industrialist and technical refugees should be discussed on a case-by-case basis with the Swiss. Dulles proposed: "Possibly such refugees would prefer to surrender to us, say at Annemasse, after they had taken refuge in Switzerland."[50]

The results of such negotiations remain shrouded in mystery, but after the war ended the Americans would take in, recruit, or use the services of German rocket scientists, Nazi intelligence operatives, and other useful ex-enemies to fight the Cold War.

Meanwhile, Swiss Foreign Minister Pilet-Golaz informed Dulles at the year's end the details of Hitler's whereabouts and relapse into illness, together with Himmler's inability to take the reins of power. Closer to home, Dulles reported:

> Regarding rumors of heavy concentrations of German troops on Swiss border, and of possible German attack via Switzerland (which SI [Secret Intelligence Branch] Paris transmitted but said discounted by SHAEF [Supreme Headquarters Allied Expeditionary Force]), source believes no basis for such rumors, and Swiss military authorities undisturbed. 2 additional Swiss divisions to be called up early January to replace other divisions, but latter will not be immediately dismissed, thus in effect substantially increasing Swiss standing army during early weeks of year.[51]

The Swiss military exhibited calm, and the uncertainty of the situation demanded they prepare for the substantial risk that retreating German armies would bring the war into Switzerland. In any event, Dulles by now considered Pilet-Golaz to be a regular enough informant to assign him a number—"518."

Dulles constantly felt the need to explain to his superiors the special situation of Switzerland and her value to the Allies. In a January 2, 1945, report to General John Magruder, OSS Deputy Director for Intelligence, Dulles urged restraint by the Allies in their demands regarding the transportation of German shipments through Switzerland. In particular, pursuant to turn-of-the-century treaties, to her status as a neutral, and to encirclement by Germany, Switzerland was forced to allow German rail traffic in coal and commercial goods to pass through the Gotthard tunnel en route to Italy, but strictly excluded German troops as well as weapons or munitions. The loosening of the noose allowed the Swiss to begin to curtail this traffic. Dulles explained:

> Traffic [has been] reduced because of changes in [the] war situation and also as result of diplomatic and economic pressure. [The] latter has obtained some results because fear [of an] attack by Germany [is] gone and because [the] Swiss vitally need certain facilities from Anglo-Saxon side, particularly food and raw material imports. Also Swiss firmly convinced of, and in great majority desire, our victory and hope it will come soon.[52]

Dulles continued that it would be a mistake "to ask [the] Swiss to give up a principle, particularly one which they consider vital to their neutral status." Neutrality saved them from two world wars in 25 years. It would be more effective to seek concessions on other specific points. The Allies themselves may need to send transit through Switzerland, particularly "if German project for final stand in Bavarian Alps materializes." He concluded with some practical advice:

> I am undoubtedly influenced by [the] fact [that] in my work, I constantly need from Swiss favors to which, under strict rules of neutrality, I am not entitled. As we now give Swiss little except dynamite and diplomatic demands, it is not easy to create best atmosphere for my work. Hence I do not favor pressing [the] Swiss to [the] wall for what seems to me to be very small military

advantages, particularly as it is a wall [through] which [the] Swiss may not jump.[53]

In other words, OSS espionage against the Axis and its promotion of resistance groups from Switzerland was not helped by "dynamite" (accidental Allied bombings) and overbearing "diplomatic demands" to Switzerland. It was unreasonable to press Switzerland to the "wall" by demanding that she violate her formal status as a neutral, when she was constantly bending the rules in favor of the Allies.

Fear of possible long-term Nazi resistance from Alpine redoubts escalated with fresh intelligence reports. General Donovan's February 14 report to President Roosevelt reflected Allied reliance on Swiss intelligence:

> When organized German military resistance collapses, there will probably be more than one "Réduit" or inner fortress of Nazi resistance which may remain. It seems generally accepted now that a delayed defense fortress will lie in the Bavarian and Austrian Alps. Swiss sources have information which they consider reliable that substantial amounts of foodstuffs [are] being collected here, and that some underground factories are being prepared to supply arms required for mountain warfare.[54]

Besides the primary redoubt, Nazi resistance would center in Thueringen, around Weimar, and in the Black Forest, "flanked by the northern frontier of Switzerland and the Rhine."

Such intelligence could hardly be ignored either by the Allies, who would have to conquer any such last stands, or the Swiss, who would have to repel any intrusions into her territory. Allied strategists must have anticipated a possible German redoubt, but day-to-day combat and rapid advances consumed their attention. It was in the interest of the Swiss to ward off a German redoubt and to help facilitate the end of the war.

Swiss intelligence would play an instrumental role in Operation Sunrise, secret negotiations over two months which resulted in the surrender of German forces in Italy. On March 8, 1945, Dulles and a Swiss intermediary met with SS General Karl Wolff at an apartment held by Dulles in Zurich. Wolff hoped to lead Germany out of the war and thought he could convince Field Marshal Albert Kesselring to join him. These two German military chieftains controlled northern Italy and western Austria, and Hitler and Himmler could not successfully counter-mand the surrender of German forces in these areas. Wolff hoped to return within the week with Kesselring to Switzerland to meet with the Allies to coordinate military surrender measures.[55]

Wolff offered to halt active warfare against the anti-German partisans and to keep up just a pretense of fighting, as well as to release to Switzerland without ransom several hundred Italian Jews interned at Bozen. This would have been consistent with Swiss plans at that time to rescue Jews from Hungary and other Nazi-occupied countries. Dulles wrote that the plan "may present very unique opportunity to shorten war and to permit occupation of North Italy and possibly even penetration Austria under most favorable conditions. Also this might wreck German plans for establishment of maquis." The term "maquis" meant the French resistance, but in this context referred to German guerilla resistance in a mountainous redoubt. Dulles firmly told Wolff that unconditional surren-der would be required.[56]

As noted above, Swiss commander-in-chief Guisan had warned Dulles of possible bacteriological warfare by the Nazis. Now, while Operation Sunrise was proceeding, an informant with close contact to the Japanese legation in Bern reported alarming intelligence to the OSS. Dulles telegraphed the following: "Members Jap legation here including their MA [military attaché] and commercial attaché reported to be spreading reports that Hitler [is] determined [to] start gas and bacterio-logical warfare which will cause epidemics throughout Europe including Switzerland. They say Japs backing up Hitler in this determination but he meeting opposition in military and some party circles."[57] This indicates the continued Nazi threat to Switzerland as well as the ability of the Allies in that neutral country to obtain intelligence of the most serious threats. Countless rumors from many informants abounded, but allegations of such serious consequences made directly by Axis sources could not be ignored.

Such threats made the success of Operation Sunrise even more urgent. Dulles believed Hitler intended to use most of the German army in Italy for defense of the German Alpine redoubt, for which some stock-ing of supplies had been made and which "seems inevitable from the force of circumstances." He thought he could use talks with "Critic" (Wolff) to help defeat Hitler in this strategy.[58] Dulles telegraphed General Donovan that "there is evidence that considerable activity has recently developed," including "that sufficient supplies and weapons have been stored in inner reduit to equip with light arms and feed approximately 25,000 men for period of year. Work on defense of important passes into reduit and on certain underground plants for light arms and on hidden depots has also been pushed." Portions of this redoubt would extend to the Swiss frontier. Hitler apparently had not yet decided "whether to make last stand there or around Berlin."[59]

It was possible that Wolff was bluffing about his plan to arrange for the surrender of German forces in Italy. Dulles wrote General Lyman Lemnitzer at Allied Force Headquarters (Caserta): "Today I consider at least 50 percent chance it is genuine but agree sufficient margin of doubt to make every precaution necessary. Swiss SI [Secret Intelligence] have rarely been fooled by Nazis in such matters."[60]

At the same time, underlying conflicts of interest among the Allies began to emerge, particularly in regard to a future occupation. In a follow-up message to Caserta, Dulles noted that the Soviets would try to block a German surrender in Italy, because it would allow "our forces" to occupy Trieste, which he thought was more important to the Russians than Berlin. If surrender negotiations failed and the Germans retreated, then the Soviets would probably reach Trieste first. "While I realize we will deal openly and fairly with our Russian allies, this should not preclude us from doing everything possible to bring about quick surrender which would save the lives of our troops and bring us into the heart of German reduit."[61]

Unfortunately for the cause of saving the lives of American troops, on April 20, 1945, OSS Washington cabled Dulles that the Joint Chiefs of Staff ordered an end to surrender talks, due to "complications which have arisen with Russians." Evidently, Roosevelt did not wish to offend Stalin. Dulles was forced to call a halt to the German surrender effort. He expressed concern about a radio operator who was transmitting intelligence for him from Milan:

> This contact, originally initiated for intelligence purposes, was largely developed through outstanding competent and Allied friendly Swiss officer who had charge of Swiss intelligence work directed toward Germany, and who is rendering us vital services in matters affecting reduit. I have task of effecting break in manner not to alienate this contact which is potentially the most useful and important we have for developing work directed against reduit.[62]

Dulles reported on April 24 about SS General Wolff's visit of the preceding week to Berlin in an attempt to persuade Hitler and the Nazi leadership to surrender. Wolff had provided this information to two Swiss intermediaries in the surrender negotiations, Swiss intelligence Major Max Weibel and Professor Max Husmann. Wolff got the same reaction from Hitler as Dulles had from the Allied leadership: German forces in Italy would not be allowed to surrender to the Americans. Hitler cared not a wit about further senseless destruction in Italy and was quoted as remarking: "In two more months the break between Anglo Saxons and Russians will come about, and then I shall join [the] party which approaches me first, it makes no difference which."[63]

Despite the intransigence on both sides to prevent the surrender of the German forces in Italy, on April 26 the Joint Chiefs of Staff relented and directed that German envoys could proceed to Allied Force Headquarters in Caserta to surrender. A Soviet representative would be present. On May 2, the Wehrmacht forces in Italy surrendered.

Instead of concentrating available German forces in a redoubt, Hitler remained in Berlin, where he committed suicide two days before the above surrender. The Third Reich unconditionally surrendered on May 8. The war in Europe was over.

Despite its strict official neutrality, Switzerland clearly played a role in the defeat of Nazism. The above represents only a sampling of Allen Dulles' OSS dispatches. These have never been so much as mentioned in studies of the role of Switzerland during World War II, much less in the two recent critical yet heavily publicized Swiss and U.S. government reports. Neither the U.S. Eizenstat-Slany report (1997) nor Switzerland's Bergier Commission report (2002)[64] make mention of Allen Dulles, the OSS, or Switzerland's role as America's window on the Reich. Perhaps in the future the full documentation of Swiss involvement with American intelligence will be brought to light.

CONCLUSION

Are the lessons offered by Switzerland during World War II relevant today? Once more, after a brief period of peace, the world is enmeshed in conflict based on religious, racial and other ideologies. The slow breakup of the old European balance of power of the nineteenth century culminated in the First and Second World Wars. Today the breakup of the Soviet empire and the rise of Islamic fundamentalism have produced new challenges for U.S. foreign policy that are still being debated. In a world wracked by new waves of turbulence, the example of a small state that stood fast in the face of tyranny is well worth remembering.

The Nazi threat to Switzerland began on Hitler's seizure of power in 1933, greatly accelerated with the Nazi takeover of neighboring Austria in 1938, and reached its zenith with the fall of France in 1940. The prospect of a Nazi attack could not be discounted until the end of the war in 1945. The United States managed to retain her neutrality until the end of 1941, when the Japanese attacked Pearl Harbor and Hitler declared that Germany would wage war on the United States. America responded and, with the sacrifice of almost half a million lives, met and defeated her enemies. Around the globe, scores of millions of people, the majority of them civilians, were left dead. The United States, separated from her enemies by oceans on each side, and defended by people of courage, was spared invasion in World War II. So was Switzerland, albeit without any oceans and despite her encirclement by larger Axis powers.

Switzerland was—and remains—a harmonious model of ethnic, linguistic and religious diversity with deep traditions of democracy, local autonomy and individual rights. During the wartime years when Switzerland, surrounded by Axis armies and economically isolated, continued to

303

function as a free and open society, she maintained her peace only through a tough-minded armed neutrality—being fully and seriously prepared for war. And she skillfully used diplomacy and negotiation to maintain herself against large and powerful enemies.

The Swiss did not make distinctions among their citizens on the basis of race, language or religion. They embodied the hard-won values of the Judeo-Christian tradition and the European Enlightenment—tolerance, equality before the law, and individual human rights.

The Swiss aversion to centralized authority derived in part from their mountain culture and the enduring legacy of the Reformation doctrines of Calvin and Zwingli. This proved to be a powerful bulwark against the Führer principle just as, in more recent times, the Swiss rejected integration into the sprawling bureaucracies of the European Union. Referenda, local control and democratic consensus are core values in Switzerland. Indeed, the Swiss are more opposed to statism than the parliamentary democracies Hitler sought to destroy.

It would be a mistake to equate neutrality—or at least Swiss armed neutrality—with lack of willpower. To the Swiss, strict armed neutrality meant that they would not participate in external wars. They would fight only defensively and only if attacked. They were not—and are not—pacifists, and during World War II held their ground hunkered down in bunkers and mountain passes with the enemy in their sights should he have dared to attack.

Because she energetically prepared for a Nazi invasion, Switzerland did not suffer the cruel fate of the neutrals that were quickly overrun by the Wehrmacht. At the peak of its mobilization, the Swiss Confederation mustered an astonishing 850,000 men under arms—out of a population of only 4.2 million! That was the highest per-capita mobilization of any country in the world. By contrast, for example, Denmark had a population of 3.8 million, and in 1939 shrunk her tiny force from 36,000 to 14,000 troops.[1] When Nazi Germany attacked in April 1940, the King of Denmark surrendered an hour later with virtually no resistance. Thereafter the workers and factories were saddled with Nazi war production. When orders came for the deportation of Jews in 1943, the Danes were able to rescue most, but not all, of Denmark's 8,000 Jews by putting them on boats to Sweden.[2]

There was never any need to rescue or hide Switzerland's Jews. The Swiss openly protected their Jewish compatriots, and armed them just as they did virtually every citizen—with both rifles and a determination to fight. Moreover, unlike the occupied European countries, Switzerland rescued many thousands of refugees fleeing from those countries—indeed, far more proportionately than any unoccupied country, including the United States.

There was no Holocaust in Switzerland. The architects of the Final Solution failed to kill any of Switzerland's Jews or to cause their exodus. Nor did the German war machine seize Swiss industry and impose forced labor in Switzerland, as it did in the countries it overran.

Being weak, being overrun, being a victim, and being relentlessly exploited are not virtues, although they may give rise to acts of heroism. Successfully refusing to be a victim by being strong—by making the cost in blood of invasion unacceptably high—is not blameworthy.[3]

To be sure, Switzerland also depended on economic and political factors to achieve the balancing act that kept her out of the war. But Switzerland's large allocation of resources to defense—to say nothing of her people's will to resist—shows how seriously the Swiss took their armed neutrality. In addition, despite their official political neutrality, the Swiss man and woman in the street was typically strongly anti-Nazi for the entire period of the German domination of Europe. The Germans were constantly protesting Swiss "provocations" and retaliating against Switzerland with the powerful economic leverage they possessed—the ability to starve the country by restricting supplies of fuel and food.

Switzerland's defense capability, moreover, did not consist of hidden resistance cells or guerrilla fighters—it was represented by a public army on the local and national level, supported by massive fortifications along the border and in the Alps, and constant efforts to upgrade weaponry and training. The Swiss could not have emerged victorious if the Nazis had devoted all their resources to an invasion; however, their efforts were sufficient to convince the Germans that a conquest of Switzerland would have required a concerted, lengthy effort of the kind that—as we only know in retrospect—the course of the war did not allow.

The Swiss survived in the very shadow of the Third Reich, and when the evidence is assessed and balanced, it is clear they not only managed to protect themselves in terrible times, they made solid contributions to the Allied cause. Of course it is possible to point out individual actions that can be questioned. But the Swiss have been open about their history and have encouraged investigation. None of the Allies, including the United States—not to mention other neutrals—have subjected their wartime decisions to such intense scrutiny.

Switzerland and the U.S. share a common heritage. Both have been from their beginnings independent republics. The births of the Swiss Confederation in 1291 and the United States in 1776 are extraordinary episodes in history in which peoples banded together to win their freedom. Despite today's vast difference in size and population, Swiss local democracy is a kind of template of American local democracy. That is why Switzerland and the United States, despite occasional bumps on the road, will inalterably remain Sister Republics.

Massive state terrorism during World War II had to be confronted and resisted by any means at hand. Like the Americans, the Swiss had their own "Greatest Generation," and it included all of those who were ready to lay down their lives had the Nazi armies come over the border. How exactly tiny Switzerland stood down the Nazi monolith is a lesson worth remembering in the annals of history.

SOURCE NOTES

INTRODUCTION

1. Winston S. Churchill, *The Second World War* (London: Cassel, 1954), VI, 616.

2. Eisenhower to Col. Albert Zublin, July 23, 1955, in Robert Gubler, *Felddivision 6: Von der Zürcher Miliz zur Felddivision, 1815–1991* (Verlag Neue Zürcher Zeitung, 1991), 309.

3. Allen Dulles, *The Secret Surrender* (London: Harper & Rowe, 1966), 25.

4. *Final Report on the Work of the Claims Resolution Tribunal for Dormant Accounts in Switzerland* (October 5, 2001). The Tribunal was the outgrowth of the Independent Committee of Eminent Persons chaired by Paul A. Volcker.

5. Halbrook, *Target Switzerland: Swiss Armed Neutrality in World War II* (Rockville Center, NY: Sarpedon Publishers, 1998).

6. Halbrook, *Die Schweiz im Visier: Die bewaffnete Neutralität im Zweiten Weltkrieg* (Verlage Novalis Schaffhausen/Rothenhäusler Stäfa, 1999); Halbrook, *La Suisse encerclée: La neutralité armée suisse durant la Deuxième Guerre mondiale* (Editions Slatkine Genève, 2000); Halbrook, *La Svizzera nel mirino: La neutralità aramata della Svizzera nella seconda guerra mondiale* (Coedizione Pedrazzini–Locarno / Alberti–Verbania, 2002); Halbrook, *Cel: Szwajcaria* (Warszawa: Dom Wydawniczy Bellona, 2003).

7. "Auszeichnung für Stephen P. Halbrook: Überreichung des Preises der Max-Geilinger-Stiftung," *Neue Zürcher Zeitung*, 31. Mai 2000, S. 47; "'Kontrapunkt zur Diffamierung der Schweiz': Preisverleihung an Stephen Halbrook und Angelo Codevilla," *Neue Zürcher Zeitung*, 11. Nov. 2002, S. 27.

8. The Bergier Commission publications are described in http://www.uek.ch/en/index.htm.

9. See Leo Schelbert, ed., *Switzerland Under Siege, 1939–1945: A Neutral Nation's Struggle for Survival* (Rockport, ME: Picton Press, 2000); Donald P. Hilty, ed., *Retrospectives on Switzerland in World War Two* (Rockport, ME: Picton Press, 2001); Angelo M. Codevilla, *Between the Alps and a Hard Place: Switzerland in World War II and the Rewriting of History* (Washington, DC: Regnery Publishing, 2000); Klaus Urner, *Let's Swallow Switzerland: Hitler's Plans Against the Swiss Confederation* (Lanham,

MD: Lexington Press, 2002); Willi Gautschi, *General Henri Guisan: Commander-in-Chief of the Swiss Army during World War Two* (Rockville Centre, NY: Front Street Press, 2003); Georges-André Chevallaz, *The Challenge of Neutrality: Diplomacy and the Defense of Switzerland* (Lanham, MD: Lexington Press, 2001); Pierre Th. Braunschweig, *Secret Channel to Berlin: The Masson–Schellenberg Connection and Swiss Intelligence in World War II* (Philadelphia: Casemate Publishers, 2004).

Chapter 1: THE EYES OF GERMAN INTELLIGENCE
1. The documents herein are from the Bundesarchiv/Militärarchiv, Freiburg am Breisgau, Germany. Documents related to Nazi subversion in Switzerland are also located in other archives. See, e.g., the excellent study Hans Rudolf Fuhrer, *Spionage gegen die Schweiz* (Frauenfeld: Huber & Co., 1982).
2. BA/MA RW 5/415, Deutsche Gesandtschaft, Das gegenwärtige Verhältnis der Schweiz zu Deutschland, 24.4.1934. "BA/MA" refers to Bundesarchiv/ Militärarchiv, Freiburg am Breisgau, Germany.
3. "Un plan d'invasion de la Suisse?" *Journal de Genève*, Sept. 27, 1933, 1. See Halbrook, *Target Switzerland*, 28–29.
4. BA/MA RW 5/415, Deutsche Gesandtschaft, Annexion der deutschen Schweiz, 20.6.1934.
5. BA/MA RW 5/415, Deutsche Gesandtschaft Der Militär-Attaché, Bericht Nr. 3/34 (Schweiz), 16.7.1934. For an almost identical report to the Armed Forces High Command, see BA/MA RW 5/415, Vortragsnotiz über Bericht Nr. 3/34 des Militärattachés Wien, 1.8.1934.
6. BA/MA RW 5/415, Deutsche Gesandtschaft Der Militär-Attaché, Bericht Nr. 4/34/ Schweiz, 27.9.1934.
7. *E.g*, BA/MA RW 6/77, Wehrmachtsamt Nr. 4107/36 J III b v. 30. Juni 1936, 23.7.1936.
8. BA/MA RW 6/81, Wehrmacht, Übersicht Nr. 46, 11.3.1937.
9. BA/MA RW 6/78, Deutsche Gesandtschaft, Schweizerische Pressehetze gegen Deutschland, 13.4.1937. The report attached a copy of the article, "La guerre? Hitler la prépare," *Le Travail*, No. 82, 9 April 1937.
10. *See* Halbrook, *Target Switzerland*, 45–63.
11. BA/MA RH2 2923, Deutsche Gesandtschaft Der Militär- und Luftattaché, Hochverehrter Herr General, 24.10.1938.
12. "Hetze der Eidgenossen gegen Deutschland," *Völkische Beobachter*, 18 December 1938.
13. BA/MA RH 26-260/48 Nachrichtendienst Ic: Schweiz. Lierin: Karten schweizer Befestigungen. 18.8 bis 28.12.1939.
14. BA/MA RW5/352, AUSL, Außen- und militärpolitische Nachrichten, 26.8.1939.
15. BA/MA RW5/352, AUSL, Außen- und militärpolitische Nachrichten, 12, (Ohne Funk- und Pressemeldungen), 2.9.1939.

16. BA/MA RW5/352, AUSL, Außen- und militärpolitische Nachrichten, 12 Uhr. (Ohne Funk- und Pressemeldungen), 5.9.1939.
17. BA/MA RW5/352, AUSL, Außen- und militärpolitische Nachrichten, 14, 7.9.1939.
18. BA/MA RW5/352, AUSL, Außen- und militärpolitische Nachrichten, 9 Uhr., 18.9.1939.
19. BA/MA RH 2/739 K-5. Lage: Schweiz am 12.10.39. Anlage 2, zum Lagebericht Nr. 86 vom 13.10.39. Updated through 16.11.39.
20. BA/MA RW 5/373, Abt. Landesverteidigung, Lagebericht Nr. 107, 14.10.1939.
21. BA/MA RW 5/357, Oberkommando der Wehrmacht, Laufende Informationen Nr. 1, 30.10.1939.
22. BA/MA RH2 2923 Deutsche Gesandtschaft Der Militärattaché, Hochverehrter Herr General, 3.11.1939. The report cited "Kleines Kriegsmosaik," *National Zeitung* (Abendausgabe), 2 Nov. 1939.
23. BA/MA RH2/1739 K-1, 11.11.39–26.11.39.
24. BA/MA RW 5/537, Oberkommando der Wehrmacht, Laufende Informationen Nr. 11, 11.11.1939.
25. BA/MA RW 5/357, Oberkommando der Wehrmacht, An Auswärtiges Amt (Informationsabteilung) über Inf.A.A. (mit I Nebenabdruck), 17.11.1939.
26. Halbrook, *Target Switzerland*, 166.
27. Bruno Grimm, *Gau Schweiz? Dokumente über die nationalsozialistischen Umtriebe in der Schweiz* (Druck der Unionsdruckerei Bern, 1939), 9–13.
28. BA/MA RW 5/358, Oberkommando der Wehrmacht, Laufende Informationen Nr. 24, 29.11.1939.
29. BA/MA RW 4/315, Stimmungsbericht gem, An das Oberkommando der Wehrmacht Abwehrabteilung III (N) z.Hd.v.Herrn Obstlt.Jacobsen, 10.1.1940.
30. BA/MA RH 2/2923, H.Qu. O.K.H., Lieber Herr v. Ilsemann, 13.1.1940.
31. BA/MA RH 19III/344, Oberkommando des Heeres, Heeresgruppe C, Taschenbuch Schweizerisches Heer, 14.1.1940. The 95th Infantry Division was listed, then changed to the 212nd, and then crossed out.
32. BA/MA RH 19III/344, Heeresgruppenkommando C, Taschenbuch "Schweizerisches Heer" (N.f.D.), 29.1.1940.
33. BA/MA RH 20-7/164, Sondermeldung der 260. Div. Am 31.1.1940, 19.55 Uhr (Oblt.Schmückle), 31.1.1940.
34. BA/MA RH 19III/366, Heeresgruppenkommando C. Abt. Ic, Sondermeldung, 1.2.1940.
35. BA/MA RH 20-7/2, Armeehauptquartier, Fall Schweiz, 9.2.1940.
36. BA/MA RH 2/1739 K-6, 5.2.40.
37. BA/MA RW 4/312/1, Amt Ausl/Abw, Bericht des deutschen Militärattachés in Bern vom 23.2.40, 2.3.1940.
38. BA/MA RW 5/357, Oberkommando der Wehrmacht, Laufende Informa-

tionen Nr. 15, 16.2.1940.

39. BA/MA RW 5/357, Oberkommando der Wehrmacht, Laufende Informationen Nr. 15, 16.2.1940.

40. BA/MA RH 2/2923, Deutsche Gesandtschaft Der Militarattaché, Hochzuverehrter Herr General, 17.2.1940.

41. BA/MA RH 20-7/2, Armeehauptquartier, Betr. T. Massnahmen, Heeresgruppenkommando C!, 22.2.1940.

42. BA/MA RH 20-7/2, Geheime Kommandefache, An H.Gr.Kdo. C, 28.2.1940.

43. BA/MA RH 20-7/166, Aufnahme: Oblt. Weick, 8.3.1940.

44. BA/MA RH 20-7/166, Aufnahme: Oblt. Weick, 8.3.1940.

45. BA/MA RH 19 III/348, Abschnitts-Kommandeur Bodensee, Die Lage im Schweizer Grenzgebiet, Allgemeine Übersicht, 26.3.1940.

46. BA/MA RH 2/2923, Deutsche Gesandtschaft Der Militärattaché, Hochzuverehrter Herr General, 8.4.1940.

Chapter 2: HANGING HITLER IN SATIRE

1. *Gegen Rote und Braune Fäuste: Das Weltgeschehen von 1932–1948 in 342 Karikaturen aus dem Nebelspalter* (Nebelspalter-Verlag Rorschach, 1949). The pages are not numbered but are in chronological order.

2. Werner Rings, *Schweiz in Krieg, 1933–1945* (Verlag Ex Libris Zurich, 1974), 274.

3. Letter to author from Hedi K. Moore, Delmar, New York, March 21, 2001.

4. Elsie Attenhofer, *Cornichon: Erinnerungen an ein Cabaret* (Benteli Verlag Bern, 1975); Elsie Attenhofer, *Réserve du Patron: Im Gespräch mit K.* (Rothenhäusler Verlag-Stäfa: Stäfa, 1989). Elisabeth Sauter-Frey, a friend of Attenhofer, has an unpublished autobiographical manuscript of her life. For a recent appreciation, see Peter Michael Keller, "Staatskritisch, staatstragend. Das Cabaret Cornichon und seine Legende: nach 50 Jahren," *Neue Zürcher Zeitung*, 17. Juli 2001, 38.

5. Attenhofer, *Cornichon*, 6–7.

6. *See* Werner Rings, *Schweiz in Krieg, 1933–1945* (Verlag Ex Libris Zurich, 1974), 27–29.

7. The excerpts and quotations from specific skits are from Attenhofer, *Cornichon*.

8. Id., 27.

9. Id., 58.

10. Id., 111.

11. Id., 114–15.

12. Id., 130–31.

13. Id., 132–33.

14. Id., 138–39.

15. Id., 154.

16. Id., 155.

17. Id., 156.

18. Id., 157.
19. Id., 159.
20. Id., 160.
21. Id., 176.
22. Id., 183.
23. Id., 210–11.
24. Id., 212.
25. Id., 213–14.
26. Id., 216–21.
27. Id., 222.
28. Id., 229–30.
29. Id., 250.

Chapter 3: COUNTERATTACK OF THE NEWSREELS

1. The author interviewed Paul Alexis Ladame, the head of the Swiss *Wochenschau* (Weekly News) during 1940–44, and received comments on this chapter by Hans Laemmel, who headed it during 1944–61. The author wishes to thank the following persons who assisted in obtaining copies of films used for this study: Cdmt. Jean Abt, Centre d'histoire et de prospective militaires; M. Markus Meister, Chef Sektion Armeefilmdienst; Dr. Yves-Alain Morel; Peter Baumgartner-Jost. This article is a revised version of "The Spirit of Resistance: The Swiss 'Wochenschau' and 'Armeefilmdienst,'" in Leo Schelbert, ed., *Switzerland Under Siege, 1939–1945: A Neutral Nation's Struggle for Survival* (Rockport, ME: Picton Press, 2000).

2. *Landesverteidigung und Ortswehren,* August 1943. **C.** Note: Boldface capital letters refer to the following videotapes:

A=VP 384.00, *Schweizer Alltag 1939–1945,* 1. Teil. Bern: Armeefilmdienst.

B=VP 384.00, *Schweizer Alltag 1939–1945,* 2. Teil. Bern: Armeefilmdienst.

C=VP 380.00, *Schweizer Armee 1939–45.* Bern: Armeefilmdienst.

D=KF 4.00, *Wehrhaft und frei.* French version: *Etre Fort pour Rester Libre.* Bern: Armeefilmdienst. Historical documentary made from various sources. Réalisation: Adolf Forter, Commentaire: Urs Schwarz.

Other significant videotapes are as follows:

VP 379.00, Schweiz *1939–45.* French version: *Suisse 1939–1945.* Film officiel Diamant. Historical documentary made from various sources.

Schweizer Alltag 1939–1945. Aus der Schweizer Filmwochenschau. Zurich: Rincovision.

Die Schweiz und der Zweite Weltkrieg. Zurich: Rincovision.

Le Général Guisan et son temps. General Guisan und seine Zeit. Il General Guisan e la sua epoca. Un film de Claude Champion. L'Association Film Général Guisan— Le Centre d'Historie et de Prospective Militaires Pully.

Die Deutsche Wochenschau, Bundesarchiv, Koblenz, Germany. Videotape reproductions: *Through Enemy Eyes: A Newsreel History of the Third Reich at War* (Chicago: International Historic Films, various dates).

Polish Internment Camps in Switzerland, professora Adama Vetulaniego (1941). Unpublished film made available by Zygmunt Prugar-Ketling.

3. Letter from Hans Laemmel to author, Nov. 5, 2000.

4. *See* Stephen P. Halbrook, *Target Switzerland* (Rockville Centre, NY: Sarpedon, 1998), 181.

5. Halbrook, *Target Switzerland*, 179–81, 189–90.

6. *Die Deutsche Wochenschau* is available in the Bundesarchiv, Koblenz, Germany. Most of the newsreels have been reproduced with English subtitles on videotape under the designation *Through Enemy Eyes: A Newsreel History of the Third Reich at War* (Chicago: International Historic Films, various dates).

7. Paul Alexis Ladame, *Une caméra contre Hitler* (Editions Slatkine Genève, 1997), 101–02.

8. *Die Deutsche Wochenschau*, No. 506, 15 May 1940, UfA, Ton-Woche.

9. Major Roland Ziegler, *Geschichte der Sektion Heer und Haus 1939–1945* (AHQ Bern 1945), 47f.

10. BA/MA RW 5/358, Oberkommando der Wehrmacht, Laufende Informationen Nr. 66, 29.10.1940.

11. "Switzerland Sits Tight," *Fortune* (Sept. 1941), vol. 24, pages 74, 112.

12. Interview with Paul Alexis Ladame, Geneva, 29 May 2000.

13. BA/MA RW 5/358, Oberkommando der Wehrmacht, Laufende Informationen Nr. 68, 5.11.1940.

14. Paul Alexis Ladame, *Une caméra contre Hitler* (Editions Slatkine Genève 1997). Further information was obtained in an interview with Ladame by the author, Geneva, 29 May 2000. *See* also Ladame, *Defending Switzerland* (Delmar, New York: Caravan Books, 1999), 10–11, 45–46, 50.

15. Interview with Paul Alexis Ladame, Geneva, 29 May 2000.

16. Ladame, *Defending Switzerland*, 45–46, 50.

17. Ladame, *Une Caméra Contre Hitler*, 41–42.

18. Letter from Hans Laemmel to author, Nov. 5, 2000.

19. Ladame, *Une Caméra Contre Hitler*, 49.

20. Hans Laemmel, "Mißverständnisse um die Filmwochenschau," *Neue Zürcher Zeitung*, Jan. 24, 2000, 11.

21. Letter from Hans Laemmel to author, Nov. 5, 2000.

22. Id.

23. On the *Armeefilmdienst*, see Yves-Alain Morel, *Aufklärung oder Indoktrination? Truppeninformation in der Schweizer Armee* (Thesis Verlag Zurich, 1996), 162–70; Oskar Felix Fritschi, *Geistige Landesverteidigung während des Zweiten Weltkrieges* (Fabag + Druckerei Winterthur AG, 1971), 174–75; Major Roland Ziegler, "Heer und Haus," *Die Schweiz in Waffen* (Vaterländischer Verlag A.G. Murten und Zurich, 1945), 190–92.

24. Letter from Hans Laemmel to author, Nov. 5, 2000.

25. Ziegler, *Geschichte der Sektion Heer und Haus*, 50.

26. Some representative films include: *Alarm! Einsatz leichter Truppen/Alerte! Mise en action des troupes légères* (18 min., premiered July 5, 1940), *Fest der Heimat/Fête du pays* (20 min., 1940), *Ausbildung und Kampf unserer Weissen Truppen/La Garde blanche* (1940), *Berge und Soldaten/Montagne et soldats* (1941), *Unsere Abwehrbereitschaft/Notre volonté de défense* (38 min., 1941), *Schulung zum Nahkampf/L'école du combat rapproché* (35 min., 1942),*Grenzwacht in den Bergen/Ceux d'en haut* (1942), *Die Hochgebirgspatrouille/Patrouille de haute montagne* (12 min., 1944), *Ortskampf/Assaut d'un village* (22 min., 1944), *Pulver/Poudre* (23 min., 1945).

27. Morel, *Aufklärung oder Indoktrination?*, 166.

28. Letter from Hans Laemmel to author, Nov. 5, 2000.

29. Letter from Hans Laemmel to author, Nov. 5, 2000.

30. **D**. Note: where the videotape does not show the film name or date, only the videotape is identified.

31. **D.**

32. **D.**

33. "Krieg," September 1940. Schweizer Filmwochenschau. Edition Cinegram S.A. Genève. **A.**

34. *Wiederverwertung alter Pneus* (Recycling Old Tires), February 1941. **A.**

35. *Strassenbahn passt sich der Zeit an* (Electric Tramway Takes over Usual Transportation), July 1941. **A.**

36. *Alte Tuben für Lötdraht* (Old Household Tubes Used for Soldering Wire), August 1941. **A.**

37. *Braunkohle wird gefördert* (Brauncoal Pits Are Reopened), November 1941. **A.**

38. *Holzgas als Benzinerstz* (Gas from Wood Replaces Gasoline), February 1942. **A.**

39. *Räppler aus Zink* (Copper Money Replaced by Zinc Coins), March 1942. **A.**

40. *Schilf für Bauindustrie* (Reed Harvest for the Building Industry), February 1943. **A.**

41. *Alteisen für Metallindustrie* (Scrap Metal for the Metal Industry), June 1943. **A.**

42. *Maikäfer als Schweinefutter* (Cockchafer as Pig Feed), March 1942. **A.**

43. *Die Wissenschaft im Dienste des Mehranbaues* (Science in the Service of Cultivation), July 1942. **A.**

44. Ladame, *Une Caméra Contre Hitler*, 57–62. Other titles included *La bataille agricole, Notre pain quotidien,* and *Retour à la Terre.*

45. Interview with Paul Alexis Ladame, Geneva, 29 May 2000.

46. *Neuerungen in der Textilindustrie* (Innovations of the Textile Industry), March 1942. **B.**

47. *Kriegswirtschafts-Aktualitäten* (Realities of the War Economy), June 1943. **A.**

48. *Lebensmittelversorgung und Rationierung* (Food Supply and Rationing), February 1944. **A.**

49. *Bei uns geht die Armut nicht in Lumpen einher* (With Us, Poverty Doesn't Mean Going Around in Rags), October 1944. **A.**

50. *Die Frau in unserer Zeit* (The Woman in Our Time), February 1945. **A.**

51. *FHD* (Women's Auxiliary Service), April 1941. **A.**

52. January 1942. **C.** Note: lack of citation to an episode title indicates that the title was not reproduced on the videotape.

53. January 1943. **C.**

54. December 1943. **C.**

55. Ladame, *Une Caméra Contre Hitler*, 63–67. Unfortunately, none of the video-tapes cited herein includes any footage from the above.

56. Id., 63-64.

57. Id., 65.

58. Letter from Hans Laemmel to author, Nov. 5, 2000.

59. *Fussballmatch: Schweiz-Deutschland* (Soccer Match: Switzerland-Germany), April 1941. **B.**

60. *Das Schweizerische Sportabzeichen* (Swiss Sport Medals), August 1941. **B.**

61. *Arbeitslosigkeit im Gastgewerbe* (Unemployment in Guest Trades), July 1942. **B.**

62. *Hilfe den Kriegsgeschädigten Kindern.* (Help for War-Victim Children), February 1942. **A.**

63. *Schaffhausen Bombardiert* (Schaffhausen Bombed), April 1944. **B.**

64. *Menschen Fliegen zu Uns* (People Flee to Us), December 1944. **A.**

65. *Austausch von Schwerverwundeten durch die Schweiz* (Exchange of the Severely Wounded Through Switzerland), March 1945. **B.**

66. *Russische Internierte* (Russian Internees), August 1945. **B.** The filming of internees was generally prohibited, but this film was an exception.

67. Letter from Hans Laemmel to author, Nov. 5, 2000. *See* "La Suisse subissait le chantage," *Journal de Genève*, 28 May 1984; "Die Schweiz und die Sowjetunion," *Neue Zürcher Zeitung*, 8 May 2000.

68. May 1941. **A.**

69. September 1941. **C.**

70. **D.**

71. *Das Eidgenössische Kavallerie-Remonten-Depot* (The Swiss Cavalry Remount Depot), February 1942. **C.**

72. April 1942. **C.**

73. *Unsere Pontonniere* (Our Pontooneers), 1943. **C.**

74. May 1941. **A.**

75. *Wer nicht schweigen kann/ Qui ne sait se taire* (Whoever Cannot Be Silent), May 1943. **A.**

76. Ladame, *Une Caméra Contre Hitler*, 83–84.

77. June 1944. **D.**

78. *Die Armee Braucht Funker* (The Army Needs Wireless Operators), July 1944. **C.**

79. *Die Grenadiere* (The Grenadiers), September 1944. **C.**

80. *Unsere Fliegerabwehr bei Nacht* (Our Antiaircraft Defense at Night), October 1944. **B**.

81. *Flieger-Grenzverletzung* (Aircraft Border Violation), November 1944. **C.**

82. *Weihnachten mit dem General* (Christmas with the General), January 1944, **C**.
83. *Ein Städtchen im Jura* (A Small Town in the Jura), January 1945. **A**.
84. *Waffenstillstand* (The Armistice), May 1945. **A**. See also untitled segments in **D**.
85. *Ein Tag M.K.P. Des General* (A Day with the General), July 1945. **C**.
86. *Der Krieg ist Vorüber* (The War Is Over), August 1945. **C**.

Chapter 4: I WAS A MILITIA SOLDIER THEN
1. Hans Köfer-Richner, *Die kleine Stadt am schwarzen Fluss* (Baden: Wanner Druck, 1992); J.J. Köfer, *Harte Kriegsjahre: Jugenderinnerungen 1939 bis 1945* (Mellingen: Druckerei Nüssli AG, 1999).
2. Interview with Hans Köfer of Bellikon/Hausen, Baden, September 28, 1999. Absent a reference to one of his books, all of the following information is from this interview.
3. J.J. Köfer, *Harte Kriegsjahre: Jugenderinnerungen 1939 bis 1945* (Mellingen: Druckerei Nüssli AG, 1999), 155.
4. Letter from Rudi Tschan, La Tour-de-Peilz, October 1999.
5. Statement by and interview with Max Salm of Umiken, Baden, September 28, 1999.
6. Wolfgang Langhoff, *Die Moorsoldaten: 13 Monate Konzentrationslager* (Schweizer Spiegel Verlag Zurich, 1935). English translation: Langhoff, *Rubber Truncheon* (New York: E.P. Dutton, 1935).
7. Edgar Bonjour, *Geschichte der Schweizerischen Neutralität* (Basel: Helbing & Lichtenhahn, 1976), IV, 472; Jakob Huber, *Bericht des Chefs des Generalstabs*, 501–13.
8. Statement of Max Salm of Umiken, 6 September 1994.
9. Interview with Ernst Jenny, Baden, September 28, 1999.
10. Interview with Hans Kleiner, Baden, September 28, 1999.
11. Interview with Dr. Hans Widmer of Wildegg, Baden, September 28, 1999.
12. Interview nach Aufzeichnung auf Archimob-Film Nr 114, aufgeschrieben von Frau FHD a.D. Lucie Schaad-Denner, Basel, den 14.2.2001; further interview by author, 5 March 2001.
13. Interview with Werner P. Auer, Baden, September 28, 1999.
14. Interview with Peter Baumgartner-Jost, Langenthal, June 8, 1999.
15. Letter from Rudolf Ursprung, retired Colonel, October 4, 1999.
16. Felix P. Bentz. *Exploring My Life* (manuscript dated 1996), 32. Dr. Bentz now resides in Tucson, Arizona.
17. Id., 38.
18. Id., 54.
19. Id., 55.
20. Id., 56.
21. Id., 60.
22. Id., 73–75.
23. Id., 76–78.

24. Statement of Bruno Capol, Windisch, Sept. 27, 1999. Born in 1922, he lived in Lucerne until July 1941 and then in Richterswil (ZH) until May 1945.

25. Wm. Ernst Herzig, ed., *Damals im Aktivdienst: Soldaten erzählen aus den Jahren 1939–1945* (Zurich: Rascher Verlag, 1959), 14.

26. Heinz Häsler, Kkdt a.D., "1939–1999: Meine Erinnerung an die Allgemeine Mobilmachung," in Halbrook, *Die Schweiz im Visier* (Verlage Novalis Schaffhausen/Rothenhäusler Stäfa), 1999, 309–12.

27. Interview with Dr. iur. Heinz Langenbacher, Bern, 27 September 1999.

28. *Der Bund* (Bern), 17 May 1995, quoted in Paul Alexis Ladame, *Defending Switzerland* (Delmar, New York: Caravan Books, 1999), 43.

29. Letter from Hans A. Hug of Weston, Mass., to author, July 4, 2000.

30. Interview with members of Aktion Aktivdienst, Stäfa, June 3, 1999.

31. Peter Vogelsanger, *Mit Leib und Seele: Erlebnisse und Einsichten einen Pfarrers* (Theologischer Verlag: Zurich, 1977), 128.

32. *Id.*, 167–70.

33. Interview with Paul Rothenhäusler, Stäfa-Zurich, June 6, 1999.

34. *The Knife and Its History: Written on the Occasion of the 100th Anniversary of Victorinox* (Ibach, CH: Victorinox, 1984), 129.

35. Interview with Karl Elsener, Sr., Victorinox factory, Schwyz, June 8, 1999.

36. Interview with Dr. h.c. Arthur T. Bill, Bern, 27 September 1999.

37. Letter from Florian E. Davatz, Minusio, February 2000.

38. *See* Halbrook, *Target Switzerland*, 109.

Chapter 5: BLITZKRIEG 1940

1. "Die deutsche Occupation in Norwegen," *Neue Zürcher Zeitung*, April 24, 1940. See also François Kersaudy, *Norway 1940* (Lincoln: University of Nebraska Press, 1990), 80; Halbrook, *Target Switzerland*, 92–93.

2. BA/MA RW 5/357, Oberkommando der Wehrmacht, Laufende Informationen Nr. 39, 16.4.1940.

3. BA/MA RW 5/353 Teil 2, Oberkommando der Wehrmacht, Aussen– und militärpolitische Nachrichten, 18.4.1940.

4. BA/MA RW 5/353 Teil 2, Oberkommando der Wehrmacht, Aussen– und militärpolitische Nachrichten, 12.5.1940.

5. BA/MA RW 5/353 Teil 2, Oberkommando der Wehrmacht, Aussen– und militärpolitische Nachrichten, 16.5.1940.

6. BA/MA RW 5/359, Oberkommando der Wehrmacht, Kurze Fassung, 17.5.1940.

7. BA/MA RW 4/313, Oberkommando der Wehrmacht, An Auswärtiges Amt. (Informationsabteilung), 17.5.1940.

8. BA/MA RW 5/359, Oberkommando der Wehrmacht, Kurze Fassung, 19.5.1940.

9. BA/MA RW 4/313, Auslandsbriefprüfstelle, Stimmungsbericht Nr. 10,

27.5.1940.
10. Halbrook, *Target Switzerland*, 105–07.
11. BA/MA RH 2/2923, Deutsche Gesandtschaft Der Militärattaché, Hochzuverehrender Herr General, 1.6.1940.
12. BA/MA RH 2/2923, H.Qu. O.K.H., Lieber Herr v. Ilsemann, 6.6.40.
13. BA/MA RW 5/359, Oberkommando der Wehrmacht, Kurze Fassung, 2.6.1940.
14. BA/MA RW 5/497, Abschrift [?].1940.
15. Halbrook, *Target Switzerland*, 109-10.
16. BA/MA RW 5/35, Oberkommando der Wehrmacht, Kurze Fassung, 7.6.1940.
17. BA/MA RH 28-1/123, Gebirgs-Division, An Generalkommando XXXXIV.A.K./Ic., 10.6.1940.
18. BA/MA RH 2/465, Fiche 2, Row 6, Rückschlüsse aus einem Schriftwechsel französischer Kommandobehörden über die Beziehungen Frankreich–Schweiz vom Oktober 1939–February 1940.
19. BA/MA RH 2/465, Fiche 2, Row 6, Rückschlüsse aus einem Schriftwechsel französischer Kommandobehörden über die Beziehungen Frankreich–Schweiz vom Oktober 1939–February 1940.
20. "Mit der Gruppe Guderian zur Schweizer Grenze, 9. bis 25.6.1940," Joachim Lemelsen et al., *29. Division* (Bad Nauheim: Podzun-Verlag, 1965).
21. BA/MA RH 19 III/128 (microfiche) Grundlegende Befehle und Weisungen, 29.6.–12.10.1940, Geheime Kommandosache, Chef des Generalstabes des Heeres, Besprechung in Versailles am 18.6.40, 29.6.1940.
22. Klaus Urner, *"Die Schweiz muss noch geschluckt werden!"* 62–63; Halbrook, *Target Switzerland*, 117.
23. Urner 66–69; Halbrook 118.
24. Urner 70–71; Halbrook 119.
25. BA/MA RH 2/465, Vortragsnotiz über Angriff gegen die Schweiz, 25.6.1940. *See* Urner, *"Die Schweiz muss noch geschluckt werden!"* 52–55, 151–54; Halbrook, *Target Switzerland*, 118.
26. BA/MA RH 2/465, Fiche 1, Row 3, Neugliederung des schweizerischen Kriegsheeres, 23.6.1940.
27. BA/MA RH 2/465, Fiche 1, Row 3, Oberkommando des Heeres Gen St d H, Abt.Fremde Heere West, Die Befestigungen an den schweizerischen Grenzen und im Inneren des Landes, 1.7.1940.
28. BA/MA RH 2/465, Fiche 1, Row 4, Bauart der schweizerischen Landesbefestigung, 1940.
29. BA/MA RH 20-12/23, Armeeoberkommando12, Armeebefehl Nr. 35, 3.7.1940.
30. Roland Kaltenegger, *Die Stammdivision der deutschen Gebirgstruppe: Weg und Kampf der 1. Gebirgs-Division 1935-1945* (Graz-Stuttgart: Leopold Stocker Verlag).

31. BA/MA RH 2/465, Fiche 2, Row 4, Durchgabe eines Fernspruchs Hptm. v. Ziehlberg–O Qu IV, 9.7.1940.

32. BA/MA RH 2/465, Fiche 2, Row 5, Betr: Grenzsperre Schweiz, 15.7.1940.

33. BA/MA RH19 III/129, Oberst i.G.Müller von Hptm.i.G. von Menges, Op. Abt., 13.7.40.

34. BA/MA RH 2/465, Fiche 2, Row 5, Lagebericht West Nr.404 vom 20.7.40., 16.00 Uhr., 20.7.1940.

35. See Halbrook, Target Switzerland, 1–2, 130–31.

36. BA/MA RW 5/354, Oberkommando der Wehrmacht, Aussen- und militär-politische Nachrichten, 31.7.1940.

37. BA/MA RH 24-27/53, Armeeoberkommando, Absperrung der Demarkationslinie und der Schweizer Grenze, 31.7.1940.

38. BA/MA RH 2/465, Fiche 2, Row 5, Page 2, Oberkommando Des Heeres, Gen St d H, Abt.Fremde Heere West, 30.7.1940.

39. BA/MA RH 20-12/183, Armeeoberkommando 12, Lagebericht West Nr. 52 vom 3.August 40, 3.8.1940.

40. BA/MA RW 5/357, Oberkommando der Wehrmacht, Laufend Informationen Nr. 51, 1.8.1940.

41. See Halbrook, Target Switzerland, 127–28.

42. BA/MA RW 5/358, Oberkommando der Wehrmacht, Laufende Informationen Nr. 56, 4.9.1940.

43. BA/MA RH 2/465, Fiche 1, Row 5, Geheime Kommandosache, Bis 3.8. eingetretene Veränderungen in der Schweiz, 3.8.1940.

44. BA/MA RH 2/465, Fiche 3, Row 2, Abwehr-Abteilung III, No. 25270/40/g.Abw III (F2), 31.8.1940.

45. BA/MA RH 2/465.

46. BA/MA RH 2/465, K-2, Kräfteansatz, 2097/482; K-3; K-13 through 19.

47. BA/MA RH 2/465, K-14, Gen Std H Fremde Heere West, Karte der Schweiz, Anlage 2, Schweizer Aufmarsch und Befestigungen. Stand: 15.6.1940.

48. BA/MA RH 2/465, K-15, Gen St d H 10.Abt (IIc), Anlage 3.

49. BA/MA RH 2/465, K-17, Anlage 5, Verfügbare Kräfte, Mitte August 1940.

50. BA/MA RH 2/465, K-18, Anlage 6, Möglicher Kräfteansatz der Italiener.

51. BA/MA RH 2/465, Fiche 2, Row 5, Page 2, Oberkommando Des Heeres, Gen St d H, Abt.Fremde Heere West/IV, Lagebericht West Nr., 16.8.1940.

52. BA/MA RH 2/465, Fiche 3, Row 3, Geheime Kommandosache, Oberkommando des Heeres, 26.8.1940.

53. BA/MA RH 24-12/51, Tagesmeldung vom 27.8.40., 27.8.1940.

54. BA/MA RH 2/465, Fiche 2, Row 7, Oberkommando Des Heeres, Gen St d H, Abt.Fremde Heere West, Lagebericht West Nr. 413, 28.8.1940.

55. BA/MA RH 2/465, K-5, Gen St d H, Abt.Fremde Heere West, Anlage zum Lagebericht West Nr. 413. Lage am 25.8.40.

56. BA/MA RH 2/465, Fiche 2, Row 7, NOTE sur la défense de BALE et de la

région S., 20.10.1939; Fiche 4, Row 3, Notiz über die Verteidigung von Basel und südlich, 20.10.1939. For the analysis of Swiss roads and terrain, *see* BA/MA RH 2/465, Fiche 3, Row 1, Renseignement Itineraires Suisses, 2.5.1940; BA/MA RH 2/465, Fiche 3, Row 1, Nachrichten über Schweizer Straßen, 2.5.1940.

57. BA/MA RH 2/465, Fiche 3, Row 2, Oberkommando Des Heeres, Lagebericht West Nr. 417, 22.9.1940.

58. BA/MA RW 5/358, Oberkommando der Wehrmacht, Laufende Informationen Nr. 58, 13.9.1940.

59. BA/MA RH 2/2923, Deutsche Gesandtschaft Der Militärattaché, Hochzuverehrender Herr General, 23.9.1940.

60. BA/MA RW 5/358, Oberkommando der Wehrmacht, Laufende Informationen Nr. 60, 24.9.1940.

61. BA/MA RH 2/2923, Deutsche Gesandtschaft Der Militärattaché, Hochverehrter Herr General, 4.10.1940.

62. BA/MA RH 2/465, Fiche 3, Row 3, Heeresgruppenkommando C, Betr.: Operationsentwurf Schweiz ("Tannenbaum"), 4.10.1940.

63. BA-MA, RH 2/465, K-10, Karte 1 zu H.Gru. Kdo. C Ia Nr. 262/40 g.K. v. 4.10.40, Operationskarte. Maps accompanying the plan are RH 2/465, K-10, K-11, K-12. Another map shows attack forces "A" and "B" at the Swiss border with France. BA/MA RH 20-1/369, K1, ANL 2 zu Nr. 3907/40, 4.10.40. GenStdH Fremde Heere West, Karte der Schweiz, Befestigungskarte.

64. BA-MA, RH 2/465, K-12, "Versammlungsräume," Karte 3 zu H.Gru. Kdo. C Ia Nr. 262/40 g.K. v. 4.10.40, Operationskarte.

65. BA/MA RH 2/465, Fiche 3, Row 3, Op.Abt. (IIa), Geheime Kommandosache, 9.10.1940.

66. BA/MA RH 19 IV/3 (MF), Anruf Hptm. Worgitzky 11.11.40 Tannenbaum.

67. BA/MA RH 20-1/368, Nr. 001, Rows 2-3, Armeeoberkommando 1; Studie über einen Aufmarsch gegen die Schweiz aus dem Raume der 1. Armee, 4.10.1940.

68. BA/MA RH 20-1/368, Microfiche Nr. 001, Rows 5-7, Microfiche Nr. 002, Rows 1-4, Übersetzung, Service géographique de l'Armee, Secret Ex.Nr. 658, 4.10.1940.

69. BA/MA RH 20-1/368, Nr. 001, Rows 2-3, Armeeoberkommando 1; Studie über einen Aufmarsch gegen die Schweiz aus dem Raume der 1. Armee, 4.10.1940.

70. BA/MA RH 20-1/368, Microfiche Nr. 1, Row 1, Ia F Zu Nr. 3907/40 geh.Kdos., 4.10.1940.

71. BA/MA RH 20-1/368, Microfiche Nr. 1, Row 4, Störungsmöglichkeit der Verschiebung schweizer Divisionen mit der Eisenbahn.

72. BA/MA RW 5/497, Abschrift, 11.10.1940.

73. Klaus Urner, *"Let's Swallow Switzerland: Hitler's Plans Against the Swiss Confederation"* (Lanham, Md.: Lexington Books, 2001), 47–48.

74. Daniel Heller, *Zwischen Unternehmertum, Politik und Überleben: Emil G. Bührle und die Werkzeugmaschinenfabrik Oerlikon Bührle & Co. 1924–1945* (Verlag Huber Frauenfeld, 2002).

75. BA/MA RW 5/358, Oberkommando der Wehrmacht, Laufende Informationen Nr. 64, 18.10.1940.

76. BA/MA RW 5/358, Oberkommando der Wehrmacht, Laufende Informationen Nr. 66, 29.10.1940.

77. BA/MA RW 5/358, Oberkommando der Wehrmacht, Laufende Informationen Nr. 70, 15.11.1940.

78. Halbrook, *Target Switzerland*, 101, 110, 136-37.

79. BA/MA RW 5/358, Oberkommando der Wehrmacht, Laufende Informationen Nr. 72. 20.11.1940.

80. BA/MA RW 5/358, Oberkommando der Wehrmacht, Laufende Informationen Nr. 72, 25.11.1940.

81. BA/MA RW 49/431, Anlage 1 za neat Bremen, B.Nr. G 6335/40/1.1 vom 3.12., 3.12.1940.

82. BA/MA RH 2/2957, Der Chef der Attachéabteilung im Generalstab des Heeres, An Herrn Major i.G. 13.12.1940.

83. BA/MA RW 5/358, Oberkommando der Wehrmacht, Laufende Informationen Nr. 77, 20.12.1940.

84. BA/MA RW 5/358, Oberkommando der Wehrmacht, Laufende Informationen Nr. 78, 24.12.1940.

Chapter 6: SWITZERLAND IS A PORCUPINE

1. Anita Daniel, "The Miracle of Switzerland," *American Mercury*, 54 (May 1942) 552, 554–55.

2. C.W.C. Oman, *The Art of War in the Middle Ages* (Ithaca: Cornell University Press, 1953), 86.

3. Jeremias Gotthelf, "Einiges aus dem eidgenössischen Lustlager zu Sursee," *Allgemeine Schweizerische Militärzeitung*, Januar 1934, 55. This article was originally published in 1838.

4. "Eidgenössischer Kampfgeist," Wehrbrief Nr. 2, Armeekommando, Generaladjutantur 5. Sektion, Heer und Haus, in Yves-Alain Morel, *Aufklärung oder Indoktrination? Truppeninformation in der Schweizer Armee* (Thesis Verlag Zurich, 1996), 285–86.

5. Werner Rings, *Schweiz in Krieg, 1933-1945* (Verlag Ex Libris Zurich, 1974), 162.

6. Ernst Frei, *Erlebter Aktivdienst 1939-1945: Auszüge aus dem Tagebuch eines Angehörigen der Fliegertruppen* (Novalis Verlag Schaffhausen: 1998), 40.

7. Eloise Engle and Lauri Paananen, *The Winter War: The Soviet Attack on Finland 1939–1940* (Harrisburg, PA: Stackpole Books, 1973), 113.

8. Id., 136.

9. Id., 142–43.

10. *Nuremberg Trial Proceedings*, Vol. 14, p. 470 (24 May 1946).

11. Interview with Dr. Max Jufer, Langenthal, June 5, 1999.

12. Günther D. Reiss, "Fortification in Switzerland from 1860 to 1945," *Fort*, Vol. 21, pp. 19, 47–51 (1993). Reports on the wartime fortifications program include *Bericht des Chefs des Generalstabes der Armee an den Oberbefehlshaber der Armee über den Aktivdienst 1939–1945* (Bern, 1946), 201–15, and *Bericht der Abteilung für Festungswesen über den Aktivdienst 1939–1945* (unpublished full-length report).

13. Interview and tour with Dr. Walter Lüem, June 7, 1999, Baden. *See* Walter Lüem and Andreas Steigmeier, *Die Limmatstellung im Zweiten Weltkrieg* (Baden: Baden-Verlag, 1997), and the accompanying tour guide, *Führer zur Limmatstellund aus dem Zweiten Weltkrieg* (Baden: Baden-Verlag, 1997).

14. *See* Christian Reinhart, Kurt Sallaz, and Michael am Rhyn, *Die Repetiergewehre der Schweiz* (Dietikon-Zurich: Stocker-Schmid, 1991); Richard D. Law, *Karabiner 98k, 1934–1945* (Dietikon-Zurich: Stocker-Schmid, 1995).

15. Interview and tour with Rolf Heller, retired from a career of 20-years service in Festung Fürigen, June 7, 1999.

16. Halbrook, *Target Switzerland*, 112–14.

17. *See Le Général Dufour et Saint-Maurice* (Musée Militaire Cantonal, Saint-Maurice, 1987).

18. Interview with Colonel Alexandre Morisod, St. Maurice, Oct. 9, 1998. Jean-Louis Hug acted as translator.

19. *See* Stephen Tanner, *Epic Retreats: From 1776 to the Evacuation of Saigon*, 162–63. (Rockville Centre, NY: Sarpedon Publishers, 2000).

20. Wannsee Protocol, January 20, 1942, Avalon Project, Yale Law School, http://www.yale.edu/lawweb/avalon/20th.htm.

21. Zsolt Keller, "'L'armée est en dehors de toutes questions de confession!' Jüdische Soldaten und Offiziere in der Schweizer Armee 1933–1945," *Bulletin der Schweizerschen Gesellschaft für Judaishsche Forschung*, Nr. 11 (2002), 17, 22–23.

22. Id., 25.

23. Id., 26–27.

24. Robert Braunschweig, letters to author, 12 and 22 September 1999, and interview, Bern, 28 September 1999.

25. Schweizerische Armee, *Offiziers-Etat auf 1. Mai 1938* (Bern: Eidg. Militär-Druckschriftenbureau, n.d.), 306. Braunschweig is also mentioned as a Lieutenant in 1938 in the Motorized Troop Transport. Id. at 201.

26. Generaladjutantur, Sektion Heer und Haus, *Die Judenfrage*, Wehrbrief Nr. 26 (25 May 1943).

27. Id., 4.

28. Id.

29. Schweizerische Armee, *Offiziersetat 1976* (Bern: Eidg. Militärbibliothek, 1976), 1387. Braunschweig authored the military report "Entwicklungstrends in Motorfahrzeugbau" in 1976.

30. R. Braunschweig, "Der Vater der 'Motorwägeler," *Automobile Revue*, 8.01.1970.

31. Information from Benoît de Montmollin-Constam, CH 2533 Evilard, Switzerland, who privately printed Constam's autobiographical *Lebenslauf*.

32. Ernst Wetter and Eduard V. Orelli, *Wer ist wer im Militär?* (Frauenfeld: Huber & CoAG, Grafische Unternehmung und Verlag, 1986), 37.

33. Sigmund Widmer, *Familie Frey: Durchhalten in schwieriger Zeit*, Erzählung Band 2 (Linda Verlag Zurich, 1997).

34. Interview with Paul Rothenhäusler, Stäfa-Zurich, June 6, 1999.

35. Interview with Georges-André Chevallaz at Epalinges near Lausanne, June 6, 1999.

36. Id.

37. Willi Gautschi, *General Henri Guisan: Die schweizerische Armeeführung im Zweiten Weltkrieg* (Verlag Neue Zürcher Zeitung, 1989), 320–22; for the English version, Gautschi, *General Henri Guisan* (Rockville Centre, NY: Front Street Press, 2003), 265–66. *See also* Hans Senn, *Der Schweizerische Generalstab. Volume VII: Anfänge einer Dissuasionsstrategie während des Zweiten Weltkrieges* (Basel: Helbing & Lichtenhahn, 1995), 319–22.

38. Id., 403–04.

39. Id., 628.

40. Interview with Alice Renold-Asper, Baden, September 28, 1999.

41. Gautschi, *General Henri Guisan*, 701–02.

42. Id., 720, 722.

43. Anlage 8, Die höheren Führer des schweizerischen Heeres, Oberkommando des Heeres, Gen St d H [Generalstab des Heeres, Army General Staff], Abt. Frd. Heere West (II) [Abteilung Führer Heere West, Section Army Command West], Dezember 1944. Schweizerisches Bundesarchiv Bern Bestand E 27, 14348 A, Kleinen Orientierungsheft Schweiz des OKH; BA/MA orientierungshefte, DV-RH/402.

44. Wilhelm Limpert-Verlag, Berlin, to M.le Colonel Command de Corps, Henri Guisan, 20.1.42, in Eidgenössische Militärbibliothek, Bern.

45. Dominic Pedrazzini, Jürg Stüssi-Lauterburg, Anne-Marie Volery, *En toute confiance . . ., Correspondance du Général et de Madame Henri Guisan avec le Major Albert R. Mayer, 1940–1959* (Brugg: Effingerhof, 1995).

46. Id., 39–40.

47. Dr. Med. David Kirchgraber, St. Gallen, *Erinnerungen an Vorkriegszeit und die Mobilisation 1939–1945* (unpublished mimeograph, 1989).

48. J.J. Köfer, *Harte Kriegsjahre: Jugenderinnerungen 1939 bis 1945* (Mellingen: Druckerei Nüssli AG, 1999), 80–84.

49. Id., 145–46.

Chapter 7: THE SPIRIT OF RESISTANCE

1. This is a revision of a paper presented to the Swiss-American Historical Society

Annual Meeting, New York City, Oct. 7, 2000. All interviews and correspondence cited herein are firsthand accounts by persons who resided in Switzerland during the period of the Third Reich.

2. Interview with Bruno Capol, Baden, Sept. 27, 1999.

3. *Collins German-English, English-German Dictionary* (Glasgow: HarperCollins, 1991), 718.

4. Carl Ludwig, *Die Flüchtlingspolitik der Schweiz in den Jahren 1933 bis 1955: Bericht an den Bundesrat zuhanden der eidgenössischen Räte von Professor Dr. Carl Ludwig* (Bern, 1957), 29.

5. Letter from Dr. Gustav T. and Margot Ammann Durrer, Nov. 2000.

6. Statement of Peter Voser, May 7, 1997.

7. *Collins German-English, English-German Dictionary*, 565.

8. Id., 567.

9. Id., 592.

10. *Webster's Ninth New Collegiate Dictionary* (Springfield, MA: Merriam-Webster, 1991), 1508.

11. Wm. Ernst Herzig, ed., *Damals im Aktivdienst: Soldaten erzählen aus den Jahren 1939–1945* (Zurich: Rascher Verlag, 1959), 50.

12. Ursprung to Halbrook, October 4, 1999 (condensed).

13. Statement of Mr. Rapold at interview with members of Aktion Aktivdienst, Stäfa-Zurich, June 3, 1999.

14. Paul Rothenhäusler, ed., *Leuchtturm in der Wüste: Die Schweiz im Zweiten Weltkrieg* (Stäfa, Switzerland: Rothenhäusler Verlag, 1997), 30.

15. Interview with Max Salm, Baden, Sept. 28, 1999.

16. Statement of Verena Rothenhäusler at interview with members of Aktion Aktivdienst, Stäfa-Zurich, June 3, 1999.

17. Inge Scholl, *The White Rose: Munich 1942–1943*, trans. Arthur R. Schultz (Hanover, NH: Wesleyan University Press, 1983), 116.

18. Statement of Peter Voser, May 7, 1997.

19. "Boche...Jerry, Boche, Hun, Kraut." *Collins-Robert French-English, English-French Dictionary* (Glasgow: HarperCollins, 1987), 76.

20. Interview with Dr. Hans Widmer, Baden, Sept. 28, 1999.

21. Audience comment, Swiss-American Historical Society Annual Meeting, New York, Oct. 7, 2000.

22. Interview with Georges-André Chevallaz at Epalinges near Lausanne, June 6, 1999.

23. James Murray Luck, *A History of Switzerland* (Palo Alto, CA: SPOSS, 1985), 108.

24. On the war, see Oberst M. Feldman and H.G. Wirz, eds., *Schweizer Kriegsgeschichte* (Bern, 1935), I, Heft 2, 203–76.

25. Albert Winkler, "The Swabian War of 1499," *Swiss-American Historical Society Review*, XXXV, No. 3, November 1999, 3, 10.

26. Interview with ex-member of Wehrmacht who wishes to remain anonymous.

27. *Collins German-English, English-German Dictionary*, 596.

28. Jürg Stüssi-Lauterburg, "The Threat of Three Totalitarianisms: The Swiss Response," in Leo Schelbert, ed., *Switzerland Under Siege* (Rockport, Maine: Picton Press, 2000), 33, n.3.

29. Interview with Armin Caminisch of Freienbach, Zurich, Jan. 14, 2000.

30. Letter from Dr. Gustav T. and Margot Ammann Durrer, Nov. 2000.

31. John McCormack, *One Million Mercenaries: Swiss Soldiers in the Armies of the World* (London: Leo Cooper, 1993), 33–34; C.W.C. Oman, *The Art of War in the Middle Ages* (Ithaca: Cornell University Press, 1953), 86, 104.

32. Winkler, "The Swabian War of 1499," 18, 21, 24.

33. Thomas A. Brady, *Turning Swiss: Cities and Empires, 1450–1550* (Cambridge: Cambridge University Press, 1985), 35.

34. Andreas Hillgruber, *Staatsmänner und Diplomaten bei Hitler* (München: DTV, 1969), 275–76.

35. Letter from Dr. Gustav T. and Margot Ammann Durrer, Nov. 2000.

36. Dr. Med. David Kirchgraber, St. Gallen, *Erinnerungen an Vorkriegszeit und die Mobilisation 1939–1945* (unpublished mimeograph, 1989).

37. Interview with Frau Cornelia Rogger, Davos, Jan. 21, 2000.

38. Interview with Anton Bueler-Smulders and Tony Anton Maria Bueler, Schwyz, Sept. 26, 1999.

39. Interview with Sigmund Widmer, Andreas Dolfuss, and Jean Planchere, Stäfa, Sept. 29, 1999.

40. Interview with Karl Elsener, Sr., Victorinox factory, Schwyz, June 8, 1999.

41. Interview with Dr. iur. Heinz Langenbacher, Bern, Sept. 27, 1999.

42. Interview with Alice Renold-Asper, Baden, Sept. 28, 1999.

43. Interview with Dr. Iur. Peter Voser, Baden, Sept. 28, 1999.

44. Personal collection of author.

45. Interview with Dr. Iur. Peter Voser, Baden, Sept. 28, 1999.

46. Interview with Frau Robert Braunschweig, Bern, Sept. 28, 1999.

47. Interview with Rita de Quervain, Davos Dorf, Jan. 21, 2000.

48. Letter from Dr. Gustav T. and Margot Ammann Durrer, Nov. 2000.

Chapter 8: GAS MASKS AND POTATO BREAD

1. Interview with members of Aktion Aktivdienst, Stäfa, June 3, 1999.

2. Interview with Fritz Wille of Gümligen, June 4, 1999.

3. Interview with Martina Wille-von Erlach of Gümligen, Canton of Berne, June 4, 1999.

4. Interview with Dr. iur. Heinz Langenbacher, Bern, September 27, 1999.

5. Statement of Robert Gasser-Hänni, Gasel bei Köniz, Canton of Berne, June 4, 1999.

6. Interview with Verena Rothenhäusler, Stäfa-Zurich, June 6, 1999.

7. See *25 Jahre FHD: 25 Jahre Schweizerischer Militärischer Frauenhilfsdienst* (Zurich: Atlantis Verlag, 1964).

8. Interview with Esther Terrier, Baden, September 28, 1999.

9. Interview with Alice Renold-Asper, Baden, September 28, 1999.

10. Alice Schelbert, "Memories of World War Two," *Swiss-American Historical Society Review*, vol. 36, No. 3, 35 (Nov. 2000).

11. Letter from Madame Denise Lecoultre, Geneva, June 18, 2000.

12. Statement of Gertrud Seiler, Gasel bei Köniz, Canton of Berne, June 4, 1999.

13. Interview with Rita de Quervain, Davos Dorf, 21 January 2000.

14. Interview with Hedwig Stamm, Zurich, June 2, 1999. Her service is summarized in a document entitled "Zeugnis" by Otto Zaugg, Der Chef der Zentralleitung, July 10, 1948.

15. Andreas Capol, notes left with his son Bruno Capol, communication to author, Sept. 27, 1999.

16. Albert H. Vogel, Ansprache anlässlich des Besuchs von Stephen Halbrook in Langenthal am 09. Juni 1999; also interview of same date.

17. Statement of Peter Voser, May 7, 1997.

18. Interview with Peter Baumgartner-Jost, Langenthal, June 8, 1999, including examination of rationing cards.

19. Statement of Arthur Oberle of Ennetbaden, 1999.

20. Interview with Hedi Köppel Moore of Delmar, New York, in Fairfax, Virginia, January 31, 2001.

Chapter 9: THE "J" STAMP, THE LIFEBOAT, AND REFUGEES

1. Ken Newman, *Swiss Wartime Work Camps: A Collection of Eyewitness Testimonies 1940–1945* (Zurich: Verlag Neue Zürcher Zeitung, 1999), 74.

2. Jean-François Bergier, Chairman, Independent Commission of Experts, Switzerland World War II, *Switzerland and Refugees in the Nazi Era* (Bern, 1999), 46.

3. Carl Ludwig, *Die Flüchtlingspolitik der Schweiz in den Jahren 1933 bis 1955: Bericht an den Bundesrat zuhanden der eidgenössischen Räte von Professor Dr. Carl Ludwig* (Bern, 1957).

4. Alfred A. Häsler, *The Lifeboat Is Full: Switzerland and the Refugees, 1933–1945*, trans. C.L. Markmann (New York: Funk & Wagnalls, 1969).

5. Ken Newman, *Swiss Wartime Work Camps: A Collection of Eyewitness Testimonies 1940–1945* (Zurich: Verlag Neue Zürcher Zeitung, 1999).

6. Meir Wagner, *The Righteous of Switzerland: Heroes of the Holocaust* (Hoboken, NJ: Ktav Publishing House, 2001).

7. Ludwig 56, 62.

8. Ludwig 52, 5; Häsler 321. *See* (n.a.) *Prominente Flüchtlinge im Schweizer Exil* (Bern: Bundesamt für Flüchtlinge, Medien un Kommunikation, 2003).

9. Ludwig 34. *See* Wolfgang Langhoff, *Die Moorsoldaten: 13 Monate Konzentrationslager* (Schweizer Spiegel Verlag Zurich, 1935); Langhoff, *Rubber Truncheon*, trans. Lilo

Linke (New York: E. P. Dutton & Co., Inc., 1935).

10. Häsler 14.

11. E.g., see Die Kilchberger "Sportschule Maag," *Ein illegales Unternehmen der Nationalsozialisten im Zweiten Weltkrieg* (Kilchberg: Gemeinde Kilchberg, 2002).

12. Ludwig 70; Häsler 322.

13. Bergier 40.

14. Bergier 74.

15. Bergier 76.

16. Bergier 75–76; Ludwig 75; Häsler 322.

17. Ludwig 95; Häsler 31–32.

18. Ludwig 98–99; Häsler 32–33; Bergier 78.

19. Bergier 40.

20. Ludwig 84–85 n.1; Häsler 26.

21. Paul Alexis Ladame, *Defending Switzerland* (Delmar, NY: Caravan Books, 1999), 26–28.

22. Häsler 27.

23. Häsler 28.

24. Bergier 76; Ludwig 90–91; Häsler 51.

25. Ludwig 90; Häsler 322.

26. Ludwig 103; Häsler 35.

27. Ludwig 90. *See* Urs Rauber, "Von der Kooperation zum Widerstand: Der Schweizerische Israelitische Gemeindebund und die Flüchtlingspolitik von 1938 bis 1942," *Neue Zürcher Zeitung* (Inland), 15.03.2000, Nr.63, 16. Hereafter cited Rauber, "Von der Kooperation zum Widerstand," 16.

28. Ludwig 102–03 n.1; Häsler 34–35.

29. Ludwig 107–08; Häsler 35–36.

30. Ludwig 110; Häsler 37.

31. Ludwig 112–13; Häsler 38–39.

32. Ludwig 114–15; Häsler 39–40.

33. Ludwig 116–17; Häsler 41–42.

34. Ludwig 117; Häsler 42.

35. Ludwig 118; Häsler 42–43.

36. Ludwig 119; Häsler 43.

37. Ludwig 119; Häsler 44.

38. Ludwig 120; Häsler 44–45.

39. Ludwig 121–22; Bergier 81.

40. Ludwig 123; Häsler 46.

41. Ludwig 125.

42. Ludwig 125 n.1.

43. Ludwig 126–27.

44. Ludwig 243 n.; Häsler 57–58.

45. Ludwig 237–38 n.2; Häsler 110–11.

46. Ludwig 128.
47. Ludwig 128–30.
48. Ludwig 133; Häsler 49–50.
49. Ludwig 156; Häsler 51–52.
50. Rauber, "Von der Kooperation zum Widerstand," 16.
51. Wannsee Protocol, January 20, 1942, Avalon Project, Yale Law School, http://www.yale.edu/lawweb/avalon/20th.htm.
52. "Eine unglaubliche Affäre," *Beobachter*, March 31, 1954, reprinted in Max Keller, *Das Ende der J-Stempel-Saga: Fall beispiel von Geschichtsprägung durch Medienmacht* (Bern: Pro Libertate, 1999), 7.
53. Ludwig 112–13; Häsler 38–39.
54. Keller, *Das Ende der J-Stempel-Saga*, 36.
55. Keller, *Das Ende der J-Stempel-Saga*, 45.
56. Ludwig 36; Häsler 60.
57. *The Holocaust, Vol. 3, The Crystal Night Pogrom*, John Mendelsohn, ed. (New York: Garland, 1982), 183–84.
58. Rauber, "Von der Kooperation zum Widerstand," 16.
59. Ludwig 169–71; Häsler 324.
60. Saul Friedländer, *Nazi Germany and the Jews: Vol. I, The Years of Persecution, 1933–1939* (New York: Harper Collins, 1997), 313–19.
61. Ludwig 183; Häsler 325.
62. Ludwig 27–28.
63. Ludwig 184–85; Häsler 325.
64. Jerzy Rucki, *Die Schweiz im Licht Die Schweiz im Schatten* (Kriens: Verlag Brunner AG, 1997), 69.
65. Bergier 102.
66. Newman, *Swiss Wartime Work Camps*, 111.
67. David S. Wyman, *The Abandonment of the Jews: America and the Holocaust, 1941–1945* (New York: Pantheon, 1984); Henry L. Feingold, *The Politics of Rescue: The Roosevelt Administration and the Holocaust, 1938–1945* (New York: Holocaust Library, 1970).
68. Ludwig 60; Häsler 19.
69. Rauber, "Von der Kooperation zum Widerstand," 16.
70. Ludwig 238 n.; Häsler 112.
71. Rauber, "Von der Kooperation zum Widerstand," 16.
72. Ludwig 234, Häsler 80.
73. Ludwig 232–45; Häsler 65–66; Bergier 237ff.
74. Ludwig 189; Häsler 326.
75. Ludwig 199; Häsler 80.
76. Ludwig 202; Häsler 81.
77. Ludwig 204; Häsler 82.
78. Ludwig 205; Häsler 82.

79. Bergier 141.
80. Ludwig 205; Häsler 326.
81. Ludwig 207–08; Häsler 126–28.
82. Rauber, "Von der Kooperation zum Widerstand," 16.
83. Ludwig 209–11; Häsler 130–32.
84. Bergier 125–27. *But see* Shraga Elam, *Paul Grüninger—Held oder korrupter Polizist und Nazi-Agent?* (Bern: Pro Libertate, 2003).
85. Ludwig 393–94; Häsler 116; Bergier 394.
86. Häsler 175.
87. Bergier 68.
88. Bergier 160.
89. Bergier 238, 242. Henry L. Feingold, *The Politics of Rescue: The Roosevelt Administration and the Holocaust, 1938–1945* (New York: Holocaust Library, 1970).
90. Ludwig 216.
91. Ludwig 216–17; Häsler 157–59.
92. Ludwig 218–21; Häsler 160–78.
93. Häsler 170.
94. Ludwig 224–26; Häsler 181.
95. Ludwig 222–23.
96. Bergier 94.
97. Ludwig 223–24.
98. Bergier 96–97.
99. Ludwig 229–231.
100. Bergier 147, 263–64.
101. Ludwig 262, 269; Häsler 328. *See also* Renata Broggini, *Frontier of Hope: Jews from Italy Seek Refuge in Switzerland, 1943–1945* (Editore Ulrico Hoepli Milano, 2003).
102. Bergier 254.
103. Ludwig 288, 299; Häsler 287, 328.
104. Theo Tschuy, *Dangerous Diplomacy: The Story of Carl Lutz, Rescuer of 62,000 Hungarian Jews* (Grand Rapids, MI: Wm. B. Eerdmans Publishing Co., 2000), 263.
105. Id., xi.
106. *See also* David Kranzler, *The Man Who Stopped the Trains to Auschwitz: George Mantello, El Salvador, and Switzerland's Finest Hour* (Syracuse, NY: Syracuse University Press, 2000).
107. Bergier 106–07, 114, 117–18.
108. Bergier 119.
109. Bergier 99.
110. Ludwig 293–96, 303.
111. Ludwig 293; Häsler 285.
112. Ludwig 294; Häsler 285.
113. Bergier 149.

114. Ludwig 299–300 n.1; Häsler 286–87.

115. Ludwig 299–300.

116. *See generally* Tschuy, *Dangerous Diplomacy: The Story of Carl Lutz, Rescuer of 62,000 Hungarian Jews.*

117. Ludwig 298–300, 310; Bergier 292.

118. Ludwig 311, 313; Häsler 330.

119. Ludwig 314; Häsler 330.

120. Ludwig 318; Häsler 292–93. *See also* Bergier 263.

121. Ludwig 366–68; Häsler 293.

122. Bergier 62.

123. Bergier 63–66, 195–96.

124. Ludwig 370, 293.

125. Alan Morris Schom, *The Unwanted Guests: Swiss Forced Labor Camps 1940–1944* (Los Angeles: Simon Wiesenthal Center, 1998).

126. Newman, *Swiss Wartime Work Camps*, 9.

127. Newman, *Swiss Wartime Work Camps*, 179–80.

128. Bergier 154 note 325. *See* Newman, *Swiss Wartime Work Camps.*

129. Bergier 163.

130. Bergier 165–66.

131. Bergier 270–71.

132. Bergier 20, 129.

133. Jean-Christian Lambelet, *A Critical Evaluation of the Bergier Report on "Switzerland and Refugees during the Nazi Era," with a New Analysis of the Issue* (Lausanne: University of Lausanne, Ecole des HEC, January 2001), 11.

134. Id., 12.

135. Id., 7.

136. Id., 15.

137. Id., 20.

138. Id., 17–18.

139. Id., 30.

140. Id., 32.

141. Id., 72

142. Newman, *Swiss Wartime Work Camps*, 135.

143. Carl J. Friedrich, "As Switzerland Sees It," *Atlantic Monthly*, 178 (Dec. 1946) 108, 109.

Chapter 10: THE CONSEQUENCES OF ENCIRCLEMENT

1. BA/MA RW 5/358, Oberkommando der Wehrmacht, Laufende Informationen Nr. 1, 9.1.1941.

2. BA/MA RW 491/431, Anlage 1 zu Nest Bremen B.Nr.g. 152/41/IH v. 10. Januar 1941, 10.1.1941.

3. Halbrook, *Target Switzerland*, 145–46.

4. BA/MA RH2/2923, Deutsche Gesandtschaft Der Militärattaché, Sehr verehrter Herr General, 28.4.41.

5. BA/MA Wi/1A3.148b, Telegramm, Paris, Deutsche Waffenstillstands-Delegation für Wirtschaft, 17.4.1941.

6. BA/MA Wi/173.148.a, Protokoll der Verhandlungen über den deutsch-schweizer, 26.5.1941.

7. BA/MA Wi/173.148a, Deutsche Waffenstillstandsfommission Wiesbaden, Schließung der französisch-schweizerischen Grenzübergänge, 3.6.1941.

8. BA/MA Wi/173.148a, Fortsetzung des Protokols der Verhandlungen über den deutsche-schweizer, 29.5.1941.

9. BA/MA Wi/173.148a, Deutsche Waffenstillstandkommission Wiesbaden, Lockerung des Geleitscheinsystems für die französische Wareneinfuhr aus der Schweiz, 11.7.1941.

10. Daniel Heller, *Zwischen Unternehmertum, Politik und Überleben: Emil G. Bührle und die Werkzeugmaschinenfabrik Oerlikon Bührle & Co. 1924–1945* (Verlag Huber Frauenfeld, 2002).

11. John Lomax, *The Diplomatic Smuggler* (London: Arthur Barker Limited, 1965), 211.

12. BA/MA RH 2/2923, Deutsche Gesandtschaft Der Militärattaché, Sehr verehrter Herr General, 27.5.1941.

13. BA/MA RH 2/2923, Entwurf einer Dienstanweisung für die K.O. Schweiz, 20 June 1941.

14. BA/MA RH 2/465, Fiche 4, Row 1, Major Wiest, Gruppenleiter 1, Oberst i.G. Heusinger, Chef d.Op.Abt.i.Gen.St.d.H. 14.7.1941.

15. BA-MA, RH 2/465, Fiche 4, Row 1. Unternehmen W., Major Wiest, 14.7. 1941, an Oberst i.G. Heusinger, Chef d.Op.Abt.i.Gen.St.d.H., Berlin, Oberkommando des Heeres.

16. Halbrook, *Target Switzerland*, 148–49.

17. Halbrook, *Target Switzerland*, 151.

18. BA/MA RH 2/465, Fiche 3, Row 7, Major Wiest Wehrersatzinspektion, Stuttgart, 21.7.1941.

19. BA/MA RW 19/1555, Dienstreise in die Schweiz vom 31.7. bis 15.8. 1941, 22.8.1941.

20. Pierre-Th. Braunschweig, *Geheimer Draht Nach Berlin* (Verlag Neue Zürcher Zeitung, 1989), 195. Some information on Berger's role concerning Switzerland is contained in *id.*, 203, 286, 416–17, and 462–63.

21. Hans Rudolf Fuhrer, *Spionage gegen die Schweiz* (Frauenfeld: Huber, 1982), 164.

22. Peter Padfield, *Himmler* (New York: MJF Books, 1990), 316.

23. SS Gruppenführer Gottlob Berger an den Reichsführer SS Himmler, 8.9.1941, U.S. National Archives, T175, roll 123, frame 2648463.

24. BA/MA RH 2/1739, K-2, Gen St d H, Fremde Heere West/IV, Anlage zu Lagebericht West Nr. 531, Das Schweizer Kriegsheer, Erläuterungen: Grenze des

Redoubt National, Stand: 31.10.41.

25. Markus Feldmann, *Tagebuch 1942–1945,* Band XIII/3 (Basel: Krebs, 2001) (diary entry for Dec. 4, 1942).

26. Karl Heinz Abshagen, *Canaris: Patriot und Weltbürger* (Stuttgart: Union Deutsche Verlagsgesellschaft, 1955), 346–47.

27. Prof. Dr. Walter Schaufelberger, "Das 'Kleine Orientierungsheft Schweiz,'" *Neue Zürcher Zeitung,* Nr. 177, 21/22 Mai 1977 (quoting chapter 8).

28. Pierre-Th. Braunschweig, *Geheimer Draht Nach Berlin,* 259–94. This study is now published in English as *Secret Channel to Berlin* (Philadelphia: Casemate, 2004.) *See also* Hans Senn, *Anfänge einer Dissuasionsstrategie während des Zweiten Weltkrieges* (Basel: Helbing & Lichtenhahn, 1995), 356–75; Halbrook, *Target Switzerland,* 180.

29. Józef Garlinski, *The Swiss Corridor: Espionage Networks in Switzerland during World War II* (London: Dent, 1981), 130–32, 195.

30. Kimche, *Spying for Peace,* 101–02; August Lindt, *Le temps du herisson,* 128–30.

31. *The Goebbels Diaries: 1942–1943,* ed. Louis P. Lochner (Garden City, New York: Doubleday, 1948), 355, 357–58.

32. BA/MA RW 5/363, Amt Ausland/Abwehr, Besorgnisse der Schweizer Fliegertruppe, 6.8.1943.

33. BA/MA RW 5/363, Amt Ausland/Abwehr, Besorgnisse der Schweizer Fliegertruppe, 6.8.1943.

34. BA/MA RW 4/687, Geheime Kommandosache, SSD-Fernschreiben an Chef des Transportwesens der Wehrmacht, 8.10.1943.

35. Halbrook, *Target Switzerland,* 194–99. The source document for the following is Ernst Uhlmann, "Angriffspläne gegen die Schweiz," *Allgemeine Schweizerische Militärzeitung* (Dec. 1949), LX, 841–49.

36. BA/MA RH 2/2907, Tätigkeitsbericht Mil. Att. Bern für die Zeit vom 15.3.–31.7.44 bis 2.10.1944.

37. BA/MA RH2/2923, Oberkommando des Heeres, Generalstab des Heeres, Notiz Die Lage der Schweiz, 22.8.1944.

38. BA/MA RH2 2907, Gruppe B, Mil. Pol. Lage und Stimmung, Bericht über die Reise vom 7. Bis 13.9.44 nach Bern, 14.9.1944.

39. Edmund Wehrli, "Respekt vor wehrhafter Neutralität," *Neue Zürcher Zeitung,* 7.9.1983.

40. U.S. National Archives, Office of Chief of Counsel for War Crimes, APO 696 A, U.S. Army, Staff Evidence Analysis, 8 December 1947, attaching NG [Nuremberg trial document] 4137.

41. *Bericht des Bundesrates an die Bundesversammlung über die antidemokratische Tätigkeit von Schweizern und Ausländern im Zusammnhang mit dem Kriegsgeschehen 1939–1945 (Motion Boerlin).* Erster Teil. (Vom 28. Dezember 1945), 94.

42. Jürg Stüssi-Lauterburg, "The Threat of Three Totalitarianisms," *Switzerland Under Siege, 1939–1945,* ed. Leo Schelbert (Rockport, Maine: 2000), 23–24.

43. Vicenz Oertle, *"Sollte ich aus Rußland nicht zurückkehren . . ." Schweizer Freiwillige*

an deutscher Seite 1939-1945, Eine Quellensuche (Thesis Verlag: Zurich, 1997), 561.

44. Oertle 477, 528, 598–99.

45. *Bericht des Bundesrates an die Bundesversammlung* 95-96. On "Aktion S," *see also* Oertle 473–88.

46. Id., 96.

47. Edgar Bonjour, *Geschichte der Schweizerischen Neutralität*, IV, 404–05; Halbrook, *Target Switzerland*, 139.

48. Oertle, 78.

49. Werner Rings, *Schweiz im Krieg, 1933–1945* (Verlag Ex Libris Zurich, 1974), 248.

50. William L. Shirer, *The Rise and Fall of the Third Reich* (New York: Touchstone, 1990), 1085.

51. *Bericht des Bundesrates*, 94–95.

52. Oertle 40.

53. Id., 108, 141, 190, 304–05, 331–37.

54. *Bericht des Bundesrates*, 96–97. *See* Oertle 27, 126 n.26, 141 n.70, 479, 592.

55. Id., 94.

56. Id., 97.

57. Padfield, *Himmler*, 474.

58. Walter Lippman, "The Faithful Witness," *New York Herald Tribune*, Jan. 26, 1943, 21.

Chapter 11: INTRUDERS IN OUR MIDST

1. Sources of the following information include: Interview with Dr. Peter Bollier, Davos, 19 January 2000; Peter Bollier, "4. Februar 1936: Das Attentat auf Wilhelm Gustloff," *Politische Attentate des 20. Jahrhunderts*, Herausgegeben von Roland Aegerter (Zurich: Verlag Neue Zürcher Zeitung, 1999), 42; Dr. Peter Bollier, *Der Kur- und Fremdenort in schwieriger Zeit 1929–1945* (n.d. MS). *See also* Andreas Saurer, "Der Mord von Davos: David Frankfurter erschiesst Nazi-Gauleiter Gustloff," *Bündner Zeitung*, 3. February 1996, 2.

2. Martin Bundi, *Bedrohung, Anpassung und Widerstand: Die Grenzregion Graubünden 1933–1946* (Verlag Bündner Monatsblatt/Desertina AG, Chur: 1996), 32–33.

3. Interview with Dr. Paul Müller, Davos, 19 January 2000.

4. Werner Rings, *Schweiz in Krieg, 1933–1945* (Verlag Ex Libris Zurich, 1974), 68–69.

5. Wolfgang Diewerge, .*Ein Jude hat geschossen . . . Augenzeugenbericht vom Mordprozess David Frankfurter* (München 1937). *See also* Wolfgang Diewerge, *Der Fall Gustloff. Vorgeschichte und Hintergründe der Bluttat von Davos* (München, 1936).

6. Marianne Frey-Hauser, "Ein Amerikaner auf der Suche nach Zeitzeugen," *Davoser Zeitung*, 8 Februar 2000.

7. Theo Haas, "Wir dürfen uns nicht beugen, vor wem es auch sei," *Bündner Zeitung* (Chur), 15 November 1980, 20. *See also* Theo Haas, "Gaudenz Canova

(1887–1962)," *Bündner Tagblatt* (Chur), Dec. 17, 1987, at 18.

8. "Die Ansprache Dr. Gaudenz Canovas," *Bündner Zeitung* (Chur), 15 November 1980, 20–21.

9. *See* Halbrook, *Target Switzerland*, 5.

10. Interview with Dr. Paul Müller, Davos, 19 January 2000.

11. Interview with Prof. Marcel de Quervain, Davosdorf, 21 January 2000.

12. Interview with: Dr. Christian Schmid (formerly of Davos), Zurich, 14 January 2000.

13. Interviews with Armin Camenisch of Freienbach, Zurich and en route to Davos, 14 and 17 January 2000.

14. Halbrook, *Target Switzerland*, 231–32.

15. Stephen Tanner, *Refuge from the Reich: American Airmen and Switzerland during World War II* (Rockville Centre, NY: Sarpedon, 2001); Hans-Heiri Stapfer & Gino Künzle, *Escape to Neutrality* (Carrollton, TX: Squadron/Signal Publications, 1992); Fredy Peter, *Jump Boys, Jump* (Ilfracombe, UK: Arthur H.Stockwell, 2003).

16. Fredy Peter, *Jump Boys, Jump*, Chapter 6: Camp Davos.

17. Interview with Hans Rostetter of Ilanz, son of Christian Rostetter, by Theo Hass of Domat/Ems, 19 April 2001.

18. *Liste verdächtiger Ausländer in der Landschaft Davos*, 5.4.40 & 15.5.40. Document supplied by the son of Christian Rostetter to Theo Haas of Domat/Ems, copy in possession of author. (Hereafter cited "Rostetter document.")

19. An Wm. Rostetter. Davos. *Abteilung Presse und Funkspruch*. Sektion Film. 4.6.1943. Rostetter document.

20. Werner Rings, *Schweiz in Krieg, 1933–1945* (Verlag Ex Libris Zurich, 1974), 204.

21. Dr. Peter Bollier, *Der Kur- und Fremdenort in schwieriger Zeit 1929–1945* (n.d. MS), 6–7.

22. Interview with Dr. Peter Bollier, Davos, 19 January 2000.

23. *Verzeichnis derjenigen deutschen Staatsangehörigen in Davos die auf Antrag der Gemeinde auf Grund von Art. 10 des BG über Aufenthalt und Niederlassung der Ausländer vom Kanton auszuweisen sind*, 12.7.45. Rostetter document. This same document is included in Gemeindearchiv Igis-Landquart, Polizeiwesen/Fremdenpolizei 46.10–Gemeinderatsprotokolle III C 2.27, S.509, 534, 543, 618, cited in Martin Bundi, *Bedrohung, Anpassung und Widerstand: Die Grenzregion Graubünden 1933–1946* (Chur: Verlag Bündner Monatsblatt/Desertina AG, 1996), 32–33.

Chapter 12: AMERICA'S WINDOW ON THE REICH
1. Józef Garlinski, *The Swiss Corridor: Espionage Networks in Switzerland During World War II* (London: Dent, 1981); Jon Kimche, *Spying for Peace: General Guisan and Swiss Neutrality* (New York: Roy Publishers, 1961); Pierre Accoce & Pierre Quet, *A Man Called Lucy* (New York: Coward-McCann, 1967); Drago Arsenijevic, *Genève Appelle Moscou* (Paris: Robert Laffont, 1969).

2. Hans Rudolf Fuhrer, *Spionage gegen die Schweiz: Die geheimen deutschen Nachrichten-dienste gegen die Schweiz im Zweiten Weltkrieg, 1939–1945* (Frauenfeld: Allgemeine Schweizerische Militärzeitschrift, 1982).

3. Pierre-Th. Braunschweig, *Geheimer Draht nach Berlin: Die Nachrichtenlinie Masson-Schellenberg und der schweizerische Nachrichtendienst im Zweiten Weltkrieg* (Verlag Neue Zürcher Zeitung, 1989).

4. John Lomax, *The Diplomatic Smuggler* (London: Arthur Barker Limited, 1965), 123–51, 194–218. *See also* Luzi Stamm et al., *Dignity and Coolness: Switzerland, 5 March 1940–5 August 1941* (Lenzburg, Switzerland: Verlag Merker im Effingerhof, 2004) (reports of British minister in Bern).

5. *See* Joseph E. Persico, *Piercing the Reich: The Penetration of Nazi Germany by American Secret Agents During World War II* (New York: Barnes & Noble, 1979).

6. See Joseph E. Persico, *Piercing the Reich*; R. Harris Smith, *OSS: The Secret History of America's First Central Intelligence Agency* (Berkeley: University of California Press, 1972); Bradley F. Smith, *The Shadow Warriors: OSS and the Origins of the CIA* (New York: Basic Books, 1983); James Srodes, *Allen Dulles: Master of Spies* (Washington, DC: Regnery, 1999).

7. *From Hitler's Doorstep: The Wartime Intelligence Reports of Allen Dulles, 1942–1945*, ed. Neal H. Petersen (University Park, PA: Pennsylvania State University Press, 1996).

8. Id., 22–23.

9. Id., 34–35.

10. Id., 53.

11. Id., 54.

12. Id., 546.

13. Halbrook, *Target Switzerland*, 179–81.

14. *From Hitler's Doorstep*, 54–55.

15. Id., 59.

16. Id., 71.

17. Id., 229.

18. Garlinski, *The Swiss Corridor*, 130–32, 195.

19. Lomax ran the British spy and smuggling ring in Switzerland. Lomax, *The Diplomatic Smuggler*, 123 ff.

20. *From Hitler's Doorstep*, 239–40.

21. Id., 258.

22. Id., 260.

23. Id., 260–61.

24. Id., 288–89.

25. Id., 302.

26. Id., 308.

27. Id., 309

28. Id.

29. Halbrook, *Target Switzerland*, 209–12.

30. *From Hitler's Doorstep*, 313–14.

31. Id., 309.

32. Id., 313.

33. Id., 331–32.

34. Anton Gill, *An Honourable Defeat: A History of the German Resistance to Hitler, 1933–1945* (New York: Henry Holt & Co., 1994), 253.

35. Hans B. Gisevius, *To the Bitter End: An Insider's Account of the Plot to Kill Hitler, 1933–1944*, Foreword by Allen W. Dulles (New York: De Capo Press, 1998; originally published in 1946).

36. Mary Bancroft, *Autobiography of a Spy* (New York: William Morrow & Co., 1983).

37. *From Hitler's Doorstep*, 348.

38. Id., 359.

39. Id., 360.

40. Id., 364.

41. Id., 366.

42. For more details, *see* Halbrook, *Target Switzerland*, 209.

43. *From Hitler's Doorstep*, 378.

44. Id., 390.

45. Id., 394.

46. Id., 398.

47. *See* the comprehensive study James H. Hutson, "Fatal Errors: The Allied Bombing of the Sister Republic," in Leo Schelbert, ed., *Switzerland under Siege, 1939–1945: A Neutral Nation's Struggle for Survival* (Rockport, ME: Picton Press, 2000), 69.

48. Id., 92–93.

49. *From Hitler's Doorstep*, 397, 405.

50. Id., 416–17.

51. Id., 420–21.

52. Id., 424.

53. Id., 424–25.

54. Id., 448.

55. Id., 468. For further sources on Sunrise, *see* Max Waibel, *Operation Sunrise: 1945 Kapitulation in Norditalien* (Basel: Helbing & Lichtenhahn Verlag, 1981; reprint: Schaffhausen: Novalis Verlag, 2002); Bradley F. Smith and Elena Agarossi, *Operation Sunrise* (London: André Deutsch, 1979); Eugen Dollmann, *Call Me Coward* (London: William Kimber, 1956); Shraga Elam, *Hitlers Fälscher* (Wien: Verlag Carl Ueberreuter, 2000), 103–119; Marino Viganò and Dominic Pedrazzini, eds., *"Operation Sunrise": Atti del convegno internazionale (Locarno, 2 maggio 2005)*.

56. Id., 469.

57. Id., 482.

58. Id., 485.

59. Id., 492–92.

60. Id., 498.

61. Id., 502.

62. Id., 508–09.

63. Id., 512.

64. Stuart E. Eizenstat and William Z. Slany: *U.S. and Allied Efforts to Recover and Restore Gold and Other Assets Stolen or Hidden by Germany During World War II* (Washington, DC: U.S. Department of State, 1997); Independent Commission of Experts, Switzerland: *Switzerland, National Socialism, and the Second World War: Final Report* (Pendo Verlag, Zurich, 2002).

CONCLUSION

1. Harold Flender, *Rescue in Denmark* (Washington, DC: U.S. Holocaust Memorial Museum, 1963), 21.

2. See generally *id.*

3. Jean Ziegler, *La Suisse, l'or, et les morts* (Paris: Éditions du Seuil, 1997), 305; Henry I. Sobel, "Neutrality, Morality, and the Holocaust," *American University International Law Review* (1998), vol. 14, 206–07.

BIBLIOGRAPHY

BOOKS

25 Jahre FHD: 25 Jahre Schweizerischer Militärischer Frauenhilfsdienst. Zurich: Atlantis Verlag, 1964.

Abshagen, Karl Heinz. *Canaris: Patriot und Weltbürger.* Stuttgart: Union Deutsche Verlagsgesellschaft, 1955.

Accoce, Pierre, and Pierre Quet. *A Man Called Lucy.* New York: Coward-McCann, 1967.

Arsenijevic, Drago. *GenPve Appelle Moscou.* Paris: Robert Laffont, 1969.

Attenhofer, Elsie. *Cornichon: Erinnerungen an ein Cabaret.* Benteli Verlag Bern, 1975.

Attenhofer, Elsie. *Réserve du Patron: Im Gespräch mit K.* Rothenhäusler Verlag-Stäfa: Stäfa, 1989.

Bancroft, Mary. *Autobiography of a Spy.* New York: William Morrow & Co., 1983.

Bentz, Felix P. *Exploring My Life.* Manuscript dated 1996.

Bericht des Bundesrates an die Bundesversammlung über die antidemokratische Tätigkeit von Schweizern und Ausländern im Zusammnhang mit dem Kriegsgeschehen 1939–1945. Motion Boerlin. Erster Teil. Vom 28. Dezember 1945.

Bollier, Dr. Peter. "4. Februar 1936: Das Attentat auf Wilhelm Gustloff." In *Politische Attentate des 20. Jahrhunderts.* Roland Aegerter, ed. Zurich: Verlag Neue Zürcher Zeitung, 1999.

Bollier, Dr. Peter. *Der Kur- und Fremdenort in schwieriger Zeit 1929–1945.* n.d. MS.

Bonjour, Edgar. *Geschichte der Schweizerischen Neutralität.* Basel: Helbing & Lichtenhahn, 1976.

Bower, Tom. *Nazi Gold.* New York: Harper Collins, 1997.

Brady, Thomas A. *Turning Swiss: Cities and Empires, 1450–1550*. Cambridge: Cambridge University Press, 1985.

Braunschweig, Pierre-Th. *Geheimer Draht Nach Berlin: Die Nachrichtenlinie Masson–Schellenberg und der schweizerische Nachrichtendienst im Zweiten Weltkrieg*. Verlag Neue Zürcher Zeitung, 1989.

Bundi, Martin. *Bedrohung, Anpassung und Widerstand: Die Grenzregion Graubünden 1933–1946*. Verlag Bündner Monatsblatt/Desertina AG, Chur: 1996.

Chevallaz, Georges-André. *The Challenge of Neutrality: Diplomacy and the Defense of Switzerland*. Lanham, MD: Lexington Press, 2001.

Churchill, Winston S. *The Second World War*. London: Cassel, 1954.

Codevilla, Angelo M. *Between the Alps and a Hard Place: Switzerland in World War II and the Rewriting of History*. Washington, DC: Regnery Publishing, 2000.

Die Kilchberger "Sportschule Maag", Ein illegales Unternehmen der Nationalsozialisten im Zweiten Weltkrieg. Kilchberg: Gemeinde Kilchberg, 2002.

Diewerge, Wolfgang. *Der Fall Gustloff. Vorgeschichte und Hintergründe der Bluttat von Davos*. München, 1936.

Diewerge, Wolfgang. *Ein Jude hat geschossen . . . Augenzeugenbericht vom Mordprozess David Frankfurter*. München, 1937.

Dulles, Allen. *Germany's Underground*. New York: Macmillan, 1947.

Dulles, Allen. *The Secret Surrender*. London: Harper & Row, 1966.

Eizenstat, Stuart E., and William Z. Slany. *U.S. and Allied Efforts to Recover and Restore Gold and Other Assets Stolen or Hidden by Germany during World War II*. Washington, DC: U.S. Department of State, 1997.

Engle, Eloise and Lauri Paananen. *The Winter War: The Soviet Attack on Finland 1939–1940*. Harrisburg, PA: Stackpole Books, 1973.

Feingold, Henry L. *The Politics of Rescue: The Roosevelt Administration and the Holocaust, 1938–1945*. New York: Holocaust Library, 1970.

Feldmann, Oberst M., and H.G. Wirz, eds. *Schweizer Kriegsgeschichte*. Bern, 1935. 1, Heft.

Flender, Harold. *Rescue in Denmark*. Washington, DC: U.S. Holocaust Memorial Museum, 1963.

Frei, Ernst. *Erlebter Aktivdienst 1939–1945: Auszüge aus dem Tagebuch eines Angehörigen der Fliegertruppen*. Novalis Verlag Schaffhausen: 1998.

Friedländer, Saul. *Nazi Germany and the Jews: Vol. I, The Years of Persecution, 1933–1939*. New York: Harper Collins, 1997.

Fritschi, Oskar Felix. *Geistige Landesverteidigung während des Zweiten Weltkrieges*. Fabag + Druckerei Winterthur AG, 1971.

From Hitler's Doorstep: The Wartime Intelligence Reports of Allen Dulles, 1942–1945. Neal H. Petersen, ed. University Park, PA: Pennsylvania State University Press, 1996.

Fuhrer, Hans Rudolf. *Spionage gegen die Schweiz*. Frauenfeld: Huber & Co., 1982.

Führer zur Limmatstellund aus dem Zweiten Weltkrieg. Baden: Baden-Verlag, 1997.

Garlinski, Józef. *The Swiss Corridor: Espionage Networks in Switzerland during World War II*. London: Dent, 1981.

Gautschi, Willi. *General Henri Guisan: Die schweizerische Armeeführung im Zweiten Weltkrieg*. Verlag Neue Zürcher Zeitung, 1989.

Gautschi, Willi. *Henri Guisan: Commander-in-Chief of the Swiss Army during World War II*. Rockville Centre, NY: Front Street Press, 2003.

Gegen Rote und Braune Fäuste: Das Weltgeschehen von 1932–1948 in 342 Karikaturen aus dem Nebelspalter. Nebelspalter-Verlag Rorschach, 1949.

Gill, Anton. *An Honourable Defeat: A History of the German Resistance to Hitler, 1933–1945*. New York: Henry Holt & Co., 1994.

Gisevius, Hans B. *To the Bitter End: An Insider's Account of the Plot to Kill Hitler, 1933–1944*. Foreword by Allen W. Dulles. New York: De Capo Press, 1998. Originally published in 1946.

The Goebbels Diaries: 1942–1943. Louis P. Lochner, ed. Garden City, NY: Doubleday, 1948.

Grimm, Bruno. *Gau Schweiz? Dokumente über die nationalsozialistischen Umtriebe in der Schweiz*. Druck der Unionsdruckerei Bern, 1939.

Gubler, Robert. *Felddivision 6: Von der Zürcher Miliz zur Felddivision, 1815–1991*. Verlag Neue Zürcher Zeitung, 1991.

Halbrook, Stephen P. *Cel: Szwajcaria*. Warszawa: Dom Wydawniczy Bellona, 2003.

Halbrook, Stephen P. *Die Schweiz im Visier: Die bewaffnete Neutralität im Zweiten Weltkrieg*. Verlag Novalis Schaffhausen/Rothenhäusler Stäfa, 1999.

Halbrook, Stephen P. *La Suisse encerclée: La neutralité armée suisse durant la DeuxiPme Guerre mondiale*. Editions Slatkine GenPve, 2000.

Halbrook, Stephen P. *La Svizzera nel mirino: La neutralitB aramata della Svizzera nella seconda guerra mondiale*. Coedizione Pedrazzini–Locarno/Alberti–Verbania, 2002.

Halbrook, Stephen P. *Target Switzerland: Swiss Armed Neutrality in World War II*. Rockville Centre, NY: Sarpedon Publishers, 1998.

Häsler, Alfred A. *The Lifeboat Is Full: Switzerland and the Refugees, 1933–1945*.

Trans. C.L. Markmann. New York: Funk & Wagnalls, 1969.

Heller, Daniel. *Zwischen Unternehmertum, Politik und Überleben: Emil G. Bührle und die Werkzeugmaschinenfabrik Oerlikon Bührle & Co. 1924–1945.* Verlag Huber Frauenfeld, 2002.

Herzig, Wm. Ernst, ed. *Damals im Aktivdienst: Soldaten erzählen aus den Jahren 1939–1945.* Zurich: Rascher Verlag, 1959.

Hillgruber, Andreas. *Staatsmänner und Diplomaten bei Hitler.* München: DTV, 1969.

Hilty, Donald P., ed. *Retrospectives on Switzerland in World War Two.* Rockport, Maine: Picton Press, 2001.

The Holocaust: Vol. 3. The Crystal Night Pogrom. John Mendelsohn, ed. New York: Garland, 1982.

Huber, Jakob. *Bericht des Chefs des Generalstabs an den oberbefehlshaber der Armee über den Aktivdienst 1939–1945.* Bern, 1946.

Kaltenegger, Roland. *Die Stammdivision der deutschen Gebirgstruppe: Weg und Kampf der 1. Gebirgs-Division 1935–1945.* Graz-Stuttgart: Leopold Stocker Verlag, 1981.

Keller, Max. *Das Ende der J-Stempel-Saga: Fall beispiel von Geschichtsprägung durch Medienmacht.* Bern: Pro Libertate, 1999.

Kersaudy, François. *Norway 1940.* Lincoln: University of Nebraska Press, 1990.

Kimche, Jon. *Spying for Peace: General Guisan and Swiss Neutrality.* New York: Roy Publishers, 1961.

Kirchgraber, Dr. Med. David. *Erinnerungen an Vorkriegszeit und die Mobilisation 1939–1945.* St. Gallen. Unpublished mimeograph, 1989.

The Knife and Its History: Written on the Occasion of the 100th Anniversary of Victorinox. Ibach, Switzerland: Victorinox, 1984.

Köfer, J.J. *Harte Kriegsjahre: Jugenderinnerungen 1939 bis 1945.* Mellingen: Druckerei Nüssli AG, 1999.

Köfer-Richner, Hans. *Die kleine Stadt am schwarzen Fluss.* Baden: Wanner Druck, 1992.

Kranzler, David. *The Man Who Stopped the Trains to Auschwitz: George Mantello, El Salvador, and Switzerland's Finest Hour.* Syracuse, NY: Syracuse University Press, 2000.

Ladame, Paul Alexis. *Defending Switzerland.* Delmar, NY: Caravan Books, 1999.

Ladame, Paul Alexis. *Une caméra contre Hitler.* Editions Slatkine GenPve 1997.

Lambelet, Jean-Christian. *A Critical Evaluation of the Bergier Report on*

"Switzerland and Refugees during the Nazi Era," with a New Analysis of the *Issue.* Lausanne: University of Lausanne, Ecole des HEC, Jan. 2001.

Langhoff, Wolfgang. *Die Moorsoldaten: 13 Monate Konzentrationslager.* Schweizer Spiegel Verlag Zurich, 1935. English translation: Langhoff. *Rubber Truncheon.* New York: E.P. Dutton, 1935.

Langhoff, Wolfgang. *Rubber Truncheon.* Trans. Lilo Linke. New York: E.P. Dutton & Co., Inc., 1935.

Law, Richard D. *Karabiner 98k, 1934–1945.* Dietikon-Zurich: Stocker-Schmid, 1995.

Le Général Dufour et Saint-Maurice. Musée Militaire Cantonal, Saint-Maurice, 1987.

LeBor, Adam. *Hitler's Secret Bankers.* Secaucus, NJ: Birch Lane Press, 1997.

Lemelsen, Joachim et al. *29. Division.* Bad Nauheim: Podzun-Verlag, 1965.

Lindt, August. *Le temps du Hérisson: Souvenirs, 1939–1945.* Geneva: Editions Zoé, 1995.

Lomax, John. *The Diplomatic Smuggler.* London: Arthur Barker Limited, 1965.

Luck, James Murray. *A History of Switzerland.* Palo Alto, CA: SPOSS, 1985.

Lüem, Walter, and Andreas Steigmeier. *Die Limmatstellung im Zweiten Weltkrieg.* Baden: Baden-Verlag, 1997.

Ludwig, Carl. *Die Flüchtlingspolitik der Schweiz in den Jahren 1933 bis 1955: Bericht an den Bundesrat zuhanden der eidgenössischen Räte von Professor Dr. Carl Ludwig.* Bern, 1957.

McCormack, John. *One Million Mercenaries: Swiss Soldiers in the Armies of the World.* London: Leo Cooper, 1993.

Morel, Yves-Alain. *Aufklärung oder Indoktrination? Truppeninformation in der Schweizer Armee.* Thesis Verlag Zurich, 1996.

Newman, Ken. *Swiss Wartime Work Camps: A Collection of Eyewitness Testimonies 1940–1945.* Zurich: Verlag Neue Zürcher Zeitung, 1999.

Nuremberg Trial Proceedings. Vol. 14. (May 24, 1946).

Oman, C.W.C. *The Art of War in the Middle Ages.* Ithaca, NY: Cornell University Press, 1953.

Oertle, Vicenz. *"Sollte ich aus Rußland nicht zurückkehren . . ." Schweizer Freiwillige an deutscher Seite 1939-1945, Eine Quellensuche.* Thesis Verlag: Zurich, 1997.

Padfield, Peter. *Himmler.* New York: MJF Books, 1990.

Pedrazzini, Dominic, Jürg Stüssi-Lauterburg, and Anne-Marie Volery. *En toute confiance . . ., Correspondance du Général et de Madame Henri Guisan avec le Major Albert R. Mayer, 1940-1959.* Brugg: Effingerhof, 1995.

Persico, Joseph E. *Piercing the Reich: The Penetration of Nazi Germany by American Secret Agents during World War II*. New York: Barnes & Noble, 1979.

Peter, Fredy. *Jump Boys, Jump*. Ilfracombe, UK: Arthur H. Stockwell, 2003.

Reinhart, Christian, Kurt Sallaz, and Michael am Rhyn. *Die Repetiergewehre der Schweiz*. Dietikon-Zurich: Stocker-Schmid, 1991.

Rings, Werner. *Schweiz in Krieg, 1933–1945*. Verlag Ex Libris Zurich, 1974.

Rothenhäusler, Paul ed. *Leuchtturm in der Wüste: Die Schweiz im Zweiten Weltkrieg*. Stäfa, CH: Rothenhäusler Verlag, 1997.

Rucki, Jerzy. *Die Schweiz im Licht Die Schweiz im Schatten*. Kriens: Verlag Brunner AG, 1997.

Schelbert, Leo, ed. *Switzerland under Siege, 1939–1945: A Neutral Nation's Struggle for Survival*. Rockport, ME: Picton Press, 2000.

Scholl, Inge. *The White Rose: Munich 1942–1943*. Trans. Arthur R. Schultz. Hanover, NH: Wesleyan University Press, 1983.

Schom, Alan Morris. *The Unwanted Guests: Swiss Forced Labor Camps 1940–1944*. Los Angeles: Simon Wiesenthal Center, 1998.

Schweizerische Armee. *Offiziers-Etat auf 1. Mai 1938*. Bern: Eidg. Militär-Druckschriftenbureau, n.d.

Schweizerische Armee. *Offiziersetat 1976*. Bern: Eidg. Militärbibliothek, 1976.

Senn, Hans. *Anfänge einer Dissuasionsstrategie während des Zweiten Weltkrieges*. Basel: Helbing & Lichtenhahn, 1995.

Senn, Hans. *Der Schweizerische Generalstab. Volume VII: Anfänge einer Dissuasionsstrategie während des Zweiten Weltkrieges*. Basel: Helbing & Lichtenhahn, 1995.

Shirer, William L. *The Rise and Fall of the Third Reich*. New York: Touchstone, 1990.

Stamm, Luzi, et al. *Dignity and Coolness: Switzerland, 5 March 1940–5 August 1941*. Lenzburg, Switzerland: Verlag Merker im Effingerhof, 2004.

Stapfer, Hans-Heiri, and Gino Künzle. *Escape to Neutrality*. Carrollton, TX: Squadron/Signal Publications, 1992.

Staub, Paul, ed., *34er Buch: Aktivdienst Gebirgs Füsilier Bataillon 34, 1939–1945*. Bern: Buchdruck W. Steiger, 1946.

Tanner, Stephen. *Refuge from the Reich: American Airmen and Switzerland during World War II*. Rockville Centre, NY: Sarpedon, 2001.

Tschuy, Theo. *Dangerous Diplomacy: The Story of Carl Lutz, Rescuer of 62,000 Hungarian Jews*. Grand Rapids, MI: Wm. B. Eerdmans Publishing Co., 2000.

Urner, Klaus. *"Die Schweiz muss noch geschluckt werden!": Hitlers Aktionpläne gegen die Schweiz.* Zurich: Neue Zürcher Zeitung, 1990.

Urner, Klaus. *"Let's Swallow Switzerland": Hitler's Plans Against the Swiss Confederation.* Lanham, MD: Lexington Press, 2002.

Vogelsanger, Peter. *Mit Leib und Seele: Erlebnisse und Einsichten einen Pfarrers.* Theologischer Verlag: Zurich, 1977.

Wagner, Meir. *The Righteous of Switzerland: Heroes of the Holocaust.* Hoboken, NJ: Ktav Publishing House, 2001.

Wetter, Ernst, and Eduard von Orelli. *Wer ist wer im Militär?* Frauenfeld: Huber & CoAG, Grafische Unternehmung und Verlag, 1986.

Widmer, Sigmund. *Familie Frey: Durchhalten in schwieriger Zeit.* Erzählung Band 2. Linda Verlag Zurich, 1997.

Wyman, David S. *The Abandonment of the Jews: America and the Holocaust, 1941–1945.* New York: Pantheon, 1984.

Ziegler, Jean. *La Suisse, l'or, et les morts.* Paris: Éditions du Seuil, 1997.

Ziegler, Major Roland. *Geschichte der Sektion Heer und Haus 1939–1945.* AHQ Bern, 1945.

Ziegler, Major Roland. "Heer und Haus." In *Die Schweiz in Waffen.* Vaterländischer Verlag A.G. Murten und Zurich, 1945.

ARTICLES

Braunschweig, Robert. "Der Vater der 'Motorwägeler'," in *Automobile Revue* (Jan. 8, 1970).

Daniel, Anita. "The Miracle of Switzerland," in *American Mercury*, 54 (May 1942).

Friedrich, Carl J. "As Switzerland Sees It," in *Atlantic Monthly*, 178, 108 (Dec. 1946).

Gotthelf, Jeremias. "Einiges aus dem eidgenössischen Lustlager zu Sursee," in *Allgemeine Schweizerische Militärzeitung*, 55 (Jan. 1934). This article was originally published in 1838.

Keller, Zsolt. "'L'armée est en dehors de toutes questions de confession!' Jüdische Soldaten und Offiziere in der Schweizer Armee 1933–1945," in *Bulletin der Schweizerschen Gesellschaft für Judaishsche Forschung*, Nr. 11, 17 (2002).

Lippmann, Walter. "The Faithful Witness," in *New York Herald Tribune*, 21 (Jan. 26, 1943).

Reiss, Günther D. "Fortification in Switzerland from 1860 to 1945," in *Fort*, Vol. 21, 19 (1993).

Schelbert, Alice. "Memories of World War Two," in *Swiss-American Historical Society Review*, Vol. 36, No. 3, 35 (Nov. 2000).
Sobel, Henry I. "Neutrality, Morality, and the Holocaust," in *American University International Law Review*, Vol. 14, 206 (1998).
"Switzerland Sits Tight," in *Fortune*, 24 (Sept. 1941).
Uhlmann, Ernst. "Angriffspläne gegen die Schweiz," in *Allgemeine Schweizerische Militärzeitung*, Vol. 60, 841 (Dec. 1949).
Winkler, Albert. "The Swabian War of 1499," in *Swiss-American Historical Society Review*, Vol. 35, No. 3, 3 (Nov. 1999).

REPORTS

Bergier, Jean-François, Chairman, Independent Commission of Experts, Switzerland in World War II. *Switzerland and Refugees in the Nazi Era.* Bern, 1999.
Bericht des Chefs des Generalstabes der Armee an den Oberbefehlshaber der Armee über den Aktivdienst 1939–1945. Bern, 1946.
Bericht der Abteilung für Festungswesen über den Aktivdienst 1939–1945 (unpublished full-length report).
Final Report on the Work of the Claims Resolution Tribunal for Dormant Accounts in Switzerland. October 5, 2001.
Generaladjutantur, Sektion Heer und Haus. *Die Judenfrage.* Wehrbrief Nr. 26. May 25, 1943.
Independent Commission of Experts. *Switzerland, National Socialism and the Second World War: Final Report.* Zurich: Pendo Verlag, 2002.

INTERVIEWS AND
PERSONAL STATEMENTS

Aktion Aktivdienst, members of. Interview. Stäfa-Zurich, June 3, 1999.
Auer, Werner P. Interview. Baden, Sept. 28, 1999.
Baumgartner-Jost, Pete. Interview. Langenthal, June 8, 1999.
Bill, Dr. h.c. Arthur T. Interview. Bern, Sept. 27, 1999.
Bollier, Dr. Peter. Interview. Davos, Jan. 19, 2000.
Braunschweig, Robert. Letters. Sept. 12 and 22, 1999. Interview. Bern, Sept. 28, 1999.
Braunschweig, Frau Robert. Interview. Bern, Sept. 28, 1999.
Bueler-Smulders, Anton, and Tony Anton Maria Bueler. Interview. Schwyz, Sept. 26, 1999.

Caminisch, Armin, of Freienbach. Interview. Zurich, Jan. 14, 2000. Interview en route to Davos. Jan. 17, 2000.

Capol, Bruno. Interview. Baden, Sept. 27, 1999. Statement. Windisch, Sept. 27, 1999.

Chevallaz, Georges-André. Interview. Epalinges, near Lausanne, June 6, 1999.

Davatz, Florian E. Letter. Minusio, Feb. 2000.

Durrer, Dr. Gustav T., and Margot Ammann Durrer. Letter. Nov. 2000.

Elsener, Karl, Sr. Interview. Victorinox factory, Schwyz, June 8, 1999.

Erlach, Martina Wille-von, of Gümligen, Canton of Berne. Interview. June 4, 1999.

Gasser-Hänni, Robert. Statement. Gasel bei Köniz, Canton of Berne, June 4, 1999.

Heller, Rolf. Interview and tour. Festung Fürigen, June 7, 1999.

Hug, Hans A. Letter. Weston, MA, July 4, 2000.

Kleiner, Hans. Interview. Baden, Sept. 28, 1999.

Köfer, Hans, of Bellikon/Hausen. Interview. Baden, Sept. 28, 1999.

Jenny, Ernst. Interview. Baden, Sept. 28, 1999.

Jufer, Dr. Max. Interview. Langenthal, June 5, 1999.

Ladame, Paul Alexis. Interview. Geneva, May 29, 2000.

Laemmel, Hans. Letter. Nov. 5, 2000.

Langenbacher, Dr. iur. Heinz. Interview. Bern, Sept. 27, 1999.

Lecoultre, Madame Denise. Letter. Geneva, June 18, 2000.

Lüem, Dr. Walter. Interview and tour. June 7, 1999, Baden.

Morisod, Colonel Alexandre. Interview. St. Maurice, Oct. 9, 1998. Jean-Louis Hug, translator.

Moore, Hedi Köppel. Interview. Fairfax, VA, Jan. 31, 2001. Letter. Delmar, NY, Mar. 21, 2001.

Müller, Dr. Paul. Interview. Davos, Jan. 19, 2000.

Oberle, Arthur. Statement. Ennetbaden, 1999.

de Quervain, Prof. Marcel. Interview. Davos Dorf, Jan. 21, 2000.

de Quervain, Rita. Interview. Davos Dorf, Jan. 21, 2000.

Rapold, Mr. Statement at interview with members of Aktion Aktivdienst. Stäfa-Zurich, June 3, 1999.

Renold-Asper, Alice. Interview. Baden, Sept. 28, 1999.

Rogger, Frau Cornelia. Interview. Davos, Jan. 21, 2000.

Rostetter, Hans, of Ilanz, son of Christian Rostetter. Interview by Theo Hass of Domat/Ems. Apr. 19, 2001.

Rothenhäusler, Paul. Interview. Stäfa-Zurich, June 6, 1999.

Rothenhäusler, Verena. Statement at interview with members of Aktion Aktivdienst. Stäfa-Zurich, June 3, 1999. Interview. Stäfa-Zurich, June 6, 1999.

Salm, Max. Statement. Umiken, Sept. 6, 1994.

Schaad-Denner, Lucie. Interview. Basel, Mar. 5, 2001.

Schmid, Dr. Christian, formerly of Davos. Interview. Zurich, Jan. 14, 2000.

Seiler, Gertrud. Statement. Gasel bei Köniz, Canton of Berne, June 4, 1999.

Stamm, Hedwig. Interview. Zurich, June 2, 1999.

Tschan, Rudi. Letter. La Tour-de-Peilz, Oct. 1999.

Ursprung, Colonel Rudolf. Letter. Oct. 4, 1999.

Salm, Max. Interview. Baden, Sept. 28, 1999.

Schaad-Denner, Lucie. Interview. Mar. 5, 2001.

Terrier, Esther. Interview. Baden, Sept. 28, 1999.

Vogel, Albert H. Interview. June 9, 1999.

Voser, Dr. Iur. Peter. Interview. Baden, Sept. 28, 1999. Statement. May 7, 1997.

Widmer, Dr. Hans. Interview. Baden, Sept. 28, 1999.

Widmer, Sigmund, Andreas Dolfuss, and Jean Planchere. Interview. Stäfa, Sept. 29, 1999.

Wille, Fritz, of Gümligen. Interview. June 4, 1999.

FILM

Die Deutsche Wochenschau, Bundesarchiv, Koblenz, Germany.

Die Schweiz und der Zweite Weltkrieg. Zurich: Rincovision.

Le Général Guisan et son temps. General Guisan und seine Zeit. Il General Guisan e la sua epoca. Un film de Claude Champion. L'Association Film Général Guisan—Le Centre d'Historie et de Prospective Militaires Pully.

Polish Internment Camps in Switzerland, professora Adama Vetulaniego (1941). Unpublished film made available by Zygmunt Prugar-Ketling.

INDEX

347

Wattenwyl, Lieutenant Colonel von (Swiss), 248
Weilenmann, Billy, 39
Weizsäcker, Ernst von, 12–14, 266–267
Wenk, Swiss Füsilier, 162
Widmer, Dr. Hans, 86, 164
Wiesenthal, Simon, 223
Wiest, Major, 240–242
"Wiking Line," 246–247, 286
Wille, Fritz, 173
Wille, Lieutenant General Ulrich (Swiss), 15, 125

Wille von Erlach, Martina, 173–175
Winkler, Albert, 165
Wochenschau (Weekly Film) (German), 51, 54–56, 57, 58, 59–71
Wolff, SS General Karl, 298–299, 300, 301
Women's Auxiliary Service (FHD), 62, 87, 153, 179–182, 196

Ziegler, Roland, 51
Zimmermann, General Staff Major Bobo (German), 128
Zimmermann invasion plan, 128–130